A BENN STUDY · DRAMA

THE NEW MERMAIDS

The Alchemist

THE NEW MERMAIDS

General Editor
BRIAN GIBBONS
Professor of English Literature, University of Leeds

The Alchemist

BEN JONSON

Edited by
DOUGLAS BROWN
Late Lecturer in English
University of Reading

LONDON/ERNEST BENN LIMITED

NEW YORK/W.W. NORTON AND COMPANY INC.

First published in this form 1966
by Ernest Benn Limited
12 Norwich Street, London, EC4A 1EJ
& Sovereign Way, Tonbridge, Kent TN9 1RW
Second impression 1968
Third impression 1971
Fourth impression 1976
Fifth impression 1978
Sixth impression 1982
Seventh impression 1983

Published in the United States of America by
W. W. Norton and Company Inc.
500 Fifth Avenue, New York, N.Y. 10110

Distributed in Canada by
The General Publishing Company Limited, Toronto

Printed in Great Britain

British Library Cataloguing in Publication Data

Jonson, Ben
The alchemist. – (The new mermaids).
I. Title II. Brown, Douglas, b. 1921 III. Series
882′3. PR2605

ISBN 0–510–33606–X
ISBN 0–393–90014–2 (U.S.A.)

This edition was left unfinished by Douglas Brown at his death in October 1964. The text was completed, annotated, and introduced by some of his colleagues at the University of Reading, and seen through the press by
Brian Morris and Philip Brockbank

CONTENTS

ACKNOWLEDGEMENTS

The primary debt must, of course, be to the eleven volumes of *Ben Jonson*, edited by Herford and Simpson, which supplies almost everything any reader might need. Use has also been made of *The Alchemist*, edited C. M. Hathaway, Jr. (Yale Studies in English XVII) New York, 1903, *Eastward Hoe and The Alchemist*, edited F. E. Schelling (Belles Lettres Series), Boston, Mass., 1909, and *The Works*, edited Gifford, Cunningham, 9 vols., 1875.

INTRODUCTION

THE AUTHOR

BEN JONSON was born a Londoner in 1572, the posthumous son of an impoverished gentleman. His mother married a bricklayer shortly afterwards, and his circumstances in youth were decidedly straitened. Through the intervention of an outsider, however, he had some education at Westminster School under William Camden, who remained a lifelong friend; but he probably did not finish school and certainly did not go on, as most of his contemporaries there did, to Oxford or Cambridge. Instead he was apprenticed, probably in his stepfather's craft, about 1589, remaining in it long enough only to learn he 'could not endure' it. Before 1597 he had volunteered to serve in Flanders where, during a lull in the fighting, 'in the face of both the camps', he met and killed one of the enemy in single combat and returned from no-man's-land with his victim's weapons. The scene is an emblem for his life: the giant figure, a party to neither faction, warring alone in the classical manner before his awed onlookers.

Sometime in the early 1590s he married. By the time he was twenty-five he was playing the lead in Kyd's *Spanish Tragedy* for the theatrical manager and entrepreneur Philip Henslowe. As a writer he may also have composed additions to Kyd's work; he certainly did so for Nashe's satirical *Isle of Dogs*, and was imprisoned for the 'slandrous matter' in it. But already by 1598 Francis Meres listed him in *Palladis Tamia* amongst 'our best for tragedy' along with Kyd himself and Shakespeare. These tragedies, and indeed all the work of his early twenties, have vanished, but in the surviving records the man bursts upon the theatrical scene with characteristic and transforming energy.

In 1598 as well his first great success in comedy, *Every Man in his Humour*, was produced; in this, as in *Sejanus*, Shakespeare played a leading role. Within the same month Jonson killed an actor in Henslowe's company, Gabriel Spencer, in a duel. He pleaded guilty to a charge of felony and saved himself from the gallows only by claiming 'benefit of clergy', that is, by proving his literacy and hence immunity by reading 'neck-verse'. His goods–such as they may have been–were confiscated and he was branded on the thumb. His career was not yet fully under way: in writing of the incident, Henslowe refers to Jonson as a 'bricklayer'.

Still in the same year *The Case is Altered* was acted, once again with great success, and in 1599 or 1600 came *Every Man Out of his Humour*, which–although it too enhanced his growing reputation–included in the targets of its satire the diction of some contemporary playwrights, notably John Marston. Marston may have annoyed his older friend by a bungled attempt to flatter him in *Histriomastix* a few months earlier, but he was in any case ready to take very unfriendly revenge for *Every Man Out* when, in late 1600, he caricatured Jonson in *Jack Drum's Entertainment*. Jonson countered with *Cynthia's Revels*, Marston with *What You Will*, Jonson with *Poetaster*, all in 1601. Thomas Dekker, previously Jonson's collaborator on the lost tragedy *Page of Plymouth*, came to Marston's aid with *Satiro-mastix*. But Jonson had gone beyond attacking his attackers: his plays, and particularly *Poetaster*, satirized influential men, and he barely escaped prosecution again. He withdrew, not yet thirty years old, from comedy and the popular stage, into the patronage and protection first of Sir Robert Townshend and later Esmé Stewart, Lord Aubigny, to whom he dedicated the fruit of his retirement, *Sejanus*.

Once again Jonson's talent for trouble caused him difficulty with the authorities, this time on the pretext of 'popery and treason'–he had become a Catholic during his imprisonment for killing Spencer–and once again powerful friends intervened to save him. Still again in 1604, when he collaborated with his reconciled friend Marston and with George Chapman on the comedy *Eastward Ho!* he was jailed, now for satirizing the Scots, for James I was king. But once more he was let off, and on the whole the accession of James I was of great benefit to Jonson: for this brilliant and learned court he wrote almost all his many masques, delicate confections of erudition and artistry in which he knew no master.

But it is to *Volpone* (1605), *Epicoene* (1609–10), *The Alchemist* (1610), *Bartholomew Fair* (1614) and *The Devil is an Ass* (1616) that we must turn for the central documents of his comic maturity, interrupted only by the tragic (and unsuccessful) *Catiline* of 1611. Jonson had by 1612 become conscious of the scope of his accomplishment, for in that year he began work on a collective edition which would enshrine in an impressive folio the authoritative text. His close connections with the court, doubtless enhanced when he gave up Catholicism about 1610, and the literary self-awareness begot by his huge reading in the classics, in part recorded in his commonplace book *Timber*, led him, unique amongst the playwrights of his age, to take such pains with his *oeuvre*.

Jonson continued writing his masques and non-dramatic poems, but no stage play appeared after *The Devil is an Ass* until *The Staple of News* in 1625. Jonson's fortune declined in the nine years between. He began them with a walking tour to Scotland in 1618, where

Drummond recorded their *Conversations*, and with a visit to Oxford in 1619, where the University made him a Master of Arts. He ended them increasingly destitute of health, money and invention. His rule over the 'tribe' that met at the Mermaid was unweakened, but he depended more and more on pensions from Crown and City, especially when he failed to maintain with Charles I the favour he had found with the scholarly James I.

There followed *The New Inn* (1629), *The Magnetic Lady* (1632), and *The Tale of a Tub* (1633); the first was a disaster the last two did little to mitigate. Apart from a few verses he wrote nothing thereafter (his *English Grammar*, a draft of which perished in the fire that destroyed his library in 1623, probably goes back to a period as Professor of Rhetoric at Gresham College), although his lifelong habit of reading was not broken. He did not complete work on the second folio which was to include his writings since 1612. No child of his survived him, and it fell to his intellectual disciples, the 'Sons of Ben', to be his literary executors.

He died on 6th August, 1637, at the age of sixty-five, and was buried in Westminster Abbey.

DATE AND SOURCES

The first performance of *The Alchemist* was by the King's Men at the Globe in 1610. The exact date is not known, but the fact that the play was entered on the Stationers' Register by Walter Burre on 3rd October, 1610,[1] indicates that the performance had taken place by that date. Internal evidence like Ananias's confused chronology at III.ii, 131–2, and V.v, 102–3 is unreliable, and the best evidence is provided by the plague, which was in London from 12th July.[2] The theatres must have been closed throughout the summer, and scholars are now generally agreed that the first performance must have taken place in the first half of the year.[3] Several passages in the play itself suggest that the action was supposed to take place in the year 1610. For example, Dame Pliant, who is said by Drugger to be 'But nineteen, at the most', implies herself that she was born in 1591:

> Never, sin' eighty-eight could I abide 'em,
> And that was some three year afore I was born, in truth.
> (IV.iv, 29–30)

There is nothing to suggest a gap between composition and first performance, and both may be assigned to the early months of 1610.

[1] Arber, *Transcript of the Stationers' Registers*, iii, 445.
[2] F. P. Wilson, *The Plague in Shakespeare's London*, 120–2.
[3] See E. K. Chambers, *The Elizabethan Stage*, iii, 371, and Herford and Simpson, *Ben Jonson*, ix, 224.

Some confirmation of this date comes from the discovery that the King's Men took *The Alchemist* and *Othello* to Oxford in September on their autumn tour.[1]

The plot is entirely original. There is no 'source' in the sense of an existing story which Jonson adapted for his own purposes,[2] though impulses from many areas of his experience and learning come together within the play. There is no doubt, for example, that the idea of rogues carrying on their intrigues in the house of a man whose unexpected return provides the resolution of the plot comes from Plautus's *Mostellaria*; there are traces in the play of Erasmus's dialogue *De Alcumista*, which Jonson probably read at school; Delrio's *Disquisitiones Magicae* provides much of the alchemical argument, and Broughton's *A Concent of Scripture* is ransacked to produce Dol's distraction in IV.v. Similarly, it has been argued that Surly is a development of the character of Bonario in *Volpone*, that Subtle is in some ways very like Volpone himself, and that Face is deeply indebted to Mosca. There is some truth in all this, just as Jonson could not have been unaware of contemporary alchemists and tricksters like John Dee, Edward Kelly and Simon Forman when creating Subtle and Face.[3] But this is only to say that no work of art can be created *ex nihilo*. Jonson's erudite mind and observant eye have synthesized the materials of his experience into a totality which is greater than the sum of them all.

THE PLAY

The time is come about, whereof *Diogenes* prophesied; when he gave the reason why he would be buried grovelling: we have made the earth's bottom powerful to the lofty skies: Gold that lay buried in the buttock of the world: is now made the head and ruler of the people:

(Feltham, *Resolves*)

Seek not Proud *Riches*, but such as thou mayest get justly, use soberly, distribute cheerfully, and leave contentedly . . . The *ways to enrich* are many, and most of them Foul.

(Bacon, *Of Riches*)

[1] The discovery was made in the Fulman papers of Corpus Christi College, Oxford, by Geoffrey Tillotson. See *The Times Literary Supplement*, 20th July, 1933.

[2] Ariosto's *Negromante* (1520) and Lyly's *Gallathea* may confidently be dismissed, but a case for Bruno's *Candelaio* (an Italian play published in Paris in 1582) has been made by Professor C. G. Child, in the New York *Nation*, 28th July, 1904. The claim is discussed and dismissed by Herford and Simpson (*Ben Jonson*, ii, 94–98) who give a summary of the plot as Appendix VI to the same volume.

[3] These points are discussed at length in the edition of *The Alchemist* by C. M. Hathaway (New York, 1903), 90–103; Herford and Simpson, though agreeing for the most part, find some of his conclusions unacceptable.

The Alchemist is a play about Avarice, and the symbol of Avarice is gold. It is this *cupiditas* which unites the cozeners and the cozened, which places Subtle and Lovewit on the same side of the moral fence, which motivates in various degrees and directions the whole complex of actions out of which the play is built. Jonson, as critic of the acquisitive society, is concerned to explore the rich variety of ways in which human energies and ingenuity can be directed towards the processes of enrichment. In his critique of Avarice he is rehearsing one of the great commonplaces of literature in the special terms of his own age; Chaucer had shown long ago, in *The Pardoner's Tale*, that 'radix malorum est cupiditas', and Molière would later point the same moral in *L'Avare*. But Renaissance writers had many ways of presenting Avarice, ranging in mode from the drama to the emblem, from the sermon to the hieroglyph, and Jonson's play represents one kind of moral picture among many.

The faces of greed

In the masques and entertainments of the seventeenth century allegories of virtue and vice are usually presented by actors, who, by their dress and appearance, inform the audience of what they represent. Certain conventions of presentation had been inherited from the Middle Ages, and even from antiquity, and these had been assembled and codified by Renaissance encyclopaedists, of whom perhaps the most important is Cesare Ripa. The first edition of Ripa's *Iconologia* was published in Rome in 1593, and by 1603 it had reached a third edition in which a number of descriptions of virtues and vices were added, together with some illustrations. The edition of 1613 was further augmented by the author, and others followed in 1618, 1620, 1625, 1630 and later years. Poets and painters, although much of the material was already familiar to them, found the *Iconologia* a useful handbook, and Jonson is known to have used a copy of the 1603 edition in his own masques. One of the five descriptions of Avarice which Ripa gives runs: 'A woman badly dressed, bare-headed, bare-footed, holding a toad in her right hand and a closed purse in her left',[1] and in Jonson's masque *The Golden Age Restored* (1615) the Iron Age enters and calls up Avarice as the 'grandame Vice of all my issue'. Jonson used Ripa's pictures and descriptions in many ways, sometimes following closely, sometimes inventing, sometimes combining the attributes of two figures in his description of a third, but always using visual images to present moral qualities, and this visual presentation of Avarice is part of the tradition.

The word Jonson most commonly uses for the symbolical figure

[1] Illustrations from Ripa may be found among the plates in Gilbert's *The Symbolic Persons in the Masques of Ben Jonson*, North Carolina, 1948.

or object is *hieroglyphic*, which he explains himself in *The Masque of Beauty* when he describes the rose as the 'hieroglyphic of splendour', and pearls and lilies as 'the special hieroglyphics of loveliness'. One of the most important books to which Jonson had recourse in this phase of his career was Pierio Valeriano's *Hieroglyphica*, first published in Latin in 1556 and translated into Italian in 1602. Valeriano lists a large number of hieroglyphics, from the lion, the serpent, the elephant, to the moon, the head, and the anchor, and shows how each one represents a wide variety of human qualities and activities. In Book XXXV, 'De Manu', he describes the hand as the hieroglyphic of Avarice:

... There are also people who paint the left hand alone, with clenched fingers, as the mark of graspingness and avarice; interpreters also give the left hand as the mark of money and increase in property, for the left hand is more appropriate for guarding things, since it is less active (than the right) and better fitted to graspingness.[1]

Valeriano's hieroglyphics are derived from classical sources and not, as the name suggests, from Egyptian, but the method of presentation is constant: the hieroglyph is the mute symbol of the quality. As A. H. Gilbert has said: 'In *The Masque of Blackness* the hieroglyphics, such as the salamander and the urn sphered with wine, indicate the "qualities" of their bearers, such as majesty and purity'.[2] Valeriano was not the only encyclopaedist interested in this form of symbolism, but he was among the best known, and since Jonson is known to have used him he may stand as a representative.

Even more numerous were the emblem writers.[3] All over Europe emblem books were published and reprinted for a seemingly insatiable public. An emblem was a drawing or picture expressing an abstract quality, or a class of persons, or a fable, or an allegory, and usually accompanied by explanatory verses. In England the best known emblem writers were probably Geoffrey Whitney, whose *Choice of Emblemes* was published at Leyden in 1586, and (later) Francis Quarles, whose *Emblems* appeared in 1635 and were constantly reprinted. On the continent, one of the most influential collections was that made by Andrea Alciati, which first appeared in the middle of the sixteenth century, and was many times reprinted. Alciati has several emblems depicting Avarice, and the first of them, Emblem LXXXIV, shows a landscape with a stream flowing through it, and Tantalus up to his armpits in the water

[1] Neque desunt qui manum tantum sinistram digitis compressis pro tenacitate et auaritia pingant: nam et coniectores laeuam lucri, et augendae rei signum ponunt, quippe que ad custodiendum magis idonea sit vtpote segnior, et tenacitati accomodatior.
[2] *Symbolic Persons*, 6.
[3] See R. Freeman, *English Emblem Books*, 1948.

reaching for fruit from a branch which hangs down over his head. Beneath the picture are four lines of Latin which comment on the situation:

The wretched Tantalus stands thirstily in the midst of the waters, and although he is hungry he cannot reach the fruit which is so close to him. Change the name, miser, and the story will be true of you; you no more enjoy your possessions than if you did not possess them at all.[1]

Alciati goes on to analyse and apply picture and comment for several pages, drawing examples from Petronius, Horace, Achilles Statius and others. Don Cameron Allen has shown[2] that Jonson made use of Alciati on at least one occasion (*Poetaster*, V.iii, 101–3), and the emblematic presentation of Avarice could be illustrated from a dozen different writers. The habit of thinking about abstract qualities in visual images was widespread and deep-rooted, and the multiplicity of iconologies, hieroglyphics, and emblems bear witness to the strength and range of the tradition.

It is against this background that the pageant of Avarice in Jonson's play should be seen. He is concerned to display the various facets of greed in his chosen social context, a context which is sharply limited and constrained. It has often been pointed out how close Jonson comes in *The Alchemist* to a strict observation of the so-called 'unities' of time, place, and action, but the dramaturgical austerity goes deeper than a mere control of surface plot. The characters, and especially the dupes, are each a brilliant compromise between realism and abstraction; outside the confines of Lovewit's house Surly and Mammon would have nothing to say to one another, but here they and the others set up a momentary pattern of desires and energies which shatters when they touch. Kastril and Drugger display Avarice at its most venial, at its lowest pitch of intensity. Kastril wants no more than an entry into 'good company' by learning how to take the altitude of a quarrel (III.iv), while Drugger is doing no more than cutting the corners in his pursuit of a lawful, if lowly, trade. Dapper stands on a higher rung in the ladder of Avarice, but his search for gold is still oblique; he is the gamester, the 'sporting man' whose greed is cheerful. He desires a fly 'for all games' but only for games, and his ambition rises no higher than 'But I do think, now, I shall leave the law'. He is superbly 'placed' in Face's description of him:

1 Heu miser in mediis sitiens stat Tantalus undis,
Et poma esuriens proxima habere nequit.
Nomine mutato de te id dicetur auare,
Qui, quasi non habeas, non frueris quod habes.

2 'Ben Jonson and the Hieroglyphics', *Philological Quarterly*, XVIII (1939), 290–300.

. . . a special gentle,
That is the heir to forty marks, a year,
Consorts with the small poets of the time,
Is the sole hope of his old grandmother,
That knows the law, and writes you six fair hands . . .

Such a man's Avarice is modest, pitiful, and his reward is apt–a gingerbread gag. Quarles once described an emblem as 'a silent parable', and the three figures of Kastril, Drugger and Dapper, though sharply and widely distinguished, are emblems and parables of Avarice, rather than Avarice personified.

Ananias and Tribulation are altogether larger figures–we have moved from the world of Alciati to the world of Valeriano and Ripa. Jonson, who professed himself a Catholic during the decade before he wrote this play, treats them with notable contempt–the more so because their Avarice is solemn, pretentious, hypocritical. They are arrogant, and Jonson understood arrogance. He exposes and deflates Puritan greed by a delicate and totally dramatic satiric device: he brings the Puritan and the Alchemist together, and shows they are one and the same:

SUBTLE
. . . Who are you?
ANANIAS
A faithful Brother, if it please you.
SUBTLE
What's that?
A Lullianist? A Ripley? *Filius artis*?
Can you sublime, and dulcify? Calcine?
Know you the *sapor pontic*? *Sapor styptic*?
Or, what is homogene, or heterogene?
ANANIAS
I understand no heathen language, truly.

(II.v, 6–12)

The key-word is 'Brother', which Ananias offers in a religious sense, and Subtle accepts as meaning a member of the alchemical fraternity. Suddenly the two frauds are identified, and in the later debates between Subtle, Ananias and Tribulation Jonson relentlessly presses home the identity, crowning it with the ironical recital (III.ii) of Puritan practices, from which possession of the stone will liberate them. In these two figures Jonson exposes the face of greed at its most ugly. Jonson's art must be judged in terms of pattern and colour, and the Puritans are set forward as the moral nadir of the play, Avarice in its blackest suit.

Mammon, on the other hand, is the play's most colourful figure; the gargantuan quality of his greed is matched by the damasked extravagance of his invention. He is non-realistic, unbelievable, and he is only viable as a dramatic character because he is underwritten and guaranteed by the credible ambitiousness of Kastril, Drugger and Dapper. Herford and Simpson point up the Marlowesque quality of his hyperbole when they describe him as 'a Faustus of the senses', and this insight is shrewdly developed by Levin, who says:

> Marlowe consistently presented the voluptuary as a hero; to Jonson, he is always either a villain like Volpone, or a dupe like Sir Epicure Mammon . . . Jonson could not have expressed his reservations more explicitly, nor hit upon a more elaborate contrivance for turning to dust and ashes all the lovely fruit of the Renaissance imagination.[1]

As an image of Avarice Mammon is a marvellously ambivalent figure. Jonson manipulates his audience's responses adroitly, so that moral disapproval is unbalanced by admiration for the wit, the imaginative energy, and, above all, the teeming fecundity of invention. Mammon's greed is a dream, and the dream liberates both the imagination and the moral sense. It is in this that Jonson, as a dramatist, can enter a dimension denied to the iconologists and the emblem writers, whose figures, once created, are unalterable and patient only of ethical application. Mammon enters the play as a stage figure–he is a man as we are–and he grows into a superman dreaming up his Elysium before our eyes.

Subtle, Face and Dol contribute little to the play's exposure of Avarice; they are the clear-sighted exploiters of the Avarice of others, sublimely careless of the perils attendant on their own greed. From the point of view of orthodox morality they are rogues and tricksters, but Jonson invites our admiration for the very vigour of their trickery, and their infinite resourcefulness in action. Primarily, they escape our calumny because they are self-confessed cheats, and the targets of Jonson's satire in *The Alchemist* are the pretentious and the hypocrites. Subtle, Face and Dol have few illusions about themselves or about each other, and their Avarice is open, not to say blatant. It is as if Jonson's spleen is raised not so much by the grasping fingers of Tantalus, as by the clenched fingers in Valeriano's description.

Surly should be the ethical arbitrator of the play. He, like Asper in *Every Man Out of his Humour*, is the exposer of vice and folly; he represents the golden mean between sharp practice and green innocence; he is the man who 'would not be gulled'. Yet Jonson allows him no status. He is no match for Subtle in argument, and at the very moment when he seems to have all the schemers in his hand, and to be about to reap his modest reward, he is foiled by Lovewit and despatched into discomfiture with the other dupes and rascals. There are dramatic reasons for this, but for the moment it is enough to observe that the absence of vicious qualities, in particular of

[1] Harry Levin, 'An Introduction to Ben Jonson', reprinted in *Ben Jonson: A Collection of Critical Essays*, ed. Barish, New Jersey, 1963, 52.

Avarice, is not enough to establish any kind of heroic stature in this play. More, we see that virtue, in itself, is powerless.

In the morality of the play there are no positives. It is Thersites' world–'such patchery, such juggling, and such knavery'[1]–yet the total impression is of a vast expenditure of energy (it is an exhausting play to watch) and nothing to show for it. The figures of greed which Jonson creates may be icons of Avarice in one sense, but they are never static; they are forever grasping, getting, spending, losing. The moral discovery which *The Alchemist* makes is concerned with the sheer *waste* which Avarice implies. The world is constantly present; getting and spending we lay waste our powers.

Comic Justice

The fifth act provides a series of verdicts upon the action. In *Volpone* Jonson had imposed a rigorous justice upon the evildoers in a court scene which sternly eschewed both charity and wit. The effect of this judgement is to enforce with great power the sense of evil and suffering which the preceding comic tones had largely masked. The end of *Volpone* declares unequivocally that the game is over, the chickens have come home to roost, and whatsoever a man sows that shall he reap. Such Levitical justice was no part of Jonson's purpose in *The Alchemist*. The comedy of *The Alchemist* is delicate, and it requires delicate resolution. In *Volpone* the fibres are of a darker and stronger twist, which can sustain the more nearly tragic vision at the end.

Yet the judgements in *The Alchemist* form a wry kind of justice. Its world is not without dangers. We should not forget the plague which hangs over the house, nor that laboratory explosions are apt to injure people, nor the angry mob pounding at the door. The cart and the whip are present fears to Dol, and quite early in the play the perils which awaited the conjurer and the false coiner are firmly established. These presences are latent rather than manifest in the action, but they serve to keep the fantasy in touch with the social realities, they constitute a yardstick by which intentions and activities might be judged. The rejection of this yardstick is one of the notable abstentions of the play. Jonson's judge is not an official representative of order and authority, but Lovewit, the 'jovy boy', 'not hide-bound', who loves a teeming wit as he loves his nourishment. This arbitrator is akin to the Justice who dispenses the rewards and punishments at the end of *Every Man in his Humour*, but whereas that play is concerned with comparatively harmless misunderstandings and fooleries *The Alchemist* has to do with crimes.

Lovewit enters with an air of authority–'Has there been such

[1] *Troilus and Cressida*, II. iii.

resort, say you?'–which immediately breaks down into curiosity as he smells a device:

What should my knave advance,
To draw this company? He hung out no banners
Of a strange calf, with five legs, to be seen?
Or a huge lobster, with six claws?
(V.i, 6–9)

His subsequent actions form a kind of 'moral slide' as he descends from investigator to bargainer to trickster to exploiter. The stations of the slide are clearly marked in his conversations with the neighbours, with the dupes, with Face over the terms of the bargain, and with Surly over the fate of Dame Pliant. The fifth act, which should see the revoking of the comic licence and the re-establishment of order, becomes a comic exploit in its own right, with Lovewit as protagonist and manipulator. Here again Jonson's economy is matchless. Lovewit's settlement with Face begets all the other judgements almost mechanically: Surly is foiled, the other dupes are all sent penniless away, Subtle and Dol disappear over the garden wall, with Face speeding the parting jest:

Let's know where you set up next; I'll send you
A customer, now and then, for old acquaintance:

Face himself is the only survivor, and he divides the spoils (unequally it is true) with Lovewit. Face, the play's prime manipulator and greatest rogue, is vindicated by his wit; the wicked and slothful servant enters into the joy of his lord. Thus the verdict in which the play comes to rest is an exaltation of Intelligence above virtue, in which the honest Surly is abashed while the impudent Face triumphs. Edmund Wilson has described it well:

There is no element of false morality to blur Jonson's acrid relish of the confidence games of his rogues: the cynicism is carried right through.[1]

'Cynicism' is a strong word, and Wilson was arguing a special case, but we have only to compare Lovewit's pardon of Face with the Duke's judgement of Lucio in *Measure for Measure* to appreciate the difference between Shakespeare's conception of comic justice and Jonson's. In *The Alchemist* Intelligence is at a premium, and creative ingenuity assumes the stature of a virtue: unto him that hath shall be given, and he shall have abundance. If we take this as a summing up of the human condition it seems both harsh and superficial. But if we see it as the savage judgement upon a viciously acquisitive society, a society where Avarice is regnant and rampant,

[1] Edmund Wilson, 'Morose Ben Jonson' in *The Triple Thinkers*, and reprinted in *Ben Jonson: A Collection of Critical Essays*, ed. Barish, 63.

where Alchemist and Puritan serve the same gods, it becomes acceptable. Instead of bringing the play's fantasy to rest on a solid ground of moral certainties Jonson has judged it by its own rules, and on its own terms. His verdict is that the acquisitive society is a vortex of greed, competition, self-seeking, out-manoeuvring, corner-cutting, swindling and cozening; its justice is unpredictable and arbitrary, and cleverness is its only virtue. But it is as it is. You must take it or leave it.

The Clash of Jargons

It was Coleridge who spoke of Jonson's 'sterling English diction',[1] and in a play like *The Alchemist* which offers a staggering display of the uses of language this is a point to bear in mind. Indeed, the range of language might be plotted between the 'sterling English' and the total gibberish of Dol's fit of talking in IV.v. The tone which Coleridge admired is set early in the first act:

But I shall put you in mind, sir, at Pie Corner,
Taking your meal of steam in, from cooks' stalls,
Where, like the Father of Hunger, you did walk
Piteously costive, with your pinched-horn-nose,
And your complexion, of the Roman wash,
Stuck full of black, and melancholic worms,
Like powder corns, shot, at th'artillery-yard.

(I.i, 25–31)

'Pie Corner' and 'th'artillery-yard' root the statements in actual, London places; they give a local habitation to the speech. This is the same impulse as Horace displays in those Odes which celebrate the Roman countryside, the famous *fons Bandusiae*, or, by contrast, the seventh Ode of Book I:

Laudabunt alii claram Rhodon aut Mytilenen
  aut Epheson bimarisve Corinthi
moenia vel Baccho Thebas vel Apolline Delphos
  insignes aut Thessala Tempe.

Levin quotes examples to show how Jonson elsewhere paraphrased the tropes of Catullus into Rumney and the Chelsea fields.[2] It is this locative impulse, attended by a sensitive simplicity of diction and allusion which allows the light colloquialisms their proper assertion, that goes to make up the basic speech of Jonsonian comedy and serves as a touchstone for the more complex uses of language elsewhere in the play.

The powerful extravagance of Dol's raving has already been mentioned, but the more subtle, and totally dramatic mode of speech can perhaps best be illustrated from Mammon's first speech

[1] *Lectures on Shakespeare* (Bohn edition), 397.
[2] In *Ben Jonson &c.*, ed. Barish, 44.

in II.i. L. C. Knights has shown[1] how what begins as comic inflation and fantastic caricature develops through a series of negatives into a richly ambiguous statement about the social world and the world of alchemy. Perhaps it is even more than that. Mammon, when he enters his dream, when he sets his foot on shore 'In *novo orbe*' takes Surly with him, and it is to convince Surly, the sceptic, that the string of negatives roll forth, culminating in the powerful, persuasive allusion which unites the Inn yard with the book of Exodus:

No more
Shall thirst of satin, or the covetous hunger
Of velvet entrails, for a rude-spun cloak,
To be displayed at Madam Augusta's, make
The sons of sword, and hazard fall before
The golden calf, and on their knees, whole nights,
Commit idolatry with wine, and trumpets:

This is the strong-knit, allusive tone, which is frequently sounded in the play, and which is the particular voice of Mammon. It modulates further in the same scene, when to the jibes of Surly are added the blandishments of Face. Both speakers are brief, and the effect of their presences and words is principally to incite Mammon to screw up his rhetoric and invention to ever higher notes, so that the language of comedy in this scene separates out on to three levels, the crude realism of Surly ('The decayed Vestals of Pict-Hatch would thank you'), Face's smooth civility ('The evening will set red, upon you, sir'), and over all the swelling chant of Mammon's personal *gloria*.

These uses of language, the plain and the ornate, are found for the most part in the first two acts. The language of the middle of the play is more violent. In the third and fourth acts it becomes dramatically important that people shall not properly understand what is said to them, and that they shall be mystified, frightened, or impressed with their failure to comprehend. Jonson's art accomplishes this by clashing together the various jargons which have already been established: the vast sprawl of technical terms which surround alchemy had been used to suppress the loquacity of Mammon in II.iii, and in II.v it is employed again, liturgically, in a catechistical exchange between Subtle and Face to baffle and control the thrustingness of Ananias:

SUBTLE
Sirrah, my varlet, stand you forth, and speak to him
Like a philosopher: answer, i' the language.

[1] 'Ben Jonson, Dramatist', in *Penguin Guide to English Literature*, ed. Boris Ford, ii, 312–4.

Name the vexations, and the martyrizations
Of metals, in the work.
FACE Sir, Putrefaction,
Solution, Ablution, Sublimation,
Cohobation, Calcination, Ceration, and
Fixation.

It is the episcopal pomp of this jargon which puts down the humble 'saint'.

The opposition is renewed in the opening scenes of Act Three. Here Jonson allows the two Puritans a scene to themselves in which to develop the separatist tropes, and they create a language of Amsterdam which is grave and impressive, rich in its biblical sonorities:–'In pure zeal', 'the language of Canaan', 'profane person', 'The visible mark of the Beast', 'holy cause', 'sanctified cause', 'sanctified course', 'The children of perdition'. The first hundred lines of the following scene (III.ii) present the attempt of Tribulation to make some kind of verbal contact with Subtle. Each of them chastens his speech, tempers his jargon, in order to communicate. But Ananias cannot be contained, and bursts out with the party line and the party slogans: 'I hate traditions: I do not trust 'em', 'They are popish, all'. Subtle and Tribulation draw back, and Subtle sets up again the impregnable rock of his jargon:

We must now increase
Our fire to *ignis ardens*, we are past
Fimus equinus, *balnei*, *cineris*,
And all those lenter heats.

Tribulation resorts to casuistic chop-logic about the relative legality of coining and casting, and as the scene ends he finds refuge in an appeal to authority, like a trade-union official going off to consult his executive:

I'll make a question of it, to the Brethren.

Jonson uses the clash of jargons to prevent communication. The high-sounding terms are impressive, but they are simply counters in a struggle for ascendancy. In scenes like this between the Alchemist and the Puritans the words, far from linking people together, drive them apart. The play has other scenes in which this movement takes place–Mammon's wooing of Dol, Subtle and Kastril on the causes of quarrels, and (in its most complex form) Subtle and Face in conversation with the disguised Surly, whose Spanish, though incomprehensible to them, is infinitely suggestive. The effect of the play's various powerful jargons is to prevent, or baffle, or mutilate meaningful communication between characters whenever the dramaturgy requires that communication should be stifled. There is a constantly recurring sense in the play of the unbridgeable distance between people; they stand, shouting at each other across the abyss.

The Metaphor of Change

The central image of the play is the figure of transmutation; the end of all things is the search for gold. Yet the image is flexible and expansive because the end of the search is an *ignis fatuus*, an illusion. In *Volpone*, the gold is real enough, a present and potent force in the action, but in *The Alchemist* all the characters are chasing a will o' the wisp. It is perhaps this very lack of substance in the search which allows the dramatist such freedom in his exploration of the image. To return for a moment to Mammon's speech in II.i, the key is provided by the line which Subtle speaks to introduce him:

> If his dream last, he'll turn the age, to gold.

This was the quest of the genuine alchemist, and despite the chicanery and pretentiousness which surrounded the pseudo-science the motives of many of its practitioners were altruistic and laudable. The alchemist had a place and a real status in Elizabethan society because an age of such scientific curiosity and economic aggressiveness could not afford to neglect the possibility of turning base metals to gold.[1] Mammon's speech, for all its delusions of grandeur and adoration of excess, displays a wide generosity; everyone will benefit when he has the philosopher's stone. The 'hollow dye' and the 'frail card' will no longer be needed, and men will be able to live without deception. This expansive movement towards a vision of the Golden Age is part of the metaphor of change within the speech, but counterpointing it, balancing it, is the ethical descent from the noble to the base. As the metal is purified and refined by fire into gold, so humanity is consumed by the growing fire of lust and concupiscence, and the vision of the Golden Age degenerates into dull Aretine's pictures. But the image of metamorphosis is not confined to the language of the play. In visual terms it is a constant procession of shifts and disguises: Face becomes the Captain who becomes Jeremy, Dol takes on the mantle of the Queen of Faery, Surly is disguised as the Diego, everyone is striving to become someone else. The final impression of the play is of an immense activity, a constant flux of language and spectacle, of things changing and being changed. There is chemical alchemy and there is human alchemy, yet it is Jonson's triumph that despite all the disguises and transformations, identities are preserved. In its dominant preoccupation with Avarice through the processes of alchemy *The*

[1] The best account of alchemists and alchemy in this play is given in the Introduction to Hathaway's edition of *The Alchemist*, New York, 1903.

Alchemist emerges as a vast gloss upon the reply of Marlowe's Bashaw in *The Jew of Malta*, when the Governor asks him 'What wind drives you thus into Malta rhode?'

> The wind that bloweth all the world besides,
> Desire of gold.

NOTE ON THE TEXT

The play was printed in a quarto (Q) in 1612 and in the collective folio (F) edition in 1616, both under Jonson's supervision and incorporating press corrections. Jonson's hand is not so clear in the posthumous second folio (F2) of 1640 on which he had done some work before he died.

This edition follows the corrected state of F. Some passages which might have given offence were altered in F; these and other substantial differences are mentioned in notes save when, as often, Q omits a stage direction. The spelling, including capitalization and the contrast of roman with italic, small capital and black letter types, is modernized throughout, as is the presentation of speeches. In F block entries precede every scene, and the first name among them is that of the first speaker. In this edition entries are supplied only as the action requires, and the first speaker has a separate speech prefix. Speech prefixes in broken lines are all on the left; Jonson had them within the line:

Dare you do this? SUB. Yes faith, yes faith. FAC. Why! Who (I.i, 12).

Abbreviations are expanded, and so are elisions within (but not between) words, but forms reflecting the colloquial speech of the time have been retained.

The punctuation follows Jonson's highly-developed system for F, considerably more explicit than Q, except that a few obvious errors have been silently corrected; the metrical apostrophe, intended to prevent elision of vowels in adjacent words, has been omitted; and the use of hyphens has been modernized.

FURTHER READING

The Jonson bibliography is vast, and the following brief list is intended only to facilitate the pursuit of some of the issues raised in the Introduction and Notes.

Barish, J. A., *Ben Jonson and the Language of Prose Comedy*, Cambridge, Mass., 1960.

Barish, J. A., ed., *Ben Jonson: A Collection of Critical Essays* (Twentieth Century Views), New Jersey, 1963.

Blissett, William, Julian Patrick, and R. W. Van Fossen, edd., *A Celebration of Ben Jonson*, Toronto and London, 1973.

Davies, Robertson, 'Ben Jonson and Alchemy', *Stratford Papers 1968–69*, ed. B. A. W. Jackson, Shannon, 1972, pp. 40–60.

Dessen, Alan C., *Jonson's Moral Comedy*, Evanston, Ill., 1971.

Donaldson, Ian, *The World Upside-Down*, Oxford, 1970.

Eliot, T. S., 'Ben Jonson', reprinted in *Elizabethan Dramatists*, 1963.

Ellis-Fermor, U., *The Jacobean Drama*, fourth edition with additional material, 1961.

Gilbert, A. H., *The Symbolic Persons in the Masques of Ben Jonson*, Duke University Press, North Carolina, 1948.

Hibbard, G. R., ed., *The Elizabethan Theatre, IV*, Toronto, London and Basingstoke, 1974.

Kernan, Alvin B., ed., *The Alchemist*, New Haven and London, 1974.

Kernan, Alvin B., 'Alchemy and Acting: the Major Plays of Ben Jonson', in *Ben Jonson: Quadricentennial Essays*, ed. Mary Olive Thomas, Atlanta, 1973.

Knights, L. C., *Drama and Society in the Age of Jonson*, 1937.

Partridge, E. B., *The Broken Compass, A Study of the Major Comedies of Ben Jonson*, New York, 1958.

Sackton, A. H., *Rhetoric as a Dramatic Language in Ben Jonson*, New York, 1948.

Thayer, C. G., *Ben Jonson: Studies in the Plays*, Norman, Okla., 1963.

THE ALCHEMIST.

A Comœdie.

Acted in the yeere 1610. By the
Kings MAIESTIES
Seruants.

The Author B. I.

LVCRET.

———*petere inde coronam,*
Vnde priùs nulli velarint tempora Musæ.

LONDON,
Printed by WILLIAM STANSBY

M. DC. XVI.

TO THE LADY, MOST DESERVING HER NAME, AND BLOOD:
Mary,
LADY WROTH

MADAM,

In the age of sacrifices, the truth of religion was not in the greatness, and fat of the offerings, but in the devotion, and zeal of the sacrificers: else, what could a handful of gums have done in the sight of a hecatomb? Or, how might I appear at this altar, except with those affections, that no less love the light and witness, than they have the conscience of your virtue? If what I offer bear an acceptable odour, and hold the first strength, it is your value of it, which remembers, where, when, and to whom it was kindled. Otherwise, as the times are, there comes rarely forth that thing, so full of authority, or example, but by assiduity and custom, grows less, and loses. This, yet, safe in your judgment (which is a Sidney's) is forbidden to speak more; lest it talk, or look like one of the ambitious faces of the time: who, the more they paint, are the less themselves.

Your Ladyship's true honourer,
Ben Jonson.

Mary, Lady Wroth. The name is also spelled 'Worth' – hence 'most deserving her name'. She was the eldest daughter of the first Earl of Leicester, niece of Sir Philip Sidney, and married Sir Robert Wroth at Penshurst on 27th September, 1604.

1–5 See Seneca, *De Beneficiis*, I.vi.2

TO THE READER

If thou beest more, thou art an understander, and then I trust thee. If thou art one that takest up, and but a pretender, beware at what hands thou receivest thy commodity; for thou wert never more fair in the way to be cozened (than in this age) in poetry, especially in plays: wherein, now, the concupiscence of dances, and antics so reigneth, as to run away from nature, and be afraid of her, is the only point of art that tickles the spectators. But how out of purpose, and place, do I name art? When the professors are grown so obstinate contemners of it, and presumers on their own naturals, as they are deriders of all diligence that way, and, by simple mocking at the terms, when they understand not the things, think to get off wittily with their ignorance. Nay, they are esteemed the more learned, and sufficient for this, by the many, through their excellent vice of judgment. For they commend writers, as they do fencers, or wrestlers; who if they come in robustiously, and put for it with a great deal of violence, are received for the braver fellows: when many times their own rudeness is the cause of their disgrace, and a little touch of their adversary gives all that boisterous force the foil. I deny not, but that these men, who always seek to do more than enough, may some time happen on something that is good, and great; but very seldom: and when it comes it doth not recompense the rest of their ill. It sticks out perhaps, and is more eminent, because all is sordid, and vile about it: as lights are more discerned in a thick darkness, than a faint shadow. I speak not this, out of a hope to do good on any man, against his will; for I know, if it were put to the question of theirs, and mine, the worse would find more suffrages: because the most favour common errors. But I give thee this warning, that there is a great difference between those, that (to gain the opinion of copie) utter all they can, however unfitly; and those that use election, and a mean. For it is only the disease of the unskilful, to think rude things greater than polished: or scattered more numerous than composed.

To the Reader

These critical comments on the popular contempt for art are paralleled in Jonson's *Discoveries* (see Herford and Simpson, *Ben Jonson*, viii, 572) and derive ultimately from Quintilian.

THE PERSONS OF THE PLAY

SUBTLE, The Alchemist
FACE, The Housekeeper
DOL COMMON, Their Colleague
DAPPER, A Clerk
DRUGGER, A Tobaccoman
LOVEWIT, Master of the House
EPICURE MAMMON, A Knight
SURLY, A Gamester
TRIBULATION, A Pastor of Amsterdam
ANANIAS, A Deacon there
KASTRIL, The Angry Boy
DAME PLIANT, His Sister: A Widow

Neighbours
Officers
Mutes

The Scene

LONDON [, inside Lovewit's house and in the street outside]

Surly. He is addressed as 'Pertinax' (i.e. obstinate) at II.i,79, and II.ii, 5. He, like Quarlous in *Bartholomew Fair*, is described as a 'Gamester', which usually implied dissolute life as well as gambling.
Ananias. According to Sir Charles Firth the name Ananias, from this play, became the accepted nickname for a Puritan. The Puritans' use of biblical names for their children was justified on the grounds that since all are tainted with original sin, children might be named after any sinner mentioned in the Bible. The Ananias 'that cozened the Apostles' is found in *Acts*, v, but there is another, and better, Ananias in *Acts*, ix, 10 ff.
Mutes. As Herford and Simpson point out (*Ben Jonson*, x, 54) Officers and Neighbours are specified, so that only the Chaplain of V.iv,99 remains. Perhaps he walks out with Lovewit at the opening of V.v.

The Alchemist

THE ARGUMENT

T he sickness hot, a master quit, for fear,
H is house in town: and left one servant there.
E ase him corrupted, and gave means to know
A cheater, and his punk; who, now brought low,
L eaving their narrow practice, were become
C ozeners at large: and, only wanting some
H ouse to set up, with him they here contract,
E ach for a share, and all begin to act.
M uch company they draw, and much abuse,
I n casting figures, telling fortunes, news,
S elling of flies, flat bawdry, with the stone:
T ill it, and they, and all in fume are gone.

PROLOGUE

Fortune, that favours fools, these two short hours
  We wish away; both for your sakes, and ours,
Judging spectators: and desire in place,
  To th'author justice, to ourselves but grace.
Our scene is London, 'cause we would make known,
  No country's mirth is better than our own.
No clime breeds better matter, for your whore,
  Bawd, squire, imposter, many persons more,
Whose manners, now called humours, feed the stage:
  And which have still been subject, for the rage
Or spleen of comic writers. Though this pen
  Did never aim to grieve, but better men;
Howe'er the age, he lives in, doth endure
  The vices that she breeds, above their cure.
But, when the wholesome remedies are sweet,
  And, in their working, gain, and profit meet,
He hopes to find no spirit so much diseased,
  But will, with such fair correctives be pleased.
For here, he doth not fear, who can apply.
  If there be any, that will sit so nigh
Unto the stream, to look what it doth run,
  They shall find things, they'd think, or wish, were done;
They are so natural follies, but so shown,
  As even the doers may see, and yet not own.

Act I, Scene i

[*Enter*] FACE, SUBTLE, DOL COMMON

FACE
Believ't, I will.

SUBTLE
Thy worst. I fart at thee.

DOL
Ha' you your wits? Why gentlemen! For love–

FACE
Sirrah, I'll strip you—

SUBTLE
What to do? Lick figs
Out at my—

FACE
Rogue, rogue, out of all your sleights.

DOL
Nay, look ye! Sovereign, General, are you madmen?

SUBTLE
O, let the wild sheep loose. I'll gum your silks
With good strong water, an' you come.

DOL
Will you have
The neighbours hear you? Will you betray all?
Hark, I hear somebody.

FACE
Sirrah—

SUBTLE
I shall mar
All that the tailor has made, if you approach.

FACE
You most notorious whelp, you insolent slave
Dare you do this?

SUBTLE
Yes faith, yes faith.

FACE
Why! Who
Am I, my mongrel? Who am I?

SUBTLE
I'll tell you,
Since you know not yourself—

FACE
Speak lower, rogue.

1 *Thy worst* Do your worst
4 *out of all your sleights* Cease all your trickery
10 *All that the tailor has made* (from the proverb) The apparel that makes you the man you are

---

3 *Lick figs.* The uncompleted allusion is to an obscene story in Rabelais, *Pantagruel*, iv. xlv.
6 *I'll gum your silks* &c. Subtle is holding a vessel containing some chemical preparation, and in lines 8–12 Face is prevented from attacking him only by fear of the chemical.

SUBTLE
Yes. You were once (time's not long past) the good,
Honest, plain, livery-three-pound-thrum; that kept
Your master's worship's house, here, in the Friars,
For the vacations—

FACE
Will you be so loud?

SUBTLE
Since, by my means, translated Suburb-Captain.

FACE
By your means, Doctor Dog?

SUBTLE
Within man's memory
All this, I speak of.

FACE
Why, I pray you, have I
Been countenanced by you? Or you, by me?
Do but collect, sir, where I met you first.

SUBTLE
I do not hear well.

FACE
Not of this, I think it.
But I shall put you in mind, sir, at Pie Corner,
Taking your meal of steam in, from cooks' stalls,
Where, like the Father of Hunger, you did walk
Piteously costive, with your pinched-horn-nose,
And your complexion, of the Roman wash,
Stuck full of black, and melancholic worms,
Like powder corns, shot, at th'artillery-yard.

SUBTLE
I wish, you could advance your voice, a little.

FACE
When you went pinned up, in the several rags,
You'd raked, and picked from dunghills, before day,

17 *Friars* Blackfriars
18 *vacations* between court terms
22 *countenanced* favoured, supported
23 *collect* recollect
24 *hear well* (bene audire) perhaps punningly
25 *Pie Corner* near Smithfield; name from a noted Inn
27 *Father of Hunger* glancing allusions to Catullus (xxi & xxiii)
28 *costive* constipated
29 *Roman wash* swarthy; hint of lotion for skin disease
31 *powder corns* grains of powder; *artillery-yard* a public place for arms practice
32 *advance your voice* speak louder
34 *You'd* ed. (Yo'had F.Q.)

---

16 *livery-three-pound-thrum.* Shabby, poorly paid servant. 'Livery' is the servant's uniform, 'three-pound' a sneer at Face's annual wage, and 'thrum' the loose end of a weaver's warp used for tufts of coarse yarn.

Your feet in mouldy slippers, for your kibes,
A felt of rug, and a thin threaden cloak,
That scare would cover your no-buttocks—

SUBTLE
So, sir!

FACE
When all your alchemy, and your algebra,
Your minerals, vegetals, and animals,
Your conjuring, cozening, and your dozen of trades,
Could not relieve your corps, with so much linen
Would make you tinder, but to see a fire;
I ga' you countenance, credit for your coals,
Your stills, your glasses, your materials,
Built you a furnace, drew you customers,
Advanced all your black arts; lent you, beside,
A house to practise in—

SUBTLE
Your master's house?

FACE
Where you have studied the more thriving skill
Of bawdry, since.

SUBTLE
Yes, in your master's house.
You, and the rats, here, kept possession.
Make it not strange. I know, you're one, could keep
The buttery-hatch still locked, and save the chippings,
Sell the dole-beer to aqua-vitae-men,
The which, together with your Christmas vails,
At post and pair, your letting out of counters,
Made you a pretty stock, some twenty marks,
And gave you credit, to converse with cobwebs,
Here, since your mistress' death hath broke up house.

FACE
You might talk softlier, rascal.

SUBTLE
No, you scarab,
I'll thunder you, in pieces. I will teach you
How to beware, to tempt a Fury again
That carries tempest in his hand, and voice.

36 *felt of rug* coarse hat
41 *corps* body
51 *Make it not strange* don't affect bewilderment, make mysteries
53 *dole-beer* meant for distribution to the poor; *aqua-vitae-men* dealers in spirits
54 *vails* tips
55 *post and pair* a card game; *counters* to facilitate gambling
59 *scarab* beetle, dung-fly

---

53 *Sell the dole-beer* &c. Cf. *The Devil is an Ass*, II.i, 4–7.
58 *your mistress' death*. Lovewit, Face's master, is thus a widower, and available for sudden marriage in Act V.

FACE
The place has made you valiant.
SUBTLE
No, your clothes.
Thou vermin, have I ta'en thee, out of dung,
So poor, so wretched, when no living thing
Would keep thee company, but a spider, or worse?
Raised thee from brooms, and dust, and watering-pots?
Sublimed thee, and exalted thee, and fixed thee
I'the third region, called our state of grace?
Wrought thee to spirit, to quintessence, with pains
Would twice have won me the philosopher's work?
Put thee in words, and fashion? Made thee fit
For more than ordinary fellowships?
Given thee thy oaths, thy quarrelling dimensions?
Thy rules, to cheat at horse-race, cock-pit, cards,
Dice, or whatever gallant tincture, else?
Made thee a second, in mine own great art?
And have I this for thank? Do you rebel?
Do you fly out, i' the projection?
Would you be gone, now?
DOL
Gentlemen, what mean you?
Will you mar all?
SUBTLE
Slave, thou hadst had no name—
DOL
Will you undo yourselves, with civil war?
SUBTLE
Never been known, past *equi clibanum*,
The heat of horse-dung, under ground, in cellars,
Or an ale-house, darker than deaf John's: been lost
To all mankind, but laundresses, and tapsters,
Had not I been.
DOL
Do you know who hears you, Sovereign?
FACE
Sirrah—

71 *philosopher's work* elixir
73 *fellowships* partnership in companies
74 *oaths* part of the alchemical mystique; *quarrelling dimensions* how far to take a quarrel (*cf.* II.vi, 65 ff.)
76 *tincture* used in alchemical sense
85 *deaf John's* now unknown (HS)

---

79 *Do you fly out* &c. Do you explode at the moment of perfection? – a disaster incident to alchemists.
83 *equi clibanum*. 'the furnace of the horse'. The heat of horse-dung was a moderate heat, used in alchemical processes.

DOL Nay, General, I thought you were civil—

FACE
I shall turn desperate, if you grow thus loud.

SUBTLE
And hang thyself, I care not.

FACE Hang thee, collier,
And all thy pots, and pans, in picture I will,
Since thou hast moved me—

DOL (O, this'll o'erthrow all.)

FACE
Write thee up bawd, in Paul's; have all thy tricks
Of cozening with a hollow coal, dust, scrapings,
Searching for things lost, with a sieve, and shears,
Erecting figures, in your rows of houses,
And taking in of shadows, with a glass,
Told in red letters: and a face, cut for thee,
Worse than Gamaliel Ratsey's.

DOL Are you sound?
Ha' you your senses, masters?

FACE I will have
A book, but barely reckoning thy impostures,
Shall prove a true philosopher's stone, to printers.

90 *collier* cheat (by inference)
91 *in picture* for public exposure
93 *in Paul's* at St. Paul's – a resort favoured by cheats and criminals
96 *Erecting figures* plotting position of planets; *houses* signs of zodiac
97 *glass* a crystal or beryl
98 *red letters* used to emphasize key passages in pamphlets; *cut for thee* drawn to represent you
99 *Gamaliel Ratsey's* highwayman publicized in pamphlets; *sound* sane
102 quintessential truth, and a means of enrichment

93–97 *have all . . . glass*. The hollow coal trick involved secreting silver filings in a piece of burnt wood, and then, miraculously, 'extracting' the silver. See Chaucer, *Canon's Yeoman's Tale*. The sieve and shears were traditional instruments for discovering thieves. Herford and Simpson quote Grose, *A Provincial Glossary*, 1811, p. 118:

> To discover a thief by the sieve and shears: Stick the points of the shears in the wood of the sieve, and let two persons support it, balanced upright, with their two fingers: then read a certain chapter of the Bible, and afterwards ask St. Peter and St. Paul if A. or B. is the thief, naming all the persons you suspect. On naming the real thief the sieve will turn suddenly round about.

'Erecting figures' in the casting of horoscopes was an astrologer's art, but astrology and alchemy were often closely connected. The 'shadows' in the glass were reputedly angels, who answered questions which had to be put to them by a virgin of pure life. Dr. Dee's 'glass' is in the British Museum. See also Johnstone Parr, *Tamburlaine's Malady and other essays on Astrology in Elizabethan Drama* (Alabama, 1953), 101–6.

SUBTLE
Away, you trencher-rascal.
FACE
Out you dog-leech,
The vomit of all prisons—
DOL
Will you be
Your own destructions, gentlemen?
FACE
Still spewed out
For lying too heavy o' the basket.
SUBTLE
Cheater.
FACE
Bawd.
SUBTLE Cow-herd.
FACE
Conjurer.
SUBTLE
Cut-purse.
FACE
Witch.
DOL
O me!
We are ruined! Lost! Ha' you no more regard
To your reputations? Where's your judgment? S'light,
Have yet, some care of me, o' your republic—
FACE
Away this brach. I'll bring thee, rogue, within
The statute of sorcery, *tricesimo tertio*,
Of Harry the Eighth: ay, and (perhaps) thy neck
Within a noose, for laundering gold, and barbing it.
DOL
You'll bring your head within a coxcomb, will you?
She catcheth out Face his sword: and breaks Subtle's glass
And you, sir, with your menstrue, gather it up.
S'death, you abominable pair of stinkards,
Leave off your barking, and grow one again,
Or, by the light that shines, I'll cut your throats.
I'll not be made a prey unto the marshal,

103 *trencher-rascal* hanger-on; *dog-leech* quack (by inference)
106 *lying too heavy o' the basket* the mean greed of prisoners who seize more than a share of scraps sent in (by basket)
110 *republic* joint interests; ironic usage
111 *brach* bitch
114 *laundering*, *barbing* 'sweating' gold or plate, mutilating coin
116 *menstrue* menstruum (for dissolving solids)
118 *grow one* be reconciled
120 *marshal* the provost-marshal

112–13 *The statute . . . of Harry the Eighth.* Passed in 1541, though a similar act had been passed in 1403. It forbade the multiplying of gold or silver, among other things, and it was confirmed by the statute of 1 James I, c. 12, in 1604. These acts were not repealed until 1689.

For ne'er a snarling dog-bolt o' you both.
Ha' you together cozened all this while,
And all the world, and shall it now be said
You've made most courteous shift, to cozen yourselves?
You will accuse him? You will bring him in
Within the statute? Who shall take your word?
A whoreson, upstart, apocryphal captain,
Whom not a puritan, in Blackfriars, will trust
So much, as for a feather! And you, too,
Will give the cause, forsooth? You will insult,
And claim a primacy, in the divisions?
You must be chief? As if you, only, had
The powder to project with? And the work
Were not begun out of equality?
The venture tripartite? All things in common?
Without priority? S'death, you perpetual curs,
Fall to your couples again, and cozen kindly,
And heartily, and lovingly, as you should,
And lose not the beginning of a term,
Or, by this hand, I shall grow factious too,
And, take my part, and quit you.

FACE
'Tis his fault,
He ever murmurs, and objects his pains,
And says, the weight of all lies upon him.

SUBTLE
Why, so it does.

DOL
How does it? Do not we
Sustain our parts?

SUBTLE
Yes, but they are not equal.

DOL
Why, if your part exceed today, I hope
Ours may, tomorrow, match it.

SUBTLE
Ay, they may.

DOL
May, murmuring mastiff? Ay, and do. Death on me!

121 *dog-bolt* meaning doubtful
127 *apocryphal* without authority
130 *give the cause* assume the right to lead in argument
133 *powder to project with* powder to consummate alchemy
137 *kindly* in brotherly spirit
139 *term* term of court (meaning increase of custom)
141 *quit* requite
142 *objects* objects because of his labours
148 *Death on me* Gods will Q

128 *Blackfriars.* The area was noted as a residence of Puritans, and the centre of the feather trade. Cf. *Bartholomew Fair*, V.v,85–6.

Help me to throttle him.

SUBTLE
Dorothy, mistress Dorothy,
'Ods precious, I'll do anything. What do you mean?

DOL
Because o' your fermentation, and cibation?

SUBTLE
Not I, by heaven—

DOL
Your Sol, and Luna–help me.

SUBTLE
Would I were hanged then. I'll conform myself.

DOL
Will you, sir, do so then, and quickly: swear.

SUBTLE
What should I swear?

DOL
To leave your faction, sir.
And labour, kindly, in the common work.

SUBTLE
Let me not breathe, if I meant ought, beside.
I only used those speeches, as a spur
To him.

DOL
I hope we need no spurs, sir. Do we?

FACE
'Slid, prove today, who shall shark best.

SUBTLE
Agreed.

DOL
Yes, and work close, and friendly.

SUBTLE
'Slight, the knot
Shall grow the stronger, for this breach, with me.

DOL
Why so, my good baboons! Shall we go make
A sort of sober, scurvy, precise neighbours,
(That scarce have smiled twice, since the king came in)
A feast of laughter, at our follies? Rascals,
Would run themselves from breath, to see me ride,
Or you t'have but a hole, to thrust your heads in,
For which you should pay ear-rent? No, agree.

152 *Sol, and Luna* gold and silver
156 *kindly* like a brother, amicably
162 *with me* (probably) where I'm concerned
164 *sort* set, clique; *precise* Puritanical
165 i.e. 1603
167 *from breath* out of breath *ride* carted, as a bawd
168 *a hole* pillory
169 *ear-rent* lose your ears

And may Don Provost ride a-feasting, long,
In his old velvet jerkin, and stained scarves
(My noble Sovereign, and worthy General)
Ere we contribute a new crewel garter
To his most worsted worship.

SUBTLE
Royal Dol!
Spoken like Claridiana, and thyself!

FACE
For which, at supper, thou shalt sit in triumph,
And not be styled Dol Common, but Dol Proper,
Dol Singular: the longest cut, at night,
Shall draw thee for his Dol Particular.

SUBTLE
Who's that? One rings. To the window, Dol. Pray heaven,
The master do not trouble us, this quarter.

FACE
O, fear not him. While there dies one, a week,
O'the plague, he's safe, from thinking toward London.
Beside, he's busy at his hop-yards, now:
I had a letter from him. If he do,
He'll send such word, for airing o' the house
As you shall have sufficient time, to quit it:
Though we break up a fortnight, 'tis no matter.

SUBTLE
Who is it, Dol?

DOL
A fine young quodling.

FACE
O,
My lawyer's clerk, I lighted on, last night,
In Holborn, at the Dagger. He would have
(I told you of him) a familiar,
To rifle with, at horses, and win cups.

DOL
O, let him in.

SUBTLE
Stay. Who shall do't?

FACE
Get you
Your robes on. I will meet him, as going out.

170 *Don Provost* in his role as executioner
173 *crewel* yarn (punningly)
174 *worsted* coarse yarn (punningly again)
188 *break up* dissolve partnership (temporarily)
189 *quodling* codling, 'green' boy
191 *Dagger* famous inn
192 *familiar* familiar spirit, at call
193 *rifle* gamble (raffle)

---

175 *Claridiana.* Heroine of the romance *The Mirror of Knighthood.*

DOL
And what shall I do?
FACE
Not be seen, away.
Seem you very reserved. [*Exit* DOL]
SUBTLE
Enough. [*Exit* SUBTLE]
FACE
God be w'you, sir.
I pray you, let him know that I was here.
His name is Dapper. I would gladly have stayed, but—

Act I, Scene ii

[*Enter*] DAPPER, FACE

DAPPER
Captain, I am here.
FACE
Who's that? He's come, I think, Doctor.
Good faith, sir, I was going away.
DAPPER
In truth,
I am very sorry, Captain.
FACE
But I thought
Sure, I should meet you.
DAPPER
Ay, I am very glad.
I had a scurvy writ, or two, to make,
And I had lent my watch last night, to one
That dines, today, at the sheriff's: and so was robbed
Of my pass-time. [*Enter* SUBTLE] Is this the cunning-man?
FACE
This is his worship.
DAPPER
Is he a Doctor?
FACE
Yes.
DAPPER
And ha' you broke with him, Captain?
FACE
Ay.
DAPPER
And how?
FACE
Faith, he does make the matter, sir, so dainty,
I know not what to say—
DAPPER
Not so, good Captain.
FACE
Would I were fairly rid on't, believe me.

9 *Doctor* in sense of high skill, learning
10 *broke* opened up the matter
11 *dainty* not anxious to touch it; dangerous
13 *rid on't* quit of the matter

---

6 *my watch.* Watches, at this time, were scarce and expensive. Dapper is boasting, or pretending, that he owns one. Cf. *Twelfth Night,* II.v.

DAPPER
Nay, now you grieve me, sir. Why should you wish so?
I dare assure you. I'll not be ungrateful.
FACE
I cannot think you will, sir. But the law
Is such a thing–and then, he says, Read's matter
Falling so lately—
DAPPER Read? He was an ass,
And dealt, sir, with a fool.
FACE It was a clerk, sir.
DAPPER
A clerk?
FACE Nay, hear me, sir, you know the law
Better, I think—
DAPPER I should, sir, and the danger.
You know I showed the statute to you?
FACE You did so.
DAPPER
And will I tell, then? By this hand, of flesh,
Would it might never write good court-hand, more,
If I discover. What do you think of me,
That I am a chouse?
FACE What's that?
DAPPER The Turk was, here—
As one would say, do you think I am a Turk?
FACE
I'll tell the Doctor so.
DAPPER Do, good sweet Captain.
FACE
Come, noble Doctor, pray thee, let's prevail,
This is the gentleman, and he is no chouse.
SUBTLE
Captain, I have returned you all my answer.

24 *court-hand* law-court script
25 *discover* reveal
26 *chouse* (or chiaus: slang from Turkish) cheat

---

17 *Read's matter.* Dr. Simon Read, physician, was pardoned by the King for having on 8th November, 1607, invoked spirits to find who had stolen £37 10s. from Toby Matthew (the 'fool' of line 19). See Rymer, *Foedera*, xvi, 666.

26 *The Turk.* A Turk named Mustafa reached England towards the end of July, 1607, saying he was an ambassador from the Sultan, though he took no higher title than *Chāush* (messenger or herald). The Levant merchants were obliged to entertain him, for fear of offending the Sultan, and he was even received at Windsor. He left in November, 1607, having added a new word to the language.

I would do much, sir, for your love–but this
I neither may, nor can.

FACE
Tut, do not say so.
You deal, now, with a noble fellow, Doctor,
One that will thank you, richly, and he's no chouse:
Let that, sir, move you.

SUBTLE
Pray you, forbear—

FACE
He has
Four angels, here—

SUBTLE
You do me wrong, good sir.

FACE
Doctor, wherein? To tempt you, with these spirits?

SUBTLE
To tempt my art, and love, sir, to my peril.
Fore heaven, I scarce can think you are my friend,
That so would draw me to apparent danger.

FACE
I draw you? A horse draw you, and a halter,
You, and your flies together—

DAPPER
Nay, good Captain.

FACE
That know no difference of men.

SUBTLE
Good words, sir.

FACE
Good deeds, sir, Doctor Dogs-meat. 'Slight I bring you
No cheating Clim o' the Cloughs, or Claribels,
That look as big as five-and-fifty, and flush,
And spit out secrets, like hot custard—

DAPPER
Captain.

FACE
Nor any melancholic under-scribe,

37 *angels* gold coin worth over 10/–
38 *spirits* angels
42 *draw you* i.e. in a cart, to Tyburn
43 *flies* familiar demons
44 *difference* distinction (social, and between honest and fraud)
45 *Dogs-meat* carrion; Q has *dogs-mouth*, with possible sense of 'barking at all comers'

---

46 *No cheating Clim* &c. Heroes of ballad and romance. Clim was a celebrated archer and outlaw of the North; see the *Ballad of Adam Bell* (Percy, *Reliques*, I.156). Sir Claribel is one of the knights contending for the false Florimel in *The Faerie Queene*, IV, ix. 'Cheating' is puzzling; Herford and Simpson suggest that some contemporary thief might have adopted Clim's name.

47 *five-and-fifty, and flush.* A complete sequence in the same suit, an invincible hand in the game of Primero.

Shall tell the vicar: but, a special gentle,
That is the heir to forty marks, a year,
Consorts with the small poets of the time,
Is the sole hope of his old grandmother,
That knows the law, and writes you six fair hands,
Is a fine clerk, and has his cyphering perfect,
Will take his oath, o' the Greek Xenophon
If need be, in his pocket: and can court
His mistress, out of Ovid.

DAPPER
Nay, dear Captain.

FACE
Did you not tell me, so?

DAPPER
Yes, but I'd ha' you
Use master Doctor, with some more respect.

FACE
Hang him proud stag, with his broad velvet head.
But, for your sake, I'd choke, ere I would change
An article of breath, with such a puck-fist—
Come let's be gone.

SUBTLE
Pray you, le' me speak with you.

DAPPER
His worship calls you, Captain.

FACE
I am sorry,
I e'er embarked myself, in such a business.

DAPPER
Nay, good sir. He did call you.

FACE
Will he take, then?

SUBTLE
First, hear me—

FACE
Not a syllable, 'less you take.

SUBTLE
Pray ye, sir—

FACE
Upon no terms, but an *assumpsit.*

SUBTLE
Your humour must be law.

He takes the money

FACE
Why now, sir, talk.
Now, I dare hear you with mine honour. Speak.
So may this gentleman too.

50 *vicar* vicar-general: chancellor, acting for bishop (HS)
51 *marks* worth (then) about 15/–
61 *head* i.e. hat
63 *article* punningly, to Dapper
67 *take* confirm the agreement
68 *'less* unless
69 *assumpsit* voluntary verbal promise

SUBTLE
Why, sir—
FACE
No whispering.
SUBTLE
'Fore heaven, you do not apprehend the loss
You do yourself, in this.
FACE
Wherein? For what?
SUBTLE
Marry, to be so importunate for one,
That, when he has it, will undo you all:
He'll win up all the money i' the town.
FACE
How!
SUBTLE Yes. And blow up gamester, after gamester,
As they do crackers, in a puppet-play.
If I do give him a familiar,
Give you him all you play for; never set him:
For he will have it.
FACE
You're mistaken, Doctor.
Why, he does ask one but for cups, and horses,
A rifling fly: none o' your great familiars.
DAPPER
Yes, Captain, I would have it, for all games.
SUBTLE
I told you so.
FACE
'Slight, that's a new business!
I understood you, a tame bird, to fly
Twice in a term, or so; on Friday nights,
When you had left the office: for a nag,
Of forty, or fifty shillings.
DAPPER
Ay, 'tis true, sir,
But I do think, now, I shall leave the law,
And therefore—
FACE
Why, this changes quite the case!
D'you think, that I dare move him?
DAPPER
If you please, sir,
All's one to him, I see.
FACE
What! For that money?
I cannot with my conscience. Nor should you
Make the request, methinks.
DAPPER
No, sir, I mean
To add consideration.

78 *blow up* ruin, explode
81 *set* stake against
84 *rifling fly* demon for raffles
92 *therefore* – so F (Q has *therefore.* i.e. on that account)
97 *consideration* payment

FACE
Why, then, sir,
I'll try. Say, that it were for all games, Doctor?

SUBTLE
I say, then, not a mouth shall eat for him
At any ordinary, but o' the score,
That is a gaming mouth, conceive me.

FACE
Indeed!

SUBTLE
He'll draw you all the treasure of the realm,
If it be set him.

FACE
Speak you this from art?

SUBTLE
Ay, sir, and reason too: the ground of art.
He's o' the only best complexion,
The Queen of Fairy loves.

FACE
What! Is he!

SUBTLE
Peace.
He'll overhear you. Sir, should she but see him—

FACE
What?

SUBTLE Do not you tell him.

FACE
Will he win at cards too?

SUBTLE
The spirits of dead Holland, living Isaac,
You'd swear, were in him: such a vigorous luck
As cannot be resisted. 'Slight he'll put
Six o' your gallants, to a cloak, indeed.

FACE
A strange success, that some man shall be born to!

SUBTLE
He hears you, man—

103 *set him* required of him (i.e. of the familiar)
105–6 i.e. favoured by supernatural powers
112 *to a cloak* strip to the cloak

99–100 *not a mouth . . . score.* i.e. at any inn he will get all the meals he orders on credit. An 'ordinary' was originally a meal prepared at an inn at a fixed price. It came to mean the inn itself.

109 *dead Holland, living Isaac.* 'John and John Isaac, surnamed Holland, reputed to have been the first Dutch alchemists in the first half of the fifteenth century' (Herford and Simpson). Their works were not published until the beginning of the seventeenth century, and this may have misled Jonson into speaking of 'living Isaac'. Several of Jonson's earlier editors doubted this identification, on the grounds that luck in gambling would not be associated with the names of two Dutch alchemists. But Subtle is simply concerned to dazzle Dapper, and does so by this reference to recondite masters of his own art.

DAPPER
Sir, I'll not be ingrateful.

FACE
Faith, I have a confidence in his good nature:
You hear, he says, he will not be ingrateful.

SUBTLE
Why, as you please, my venture follows yours.

FACE
Troth, do it, Doctor. Think him trusty, and make him.
He may make us both happy in an hour:
Win some five thousand pound, and send us two on't.

DAPPER
Believe it, and I will, sir.

FACE
And you shall, sir.
You have heard all?

DAPPER
No, what was't? Nothing, I sir.

Face takes him aside

FACE
Nothing?

DAPPER
A little, sir.

FACE
Well, a rare star
Reigned, at your birth.

DAPPER
At mine, sir? No.

FACE
The Doctor
Swears that you are—

SUBTLE
Nay, Captain, you'll tell all, now.

FACE
Allied to the Queen of Fairy.

DAPPER
Who? That I am?
Believe it, no such matter—

FACE
Yes, and that
Yo' were born with a caul o' your head.

DAPPER
Who says so?

FACE
Come.
You know it well enough, though you dissemble it.

DAPPER
I'fac, I do not. You are mistaken.

FACE
How!
Swear by your fac? And in a thing so known
Unto the Doctor? How shall we, sir, trust you
I' the other matter? Can we ever think,

119 *happy* rich like the Latin *beatus* (HS)
130 *fac* coy corruption of faith

---

128 *born with a caul.* A sign of good fortune. Cf. French *né coiffé.*

When you have won five, or six thousand pound,
You'll send us shares in't, by this rate?

DAPPER By Jove, sir,
I'll win ten thousand pound, and send you half.
I'fac's no oath.

SUBTLE No, no, he did but jest.

FACE
Go to. Go, thank the Doctor. He's your friend
To take it so.

DAPPER I thank his worship.

FACE So?
Another angel.

DAPPER Must I?

FACE Must you? 'Slight,
What else is thanks? Will you be trivial? Doctor,
When must he come, for his familiar?

DAPPER
Shall I not ha' it with me?

SUBTLE O, good sir!
There must a world of ceremonies pass,
You must be bathed, and fumigated, first;
Besides, the Queen of Fairy does not rise,
Till it be noon.

FACE Not, if she danced, tonight.

SUBTLE
And she must bless it.

FACE Did you never see
Her royal Grace, yet?

DAPPER Whom?

FACE Your aunt of Fairy?

SUBTLE
Not, since she kissed him, in the cradle, Captain,
I can resolve you that.

FACE Well, see her Grace,
Whate'er it cost you, for a thing that I know!
It will be somewhat hard to compass: but,
How ever, see her. You are made, believe it,
If you can see her. Her Grace is a lone woman,
And very rich, and if she take a fancy,

147 *tonight* last night

---

137 *I'fac's no oath.* A strict Puritan did not allow himself to swear at all. His yea was yea, and his nay, nay (*Matthew*, v,34, and *James*, v,12). It became a sign of 'respectability' to limit one's oaths, and Dapper's coyness exemplifies his pretended status.

She will do strange things. See her, at any hand.
'Slid, she may hap to leave you all she has!
It is the Doctor's fear.

DAPPER
How will't be done, then?

FACE
Let me alone, take you no thought. Do you
But say to me, Captain, I'll see her Grace.

DAPPER
Captain, I'll see her Grace.

FACE
Enough. *One knocks without*

SUBTLE
Who's there?
Anon. (Conduct him forth, by the back way)
Sir, against one o'clock, prepare yourself.
Till when you must be fasting; only, take
Three drops of vinegar, in, at your nose;
Two at your mouth; and one, at either ear;
Then, bathe your fingers' ends; and wash your eyes;
To sharpen your five senses; and, cry *hum*,
Thrice; and then *buz*, as often; and then, come.

FACE
Can you remember this?

DAPPER
I warrant you.

FACE
Well, then, away. 'Tis, but your bestowing
Some twenty nobles, 'mong her Grace's servants;
And, put on a clean shirt: you do not know
What grace her Grace may do you in clean linen. [*Exeunt*]

Act I, Scene iii

[*Enter*] SUBTLE

SUBTLE
Come in (Good wives, I pray you forbear me, now.
Troth I can do you no good, till afternoon)

[*Enter* DRUGGER]

What is your name, say you, Abel Drugger?

169–70 *hum, buz* noises for magic formulae
173 *nobles* coin worth about 8/6

---

1 *Good wives.* This is addressed to some women (probably imaginary) waiting in another room, and it is one of the few moments in the play when we are made aware of another world outside the immediate, tight circle of the cozeners and the cozened.

DRUGGER
Yes, sir.

SUBTLE
A seller of tobacco?

DRUGGER
Yes, sir.

SUBTLE
'Umh.
Free of the grocers?

DRUGGER
Ay, and't please you.

SUBTLE
Well—
Your business, Abel?

DRUGGER
This, and't please your worship,
I am a young beginner, and am building
Of a new shop, and't like your worship; just,
At corner of a street: (here's the plot on't.)
And I would know, by art, sir, of your worship,
Which way I should make my door, by necromancy.
And, where my shelves. And, which should be for boxes.
And, which for pots. I would be glad to thrive, sir.
And, I was wished to your worship, by a gentleman,
One Captain Face, that says you know men's planets,
And their good angels, and their bad.

SUBTLE
I do,
If I do see 'em—

[*Enter* FACE]

FACE
What! My honest Abel?
Thou art well met, here!

DRUGGER
Troth, sir, I was speaking,
Just, as your worship came here, of your worship.
I pray you, speak for me to master Doctor.

FACE
He shall do anything. Doctor, do you hear?
This is my friend, Abel, an honest fellow,
He lets me have good tobacco, and he does not
Sophisticate it, with sack-lees, or oil,
Nor washes it in muscadel, and grains,

5 *Free of the grocers* member of the Grocers' Company
9 *plot* ground plan
11 *necromancy* magic, especially divination of the future
15 *planets* i.e. can cast horoscopes
24 *Sophisticate* adulterate

---

5 *the grocers.* Grocers, apothecaries, chandlers, and innkeepers all sold tobacco, as well as specialists like Drugger. Subtle is establishing that Drugger has served a proper apprenticeship.

24 *Sophisticate.* Tobacco-curing was not widely understood in the seventeenth century, and because it was transported between continents it frequently became too dry, or mouldy. Dry tobacco could be disguised (and increased in weight) by adulteration with wines or oils.

Nor buries it, in gravel, under ground,
Wrapped up in greasy leather, or pissed clouts:
But keeps it in fine lily-pots, that opened,
Smell like conserve of roses, or French beans.
He has his maple block, his silver tongs,
Winchester pipes, and fire of Juniper.
A neat, spruce-honest-fellow, and no gold-smith.

SUBTLE
He's a fortunate fellow, that I am sure on—

FACE
Already, sir, ha' you found it? Lo' thee Abel!

SUBTLE
And, in right way toward riches—

FACE
Sir.

SUBTLE
This summer,
He will be of the clothing of his company:
And, next spring, called to the scarlet. Spend what he can.

FACE
What, and so little beard?

SUBTLE
Sir, you must think,
He may have a receipt, to make hair come.
But he'll be wise, preserve his youth, and fine for't:
His fortune looks for him, another way.

FACE
'Slid, Doctor, how canst thou know this so soon?
I am amused, at that!

SUBTLE
By a rule, Captain,
In metoposcopy, which I do work by,
A certain star i'the forehead, which you see not.
Your chestnut, or your olive-coloured face

29 *French beans* broad beans
32 *gold-smith* usurer
37 *scarlet* i.e. made sheriff
40 *fine* pay the fine for refusing the office (HS)
43 *amused* set musing, puzzled
44 *metoposcopy* branch of physiognomy

---

30 *He has his maple block* &c. Drugger's shop is well equipped to teach the art of smoking. The maple block was for shredding the tobacco leaf, the tongs for holding the lighted coal, and the fire of juniper for lighting the pipes (juniper wood burns very slowly and steadily). For 'Winchester pipes' see *Notes and Queries*, clxxxii (1942) p.x.

45–49 *A certain . . . finger*. Herford and Simpson quote Richard Sanders, *Physiognomie and Chiromancie, Metoposcopie*, 1653: 'The colours of the Body, and especially of the face, denote the Humour and inclination of the person; . . . Those that be chestnut or olive colour are Jovialists and honest people, open without painting or cheating.'

Does never fail: and your long ear doth promise.
I knew't, by certain spots too, in his teeth,
And on the nail of his mercurial finger.

FACE
Which finger's that?

SUBTLE
His little finger. Look.
You're born upon a Wednesday?

DRUGGER
Yes, indeed, sir.

SUBTLE
The thumb, in chiromanty, we give Venus;
The forefinger to Jove; the midst, to Saturn;
The ring to Sol; the least, to Mercury:
Who was the lord, sir, of his horoscope,
His house of life being Libra. which foreshowed,
He should be a merchant, and should trade with balance.

FACE
Why, this is strange! Is't not, honest Nab?

SUBTLE
There is a ship now, coming from Ormus,
That shall yield him, such a commodity
Of drugs–this is the west, and this the south?

DRUGGER
Yes, sir.

SUBTLE
And those are your two sides?

DRUGGER
Ay, sir.

SUBTLE
Make me your door, then, south; your broad side, west:
And, on the east side of your shop, aloft,
Write *Mathlai*, *Tarmiel*, and *Baraborat*;
Upon the north part, *Rael*, *Velel*, *Thiel*.
They are the names of those mercurial spirits,
That do fright flies from boxes.

DRUGGER
Yes, sir.

SUBTLE
And
Beneath your threshold, bury me a loadstone
To draw in gallants, that wear spurs: the rest,

47 *promise* i.e. promise well
52 *chiromanty* palmistry
58 *Nab* (slang) head, head-piece

---

56 *His house of life* &c. If Libra governed the house of life, Venus ruled Libra, and not Mercury. Subtle, trading on Drugger's ignorance, substitutes the more appropriate Mercury, the god of business men.

65 *Write Mathlai* &c. Quoted, as Gifford points out, from *Heptameron, seu Elementa magica Pietri de Abano philosophi*, appended to Cornelius Agrippa's *De Occulta Philosophia*, Paris? 1567?

They'll seem to follow.

FACE
That's a secret, Nab!

SUBTLE
And, on your stall, a puppet, with a vice,
And a court-fucus, to call city-dames.
You shall deal much, with minerals.

DRUGGER
Sir, I have,
At home, already—

SUBTLE
Ay, I know, you have arsenic,
Vitriol, sal-tartar, argaile, alkali,
Cinoper: I know all. This fellow, Captain,
Will come, in time, to be a great distiller,
And give a say (I will not say directly,
But very fair) at the philosopher's stone.

FACE
Why, how now, Abel! Is this true?

DRUGGER
Good Captain,
What must I give?

FACE
Nay, I'll not counsel thee.
Thou hear'st what wealth (he says, spend what thou canst)
Th'art like to come to.

DRUGGER
I would gi' him a crown.

FACE
A crown! And toward such a fortune? Heart,
Thou shalt rather gi' him thy shop. No gold about thee?

DRUGGER
Yes, I have a portague, I ha' kept this half year.

FACE
Out on thee, Nab; 'Slight, there was such an offer—
Shalt keep't no longer, I'll gi'it him for thee?
Doctor, Nab prays your worship, to drink this: and swears
He will appear more grateful, as your skill
Does raise him in the world.

DRUGGER
I would entreat
Another favour of his worship.

FACE
What is't, Nab?

DRUGGER
But, to look over, sir, my almanack,

71 *seem* be seen in public
72 *puppet, with a vice* doll worked by wire mechanism
73 *fucus* a cosmetic
76 *sal-tartar* carbonate of potash; *argaile* crude cream of tartar; *alkali* soda-ash (HS)
77 *Cinoper* mercuric sulphide crystals
79 *a say* trial; i.e. make an attempt
87 *portague* Portuguese gold coin, worth some £4

And cross out my ill days, that I may neither
Bargain, nor trust upon them.

FACE
That he shall, Nab.
Leave it, it shall be done, 'gainst afternoon.

SUBTLE
And a direction for his shelves.

FACE
Now, Nab?
Art thou well pleased, Nab?

DRUGGER
Thank, sir, both your worships.

FACE
Away.

[*Exit* DRUGGER]

Why, now, you smoky persecutor of nature!
Now, do you see, that something's to be done,
Beside your beech-coal, and your corsive waters,
Your crosslets, crucibles, and cucurbites?
You must have stuff, brought home to you, to work on?
And, yet, you think, I am at no expense,
In searching out these veins, then following 'em,
Then trying 'em out. 'Fore God, my intelligence
Costs me more money, than my share oft comes to,
In these rare works.

SUBTLE
You are pleasant, sir. How now?

Act I, Scene iv

[*Enter*] DOL

SUBTLE
What says, my dainty Dolkin?

DOL
Yonder fish-wife
Will not away. And there's your giantess,
The bawd of Lambeth.

SUBTLE
Heart, I cannot speak with 'em.

102 *corsive* corrosive
103 *crosslets* melting-pots; *cucurbites* retorts
107 *intelligence* i.e. what I discover, report of findings

---

100 *persecutor of nature.* Both 'follower' and 'afflicter' of nature. Alchemy could be thought of as following nature, since it was based on the premise that all metals would have been gold if they could (cf. I.iv, 25–8), and the alchemist's 'art' is only perfecting the natural process. Yet he could also be seen as an 'afflicter' of metals, torturing them through furnace, alembic and still.

DOL
Not, afore night, I have told 'em, in a voice,
Thorough the trunk, like one of your familiars.
But I have spied Sir Epicure Mammon—

SUBTLE
Where?

DOL
Coming along, at the far end of the lane,
Slow of his feet, but earnest of his tongue,
To one, that's with him.

SUBTLE
Face, go you, and shift.
Dol, you must presently make ready, too—

DOL
Why, what's the matter?

SUBTLE
O, I did look for him
With the sun's rising: marvel, he could sleep!
This is the day, I am to perfect for him
The *magisterium*, our great work, the stone;
And yield it, made, into his hands: of which,
He has, this month, talked, as he were possessed.
And, now, he's dealing pieces on't, away.
Methinks, I see him, entering ordinaries,
Dispensing for the pox; and plaguey-houses,
Reaching his dose; walking Moorfields for lepers;
And offering citizens' wives pomander-bracelets,
As his preservative, made of the elixir;
Searching the spittle, to make old bawds young;
And the highways, for beggars, to make rich:
I see no end of his labours. He will make
Nature ashamed, of her long sleep: when art,
Who's but a step-dame, shall do more, than she,
In her best love to mankind, ever could.
If his dream last, he'll turn the age, to gold. [*Exeunt*]

5 *trunk* tube
9 *shift* change uniform
20 *Reaching* extending, offering
21 *pomander-bracelets* i.e. as talismans
23 *spittle* hospital

Act II, Scene i

[*Enter*] MAMMON, SURLY

MAMMON

Come on, sir. Now, you set your foot on shore
In *novo orbe*; here's the rich Peru:
And there within, sir, are the golden mines,
Great Solomon's Ophir! He was sailing to't,
Three years, but we have reached it in ten months.
This is the day, wherein, to all my friends,
I will pronounce the happy word, be rich.
This day, you shall be *spectatissimi*.
You shall no more deal with the hollow die,
Or the frail card. No more be at charge of keeping
The livery-punk, for the young heir, that must
Seal, at all hours, in his shirt. No more
If he deny, ha' him beaten to't, as he is
That brings him the commodity. No more
Shall thirst of satin, or the covetous hunger
Of velvet entrails, for a rude-spun cloak,
To be displayed at Madam Augusta's, make
The sons of sword, and hazard fall before
The golden calf, and on their knees, whole nights,
Commit idolatry with wine, and trumpets:
Or go a-feasting, after drum and ensign.

8 *spectatissimi* most honoured
9 *hollow die* (plural dice) leaded dice
10 *frail card* prepared for cheating
16 *entrails* i.e. lining
17 *Madam Augusta's* mistress of a brothel
18 *of sword, and hazard* fighting men and gamblers (*cf.* Face)

1–5 *Now, you set your foot* &c. Pizarro conquered Peru in 1532, and its name had become a symbol for boundless wealth. Solomon was believed to have had the philosopher's stone (II.ii, 36) and to have made gold with it in far-away Ophir, because he could not trust his courtiers with the secret. Mammon's speech takes some of its impetus from the account of Solomon's wealth, 1 *Kings*, x.

10–14 *No more* &c. This passage describes, obliquely, the 'commodity' swindle, in which a borrower was compelled to take part or all of his loan in merchandise, and realize what he could by the resale of it. The goods were usually of some quite unsaleable nature. Cf. III.iv, 90. In Middleton's *Michaelmas Term* Quomodo, the moneylender, sends one of his servants to buy back the commodity at far less than it cost his victim. Here, the 'livery-punk' is a woman employed to persuade the young heir who is too wary to sign the mortgages in cold blood to do so in the heat of passion.

No more of this. You shall start up young viceroys,
And have your punks, and punketees, my Surly.
And unto thee, I speak it first, be rich.
Where is my Subtle, there? Within ho?

FACE Sir. *Within*
He'll come to you, by and by.

MAMMON That's his fire-drake,
His lungs, his Zephyrus, he that puffs his coals,
Till he firk nature up, in her own centre.
You are not faithful, sir. This night, I'll change
All, that is metal, in thy house, to gold.
And, early in the morning, will I send
To all the plumbers, and the pewterers,
And buy their tin, and lead up: and to Lothbury,
For all the copper.

SURLY What, and turn that too?

MAMMON
Yes, and I'll purchase Devonshire, and Cornwall,
And make them perfect Indies! You admire now?

SURLY
No faith.

MAMMON But when you see th'effects of the great medicine!
Of which one part projected on a hundred
Of Mercury, or Venus, or the moon,
Shall turn it, to as many of the sun;
Nay, to a thousand, so *ad infinitum:*
You will believe me.

SURLY Yes, when I see't, I will.
But, if my eyes do cozen me so (and I
Giving 'em no occasion) sure, I'll have
A whore, shall piss 'em out, next day.

MAMMON Ha! Why?
Do you think, I fable with you? I assure you,
He that has once the flower of the sun,
The perfect ruby, which we call elixir,
Not only can do that, but by its virtue,

23 *punketees* slang term – 'punquettes'
28 *firk* drive, force (also, cheat)
36 *perfect Indies* i.e. change their tin and copper to gold
49 *virtue* power

---

33 *Lothbury*. An area noted for its foundries. See Stow, *A Survey of London*, 1598, p. 220.
37–40 *But when . . . sun*. Cf. Chaucer, *Canon's Yeoman's Tale*, 272–6.

Can confer honour, love, respect, long life,
Give safety, valour: yea, and victory,
To whom he will. In eight, and twenty days,
I'll make an old man, of fourscore, a child.

SURLY
No doubt, he's that already.

MAMMON
Nay, I mean,
Restore his years, renew him, like an eagle,
To the fifth age; make him get sons, and daughters,
Young giants; as our philosophers have done
(The ancient patriarchs afore the flood)
But taking, once a week, on a knive's point,
The quantity of a grain of mustard, of it:
Become stout Marses, and beget young Cupids.

SURLY
The decayed Vestals of Pict-Hatch would thank you,
That keep the fire alive, there.

MAMMON
'Tis the secret
Of nature, naturized 'gainst all infections,
Cures all diseases, coming of all causes,
A month's grief, in a day; a year's, in twelve:
And, of what age soever, in a month.
Past all the doses, of your drugging Doctors.
I'll undertake, withal, to fright the plague
Out o' the kingdom, in three months.

SURLY
And I'll
Be bound the players shall sing your praises, then,
Without their poets.

MAMMON
Sir, I'll do't. Meantime,
I'll give away so much, unto my man,
Shall serve th' whole city, with preservative,
Weekly, each house his dose, and at the rate—

57 *philosophers* alchemists (here)
62 *Pict-Hatch* near Clerkenwell; resort of prostitutes
64 *naturized* naturata, as distinct from naturans
74 *preservative* i.e. medicinal

---

55 *like an eagle.* This refers to the idea that every ten years the eagle soars into the 'fiery region', then plunges into the sea, where, moulting its feathers, it acquires new life. But there is also an unmistakable allusion to *Psalms*, ciii, 5, and a suitably blasphemous irony.

58 The patriarchs, from Adam to Noah, were believed to have understood alchemy among other mysteries. Their great ages, as recorded in *Genesis*, were taken as proof that they possessed the philosopher's stone.

71 *the players shall sing your praises.* For fear of spreading infection the London theatres were closed when the number of cases of plague reached a statutory limit, variously given as thirty and forty.

SURLY
As he that built the waterwork, does with water?
MAMMON
You are incredulous.
SURLY
Faith, I have a humour,
I would not willingly be gulled. Your stone
Cannot transmute me.
MAMMON
Pertinax, Surly,
Will you believe antiquity? Records?
I'll show you a book, where Moses, and his sister,
And Solomon have written, of the art;
Ay, and a treatise penned by Adam.
SURLY
How!
MAMMON
O' the philosopher's stone, and in High Dutch.
SURLY
Did Adam write, sir, in High Dutch?
MAMMON
He did:
Which proves it was the primitive tongue.
SURLY
What paper?
MAMMON
On cedar board.
SURLY
O that, indeed (they say)
Will last 'gainst worms.
MAMMON
'Tis like your Irish wood,
'Gainst cobwebs. I have a piece of Jason's fleece, too,
Which was no other, than a book of alchemy,
Writ in large sheepskin, a good fat ram-vellum.
Such was Pythagoras' thigh, Pandora's tub;
And, all that fable of Medea's charms,
The manner of our work: the bulls, our furnace,

77 *humour* i.e. it is my nature 79 *Pertinax* pertinacity
91 *ram-vellum* parchment of ram's hide

---

76 *waterwork.* Waterworks supplying different parts of London with water from the Thames were built in 1582 and 1594. See Stow, *A Survey of London*, 1598, p. 18.

81–83 *I'll show . . . Adam.* Writers on alchemy frequently claimed Adam, Moses, Miriam and Solomon as masters in that art. Many of the works attributed to them are collected in J. A. Fabricius, *Codex Pseudepigraphus Veteris Testamenti*, 1713.

85 *High Dutch.* 'Ioannes Goropius Becanus, a man very learned . . . letted not to maintaine it [the German language] to bee the first and moste ancient language of the world; yea the same that Adam spake in Paradise.' Richard Verstegan, *A Restitution of Decayed Intelligence*, 1605, p. 190.

89–100 *I have a piece . . . fixed.* All these interpretations could be found in a book like Martin Delrio, *Disquisitiones Magicae*, 1599.

Still breathing fire; our argent-vive, the dragon:
The dragon's teeth, mercury sublimate,
That keeps the whiteness, hardness, and the biting;
And they are gathered, into Jason's helm,
(Th' alembic) and then sowed in Mars his field,
And, thence, sublimed so often, till they are fixed.
Both this, th' Hesperian garden, Cadmus' story,
Jove's shower, the boon of Midas, Argus' eyes,
Boccace his Demogorgon, thousands more,
All abstract riddles of our stone. How now?

Act II, Scene ii

[*Enter*] FACE

MAMMON
Do we succeed? Is our day come? And holds it?

FACE
The evening will set red, upon you, sir;
You have colour for it, crimson: the red ferment
Has done his office. Three hours hence, prepare you
To see projection.

MAMMON
Pertinax, my Surly,
Again, I say to thee, aloud: be rich.
This day, thou shalt have ingots: and, tomorrow,
Give lords th'affront. Is it, my Zephyrus, right?
Blushes the bolt's head?

FACE
Like a wench with child, sir,
That were, but now, discovered to her master.

MAMMON
Excellent witty Lungs! My only care is,
Where to get stuff, enough now, to project on,
This town will not half serve me.

FACE
No, sir? Buy
The covering off o' churches.

MAMMON
That's true.

FACE
Yes.
Let 'em stand bare, as do their auditory.
Or cap 'em, new, with shingles.

MAMMON
No, good thatch:
Thatch will lie light upo' the rafters, Lungs.

95 *argent-vive* mercury 99 *alembic* distilling apparatus
102 *Jove's shower* i.e. the Danae 3 *crimson cf.* II.i, 48
5 *projection* last stage in alchemy 8 *affront* look in the eye
9 *bolt's head* globular flask

101–4 *th' Hesperian garden* &c. From Robertus Vallensis, *De Veritate et Antiquitate Artis Chemiae*, Paris, 1561.

Lungs, I will manumit thee, from the furnace;
I will restore thee thy complexion, Puff,
Lost in the embers; and repair this brain,
Hurt wi' the fume o' the metals.

FACE I have blown, sir,
Hard, for your worship; thrown by many a coal,
When 'twas not beech; weighed those I put in, just,
To keep your heat, still even; these bleared eyes
Have waked, to read your several colours, sir,
Of the pale citron, the green lion, the crow,
The peacock's tail, the plumed swan.

MAMMON And, lastly,
Thou hast descried the flower, the *sanguis agni*?

FACE
Yes, sir.

MAMMON Where's master?

FACE At's prayers, sir, he,
Good man, he's doing his devotions,
For the success.

MAMMON Lungs, I will set a period,
To all thy labours: thou shalt be the master
Of my seraglio.

FACE Good, sir.

MAMMON But do you hear?
I'll geld you, Lungs.

FACE Yes, sir.

MAMMON For I do mean
To have a list of wives, and concubines,
Equal with Solomon; who had the stone
Alike, with me: and I will make me, a back
With the elixir, that shall be as tough
As Hercules, to encounter fifty a night.
Th'art sure, thou saw'st it blood?

FACE Both blood, and spirit, sir.

18 *manumit* release 31 *period* stop, end
40 *blood cf.* line 28

---

23 *not beech.* It was crucial that the alchemist's fire should be made of beech, which was thought to be the best wood for maintaining a steady heat.

25 *several colours.* These colours showed the various degrees of fermentation. There seems to have been no fixed scale common to all alchemists, but black (the crow) and green (the lion) were matters for congratulation when achieved, while white (the swan) and yellow (citron) were ascending stages towards red, the colour of projection. Jonson's audience would have been mystified by all these terms except *sanguis agni*, the associations of which would have been quite clear.

MAMMON

I will have all my beds, blown up; not stuffed:
Down is too hard. And then, mine oval room,
Filled with such pictures, as Tiberius took
From Elephantis: and dull Aretine
But coldly imitated. Then, my glasses,
Cut in more subtle angles, to disperse,
And multiply the figures, as I walk
Naked between my succubae. My mists
I'll have of perfume, vapoured 'bout the room,
To lose ourselves in; and my baths, like pits
To fall into: from whence, we will come forth,
And roll us dry in gossamer, and roses.
(Is it arrived at ruby?)–Where I spy
A wealthy citizen, or rich lawyer,
Have a sublimed pure wife, unto that fellow
I'll send a thousand pound, to be my cuckold.

FACE

And I shall carry it?

MAMMON

No. I'll ha' no bawds,
But fathers, and mothers. They will do it best.
Best of all others. And, my flatterers
Shall be the pure, and gravest of Divines,
That I can get for money. My mere fools,
Eloquent burgesses, and then my poets
The same that writ so subtly of the fart,

48 *succubae* both female demon, and harlot – double sense intended
55 *sublimed* sublimated (alchemical), refined (figuratively)
57 *carry it?* so F (Q carry it.)
62 *burgesses* members of Parliament

---

41 *beds, blown up*. Lampridius, *Heliogabalus*, 19 and 25.
43 *Tiberius* &c. Suetonius, *Tiberius*, 43. Elephantis was a Roman author, known only from the references in Suetonius and Martial (*Epigrams*, XII, xliii).
44 *Aretine*. Pietro Aretino (1492–1556), playwright and journalist. The reference is to the sixteen obscene designs by Giulio Romano engraved by Raimondi, for which Aretino wrote sixteen *Sonnetti lussuriosi*, 1523. Cf. *Volpone*, III.iv, 96.
45 See Seneca, *Naturales Quaestiones*, I,xvi.
48 *mists*. Suetonius, *Nero*, xxxi.
58 *fathers, and mothers*. Juvenal, *Satires*, x, 304–6.
63 *the fart*. One of the most popular pieces in seventeenth century commonplace books. It is headed 'A discussion in the House of Commons on the peculiar manner in which Henry Ludlow said "noe" to a message brought by the Serjeant from the Lords' in MS. Ashmole 36–7, f.131, and dated 1607 in MS. Harley 5191, f.17. Versions were later printed in the miscellanies: see Mennis and Smith, *Musarum Deliciae*, 1656.

Whom I will entertain, still, for that subject.
The few, that would give out themselves, to be
Court, and town stallions, and, each-where, belie
Ladies, who are known most innocent, for them;
Those will I beg, to make me eunuchs of:
And they shall fan me with ten ostrich tails
Apiece, made in a plume, to gather wind.
We will be brave, Puff, now we ha' the medicine.
My meat, shall all come in, in Indian shells,
Dishes of agate, set in gold, and studded,
With emeralds, sapphires, hyacinths, and rubies.
The tongues of carps, dormice, and camels' heels,
Boiled i' the spirit of Sol, and dissolved pearl,
(Apicius' diet, 'gainst the epilepsy)
And I will eat these broths, with spoons of amber,
Headed with diamond, and carbuncle.
My footboy shall eat pheasants, calvered salmons,
Knots, godwits, lampreys: I myself will have
The beards of barbels, served, instead of salads;
Oiled mushrooms; and the swelling unctuous paps
Of a fat pregnant sow, newly cut off,
Dressed with an exquisite, and poignant sauce;
For which, I'll say unto my cook, there's gold,
Go forth, and be a knight.

FACE Sir, I'll go look
A little, how it heightens. [*Exit* FACE]

MAMMON Do. My shirts
I'll have of taffeta-sarsnet, soft, and light
As cobwebs; and for all my other raiment
It shall be such, as might provoke the Persian;
Were he to teach the world riot, anew.

66 *belie* slander (to sustain the proposed reputation)
74 *hyacinths* species of gem
76 *Sol* i.e. gold
77 *Apicius'* a Roman gourmand
80 *calvered* carved while still alive
89 *taffeta-sarsnet* (or sarcenet) fine, soft silk

---

75 *camels' heels*. Lampridius, *Heliogabalus*, 20.
83 *unctuous paps* &c. Herford and Simpson quote Holland's translation of Pliny (1601): 'sows were killed even upon the point of their farrowing, and being readie to Pig [as our monstrous gluttons doe nowadaies, because they would have the teats soft, tender, and full of milke].' The air of degenerate luxury in Mammon's speeches is created for the most part by allusion to the excesses of Roman emperors. Jonson's judgement is the same as Gibbon's.

My gloves of fishes', and birds' skins, perfumed
With gums of paradise, and eastern air—

SURLY
And do you think to have the stone, with this?

MAMMON
No, I do think, t' have all this, with the stone.

SURLY
Why, I have heard, he must be *homo frugi*,
A pious, holy, and religious man,
One free from mortal sin, a very virgin.

MAMMON
That makes it, sir, he is so. But I buy it.
My venture brings it me. He, honest wretch,
A notable, superstitious, good soul,
Has worn his knees bare, and his slippers bald,
With prayer, and fasting for it: and, sir, let him
Do it alone, for me, still. Here he comes,
Not a profane word, afore him: 'tis poison.

Act II, Scene iii

[*Enter*] SUBTLE

MAMMON
Good morrow, Father.

SUBTLE
Gentle son, good morrow,
And, to your friend, there. What is he, is with you?

MAMMON
An heretic, that I did bring along,
In hope, sir, to convert him.

SUBTLE
Son, I doubt
You're covetous, that thus you meet your time
I' the just point: prevent your day, at morning.
This argues something, worthy of a fear
Of importune, and carnal appetite.
Take heed, you do not cause the blessing leave you,
With your ungoverned haste. I should be sorry,
To see my labours, now, e'en at perfection,
Got by long watching, and large patience,

93 i.e. cheverel or silk 100 *That makes* He that makes
101 *venture* financial investment 105 *alone* only
5 *meet your time* prove so punctual 6 *prevent* anticipate
8 *importune* importunate

---

97 *homo frugi*. The necessity of piety and austerity of life in the would-be alchemist was insisted upon by all who taught the art.

Not prosper, where my love, and zeal hath placed 'em.
Which (heaven I call to witness, with yourself,
To whom, I have poured my thoughts) in all my ends,
Have looked no way, but unto public good,
To pious uses, and dear charity,
Now grown a prodigy with men. Wherein
If you, my son, should now prevaricate,
And, to your own particular lusts, employ
So great, and catholic a bliss: be sure,
A curse will follow, yea, and overtake
Your subtle, and most secret ways.

MAMMON I know, sir,
You shall not need to fear me. I but come,
To ha' you confute this gentleman.

SURLY Who is,
Indeed, sir, somewhat costive of belief
Toward your stone: would not be gulled.

SUBTLE Well, son,
All that I can convince him in, is this,
The work is done: bright Sol is in his robe.
We have a medicine of the triple soul,
The glorified spirit. Thanks be to heaven,
And make us worthy of it. Eulenspiegel.

[*Enter* FACE]

FACE
Anon, sir.

SUBTLE Look well to the register,
And let your heat, still, lessen by degrees,
To the aludels.

FACE Yes, sir.

SUBTLE Did you look
O' the bolt's head yet?

19 *prevaricate* take a crooked path
21 *catholic* universal
26 *costive* (figuratively) reticent
32 *Eulenspiegel* (owlglass) folklore name for a jesting knave
33 *register* damper
35 *aludels* pots, open at both ends (HS)

30–31 *the triple soul, The glorified spirit.* i.e. the elixir. Norton, in his *Ordinall* (ed. Ashmole, 1652) speaks of a 'treble Spirit', vital, natural and animal, by which the soul was knit to the body:

> Therefore in our worke as Auctors teach us,
> There must be *Corpus, Anima & Spiritus.*

FACE
Which, on D, sir?

SUBTLE
Ay.
What's the complexion?

FACE
Whitish.

SUBTLE
Infuse vinegar,
To draw his volatile substance, and his tincture:
And let the water in glass E be filtered,
And put into the gripe's egg. Lute him well;
And leave him closed in *balneo*.

FACE
I will, sir.

SURLY
What a brave language here is? Next to canting?

SUBTLE
I have another work; you never saw, son,
That, three days since, passed the philosopher's wheel,
In the lent heat of Athanor; and's become
Sulphur o' nature.

MAMMON
But 'tis for me?

SUBTLE
What need you?
You have enough, in that is, perfect.

MAMMON
O, but—

SUBTLE
Why, this is covetise!

MAMMON
No, I assure you,
I shall employ it all, in pious uses,
Founding of colleges, and grammar schools,
Marrying young virgins, building hospitals,
And now, and then, a church.

SUBTLE
How now?

FACE
Sir, please you,
Shall I not change the filter?

SUBTLE
Marry, yes.
And bring me the complexion of glass B. [*Exit* FACE]

MAMMON
Ha' you another?

40 *gripe's egg* pot shaped like griffin's egg;
Lute make clay covering
41 *balneo* sand-bath or water-bath for gradual heating
42 *canting* thieves' jargon; possibly also puritans'
44 *philosopher's wheel* alchemical cycle
45 *lent heat* (Latin) slow fire
48 *covetise* covetousness

---

36 *on D sir?* Several different furnaces are supposed to be operating in the adjoining room, distinguished by different letters.

SUBTLE Yes, son, were I assured
Your piety were firm, we would not want
The means to glorify it. But I hope the best:
I mean to tinct C in sand-heat, tomorrow,
And give him imbibition.

MAMMON Of white oil?

SUBTLE
No, sir, of red. F is come over the helm too,
I thank my Maker, in S. Mary's bath,
And shows *lac virginis.* Blessed be heaven.
I sent you of his faeces there, calcined.
Out of that calx, I ha' won the salt of mercury.

MAMMON
By pouring on your rectified water?

SUBTLE
Yes, and reverberating in Athanor.

[*Enter* FACE]

How now? What colour says it?

FACE The ground black, sir.

MAMMON
That's your crow's head?

SURLY Your cockscomb's, is't not?

SUBTLE
No, 'tis not perfect, would it were the crow.
That work wants something.

SURLY (O, I looked for this.
The hay is a-pitching.)

SUBTLE Are you sure, you loosed 'em
I' their own menstrue?

FACE Yes, sir, and then married 'em,
And put 'em in a bolt's head, nipped to digestion,
According as you bade me; when I set
The liquor of Mars to circulation,
In the same heat.

SUBTLE The process, then, was right.

59 *imbibition* soaking 60 *helm* cap of a retort
61 *Mary's bath* heat-bath
63 *sent you* (used impersonally)
faeces sediment
64 *calx* thoroughly burnt powder; *salt* oxide
66 *reverberating* reflected heat 67 *ground* putrefying
68 *crow's head* symbolizing total calcination
71 *hay* netted snare for rabbits
73 *digestion* (chemically) substance exposed to liquid, heated
75 *liquor of Mars* molten iron

FACE
Yes, by the token, sir, the retort broke,
And what was saved, was put into the pelican,
And signed with Hermes' seal.

SUBTLE
I think 'twas so.
We should have a new amalgama.

SURLY
O, this ferret
Is rank as any pole-cat.

SUBTLE
But I care not.
Let him e'en die; we have enough beside,
In embrion. H has his white shirt on?

FACE
Yes, sir,
He's ripe for inceration: he stands warm,
In his ash-fire. I would not, you should let
Any die now, if I might counsel, sir,
For luck's sake to the rest. It is not good.

MAMMON
He says right.

SURLY
Ay, are you bolted?

FACE
Nay, I know't, sir,
I have seen th' ill fortune. What is some three ounces
Of fresh materials?

MAMMON
Is't no more?

FACE
No more, sir,
Of gold, t'amalgam, with some six of mercury.

MAMMON
Away, here's money. What will serve?

FACE
Ask him, sir.

MAMMON
How much?

SUBTLE
Give him nine pound: you may gi' him ten.

SURLY
Yes, twenty, and be cozened, do.

MAMMON
There 'tis.

SUBTLE
This needs not. But that you will have it, so,
To see conclusions of all. For two
Of our inferior works, are at fixation.

78 *pelican* vessel so shaped 79 i.e. hermetically sealed
80 *amalgama* mixture of metals with mercury; *ferret* (see line 71) to drive the rabbit out and (line 88) 'bolt' it
83 *embrion* (chemically) metal still in combination
84 *inceration* making into moist wax 94 *cozened* cheated
97 *fixation* reduction of the volatile to permanent form, conversion (of mercury) into solid

A third is in ascension. Go your ways.
Ha' you set the oil of Luna in kemia?

FACE
Yes, sir.

SUBTLE And the philosopher's vinegar?

FACE
Ay. [*Exit* FACE]

SURLY
We shall have a salad.

MAMMON When do you make projection?

SUBTLE
Son, be not hasty, I exalt our medicine,
By hanging him in *balneo vaporoso*;
And giving him solution; then congeal him;
And then dissolve him; then again congeal him;
For look, how oft I iterate the work,
So many times, I add unto his virtue.
As, if at first, one ounce convert a hundred,
After his second loose, he'll turn a thousand;
His third solution, ten; his fourth, a hundred.
After his fifth, a thousand thousand ounces
Of any imperfect metal, into pure
Silver, or gold, in all examinations,
As good, as any of the natural mine.
Get you your stuff here, against afternoon,
Your brass, your pewter, and your andirons.

MAMMON
Not those of iron?

SUBTLE Yes, you may bring them, too.
We'll change all metals.

SURLY I believe you, in that.

MAMMON
Then I may send my spits?

SUBTLE Yes, and your racks.

SURLY
And dripping pans, and pot-hangers, and hooks?
Shall he not?

SUBTLE If he please.

SURLY To be an ass.

SUBTLE
How, sir!

MAMMON This gentleman, you must bear withal.

98 *ascension* distillation
99 *oil of Luna* white elixir; *kemia* a cucurbit (chymia)
100 *philosopher's vinegar* universal dissolvent
101 *salad* punningly also sallad, a recognized alchemical compound
109 *loose* i.e. in solution 116 *andirons* bars to support fire

I told you, he had no faith.

SURLY
And little hope, sir,
But, much less charity, should I gull myself.

SUBTLE
Why, what have you observed, sir, in our art,
Seems so impossible?

SURLY
But your whole work, no more.
That you should hatch gold in a furnace, sir,
As they do eggs, in Egypt!

SUBTLE
Sir, do you
Believe that eggs are hatched so?

SURLY
If I should?

SUBTLE
Why, I think that the greater miracle.
No egg, but differs from a chicken, more,
Than metals in themselves.

SURLY
That cannot be.
The egg's ordained by nature, to that end:
And is a chicken in *potentia*.

SUBTLE
The same we say of lead, and other metals,
Which would be gold, if they had time.

MAMMON
And that
Our art doth further.

SUBTLE
Ay, for 'twere absurd
To think that nature, in the earth, bred gold
Perfect, i' the instant. Something went before.
There must be remote matter.

SURLY
Ay, what is that?

126 *But* only 139 *Perfect* (here, and passim) complete
140 *remote* prima materia, the first matter

---

128 *eggs, in Egypt*. The Egyptians hatched eggs by incubation in an oven heated by burning dung. See Pliny, *Natural History*, trans. Holland, 1635, x.liv.

131–76 *No egg, but differs* &c. This is the orthodox theory of alchemy, so Subtle can afford to set it forth quite clearly. If we grant the principles (1) the ultimate convertibility of matter from one state into another (2) the properties of a substance are due to the existence of universal principles in that substance (e.g. honey is sweet because it contains some portion of that sweetness which exists apart from all sweet things) then the argument is logical. As the egg strives to become a chicken, so all metals strive to become gold. Subtle does no more than develop these commonplaces, and locks up the argument by appeal to the theory of spontaneous generation (171–6), which was widely believed at the time. Herford and Simpson point out that the whole of this passage is taken from Delrio, *Disquisitiones Magicae*, i.83. It is explained in detail in Hathaway's edition of *The Alchemist*, pp. 20–23.

SUBTLE

Marry, we say—

MAMMON Ay, now it heats: stand Father.

Pound him to dust—

SUBTLE It is, of the one part,

A humid exhalation, which we call
Materia liquida, or the unctuous water;
On th' other part, a certain crass, and viscous
Portion of earth; both which, concorporate,
Do make the elementary matter of gold:
Which is not, yet, *propria materia*,
But common to all metals, and all stones.
For, where it is forsaken of that moisture
And hath more dryness, it becomes a stone;
Where it retains more of the humid fatness,
It turns to sulphur, or to quicksilver:
Who are the parents of all other metals.
Nor can this remote matter, suddenly,
Progress so from extreme, unto extreme,
As to grow gold, and leap o'er all the means.
Nature doth, first, beget th' imperfect; then
Proceeds she to the perfect. Of that airy,
And oily water, mercury is engendered;
Sulphur o' the fat, and earthy part: the one
(Which is the last) supplying the place of male,
The other of the female, in all metals.
Some do believe hermaphrodeity,
That both do act, and suffer. But, these two
Make the rest ductile, malleable, extensive.
And, even in gold, they are; for we do find
Seeds of them, by our fire, and gold in them:
And can produce the species of each metal
More perfect thence, than nature doth in earth.
Beside, who doth not see, in daily practice,
Art can beget bees, hornets, beetles, wasps,
Out of the carcasses, and dung of creatures;
Yea, scorpions, of an herb, being rightly placed:
And these are living creatures, far more perfect,
And excellent, than metals.

MAMMON Well said, Father!

Nay, if he take you in hand, sir, with an argument,

145 *crass* dense, thick 157 *means* intermediate stages
164 *hermaphrodeity* combining characteristics of either sex
166 *extensive* i.e. can permeate, or be drawn out, spread out
174 *herb* i.e. basil

He'll bray you in a mortar.

SURLY
Pray you, sir, stay.
Rather, than I'll be brayed, sir, I'll believe,
That alchemy is a pretty kind of game,
Somewhat like tricks o' the cards, to cheat a man,
With charming.

SUBTLE
Sir?

SURLY
What else are all your terms,
Whereon no one o' your writers 'grees with other?
Of your elixir, your *lac virginis*,
Your stone, your medicine, and your chrysosperm,
Your sal, your sulphur, and your mercury,
Your oil of height, your tree of life, your blood,
Your marcasite, your tutty, your magnesia,
Your toad, your crow, your dragon, and your panther,
Your sun, your moon, your firmament, your adrop,
Your lato, azoch, zernich, chibrit, autarit,
And then, your red man, and your white woman,
With all your broths, your menstrues, and materials,
Of piss, and eggshells, women's terms, man's blood,
Hair o' the head, burnt clouts, chalk, merds, and clay,
Powder of bones, scalings of iron, glass,
And worlds of other strange ingredients,
Would burst a man to name?

SUBTLE
And all these, named
Intending but one thing: which art our writers
Used to obscure their art.

MAMMON
Sir, so I told him,
Because the simple idiot should not learn it,
And make it vulgar.

SUBTLE
Was not all the knowledge
Of the Egyptians writ in mystic symbols?
Speak not the Scriptures, oft, in parables?
Are not the choicest fables of the poets,
That were the fountains, and first springs of wisdom,
Wrapped in perplexed allegories?

178 *bray . . . mortar* i.e. crush with pestle, pound. Vide *Proverbs* xxvii, 22
182 *charming* casting a spell, beguiling
184 *lac virginis* water of mercury 185 *chrysosperm* seed of gold
188 *tutty* impure zinc
190 *adrop* lead
191 *lato* latten, a mixed metal; *azoch* quicksilver; *zernich* trisulphide of arsenic; *chibrit* sulphur; *autarit*(*e*) mercury
192 *red man . . . white woman* sulphur and mercury
195 *merds* ordure

MAMMON I urged that,
And cleared to him, that Sisyphus was damned
To roll the ceaseless stone, only, because
He would have made ours common. Who is this?

Dol is seen

SUBTLE
God's precious–What do you mean? Go in, good lady,
Let me entreat you. Where's this varlet?

[*Enter* FACE]

FACE Sir?

SUBTLE
You very knave! Do you use me, thus?

FACE Wherein, sir?

SUBTLE
Go in, and see, you traitor. Go. [*Exit* FACE]

MAMMON Who is it, sir?

SUBTLE
Nothing, sir. Nothing.

MAMMON What's the matter? Good, sir!
I have not seen you thus distempered. Who is 't?

SUBTLE
All arts have still had, sir, their adversaries,

FACE *returns*

But ours the most ignorant. What now?

FACE
'Twas not my fault, sir, she would speak with you.

SUBTLE
Would she, sir? Follow me.

MAMMON Stay, Lungs.

FACE I dare not, sir.

MAMMON
How! Pray thee stay

FACE She's mad, sir, and sent hither—

MAMMON
Stay man, what is she?

FACE A lord's sister, sir.
(He'll be mad too.

MAMMON I warrant thee.) Why sent hither?

FACE
Sir, to be cured.

SUBTLE [*within*] Why, rascal!

208 *Sisyphus*. Again, from Delrio, *Disquisit*. *Mag*. i.66.

FACE
Lo you. Here, sir.

He goes out

MAMMON
'Fore God, a Bradamante, a brave piece.

SURLY
Heart, this is a bawdyhouse! I'll be burnt else.

MAMMON
O, by this light, no. Do not wrong him. He's
Too scrupulous, that way. It is his vice.
No, he's a rare physician, do him right.
An excellent Paracelsian! And has done
Strange cures with mineral physic. He deals all
With spirits, he. He will not hear a word
Of Galen, or his tedious recipes.

FACE *again*

How now, Lungs!

FACE
Softly, sir, speak softly. I meant
To ha' told your worship all. This must not hear.

MAMMON
No, he will not be gulled; let him alone.

FACE
You're very right, sir, she is a most rare scholar;
And is gone mad, with studying Broughton's works.
If you but name a word, touching the Hebrew,
She falls into her fit, and will discourse
So learnedly of genealogies,
As you would run mad, too, to hear her, sir.

MAMMON
How might one do t'have conference with her, Lungs?

FACE
O, divers have run mad upon the conference.
I do not know, sir: I am sent in haste,
To fetch a vial.

SURLY
Be not gulled, Sir Mammon.

MAMMON
Wherein? Pray ye, be patient.

SURLY
Yes, as you are.
And trust confederate knaves, and bawds, and whores.

225 *Bradamante* an Amazon (in *Orlando Furioso*)
230 *Paracelsian* Paracelsus (1493–1541) united chemistry with medicine
233 i.e. traditional herbs and drugs
235 *This* i.e. Surly
236 *gulled* (ironically intended)
238 *Broughton* a contemporary O.T. theologian
244 i.e. upon merely meeting her

MAMMON
You are too foul, believe it. Come, here, Eulen.
One word.

FACE I dare not, in good faith.

MAMMON Stay, knave.

FACE
He's extreme angry, that you saw her, sir.

MAMMON
Drink that. What is she, when she's out of her fit?

FACE
O, the most affablest creature, sir! So merry!
So pleasant! She'll mount you up, like quicksilver,
Over the helm; and circulate, like oil,
A very vegetal: discourse of state,
Of mathematics, bawdry, anything—

MAMMON
Is she no way accessible? No means,
No trick, to give a man a taste of her–wit—
Or so?

SUBTLE [*within*] Eulen!

FACE I'll come to you again, sir. [*Exit* FACE]

MAMMON
Surly, I did not think, one o' your breeding
Would traduce personages of worth.

SURLY Sir Epicure,
Your friend to use: yet, still, loth to be gulled.
I do not like your philosophical bawds.
Their stone is lechery enough, to pay for,
Without this bait.

MAMMON Heart, you abuse yourself.
I know the lady, and her friends, and means,
The original of this disaster. Her brother
Has told me all.

SURLY And yet, you ne'er saw her
Till now?

MAMMON O, yes, but I forgot. I have (believe it)
One of the treacherous'st memories, I do think,
Of all mankind.

SURLY What call you her, brother?

MAMMON My lord—

249 *Eulen* so F (Q has Zephyrus) 252 *Drink that* i.e. a bribe
256 *vegetal* perhaps (Latin) active

259–60 Q has 'Wit? or so?' as the beginning of line 260. In F 'Eulen' is made a part of Mammon's speech; Q omits the word altogether. The present emendation is Gifford's.

He wi' not have his name known, now I think on't.

SURLY
A very treacherous memory!

MAMMON
O' my faith—

SURLY
Tut, if you ha' it not about you, pass it,
Till we meet next.

MAMMON
Nay, by this hand, 'tis true.
He's one I honour, and my noble friend,
And I respect his house.

SURLY
Heart! Can it be,
That a grave sir, a rich, that has no need,
A wise sir, too, at other times, should thus
With his own oaths, and arguments, make hard means
To gull himself? And, this be your elixir,
Your *lapis mineralis*, and your lunary,
Give me your honest trick, yet, at primero,
Or gleek; and take your *lutum sapientis*,
Your *menstruum simplex:* I'll have gold, before you,
And, with less danger of the quicksilver;
Or the hot sulphur.

[*Enter* FACE]

FACE
Here's one from Captain Face, sir,
To SURLY
Desires you meet him i' the Temple Church,
Some half hour hence, and upon earnest business.
Sir, if you please to quit us, now; and come,
He whispers MAMMON
Again, within two hours: you shall have,
My master busy examining o' the works;
And I will steal you in, unto the party,
That you may see her converse. [*To* SURLY]
Sir, shall I say,
You'll meet the Captain's worship?

SURLY
Sir, I will.
But, by attorney, and to a second purpose.

281 *hard* harsh
283 *lunary* the fern, moonwort, whose 'liquor' was connected with making silver
285 *gleek* a card game; *lutum* philosopher's lute, or clay
286 *menstruum* plain solvent
287 (with side-glance at venereal diseases and scabies)
289 *Temple Church* the Round, a usual meeting-place
295 *converse* euphemistically, for sexual attractions
297 *attorney* in another's person

Now, I am sure, it is a bawdy house;
I'll swear it, were the Marshal here, to thank me:
The naming this Commander, doth confirm it.
Don Face! Why, he's the most authentic dealer
I' these commodities! The Superintendent
To all the quainter traffickers, in town.
He is their Visitor, and does appoint
Who lies with whom; and at what hour; what price;
Which gown; and in what smock; what fall; what tire.
Him, will I prove, by a third person, to find
The subleties of this dark labyrinth:
Which, if I do discover, dear Sir Mammon,
You'll give your poor friend leave, though no philosopher,
To laugh: for you that are, 'tis thought, shall weep.

FACE
Sir. He does pray, you'll not forget.

SURLY
I will not, sir.
Sir Epicure, I shall leave you? [*Exit* SURLY]

MAMMON
I follow you, straight.

FACE
But do so, good sir, to avoid suspicion.
This gentleman has a parlous head.

MAMMON
But wilt thou, Eulen,
Be constant to thy promise?

FACE
As my life, sir.

MAMMON
And wilt thou insinuate what I am? And praise me?
And say I am a noble fellow?

FACE
O, what else, sir?
And, that you'll make her royal, with the stone,
An empress; and yourself King of Bantam.

MAMMON
Wilt thou do this?

FACE
Will I, sir?

MAMMON
Lungs, my Lungs!
I love thee.

FACE
Send your stuff, sir, that my master
May busy himself, about projection.

299 *Marshal* provost
300 *Commander* another euphemism; so *Superintendent*, *quainter*, *Visitor*
306 *fall* loose collar, as against stiff ruff; *tire* apron (primarily; but see *O.E.D.* for euphemistic suggestions)
315 *parlous* (perilous) here, shrewd, penetrating
320 *Bantam* Javanese city, newly opened to trade: associated with dreams of wealth

MAMMON

Th'hast witched me, rogue: take, go.

FACE

Your jack, and all, sir.

MAMMON

Thou art a villain–I will send my jack;
And the weights too. Slave, I could bite thine ear.
Away, thou dost not care for me.

FACE

Not I, sir?

MAMMON

Come, I was born to make thee, my good weasel;
Set thee on a bench: and, ha' thee twirl a chain
With the best lord's vermin, of 'em all.

FACE

Away, sir.

MAMMON

A count, nay, a count-palatine—

FACE

Good sir, go.

MAMMON

Shall not advance thee, better: no, nor faster.

[*Exit* MAMMON]

Act II, Scene iv

[*Enter*] SUBTLE, DOL

SUBTLE

Has he bit? Has he bit?

FACE

And swallowed too, my Subtle.
I ha' given him line, and now he plays, i' faith.

SUBTLE

And shall we twitch him?

FACE

Thorough both the gills.
A wench is a rare bait, with which a man
No sooner's taken, but he straight firks mad.

SUBTLE

Dol, my Lord Wha'ts'hum's sister, you must now
Bear yourself *statelich.*

DOL

O, let me alone.
I'll not forget my race, I warrant you.
I'll keep my distance, laugh, and talk aloud;
Have all the tricks of a proud scurvy lady,
And be as rude's her woman.

324 *jack* mechanism to regulate heat supply
326 *bite thine ear* i.e. amorously
330 *vermin* punning on ermine
5 *firks mad* is stirred to raging madness
7 *statelich* stately (German, or Dutch: printed as German in F)

FACE
Well said, Sanguine.

SUBTLE
But will he send his andirons?

FACE
His jack too;
And's iron shoeing horn: I ha' spoke to him. Well,
I must not lose my wary gamester, yonder.

SUBTLE
O Monsieur Caution, that will not be gulled?

FACE
Ay, if I can strike a fine hook into him, now,
The Temple Church, there I have cast mine angle.
Well, pray for me. I'll about it.

SUBTLE
What, more gudgeons!

One knocks

Dol, scout, scout; stay Face, you must go to the door:
Pray God, it be my Anabaptist. Who is't, Dol?

DOL
I know him not. He looks like a gold-end-man.

SUBTLE
Gods so! 'Tis he, he said he would send. What call you him?
The sanctified Elder, that should deal
For Mammon's jack, and andirons! Let him in.
Stay, help me off, first, with my gown. Away
Madam, to your withdrawing chamber. Now, [*Exit* DOL]
In a new tune, new gesture, but old language.
This fellow is sent, from one negotiates with me
About the stone, too; for the holy Brethren
Of Amsterdam, the exiled Saints: that hope
To raise their discipline, by it. I must use him
In some strange fashion, now, to make him admire me.

11 *Sanguine* i.e. (here) amorous of disposition
18 *gudgeons* (will swallow anything)
21 *gold-end-man* like modern collector of 'old gold and silver, brassware, etc.'
30 *exiled Saints* puritans who had fled abroad (to Geneva, Amsterdam and elsewhere)

---

20 *Anabaptist*. This sect is first known in Germany in 1521, and began to appear in England around 1534. It attempted to set up a theocracy, and advocated adult baptism and community of goods.

Act II, Scene v

[*Enter*] ANANIAS

SUBTLE
Where is my drudge?
FACE
Sir.
SUBTLE
Take away the recipient,
And rectify your menstrue, from the phlegma.
Then pour it, o' the Sol, in the cucurbite,
And let 'em macerate, together.
FACE
Yes, sir.
And save the ground?
SUBTLE
No. *Terra damnata*
Must not have entrance, in the work. Who are you?
ANANIAS
A faithful Brother, if it please you.
SUBTLE
What's that?
A Lullianist? A Ripley? *Filius artis*?
Can you sublime, and dulcify? Calcine?
Know you the *sapor pontic*? *Sapor styptic*?
Or, what is the homogene, or heterogene?
ANANIAS
I understand no heathen language, truly.
SUBTLE
Heathen, you Knipperdoling? Is *Ars sacra*,
Or *chrysopoeia*, or *spagyrica*,

1 *recipient* receptacle
2 *phlegma* watery product of distillation
4 *macerate* soften by soaking
5 *ground . . . Terra* i.e. the sediment
9 *sublime* process for solids similar to distillation for liquids; *dulcify* neutralize acidity; eliminate salts; *Calcine* reduce to powder by intense heat
10 *sapor* i.e. trial by taste; *pontic* sour; *styptic* astringent
14 *chrysopoeia* making of gold; *spagyrica* alchemical wisdom

---

8 *A Lullianist? A Ripley?* Two celebrated alchemists. Subtle deliberately misunderstands Ananias's 'A faithful Brother' as meaning an alchemist. Raymond Lully (1235–1315) was a Spanish courtier, missionary, alchemist, and inventor of a machine for logic, by which one could try mechanically all possible aspects of a given proposition. Sir George Ripley, canon of Bridlington, died *circa* 1490. His chief works are *The Compound of Alchemie* (written 1471, published 1591), and *Medulla Alchemiae*, 1476.
13 *Knipperdoling*. Bernt Knipperdollinck, a draper, was an Anabaptist leader in the Munster Rising (1534), when 'the Kingdom of God' was established there under John of Leyden. The main features of this kingdom were debauchery and despotism.

Of the pamphysic, or panarchic knowledge,
A heathen language?

ANANIAS Heathen Greek, I take it.

SUBTLE
How? Heathen Greek?

ANANIAS All's heathen, but the Hebrew.

SUBTLE
Sirrah, my varlet, stand you forth, and speak to him
Like a philosopher: answer, i' the language.
Name the vexations, and the martyrizations
Of metals, in the work.

FACE Sir, Putrefaction,
Solution, Ablution, Sublimation,
Cohobation, Calcination, Ceration, and
Fixation.

SUBTLE This is heathen Greek, to you, now?
And when comes Vivification?

FACE After Mortification.

SUBTLE
What's Cohobation?

FACE 'Tis the pouring on
Your *Aqua Regis*, and then drawing him off,
To the trine circle of the seven spheres.

SUBTLE
What's the proper passion of metals?

FACE Malleation.

SUBTLE
What's your *ultimum supplicium auri*?

FACE *Antimonium.*

SUBTLE
This 's heathen Greek, to you? And, what's your mercury?

FACE
A very fugitive, he will be gone, sir.

15 *pamphysic* relating to all nature; *panarchic* sovereign, entire
19 *philosopher* i.e. alchemist
20 i.e. the chemical processes undergone
21 *Putrefaction* decomposition caused by chemical action
22 *Ablution* washing away impure accretions
23 *Cohobation* redistillation; *Ceration* fixation of mercury
24 *Fixation* reduction to permanent form by combination
25 *Vivification* restoring to natural state; *Mortification* alteration of form of metals; destruction or neutralization of active qualities of chemicals
27 *Aqua Regis* chemical solvent for gold
28 *trine circle* triple; also ('trinity') planets in benign conjunction
29 *passion* natural susceptibility; *Malleation* malleability
30 Gold loses malleability when alloyed with antimony (HS)

SUBTLE
How know you him?

FACE
By his viscosity,
His oleosity, and his suscitability.

SUBTLE
How do you sublime him?

FACE
With the calce of eggshells,
White marble, talc.

SUBTLE
Your *magisterium*, now?
What's that?

FACE
Shifting, sir, your elements,
Dry into cold, cold into moist, moist into
Hot, hot into dry.

SUBTLE
This 's heathen Greek to you, still?
Your *lapis philosophicus*?

FACE
'Tis a stone, and not
A stone; a spirit, a soul, and a body:
Which, if you do dissolve, it is dissolved,
If you coagulate, it is coagulated,
If you make it to fly, it flieth.

SUBTLE
Enough. [*Exit* FACE]
This 's heathen Greek, to you? What are you, sir?

ANANIAS
Please you, a servant of the exiled Brethren,
That deal with widows; and with orphans' goods;
And make a just account, unto the Saints:
A Deacon.

SUBTLE
O, you are sent from master Wholesome,
Your teacher?

ANANIAS
From Tribulation Wholesome,
Our very zealous Pastor.

SUBTLE
Good. I have
Some orphans' goods to come here.

ANANIAS
Of what kind, sir?

SUBTLE
Pewter, and brass, andirons, and kitchen ware,
Metals, that we must use our medicine on:
Wherein the Brethren may have a penn'orth,
For ready money.

ANANIAS
Were the orphans' parents

34 *oleosity* oiliness; *suscitability* excitability
35 *calce* calx, powder
36 *magisterium* token of alchemical mastery
37 *elements* i.e. the four elements
48 *Saints* i.e. the Faithful of the sect. N.T. usage

Sincere professors?

SUBTLE
Why do you ask?

ANANIAS
Because
We then are to deal justly, and give (in truth)
Their utmost value.

SUBTLE
'Slid, you'd cozen, else,
And, if their parents were not of the faithful?
I will not trust you, now I think on 't,
Till I ha' talked with your Pastor. Ha' you brought money
To buy more coals?

ANANIAS
No, surely.

SUBTLE
No? How so?

ANANIAS
The Brethren bid me say unto you, sir.
Surely, they will not venture any more,
Till they may see projection.

SUBTLE
How!

ANANIAS
You've had,
For the instruments, as bricks, and loam, and glasses,
Already thirty pound; and, for materials,
They say, some ninety more: and, they have heard, since,
That one, at Heidelberg, made it, of an egg,
And a small paper of pin-dust.

SUBTLE
What's your name?

ANANIAS
My name is Ananias.

SUBTLE
Out, the varlet
That cozened the Apostles! Hence, away,
Flee mischief; had your holy Consistory
No name to send me, of another sound;
Than wicked Ananias? Send your Elders,
Hither, to make atonement for you, quickly.
And gi' me satisfaction; or out goes
The fire: and down th' alembics, and the furnace,
Piger Henricus, or what not. Thou wretch,
Both Sericon, and Bufo, shall be lost,
Tell 'em. All hope of rooting out the Bishops,

57 *professors* i.e. of the Faith
67 *instruments* necessary materials, means
70 *one, at Heidelberg* not traced. Mere rumour?
71 *pin-dust* fine metallic dust (used in making pins)
73 *That cozened* See *Acts* v (for Subtle's view) and ix (for Ananias's, no doubt)
80 *Piger Henricus* (lazy Henry) a composite furnace
81 *Sericon* ingredient in Alchemists' gold: red tincture; *Bufo* (toad) black tincture

Or th' Antichristian Hierarchy shall perish,
If they stay threescore minutes. The Aqueity,
Terreity, and Sulphureity
Shall run together again, and all be annulled
Thou wicked Ananias. This will fetch 'em,
[*Exit* ANANIAS]
And make 'em haste towards their gulling more.
A man must deal like a rough nurse, and fright
Those, that are froward, to an appetite.

Act II, Scene vi

[*Enter*] DRUGGER, FACE

FACE
He's busy with his spirits, but we'll upon him.

SUBTLE
How now! What mates? What Bayards ha' we here?

FACE
I told you, he would be furious. Sir, here's Nab,
Has brought you another piece of gold, to look on:
(We must appease him. Give it me) and prays you,
You would devise (what is it Nab?)

DRUGGER
A sign, sir.

FACE
Ay, a good lucky one, a thriving sign, Doctor.

SUBTLE
I was devising now.

FACE
('Slight, do not say so,
He will repent he ga' you any more.)
What say you to his constellation, Doctor?
The Balance?

SUBTLE
No, that way is stale, and common.
A townsman, born in Taurus, gives the bull;
Or the bull's head: in Aries, the ram.
A poor device. No, I will have his name

84 *Aqueity* clarified mercury
2 *Bayards* ('Bold as blind Bayards') from the legendary horse of Charlemagne
11 *The Balance* see I.iii, 56 ff.

---

83 *Antichristian Hierarchy*. Puritan opposition to episcopacy, which came to a climax in the Civil War, was present from much earlier times. Herford and Simpson quote from a work of John Udall, dated 1588. The use which Ananias and Tribulation intended for the stone is detailed in the opening scenes of Act III.

Formed in some mystic character; whose radii,
Striking the senses of the passers-by,
Shall, by a virtual influence, breed affections,
That may result upon the party owns it:
As thus—

FACE Nab!

SUBTLE He first shall have a bell, that's Abel;
And, by it, standing one, whose name is Dee,
In a rug gown; there's D and Rug, that's Drug:
And, right anenst him, a dog snarling Er;
There's Drugger, Abel Drugger. That's his sign.
And here's now mystery, and hieroglyphic!

FACE
Abel, thou art made.

DRUGGER Sir, I do thank his worship.

FACE
Six o' thy legs more, will not do it, Nab.
He has brought you a pipe of tobacco, Doctor.

DRUGGER Yes, sir:
I have another thing, I would impart—

FACE
Out with it, Nab.

DRUGGER Sir, there is lodged, hard by me
A rich young widow—

FACE Good! A *bona roba*?

DRUGGER
But nineteen, at the most.

FACE Very good, Abel.

DRUGGER
Marry, she's not in fashion, yet; she wears
A hood: but 't stands a cop.

FACE No matter, Abel.

DRUGGER
And, I do, now and then give her a fucus—

FACE
What! Dost thou deal, Nab?

SUBTLE I did tell you, Captain.

17 *virtual* powerful, of virtue; *affections* inclinations, appetites
22 *anenst* opposite 26 *legs* bows
30 *bona roba* (buona roba) lit. finely dressed girl; loosely, comely girl, 'fine piece'
33 *hood* (as opposed to fashionable hats); *a cop* high on the head
34 *fucus* cosmetic 35 *deal* i.e. in cosmetics, philtres, etc.

---

20 *Dee.* John Dee (1527–1608) was an astrologer and mathematician, part scholar and part quack, who was employed by Queen Elizabeth.

DRUGGER
And physic too sometime, sir: for which she trusts me
With all her mind. She's come up here, of purpose
To learn the fashion.

FACE
Good (his match too!) on, Nab.

DRUGGER
And she does strangely long to know her fortune.

FACE
God's lid, Nab, send her to the Doctor, hither.

DRUGGER
Yes, I have spoke to her of his worship, already:
But she's afraid, it will be blown abroad
And hurt her marriage.

FACE
Hurt it? 'Tis the way
To heal it, if 'twere hurt; to make it more
Followed, and sought: Nab, thou shalt tell her this.
She'll be more known, more talked of, and your widows
Are ne'er of any price till they be famous;
Their honour is their multitude of suitors:
Send her, it may be thy good fortune. What?
Thou dost not know.

DRUGGER
No, sir, she'll never marry
Under a knight. Her brother has made a vow.

FACE
What, and dost thou despair, my little Nab,
Knowing, what the Doctor has set down for thee,
And, seeing so many, o' the city, dubbed?
One glass o' thy water, with a Madam, I know,
Will have it done, Nab. What's her brother? A knight?

DRUGGER
No, sir, a gentleman, newly warm in his land, sir,
Scarce cold in his one and twenty; that does govern
His sister, here: and is a man himself
Of some three thousand a year, and is come up
To learn to quarrel, and to live by his wits,
And will go down again, and die i' the country.

FACE
How! To quarrel?

DRUGGER
Yes, sir, to carry quarrels,
As gallants do, and manage 'em, by line.

FACE
'Slid, Nab! The Doctor is the only man

54 *dubbed* knighted
55 *thy water* probably a love philtre
64 *by line* conforming accurately to etiquette

In Christendom for him. He has made a table,
With mathematical demonstrations,
Touching the art of quarrels. He will give him
An instrument to quarrel by. Go, bring 'em, both:
Him, and his sister. And, for thee, with her
The Doctor haply may persuade. Go to.
Shalt give his worship, a new damask suit
Upon the premises.

SUBTLE
O, good Captain.

FACE
He shall,
He is the honestest fellow, Doctor. Stay not,
No offers, bring the damask, and the parties.

DRUGGER
I'll try my power, sir.

FACE
And thy will too, Nab.

SUBTLE
'Tis good tobacco this! What is't an ounce?

FACE
He'll send you a pound, Doctor.

SUBTLE
O, no.

FACE
He will do't.
It is the goodest soul. Abel, about it.
(Thou shalt know more anon. Away, be gone.)
[*Exit* DRUGGER]
A miserable rogue, and lives with cheese,
And has the worms. That was the cause indeed
Why he came now. He dealt with me, in private,
To get a medicine for 'em.

SUBTLE
And shall, sir. This works.

FACE
A wife, a wife, for one on's, my dear Subtle:
We'll e'en draw lots, and he, that fails, shall have
The more in goods, the other has in tail.

SUBTLE
Rather the less. For she may be so light
She may want grains.

FACE
Ay, or be such a burden,
A man would scarce endure her, for the whole.

SUBTLE
Faith, best let's see her first, and then determine.

71 *haply* ed. (F, Q have *happ'ly*)
73 *premises* here, promising grounds for hope
88 *light* wanton (punningly). Bawdy insinuations continue in lines following

FACE
Content. But Dol must ha' no breath on't.
SUBTLE
Mum.
Away, you to your Surly yonder, catch him.
FACE
Pray God, I ha' not stayed too long.
SUBTLE
I fear it.

[*Exeunt*]

Act III, Scene i

[*Enter*] TRIBULATION, ANANIAS

TRIBULATION
These chastisements are common to the Saints,
And such rebukes we of the Separation
Must bear, with willing shoulders, as the trials
Sent forth, to tempt our frailties.
ANANIAS
In pure zeal,
I do not like the man: he is a heathen.
And speaks the language of Canaan, truly.
TRIBULATION
I think him a profane person, indeed.
ANANIAS
He bears
The visible mark of the Beast, in his forehead.
And for his stone, it is a work of darkness,
And, with philosophy, blinds the eyes of man.
TRIBULATION
Good Brother, we must bend unto all means,
That may give furtherance, to the holy cause.
ANANIAS
Which his cannot: the sanctified cause
Should have a sanctified course.
TRIBULATION
Not always necessary.
The children of perdition are ofttimes,
Made instruments even of the greatest works.
Beside, we should give somewhat to man's nature,
The place he lives in, still about the fire,
And fume of metals, that intoxicate
The brain of man, and make him prone to passion.

4 *pure zeal* i.e. without personal malice
6 *of Canaan* see *Isaiah* xix
8 *mark of the Beast* see *Revelation* xvi and xix; allusion to Subtle's velvet cap
10 extreme Puritans damned all learning
11 *bend* shape ourselves, concede
17 *give* make allowances

Where have you greater atheists, than your cooks?
Or more profane, or choleric than your glassmen?
More antichristian, than your bellfounders?
What makes the Devil so devilish, I would ask you,
Satan, our common enemy, but his being
Perpetually about the fire, and boiling
Brimstone, and arsenic? We must give, I say,
Unto the motives, and the stirrers up
Of humours in the blood. It may be so.
When as the work is done, the stone is made,
This heat of his may turn into a zeal,
And stand up for the beauteous discipline,
Against the menstruous cloth, and rag of Rome.
We must await his calling, and the coming
Of the good spirit. You did fault, t' upbraid him
With the Brethren's blessing of Heidelberg, weighing
What need we have, to hasten on the work,
For the restoring of the silenced Saints,
Which ne'er will be, but by the philosopher's stone.
And, so a learned Elder, one of Scotland,
Assured me; *aurum potabile* being
The only medicine, for the civil magistrate,
T' incline him to a feeling of the cause:
And must be daily used, in the disease.

ANANIAS

I have not edified more, truly, by man;
Not, since the beautiful light, first, shone on me:
And I am sad, my zeal hath so offended.

TRIBULATION

Let us call on him, then.

ANANIAS

The motion's good,
And of the spirit; I will knock first: peace be within.

21 *atheists* (loosely used) profane or godless men
28 *motives* forces (as here the fire) that stimulate, generate, move one
36 see II.v, 70
41 *aurum potabile* medicinal gold; a term for the elixir common in alchemy. Side glance at bribery
45 *edified* taken more wholesome spiritual fare
48 *motion* impulse

---

38 *silenced Saints*. After the Hampton Court conference (1604) the clergy in convocation passed canons regulating public worship and excommunicating all who denied the supremacy of the King, refused the Prayer Book or the Thirty Nine Articles, or separated from the church. Estimates of those affected vary from fifty to three hundred. They, and their followers, were the 'silenced ministers'. Cf. *Epicoene*, II.ii, 80.

Act III, Scene ii

[*Enter*] SUBTLE, TRIBULATION, ANANIAS

SUBTLE
O, are you come? 'Twas time. Your threescore minutes
Were at the last thread, you see; and down had gone
Furnus acediae, turris circulatorius:
Lembic, bolt's head, retort, and pelican
Had all been cinders. Wicked Ananias!
Art thou returned? Nay then, it goes down, yet.

TRIBULATION
Sir, be appeased, he is come to humble
Himself in spirit, and to ask your patience,
If too much zeal hath carried him, aside,
From the due path.

SUBTLE
Why, this doth qualify!

TRIBULATION
The Brethren had no purpose, verily,
To give you the least grievance: but are ready
To lend their willing hands, to any project
The spirit, and you direct.

SUBTLE
This qualifies more!

TRIBULATION
And, for the orphans' goods, let them be valued,
Or what is needful, else, to the holy work,
It shall be numbered: here, by me, the Saints
Throw down their purse before you.

SUBTLE
This qualifies, most!
Why, thus it should be, now you understand.
Have I discoursed so unto you, of our stone?
And, of the good that it shall bring your cause?
Showed you, (beside the main of hiring forces
Abroad, drawing the Hollanders, your friends,
From th' Indies, to serve you, with all their fleet)
That even the medicinal use shall make you a faction,
And party in the realm? As, put the case,
That some great man in state, he have the gout,
Why, you but send three drops of your elixir,

3 *Furnus acediae* a compound furnace. See II.v, 80 ('lazy Henry'); *turris circulatorius* circulatory, special retort for distillation
4 *Lembic* alembic
17 *numbered* added, included
25 *make you a faction* create partisan supporters

You help him straight: there you have made a friend.
Another has the palsy, or the dropsy,
He takes of your incombustible stuff,
He's young again: there you have made a friend.
A lady, that is past the feat of body,
Though not of mind, and hath her face decayed
Beyond all cure of paintings, you restore
With the oil of talc; there you have made a friend:
And all her friends. A lord, that is a leper,
A knight, that has the bone-ache, or a squire
That hath both these, you make 'em smooth, and sound,
With a bare fricace of your medicine: still,
You increase your friends.

TRIBULATION
Ay, 'tis very pregnant.

SUBTLE
And, then, the turning of this lawyer's pewter
To plate, at Christmas—

ANANIAS
Christ-tide, I pray you.

SUBTLE
Yet, Ananias?

ANANIAS
I have done.

SUBTLE
Or changing
His parcel gilt, to massy gold. You cannot
But raise you friends. With all, to be of power
To pay an army, in the field, to buy
The King of France, out of his realms; or Spain,
Out of his Indies: what can you not do,
Against lords spiritual, or temporal,
That shall oppone you?

TRIBULATION
Verily, 'tis true.
We may be temporal lords, ourselves, I take it.

SUBTLE
You may be anything, and leave off to make
Long-winded exercises: or suck up,

31 *incombustible stuff* incombustible oil was among the forms of the final alchemical 'miracle'
33 *feat* featness, fitness, elegance
36 *oil of talc* the philosopher's oil, again; 'the white elixir'
40 *fricace* light friction
45 *parcel gilt* partly gilded silverware
51 *oppone* oppose
54 *exercises* extempore effusions of the 'moved' spirit, perhaps sermons also

---

43 *Christ-tide*. The 'Popish' word *mass* was scrupulously avoided by the Puritans. Similarly, they refused to use saints' names for streets; St. Anne's Street became Anne Street.

Your ha, and hum, in a tune. I not deny,
But such as are not graced, in a state,
May, for their ends, be adverse in religion,
And get a tune, to call the flock together:
For (to say sooth) a tune does much, with women,
And other phlegmatic people, it is your bell.

ANANIAS
Bells are profane: a tune may be religious.

SUBTLE
No warning with you? Then, farewell my patience.
'Slight, it shall down: I will not be thus tortured.

TRIBULATION
I pray you, sir.

SUBTLE
All shall perish. I have spoke it.

TRIBULATION
Let me find grace, sir, in your eyes; the man
He stands corrected: neither did his zeal
(But as yourself) allow a tune, somewhere.
Which, now, being toward the stone, we shall not need.

SUBTLE
No, nor your holy vizard, to win widows
To give you legacies; or make zealous wives
To rob their husbands, for the common cause:
Nor take the start of bonds, broke but one day,
And say, they were forfeited, by providence.
Nor shall you need, o'er night, to eat huge meals,
To celebrate your next day's fast the better:
The whilst the Brethren, and the Sisters, humbled,
Abate the stiffness of the flesh. Nor cast
Before your hungry hearers, scrupulous bones,
As whether a Christian may hawk, or hunt;
Or whether, matrons, of the holy assembly,

55 alludes to preaching mannerisms; *not deny* do not deny
56 *graced* advantaged, as by established religious forms
63 *shall down* alludes to earlier threat of demolition
67 (*But as . . .*) except in so far as
69 *vizard* feigned facial expression
72 *take the start* gain the advantage, by acting smartly
77 *Abate the stiffness* beat down the rigid, inflexible (disposition, unchastened desire, will)
78 *scrupulous bones* contentious issues depending on fine scruples, minute distinctions

---

69–82 *No, nor your holy vizard* &c. A catalogue of the common charges against Puritans. Compare Dame Purecraft's speech on the same subject in *Bartholomew Fair*, V.ii.

May lay their hair out, or wear doublets:
Or have that idol Starch, about their linen.

ANANIAS
It is, indeed, an idol.

TRIBULATION Mind him not, sir.
I do command thee, spirit (of zeal, but trouble)
To peace within him. Pray you, sir, go on.

SUBTLE
Nor shall you need to libel 'gainst the prelates,
And shorten so your ears, against the hearing
Of the next wire-drawn grace. Nor, of necessity,
Rail against plays, to please the alderman,
Whose daily custard you devour. Nor lie
With zealous rage, till you are hoarse. Not one
Of these so singular arts. Nor call yourselves,
By names of Tribulation, Persecution,
Restraint, Long-Patience, and such like, affected
By the whole family, or wood of you,
Only for glory, and to catch the ear
Of the Disciple.

TRIBULATION Truly, sir, they are
Ways, that the godly Brethren have invented,
For propagation of the glorious cause,
As very notable means, and whereby, also,
Themselves grow soon, and profitably famous.

SUBTLE
O, but the stone, all's idle to it! Nothing!
The art of Angels, nature's miracle,
The divine secret, that doth fly in clouds,
From east to west: and whose tradition
Is not from men, but spirits.

ANANIAS I hate traditions:
I do not trust 'em—

TRIBULATION Peace.

ANANIAS They are popish, all.
I will not peace. I will not—

87 *shorten so* alludes to punishment of cutting off ears
88 *wire-drawn grace* i.e. long-drawn-out, and thin, tenuous: as in the extraction of wire: a frequent metaphoric jibe at the time
89 *alderman* used to connote the plural; city magistrates
95 *wood* crowd
100 *notable* likely to catch attention

---

106 *I hate traditions.* Puritans held the Bible to be the only rule of faith and practice. The Jews and the Roman Church believed religious traditions to be of some value. Hence they were Popish and anathema.

TRIBULATION
Ananias.

ANANIAS
Please the profane, to grieve the godly: I may not.

SUBTLE
Well, Ananias, thou shalt overcome.

TRIBULATION
It is an ignorant zeal, that haunts him, sir.
But truly, else, a very faithful Brother,
A botcher: and a man, by revelation,
That hath a competent knowledge of the truth

SUBTLE
Has he a competent sum, there, i' the bag,
To buy the goods, within? I am made guardian,
And must, for charity, and conscience' sake,
Now, see the most be made, for my poor orphan:
Though I desire the Brethren, too, good gainers.
There, they are, within. When you have viewed, and bought 'em,
And ta'en the inventory of what they are,
They are ready for projection; there's no more
To do: cast on the medicine, so much silver
As there is tin there, so much gold as brass,
I'll gi' it you in, by weight.

TRIBULATION
But how long time,
Sir, must the Saints expect, yet?

SUBTLE
Let me see,
How's the moon, now? Eight, nine, ten days hence
He will be silver potate; then, three days,
Before he citronize: some fifteen days,
The *magisterium* will be perfected.

ANANIAS
About the second day, of the third week,
In the ninth month?

SUBTLE
Yes, my good Ananias.

TRIBULATION
What will the orphan's goods arise to, think you?

SUBTLE
Some hundred marks; as much as filled three cars,
Unladed now: you'll make six millions of 'em.
But I must ha' more coals laid in.

110 N.T. phrase used punningly: 'you will be too much for us'
113 *botcher* repairing tailor
126 *expect* await the consummation
128 *silver potate* liquefied silver (HS)
129 *citronize* achieve the colour denoting alchemical consummation

TRIBULATION
How!

SUBTLE
Another load,
And then we ha' finished. We must now increase
Our fire to *ignis ardens*, we are past
Fimus equinus, *balnei*, *cineris*,
And all those lenter heats. If the holy purse
Should, with this draught, fall low, and that the Saints
Do need a present sum, I have a trick
To melt the pewter, you shall buy now, instantly,
And, with a tincture, make you as good Dutch dollars,
As any are in Holland.

TRIBULATION
Can you so?

SUBTLE
Ay, and shall bide the third examination.

ANANIAS
It will be joyful tidings to the Brethren.

SUBTLE
But you must carry it, secret.

TRIBULATION
Ay, but stay,
This act of coining, is it lawful?

ANANIAS
Lawful?
We know no magistrate. Or, if we did,
This 's foreign coin.

SUBTLE
It is no coining, sir.
It is but casting.

TRIBULATION
Ha? You distinguish well.
Casting of money may be lawful.

ANANIAS
'Tis, sir.

TRIBULATION
Truly, I take it so.

138 *ignis ardens* the hottest fire
139 *Fimus equinus* moist heat (from 'horse dung'); *balnei* warmth (of water) just below boiling; *cineris* denotes the next stage of heat (see II.iii, 41, 85)
140 *lenter* slower
142 *a trick* so F2 (F1, Q, have *I have trick*)
146 i.e. survive legal or police investigation
150 *know* acknowledge

---

150 *We know no magistrate.* Some Puritans rejected all human forms of government as carnal ordinances, and set up the scripture as the only civil code. The Confession of Faith of the English Baptists at Amsterdam in 1611 expressly stated that 'the magistrate is not to meddle in religion or matters of conscience'. A surprising variety of things could become 'matters of conscience'.
151 *foreign coin.* Counterfeiting of *foreign* coin first became high treason in the reign of Queen Mary. 'Coining' was already a capital offence, and as late as 1786 a woman was executed for coining silver.

SUBTLE There is no scruple,
Sir, to be made of it; believe Ananias:
This case of conscience he is studied in.

TRIBULATION
I'll make a question of it, to the Brethren.

ANANIAS
The Brethren shall approve it lawful, doubt not.
Where shall't be done?

SUBTLE For that we'll talk, anon.
Knock without
There's some to speak with me. Go in, I pray you,
And view the parcels. That's the inventory.
[*Exeunt* ANANIAS, TRIBULATION]
I'll come to you straight. Who is it? Face! Appear.

Act III, Scene iii

[*Enter*] FACE

SUBTLE
How now? Good prize?

FACE Good pox! Yond' costive cheater
Never came on.

SUBTLE How then?

FACE I ha' walked the round,
Till now, and no such thing.

SUBTLE And ha' you quit him?

FACE
Quit him? And hell would quit him too, he were happy.
'Slight would you have me stalk like a mill-jade,
All day, for one, that will not yield us grains?
I know him of old.

SUBTLE O, but to ha' gulled him,
Had been a mastery.

FACE Let him go, black boy,
And turn thee, that some fresh news may possess thee.
A noble count, a don of Spain (my dear

2 *walked the round* kept a look out (with side glance at the Temple Church 'round')
4 i.e. I certainly have
5 *mill-jade* tired old horse moving round and round
6 food, weight (sustaining the metaphor)

---

8 *black boy*. Horace, *Satires*, I.iv. 85, 'hic niger est, hunc tu, Romane, caveto'. Cf. *Every Man Out of his Humour*, I.ii, 210.

Delicious compeer, and my party-bawd)
Who is come hither, private, for his conscience,
And brought munition with him, six great slops,
Bigger than three Dutch hoys, beside round trunks,
Furnished with pistolets, and pieces of eight,
Will straight be here, my rogue, to have thy bath
(That is the colour,) and to make his battery
Upon our Dol, our castle, our Cinque-Port,
Our Dover pier, our what thou wilt. Where is she?
She must prepare perfumes, delicate linen,
The bath in chief, a banquet, and her wit,
For she must milk his epididymis.
Where is the doxy?

SUBTLE
I'll send her to thee:
And but despatch my brace of little John Leydens,
And come again myself.

FACE
Are they within then?

SUBTLE
Numbering the sum.

FACE
How much?

SUBTLE
A hundred marks, boy.
[*Exit* SUBTLE]

FACE
Why, this 's a lucky day! Ten pounds of Mammon!
Three o' my clerk! A portague o' my grocer!
This o' the Brethren! Beside reversions,
And states, to come i' the widow, and my count!
[*Enter* DOL]
My share, today, will not be bought for forty—

DOL
What?

FACE
Pounds, dainty Dorothy, art thou so near?

11 *compeer* comrade (properly, godfather); *party-bawd* partner in bawdry
13 *slops* fashionable nether garment
14 *hoys* small vessels, usually sloop-rigged (see previous line); *round trunks* large breeches, worn padded
15 *pistolets* Spanish gold pieces, worth nearly £1
17 *colour* official pretext
18 *Cinque-Port* five privileged sea ports on the south coast
19 the metaphor implies piracy
23 *doxy* mistress of a ne'er-do-well
30 *states* estates

---

24 *John Leydens*. Ananias and Tribulation. Jan Bockelson of Leyden was one of the leaders of the Anabaptists at Munster (see II.v, 13), and many English Puritans found refuge in the town of Leyden itself.

DOL
Yes, say lord General, how fares our camp?
FACE
As, with the few, that had entrenched themselves
Safe, by their discipline, against a world, Dol:
And laughed, within those trenches, and grew fat
With thinking on the booties, Dol, brought in
Daily, by their small parties. This dear hour,
A doughty don is taken, with my Dol;
And thou may'st make his ransom, what thou wilt,
My Dousabell: he shall be brought here, fettered
With thy fair looks, before he sees thee; and thrown
In a downbed, as dark as any dungeon;
Where thou shalt keep him waking, with thy drum;
Thy drum, my Dol; thy drum; till he be tame
As the poor blackbirds were i' the great frost,
Or bees are with a basin: and so hive him
I' the swanskin coverlid, and cambric sheets,
Till he work honey, and wax, my little God's-gift.
DOL
What is he, General?
FACE
An adalantado,
A grandee, girl. Was not my Dapper here, yet?
DOL
No.
FACE Nor my Drugger?
DOL
Neither.
FACE
A pox on 'em,
They are so long a-furnishing! Such stinkards
Would not be seen, upon these festival days.
[*Enter* SUBTLE]
How now! Ha' you done?
SUBTLE
Done. They are gone. The sum
Is here in bank, my Face. I would, we knew
Another chapman, now, would buy 'em outright.

33 *Yes, say lord General.* Dol quotes the opening line of Kyd's *Spanish Tragedy*.
39 *taken* attracted by (punningly sustaining piratic image)
44 *drum* (*cf.* line 22) bawdy innuendo. See *O.E.D.*
46 *frost* of 1608
49 *God's-gift* Greek meaning of Dorothy
50 *adalantado* (loosely) Governor of a Province
53 *a-furnishing* equipping themselves, preparing (to be gulled)
54 *Would* probably with the force of *should*

---

47 *Or bees are with a basin.* The sound of a metal basin being tapped attracted bees. See Virgil, *Georgics*, 4.64.

FACE

'Slid, Nab shall do't, against he ha' the widow,
To furnish household.

SUBTLE

Excellent, well thought on,
Pray God, he come.

FACE

I pray, he keep away
Till our new business be o'erpast.

SUBTLE

But, Face,
How camest thou, by this secret don?

FACE

A spirit
Brought me th' intelligence, in a paper, here,
As I was conjuring, yonder, in my circle
For Surly: I ha' my flies abroad. Your bath
Is famous, Subtle, by my means. Sweet Dol,
You must go tune your virginal, no losing
O' the least time. And, do you hear? Good action.
Firk, like a flounder; kiss, like a scallop, close:
And tickle him with thy mother-tongue. His great
Verdugoship has not a jot of language:
So much the easier to be cozened, my Dolly.
He will come here, in a hired coach, obscure,
And our own coachman, whom I have sent, as guide,

One knocks

No creature else. Who's that?

SUBTLE

It i' not he?

FACE

O no, not yet this hour.

SUBTLE

Who is't?

DOL

Dapper,
Your clerk.

FACE

God's will, then, Queen of Fairy,
On with your tire; and, Doctor, with your robes.
Let's despatch him, for God's sake.

SUBTLE

'Twill be long.

FACE

I warrant you, take but the cues I give you,

59 *furnish* provide (nearer to modern sense than at line 53)
64 *my circle* see III.iii, 2
66 *famous*, ed. (F, Q have no comma)
67–8 *tune . . . virginal . . . action* metaphor of preparing 16th century keyboard instrument for entertainment, with bawdy innuendo
69 *Firk* stir up (tr.) move about (intr.); *flounder* a small fish; *scallop* a shell-fish
71 *Verdugoship* verdugo is Spanish for executioner, used slangily; *language* i.e. English
73 *obscure* secretly, unobserved, unlike a grandee

It shall be brief enough. 'Slight, here are more!
Abel, and I think, the angry boy, the heir,
That fain would quarrel.

SUBTLE
And the widow?

FACE
No,
Not that I see. Away. O sir, you are welcome. [*Exit* SUBTLE]

Act III, Scene iv

[*Enter*] DAPPER

FACE
The Doctor is within, a-moving for you;
(I have had the most ado to win him to it)
He swears, you'll be the darling o' the dice:
He never heard her Highness dote, till now (he says.)
Your aunt has given you the most gracious words,
That can be thought on.

DAPPER
Shall I see her Grace?

[*Enter* DRUGGER *and* KASTRIL]

FACE
See her, and kiss her, too. What? Honest Nab!
Hast brought the damask?

DRUGGER
No, sir, here's tobacco.

FACE
'Tis well done, Nab: thou'lt bring the damask too?

DRUGGER
Yes, here's the gentleman, Captain, master Kastril,
I have brought to see the Doctor.

FACE
Where's the widow?

DRUGGER
Sir, as he likes, his sister (he says) shall come.

FACE
O, is it so? Good time. Is your name Kastril, sir?

KASTRIL
Ay, and the best o' the Kastrils, I'd be sorry else,
By fifteen hundred, a year. Where is this Doctor?
My mad tobacco-boy, here, tells me of one,
That can do things. Has he any skill?

FACE
Wherein, sir?

12 *as he likes* according to his wishes
13 *Good time* all in good time
14 i.e. his fortune outbids the rest by the sum named

KASTRIL
To carry a business, manage a quarrel, fairly,
Upon fit terms.

FACE
It seems sir, you're but young
About the town, that can make that a question!

KASTRIL
Sir, not so young, but I have heard some speech
Of the angry boys, and seen 'em take tobacco;
And in his shop: and I can take it too.
And I would fain be one of 'em, and go down
And practise i' the country.

FACE
Sir, for the *duello*,
The Doctor, I assure you, shall inform you,
To the least shadow of a hair; and show you,
An instrument he has, of his own making,
Wherewith, no sooner shall you make report
Of any quarrel, but he will take the height on't,
Most instantly; and tell in what degree,
Of safety it lies in, or mortality.
And, how it may be borne, whether in a right line,
Or a half-circle; or may, else, be cast
Into an angle blunt, if not acute:
All this he will demonstrate. And then, rules,
To give, and take the lie, by.

KASTRIL
How? To take it?

FACE
Yes, in oblique, he'll show you; or in circle:
But never in diameter. The whole town
Study his theorems, and dispute them, ordinarily,

18 *carry a business* duelling jargon 19 *fit* socially accepted
37 *and take* i.e. receive challenges
40 *ordinarily* punning on 'ordinaries', i.e. public houses of refreshment; pun continued into line 41

---

22 *angry boys*. Sometimes called the 'roaring boys', these were young bucks who gained reputations for quarrels, assaults, and stylized thuggery. They have their counterparts in every century and society.

22 *take tobacco*. Abel's shop accommodated both the novice and the adept in the art of smoking. Here the adept practised the 'gulan ebolitio, the euripus, the whiff', and many other methods of retaining or emitting smoke.

25–39 *for the duello* &c. This collection of duelling jargon and punctilio is intended to 'blind with science'. The leading contemporary authority on the subject was *Vincentio Saviolo his Practise. In two Bookes. The first intreating of the use of the Rapier and Dagger. The second, of Honor and honorable Quarrels*, 1595. Cf. the degrees of the lie denominated by Touchstone in *As You Like It*, V.iv, and Fletcher's *The Queen of Corinth*, IV.i.

At the eating academies.

KASTRIL But, does he teach
Living, by the wits, too?

FACE Anything, whatever.
You cannot think that subtlety, but he reads it.
He made me a Captain. I was a stark pimp,
Just o' your standing, 'fore I met with him:
It i' not two months since. I'll tell you his method.
First, he will enter you, at some ordinary.

KASTRIL
No, I'll not come there. You shall pardon me.

FACE For why, sir?

KASTRIL
There's gaming there, and tricks.

FACE Why, would you be
A gallant, and not game?

KASTRIL Ay, 'twill spend a man.

FACE
Spend you? It will repair you, when you are spent.
How do they live by their wits, there, that have vented
Six times your fortunes?

KASTRIL What, three thousand a year!

FACE
Ay, forty thousand.

KASTRIL Are there such?

FACE Ay, sir.
And gallants, yet. Here's a young gentleman,
Is born to nothing, forty marks a year,
Which I count nothing. He's to be initiated,
And have a fly o' the Doctor. He will win you
By unresistable luck, within this fortnight,
Enough to buy a barony. They will set him
Upmost, at the Groom-porter's, all the Christmas!
And, for the whole year through, at every place,
Where there is play, present him with the chair;
The best attendance, the best drink, sometimes
Two glasses of canary, and pay nothing;
The purest linen, and the sharpest knife,
The partridge next his trencher: and, somewhere,
The dainty bed, in private, with the dainty.

44 *stark pimp* penniless go-between (pimp, with a less developed sense than now)
52 *vented* spent (ventured, adventured), made empty
61 *Groom-porter's* an officer of the royal household, especially concerned to regulate gaming

You shall ha' your ordinaries bid for him,
As playhouses for a poet; and the master
Pray him, aloud, to name what dish he affects,
Which must be buttered shrimps: and those that drink
To no mouth else, will drink to his, as being
The goodly, president mouth of all the board.

KASTRIL
Do you not gull one?

FACE
'Od's my life! Do you think it?
You shall have a cast commander, (can but get
In credit with a glover, or a spurrier,
For some two pair, of either's ware, aforehand)
Will, by most swift posts, dealing with him,
Arrive at competent means, to keep himself,
His punk, and naked boy, in excellent fashion.
And be admired for it.

KASTRIL
Will the Doctor teach this?

FACE
He will do more, sir, when your land is gone,
(As men of spirit hate to keep earth long)
In a vacation, when small money is stirring,
And ordinaries suspended till the term,
He'll show a perspective, where on one side
You shall behold the faces, and the persons
Of all sufficient young heirs, in town,
Whose bonds are current for commodity;
On th' other side, the merchants' forms, and others,
That, without help of any second broker,
(Who would expect a share) will trust such parcels:
In the third square, the very street, and sign
Where the commodity dwells, and does but wait
To be delivered, be it pepper, soap,
Hops, or tobacco, oatmeal, woad, or cheeses.
All which you may so handle, to enjoy,
To your own use, and never stand obliged.

KASTRIL
I' faith! Is he such a fellow?

76 *cast* cashiered 77 *spurrier* spur maker
78 i.e. once he can obtain advance of goods
79 *swift posts* with speed in delivery and exchange, like post-horses
85 *vacation* i.e. from law terms 90 *current* at present in the market
93 *parcels* i.e. of goods 97 *woad* plant yielding blue dye

---

87 *perspective*. A specially devised optical instrument, or, perhaps primarily, a design constructed to produce remarkable effects. See *O.E.D.*
90 *commodity*. See note to II.i, 10–14.

FACE
Why, Nab here knows him.
And then for making matches, for rich widows,
Young gentlewomen, heirs, the fortunat'st man!
He's sent to, far, and near, all over England,
To have his counsel, and to know their fortunes.

KASTRIL
God's will, my suster shall see him.

FACE
I'll tell you, sir,
What he did tell me of Nab. It's a strange thing!
(By the way you must eat no cheese, Nab, it breeds melancholy:
And that same melancholy breeds worms) but pass it–
He told me, honest Nab, here, was ne'er at tavern,
But once in's life.

DRUGGER
Truth, and no more I was not.

FACE
And, then he was so sick—

DRUGGER
Could he tell you that, too?

FACE
How should I know it?

DRUGGER
In troth we had been a-shooting,
And had a piece of fat ram-mutton, to supper,
That lay so heavy o' my stomach—

FACE
And he has no head
To bear any wine; for, what with the noise o' the fiddlers,
And care of his shop, for he dares keep no servants—

DRUGGER
My head did so ache—

FACE
As he was fain to be brought home,
The Doctor told me. And then, a good old woman—

DRUGGER
(Yes, faith, she dwells in Sea-coal Lane) did cure me,
With sodden ale, and pellitory o' the wall:
Cost me but two pence. I had another sickness,
Was worse than that.

104 *and to know* i.e. by those who wish to know
105 *suster* sister; intended to suggest rustic dialect
108 *pass it* let it pass
112 *How should* how else should
119 *Sea-coal Lane* a lane between Snow Hill and Fleet Street
120 *pellitory* the wall-pellitory, a plant used to prepare demulcents and emollients

---

107 *breeds melancholy.* 'Milk, and all that comes of milk, as butter and cheese, curds, &c., increase melancholy'. Burton, *Anatomy of Melancholy*, part 1, sec. 2, mem. 2, subs. 1.

FACE Ay, that was with the grief
Thou took'st for being 'sessed at eighteen pence,
For the water-work.
DRUGGER In truth, and it was like
T'have cost me almost my life.
FACE Thy hair went off?
DRUGGER
Yes, sir, 'twas done for spite.
FACE Nay, so says the Doctor.
KASTRIL
Pray thee, tobacco-boy, go fetch my suster,
I'll see this learned boy, before I go:
And so shall she.
FACE Sir, he is busy now:
But, if you have a sister to fetch hither,
Perhaps, your own pains may command her sooner;
And he, by that time, will be free.
KASTRIL I go. [*Exit* KASTRIL]
FACE
Drugger, she's thine: the damask. (Subtle, and I
[*Exit* DRUGGER]
Must wrestle for her.) Come on, master Dapper.
You see, how I turn clients, here, away,
To give your cause despatch. Ha' you performed
The ceremonies were enjoined you?
DAPPER Yes, o' the vinegar,
And the clean shirt.
FACE 'Tis well: that shirt may do you
More worship than you think. Your aunt's afire
But that she will not show it, t'have a sight on you.
Ha' you provided for her Grace's servants?
DAPPER
Yes, here are six score Edward shillings.
FACE Good.
DAPPER
And an old Harry's sovereign.
FACE Very good.
DAPPER
And three James shillings, and an Elizabeth groat,

123 *'sessed* assessed
132 *I go* so F (Q has *I go, sir*)
143 *old Harry's sovereign* debased currency: worth ten shillings

124 *the water-work.* Sir Hugh Myddleton's New River, begun in 1609 and completed in 1613.

Just twenty nobles.

FACE
O, you are too just.
I would you had had the other noble in Marys.

DAPPER
I have some Philip, and Marys.

FACE
Ay, those same
Are best of all. Where are they? Hark, the Doctor.

Act III, Scene v

[*Enter*] SUBTLE *disguised like a Priest of Fairy*

SUBTLE
Is yet her Grace's cousin come?

FACE
He is come.

SUBTLE
And is he fasting?

FACE
Yes.

SUBTLE
And hath cried *hum*?

FACE
Thrice, you must answer.

DAPPER
Thrice.

SUBTLE
And as oft *buz*?

FACE
If you have, say.

DAPPER
I have.

SUBTLE
Then, to her coz,
Hoping, that he hath vinegared his senses,
As he was bid, the Fairy Queen dispenses,
By me, this robe, the petticoat of Fortune;
Which that he straight put on, she doth importune.
And though to Fortune near be her petticoat,
Yet, nearer is her smock, the Queen doth note:
And, therefore, even of that a piece she hath sent,
Which, being a child, to wrap him in, was rent;

4 *coz* cousin, (any close or distant kin)
8 *importune* beg, request
10 (proverbial) *cf.* 'Though ny be my kyrtell, yet nere is my smock' (HS)
12 *being a* i.e. when he was yet a

145 *twenty nobles.* (at six shillings and eightpence each) £6 13s 4d Dapper's totalling is accurate. The 'Marys' (line 146) are to fill the gap in successive reigns. Face's numismatics divert attention from the money itself.

And prays him, for a scarf, he now will wear it
They blind him with a rag
(With as much love, as then her Grace did tear it)
About his eyes, to show, he is fortunate.
And, trusting unto her to make his state,
He'll throw away all worldly pelf, about him;
Which that he will perform, she doth not doubt him.

FACE
She need not doubt him, sir. Alas, he has nothing,
But what he will part withall, as willingly,
Upon her Grace's word (throw away your purse)
As she would ask it: (handkerchiefs, and all)
She cannot bid that thing, but he'll obey.
(If you have a ring, about you, cast it off,
Or a silver seal, at your wrist, her Grace will send
He throws away, as they bid him
Her fairies here to search you, therefore deal
Directly with her Highness. If they find
That you conceal a mite, you are undone.)

DAPPER
Truly, there's all.

FACE
All what?

DAPPER
My money, truly.

FACE
Keep nothing, that is transitory, about you.
(Bid Dol play music.) Look, the elves are come
Dol enters with a cithern: they pinch him
To pinch you, if you tell not truth. Advise you.

DAPPER
O, I have a paper with a spur-rial in't.

FACE
Ti, ti,
They knew't, they say.

SUBTLE
Ti, ti, ti, ti, he has more yet.

FACE
Ti, ti-ti-ti. I' the t'other pocket?

SUBTLE
Titi, titi, titi, titi.
They must pinch him, or he will never confess, they say.

DAPPER
O, O.

FACE Nay, pray you hold. He is her Grace's nephew.

16 *state* high rank, status, wealth
17 *pelf* money, jewellery, valuable gear
27 *Directly* frankly, honourably
31 *cithern* (or cittern) species of guitar. Cf. Tyrolean Zither
33 *spur-rial* Edward IV noble, value about fifteen shillings

Ti, ti, ti? What care you? Good faith, you shall care.
Deal plainly, sir, and shame the fairies. Show
You are an innocent.

DAPPER
By this good light, I ha' nothing.

SUBTLE
Ti ti, ti ti to ta. He does equivocate, she says:
Ti, ti do ti, ti ti do, ti da. And swears by the light, when he is blinded.

DAPPER
By this good dark, I ha' nothing but a half crown
Of gold, about my wrist, that my love gave me;
And a leaden heart I wore, sin' she forsook me.

FACE
I thought, 'twas something. And, would you incur
Your aunt's displeasure for these trifles? Come,
I had rather you had thrown away twenty half crowns.
You may wear your leaden heart still. How now?

SUBTLE
What news, Dol?

DOL
Yonder's your knight, sir Mammon.

FACE
God's lid, we never thought of him, till now.
Where is he?

DOL
Here, hard by. He's at the door.

SUBTLE
And, you are not ready, now? Dol, get his suit.
He must not be sent back.

FACE
O, by no means.
What shall we do with this same puffin, here,
Now he's o' the spit?

SUBTLE
Why, lay him back a while,
With some device. *Ti, ti ti, ti ti ti.* Would her Grace speak with me?
I come. Help, Dol.

FACE
Who's there? Sir Epicure;

He speaks through the keyhole, the other knocking

My master's i' the way. Please you to walk
Three or four turns, but till his back be turned,
And I am for you. Quickly, Dol.

SUBTLE
Her Grace

40 *innocent* (ironically playing on both senses)
43 *half crown/Of gold* first coined in Henry VIII's reign
53 *his suit* i.e. Face's costume for the role of servant
55 *puffin* derisive term for a puffed-up 'gull'; the Didapper was a near-species, in Elizabethan ornithology

Commends her kindly to you, master Dapper.

DAPPER
I long to see her Grace.

SUBTLE
She, now, is set
At dinner, in her bed; and she has sent you,
From her own private trencher, a dead mouse,
And a piece of gingerbread, to be merry withal,
And stay your stomach, lest you faint with fasting:
Yet, if you could hold out, till she saw you (she says)
It would be better for you.

FACE
Sir, he shall
Hold out, and 'twere this two hours, for her Highness;
I can assure you that. We will not lose
All we ha' done—

SUBTLE
He must nor see, nor speak
To anybody, till then.

FACE
For that, we'll put, sir,
A stay in 's mouth.

SUBTLE
Of what?

FACE
Of gingerbread.
Make you it fit. He that hath pleased her Grace,
Thus far, shall not now crinkle, for a little.
Gape sir, and let him fit you.

SUBTLE
Where shall we now
Bestow him?

DOL
I' the privy.

SUBTLE
Come along, sir,
I now must show you Fortune's privy lodgings.

FACE
Are they perfumed? And his bath ready?

SUBTLE
All.
Only the fumigation's somewhat strong.

FACE
Sir Epicure, I am yours, sir, by and by. [*Exeunt*]

Act IV, Scene i

[*Enter*] FACE, MAMMON

FACE
O, sir, you're come i' the only, finest time—

MAMMON
Where's master?

74 *stay* gag
76 *crinkle* curl away, recoil, shrink
1 *only* (onely) singularly, uniquely

FACE
Now preparing for projection, sir.
Your stuff will b' all changed shortly.
MAMMON
Into gold?
FACE
To gold, and silver, sir.
MAMMON
Silver, I care not for.
FACE
Yes, sir, a little to give beggars.
MAMMON
Where's the lady?
FACE
At hand, here. I ha' told her such brave things, o' you,
Touching your bounty and your noble spirit—
MAMMON
Hast thou?
FACE
As she is almost in her fit to see you.
But, good sir, no divinity i' your conference,
For fear of putting her in rage—
MAMMON
I warrant thee.
FACE
Six men will not hold her down. And, then,
If the old man should hear, or see you—
MAMMON
Fear not.
FACE
The very house, sir, would run mad. You know it
How scrupulous he is, and violent,
'Gainst the least act of sin. Physic, or mathematics,
Poetry, state, or bawdry (as I told you)
She will endure, and never startle: but
No word of controversy.
MAMMON
I am schooled, good Eulen.
FACE
And you must praise her house, remember that,
And her nobility.
MAMMON
Let me, alone:
No Herald, no nor Antiquary, Lungs,
Shall do it better. Go.
FACE
Why, this is yet
A kind of modern happiness, to have
Dol Common for a great lady.
MAMMON
Now, Epicure,
Heighten thyself, talk to her, all in gold;

14 *scrupulous* piously conscientious, *plus* attentive to detail
23 *modern* ordinary, common (punning on her name) as well as fashionable, modish; *happiness* includes the sense fitness, aptness

Rain her as many showers, as Jove did drops
Unto his Danae: show the God a miser,
Compared with Mammon. What? The stone will do't.
She shall feel gold, taste gold, hear gold, sleep gold:
Nay, we will *concumbere* gold. I will be puissant,
And mighty in my talk to her! Here she comes.

[*Enter* DOL]

FACE
To him, Dol, suckle him. This is the noble knight,
I told your ladyship—

MAMMON
Madam, with your pardon,
I kiss your vesture.

DOL
Sir, I were uncivil
If I would suffer that, my lip to you, sir.

MAMMON
I hope, my lord your brother be in health, lady?

DOL
My lord, my brother is, though I no lady, sir.

FACE
(Well said my Guinea bird.)

MAMMON
Right noble madam—

FACE
(O, we shall have most fierce idolatry!)

MAMMON
'Tis your prerogative.

DOL
Rather your courtesy.

MAMMON
Were there nought else t'enlarge your virtues, to me,
These answers speak your breeding, and your blood.

DOL
Blood we boast none, sir, a poor baron's daughter.

MAMMON
Poor! And gat you? Profane not. Had your father
Slept all the happy remnant of his life
After that act, lain but there still, and panted,
He'd done enough, to make himself, his issue,
And his posterity noble.

DOL
Sir, although
We may be said to want the gilt, and trappings,
The dress of honour; yet we strive to keep
The seeds, and the materials.

30 *concumbere* breed, lying together
38 *Guinea bird* guinea-hen was slang for prostitute
44 *gat* begat

MAMMON I do see
The old ingredient, virtue, was not lost,
Nor the drug money, used to make your compound.
There is a strange nobility, i' your eye,
This lip, that chin! Methinks you do resemble
One o' the Austriac princes.

FACE (Very like,
Her father was an Irish costermonger.)

MAMMON
The house of Valois, just, had such a nose.
And such a forehead, yet, the Medici
Of Florence boast.

DOL Troth, and I have been likened
To all these princes.

FACE (I'll be sworn, I heard it.)

MAMMON
I know not how. It is not any one,
But e'en the very choice of all their features.

FACE
(I'll in, and laugh.) [*Exit* FACE]

MAMMON A certain touch, or air,
That sparkles a divinity, beyond
An earthly beauty!

DOL O, you play the courtier.

MAMMON
Good lady, gi' me leave—

DOL In faith, I may not,
To mock me, sir.

MAMMON To burn i' this sweet flame:
The Phoenix never knew a nobler death.

DOL
Nay, now you court the courtier: and destroy
What you would build. This art, sir, i' your words,
Calls your whole faith in question.

MAMMON By my soul—

53 Mammon turns even his compliments alchemically
56 *Austriac* Austrian
57 *Irish* (as all costermongers were colloquially said to be)
70 *court* seek to be, mimic
71 *art* i.e. decorative, mannered; with suggestion of guile

---

56 *the Austriac princes.* '... The *Austrian* Lip at this day is by good right in high esteem; it being observed, that all the House of *Austria* have a sweet fulnesse of the Nether lip'. John Bulwer, *Anthropometamorphosis*, 1650, p. 106. The Valois nose and the Medici forehead which follow (lines 58, 59) are Jonson's joke; neither feature is distinctive in those families (Herford and Simpson).

DOL
Nay, oaths are made o' the same air, sir.

MAMMON
Nature
Never bestowed upon mortality,
A more unblamed, a more harmonious feature:
She played the stepdame in all faces, else.
Sweet madam, le' me be particular—

DOL
Particular, sir? I pray you, know your distance.

MAMMON
In no ill sense, sweet lady, but to ask
How your fair graces pass the hours? I see
You're lodged, here, i' the house of a rare man,
An excellent artist: but, what's that to you?

DOL
Yes, sir. I study here the mathematics,
And distillation.

MAMMON
O, I cry your pardon.
He's a divine instructor! Can extract
The souls of all things, by his art; call all
The virtues, and the miracles of the sun,
Into a temperate furnace: teach dull nature
What her own forces are. A man, the Emperor
Has courted, above Kelley: sent his medals,
And chains, t' invite him.

DOL
Ay, and for his physic, sir—

MAMMON
Above the art of Æsculapius,
That drew the envy of the Thunderer!
I know all this, and more.

75 *feature* form, proportions, shape, composition
76 *else* i.e. in all other faces
77 *particular* intimate, private, personal
80 i.e. the person who gathers these graces to herself
82 *artist* here, practiser of the secret arts, the mysteries
83 *mathematics* astrology (essentially)
84 *distillation* chemistry (essentially)
88 *temperate* controlled, regulated
89 *Emperor* Rudolph II of Germany

---

90 *Kelley*. Edward Kelley (1555–95), the partner of John Dee, was an energetic man who procured the favour of Rudolph II by boasting that he possessed the philosopher's stone. Rudolph twice imprisoned him to force him into some action. On the second occasion Kelley attempted escape and was killed.

92 *Æsculapius*. The god, or 'patron saint' of the doctors, who restored men to life until Zeus (the Thunderer) killed him with a flash of lightning, lest men should escape death altogether.

DOL
Troth, I am taken, sir,
Whole, with these studies, that contemplate nature:
MAMMON
It is a noble humour. But, this form
Was not intended to so dark a use!
Had you been crooked, foul, of some coarse mould,
A cloister had done well: but, such a feature
That might stand up the glory of a kingdom,
To live recluse! Is a mere solecism,
Though in a nunnery. It must not be.
I muse, my lord your brother will permit it!
You should spend half my land first, were I he.
Does not this diamond better, on my finger,
Than i' the quarry?
DOL
Yes.
MAMMON
Why, you are like it.
You were created, lady, for the light!
Here, you shall wear it; take it, the first pledge
Of what I speak: to bind you, to believe me.
DOL
In chains of adamant?
MAMMON
Yes, the strongest bands.
And take a secret, too. Here, by your side,
Doth stand, this hour, the happiest man, in Europe.
DOL
You are contented, sir?
MAMMON
Nay, in true being:
The envy of princes, and the fear of states.
DOL
Say you so, Sir Epicure!
MAMMON
Yes, and thou shalt prove it,
Daughter of honour. I have cast mine eye
Upon thy form, and I will rear this beauty,
Above all styles.
DOL
You mean no treason, sir!

95 *Whole* wholly
96 *this form* i.e. her person
101 *solecism* incongruity, quite unfitting
102 *Though* even if, although it be
103 *muse* am bemused, astonished
109 *speak* shall now say
110 *adamant* punning on old form of diamond, then in use: diamant; *bands* bonds
112 *happiest* (beatus) wealthiest, as well as happiest
118 *styles* fashions of beauty, cults (glancing, perhaps, at the older meaning, engravings)

MAMMON

No, I will take away that jealousy.
I am the lord of the philosopher's stone,
And thou the lady.

DOL

How sir! Ha' you that?

MAMMON

I am the master of the mastery.
This day, the good old wretch, here, o' the house
Has made it for us. Now, he's at projection.
Think therefore, thy first wish, now; let me hear it:
And it shall rain into thy lap, no shower,
But floods of gold, whole cataracts, a deluge,
To get a nation on thee!

DOL

You are pleased, sir,
To work on the ambition of our sex.

MAMMON

I am pleased, the glory of her sex should know,
This nook, here, of the Friars, is no climate
For her, to live obscurely in, to learn
Physic, and surgery, for the Constable's wife
Of some odd Hundred in Essex; but come forth,
And taste the air of palaces; eat, drink
The toils of empirics, and their boasted practice;
Tincture of pearl, and coral, gold, and amber;
Be seen at feasts, and triumphs; have it asked,
What miracle she is? Set all the eyes
Of court afire, like a burning glass,
And work 'em into cinders; when the jewels
Of twenty states adorn thee; and the light
Strikes out the stars; that, when thy name is mentioned,
Queens may look pale: and, we but showing our love,
Nero's Poppæa may be lost in story!

119 *jealousy* suspicion
126 as in the myth of Danae (HS)
131 *the Friars* i.e. Blackfriars (with glancing pun, perhaps)

---

122 *the mastery.* The *magisterium*, the mystery of the stone, the master-touch. The word also carries its older sense of 'mystery' or 'trade'. Cf. Abhorson on the executioner's trade in *Measure for Measure*, IV.ii: 'A bawd, sir? Fie upon him; he will discredit our mystery'.

136 *empirics.* An empiric is literally one who makes experiments, but the word had come to mean a quack: cf. Burton. *Anatomy of Melancholy*, part 2, sec. 1, mem. 4, subs. 1 'There be many Mountebanks, Quack-salvers, Empiricks, in every street'.

145 *Nero's Poppæa.* Mammon calls to mind the legendary splendour and luxury of their amour. It was said that she was so anxious to preserve her beauty that five hundred asses were kept to provide the milk in which she used daily to bathe. But see *Oxford Classical Dictionary.*

Thus, will we have it.

DOL
I could well consent, sir.
But, in a monarchy, how will this be?
The Prince will soon take notice; and both seize
You, and your stone: it being a wealth unfit
For any private subject.

MAMMON
If he knew it.

DOL
Yourself do boast it, sir.

MAMMON
To thee, my life.

DOL
O, but beware, sir! You may come to end
The remnant of your days, in a loathed prison,
By speaking of it.

MAMMON
'Tis no idle fear!
We'll therefore go with all, my girl, and live
In a free state; where we will eat our mullets,
Soused in high-country wines, sup pheasants' eggs,
And have our cockles, boiled in silver shells,
Our shrimps to swim again, as when they lived,
In a rare butter, made of dolphins' milk,
Whose cream does look like opals: and, with these
Delicate meats, set ourselves high for pleasure,
And take us down again, and then renew
Our youth, and strength, with drinking the elixir,
And so enjoy a perpetuity
Of life, and lust. And, thou shalt ha' thy wardrobe,
Richer than nature's, still, to change thyself,
And vary oftener, for thy pride, than she:
Or art, her wise, and almost equal servant.

[*Enter* FACE]

FACE
Sir, you are too loud. I hear you, every word,
Into the laboratory. Some fitter place.
The garden, or great chamber above. How like you her?

MAMMON
Excellent! Lungs. There's for thee.

FACE
But, do you hear?
Good sir, beware, no mention of the Rabbins.

148–50 several vouched-for cases could be cited
156 *mullets* fish; a reputed delicacy of Roman feasting
160 *dolphins' milk* (both rare, and rich)
171 *Into* i.e. right through into
174 *Rabbins* Rabbis, especially the more learned

MAMMON
We think not on 'em.
[*Exeunt* DOL, MAMMON]
FACE
O, it is well, sir. Subtle!

Act IV, Scene ii

[*Enter*] SUBTLE

FACE
Dost thou not laugh?
SUBTLE
Yes. Are they gone?
FACE
All's clear.
SUBTLE
The widow is come.
FACE
And your quarrelling disciple?
SUBTLE
Ay.
FACE
I must to my Captainship again, then.
SUBTLE
Stay, bring 'em in, first.
FACE
So I meant. What is she?
A bonnibell?
SUBTLE
I know not.
FACE
We'll draw lots,
You'll stand to that?
SUBTLE
What else?
FACE
O, for a suit,
To fall now, like a curtain: flap.
SUBTLE
To th' door, man.
FACE
You'll ha' the first kiss, 'cause I am not ready.
[*Exit* FACE]
SUBTLE
Yes, and perhaps hit you through both the nostrils.
FACE [*within*]
Who would you speak with?
KASTRIL [*within*]
Where's the Captain?

3 *Captainship* i.e. the appropriate costume
5 *bonnibell* colloquial (rustic) term of endearment for a Beauty
7 *flap* a term to mime the sudden 'arrival' of the uniform

---

9 *through both the nostrils*. Probably 'lead you by the nose'. See *Isaiah*, xxxvii, 29, and cf. *Othello*, I.iii 'And will as tenderly be led by the nose as asses are'.

FACE
Gone, sir.
About some business.

KASTRIL
Gone?

FACE
He'll return straight.
But master Doctor, his lieutenant, is here.

[*Enter* KASTRIL, DAME PLIANT]

SUBTLE
Come near, my worshipful boy, my *terrae fili*,
That is, my boy of land; make thy approaches:
Welcome, I know thy lusts, and thy desires,
And I will serve, and satisfy 'em.
Charge me from thence, or thence, or in this line;
Here is my centre: ground thy quarrel.

KASTRIL
You lie.

SUBTLE
How, child of wrath, and anger! The loud lie?
For what, my sudden boy?

KASTRIL
Nay, that look you to,
I am aforehand.

SUBTLE
O, this 's no true grammar,
And as ill logic! You must render causes, child,
Your first, and second intentions, know your canons,
And your divisions, moods, degrees, and differences,
Your predicaments, substance, and accident,
Series extern, and intern, with their causes
Efficient, material, formal, final,
And ha' your elements perfect—

KASTRIL
What is this!
The angry tongue he talks in?

SUBTLE
That false precept,
Of being aforehand, has deceived a number;
And made 'em enter quarrels, oftentimes,
Before they were aware: and, afterward,
Against their wills.

KASTRIL
How must I do then, sir?

13 *terrae fili* landed proprietor; but the term also had a colloquial significance – man of mean birth
17 resuming Face's geometrical jargon for duelling punctilio
20 *sudden* impetuous
21 *aforehand* made the first move; *grammar* from this point Subtle deploys the terms of scholastic argument to constitute a fresh pseudo-science of duelling punctilio
23 *canons* general axioms
25 *predicaments* what is predicated or asserted (in technical argument)
28 *elements* first principles
29 *angry* i.e. baffling, and also relating to quarrel-techniques

SUBTLE

I cry this lady mercy. She should, first,
Have been saluted. I do call you lady,
Because you are to be one, ere 't be long,

He kisses her

My soft, and buxom widow.

KASTRIL

Is she, i'faith?

SUBTLE

Yes, or my art is an egregious liar.

KASTRIL

How know you?

SUBTLE

By inspection, on her forehead,
And subtlety of her lip, which must be tasted

He kisses her again

Often, to make a judgement. 'Slight, she melts
Like a myrobalan! Here is, yet, a line
In *rivo frontis*, tells me, he is no knight.

PLIANT

What is he then, sir?

SUBTLE

Let me see your hand.
O, your *linea Fortunae* makes it plain;
And *stella* here, in *monte Veneris*:
But, most of all, *iunctura annularis*.
He is a soldier, or a man of art, lady:
But shall have some great honour, shortly.

PLIANT

Brother,
He's a rare man, believe me!

KASTRIL

Hold your peace.

[*Enter* FACE]

Here comes the tother rare man. Save you Captain.

FACE

Good master Kastril. Is this your sister?

KASTRIL

Ay, sir.
Please you to kuss her, and be proud to know her?

FACE

I shall be proud to know you, lady.

38 *egregious* gross, conspicuous
40 *subtlety* (carries a lascivious intention) a refined species of confectionery
42 *myrobalan* a sweetmeat 43 *rivo frontis* the frontal vein (HS)
45 *linea Fortunae* the line of fortune, in palmistry, runs from beneath the little finger towards the index finger
46 *stella* a star on the hill of Venus (at the root of the thumb): equivocal terminology
47 *iunctura* the joint of the ring finger
54 *know* (used equivocally)

PLIANT
Brother,
He calls me lady, too.

KASTRIL
Ay, peace. I heard it.

FACE
The Count is come.

SUBTLE
Where is he?

FACE
At the door.

SUBTLE
Why, you must entertain him.

FACE
What'll you do
With these the while?

SUBTLE
Why, have 'em up, and show 'em
Some fustian book, or the dark glass.

FACE
'Fore God,
She is a delicate dab-chick! I must have her.

[*Exit* FACE]

SUBTLE
Must you? Ay, if your fortune will, you must.
Come sir, the Captain will come to us presently.
I'll ha' you to my chamber of demonstrations,
Where I'll show you both the grammar, and logic,
And rhetoric of quarrelling; my whole method,
Drawn out in tables; and my instrument,
That hath the several scale upon't, shall make you
Able to quarrel, at a straw's breadth, by moonlight.
And, lady, I'll have you look in a glass,
Some half an hour, but to clear your eyesight,
Against you see your fortune: which is greater,
Than I may judge upon the sudden, trust me.

[*Exeunt* SUBTLE, KASTRIL, PLIANT]

Act IV, Scene iii

[*Enter*] FACE

FACE
Where are you, Doctor?

SUBTLE [*within*]
I'll come to you presently.

FACE
I will ha' this same widow, now I ha' seen her,
On any composition.

59 *fustian* bombastic, jargon-laden
60 *dab-chick* little grebe, 'hence a synonym for daintiness' (HS)
67 *several* divided up, partitioned
71 *Against* in preparation for
3 *composition* barter arrangement, agreement

[*Enter* SUBTLE]

SUBTLE
What do you say?

FACE
Ha' you disposed of them?

SUBTLE
I ha' sent 'em up.

FACE
Subtle, in troth, I needs must have this widow.

SUBTLE
Is that the matter?

FACE
Nay, but hear me.

SUBTLE
Go to,
If you rebel once, Dol shall know it all.
Therefore be quiet, and obey your chance.

FACE
Nay, thou art so violent now–Do but conceive:
Thou art old, and canst not serve—

SUBTLE
Who, cannot, I?
'Slight, I will serve her with thee, for a—

FACE
Nay,
But understand: I'll gi' you composition.

SUBTLE
I will not treat with thee: what, sell my fortune?
'Tis better than my birthright. Do not murmur.
Win her, and carry her. If you grumble, Dol
Knows it directly.

FACE
Well sir, I am silent.
Will you go help, to fetch in Don, in state? [*Exit* FACE]

SUBTLE
I follow you, sir: we must keep Face in awe,
Or he will overlook us like a tyrant.

[*Enter* FACE,] SURLY *like a Spaniard*

Brain of a tailor! Who comes here? Don John!

SURLY
Señores, beso las manos, á vuestras mercedes.

SUBTLE
Would you had stooped a little, and kissed our *anos.*

FACE
Peace Subtle.

SUBTLE
Stab me; I shall never hold, man.

10 *serve* (used equivocally)
15 *and carry* and then take, after winning
17 *state* in style
21 i.e. I kiss your hands, gentlemen
23 i.e. Let me blood: I shall burst

He looks in that deep ruff, like a head in a platter,
Served in by a short cloak upon two trestles!

FACE
Or, what do you say to a collar of brawn, cut down
Beneath the souse, and wriggled with a knife?

SUBTLE
'Slud, he does look too fat to be a Spaniard.

FACE
Perhaps some Fleming, or some Hollander got him
In d'Alva's time: Count Egmont's bastard.

SUBTLE
Don,
Your scurvy, yellow, Madrid face is welcome.

SURLY
Gratia.

SUBTLE He speaks, out of a fortification.
Pray God, he ha' no squibs in those deep sets.

SURLY
Por Dios, Señores, muy linda casa!

SUBTLE
What says he?

FACE
Praises the house, I think,
I know no more but's action.

SUBTLE
Yes, the *casa,*
My precious Diego, will prove fair enough,
To cozen you in. Do you mark? You shall
Be cozened, Diego.

FACE
Cozened, do you see?
My worthy Donzel, cozened.

SURLY
Entiendo.

SUBTLE
Do you intend it? So do we, dear Don.
Have you brought pistolets? Or portagues?
He feels his pockets

25 instead of servers and legs
27 *souse* ears (of pig)
32 *Gratia* Thanks; *fortification* see previous mock analogies. Enormous Spanish ruffs were a frequent occasion of jests
33 *sets* plaits, or folds of ruff
34 'Fore God, gentlemen, a very fine house
37 *Diego* (James) English 'name' for a Spaniard, applied at random
40 *Donzel* (Italian) squire; *Entiendo* I understand

29–30 *Perhaps some Fleming* &c. Netherlanders were proverbially fat. Fernando Alvarez, Duke of Alva, was governor of the Netherlands from 1567 to 1573. Lamoral, Count of Egmont, was a Flemish patriot executed by Alva in 1568.

My solemn Don? Dost thou feel any?

FACE
Full.

SUBTLE
You shall be emptied, Don; pumped, and drawn,
Dry, as they say.

FACE
Milked, in troth, sweet Don.

SUBTLE
See all the monsters; the great lion of all, Don.

SURLY
Con licencia, se puede ver á esta señora?

SUBTLE
What talks he now?

FACE
O' the *Señora.*

SUBTLE
O, Don,
That is the lioness, which you shall see
Also, my Don.

FACE
'Slid, Subtle, how shall we do?

SUBTLE
For what?

FACE
Why, Dol's employed, you know.

SUBTLE
That's true!
'Fore heaven I know not: he must stay, that's all.

FACE
Stay? That he must not by no means.

SUBTLE
No, why?

FACE
Unless you'll mar all. 'Slight, he'll suspect it.
And then he will not pay, not half so well.
This is a travelled punk-master, and does know
All the delays: a notable hot rascal,
And looks, already, rampant.

SUBTLE
'Sdeath, and Mammon
Must not be troubled.

FACE
Mammon, in no case!

SUBTLE
What shall we do then?

FACE
Think: you must be sudden.

SURLY
Entiendo, que la señora es tan hermosa, que codicio tan á verla, como la bien aventuranza de mi vida.

FACE
Mi vida? 'Slid, Subtle, he puts me in mind o' the widow.

47 With your permission, may I see the lady?
61 I understand that the lady is so beautiful, that I am as eager to see her, as for whatever good fortune life brings

What dost thou say to draw her to't? Ha?
And tell her, it is her fortune. All our venture
Now lies upon 't. It is but one man more,
Which on's chance to have her: and, beside,
There is no maidenhead, to be feared, or lost.
What dost thou think on 't, Subtle?

SUBTLE
Who, I? Why—

FACE
The credit of our house too is engaged.

SUBTLE
You made me an offer for my share erewhile.
What wilt thou gi' me, i'faith?

FACE
O, by that light,
I'll not buy now. You know your doom to me.
E'en take your lot, obey your chance, sir; win her,
And wear her, out for me.

SUBTLE
'Slight. I'll not work her then.

FACE
It is the common cause, therefore bethink you.
Dol else must know it, as you said.

SUBTLE
I care not.

SURLY
Señores, por qué se tarda tanto?

SUBTLE
Faith, I am not fit, I am old.

FACE
That's now no reason, sir.

SURLY
Puede ser, de hacer burla de mi amor?

FACE
You hear the Don, too? By this air, I call.
And loose the hinges, Dol.

SUBTLE
A plague of hell—

FACE
Will you then do?

SUBTLE
You're a terrible rogue,
I'll think of this: will you, sir, call the widow?

65 *venture* undertaking, risk, investment 66 *lies* hangs
67 *Which on's* whichever of us's chance it is 73 *doom* lot, fate
78 Why is there so much delay, sirs?; *tanto* F, Q have *tanta*, perhaps indicating current pronunciation
80 Is it possible you are mocking at my love?
82 i.e. I will give the game away, and loudly

74–75 *win her, And wear her, out.* Face is probably glancing at the proverbial 'Win her and wear her' (of a man and his bride) and turning it coarsely.

FACE
Yes, and I'll take her too, with all her faults,
Now I do think on't better.
SUBTLE
With all my heart, sir,
Am I discharged o' the lot?
FACE
As you please.
SUBTLE
Hands.
FACE
Remember now, that upon any change,
You never claim her.
SUBTLE
Much good joy, and health to you, sir.
Marry a whore? Fate, let me wed a witch first.
SURLY
Por estas honradas barbas—
SUBTLE
He swears by his beard.
Despath, and call the brother too. [*Exit* FACE]
SURLY
Tengo dúda, Señores,
Que no me hágan alguna traición.
SUBTLE
How, issue on? Yes, *presto Señor*. Please you
Enthratha the *chambratha*, worthy Don;
Where if it please the Fates, in your *bathada*,
You shall be soaked, and stroked, and tubbed, and rubbed:
And scrubbed, and fubbed, dear Don, before you go.
You shall, in faith, my scurvy baboon Don:
Be curried, clawed, and flawed, and tawed, indeed.
I will the heartilier go about it now,
And make the widow a punk, so much the sooner,
To be revenged on this impetuous Face:
The quickly doing of it is the grace.
[*Exeunt* SUBTLE, SURLY]

Act IV, Scene iv

[*Enter*] FACE, KASTRIL, DAME PLIANT

FACE
Come lady: I knew, the Doctor would not leave,
Till he had found the very nick of her fortune.

87 *Hands* Your hand on it
91 By this honoured beard; I fear, sirs, you are practising treachery upon me
98 *fubbed* (fobbed) cheated, deceived
100 *flawed* flayed; *tawed* suppled, as leather is when dressed with alum
2 *nick* critical moment, turning point

KASTRIL
To be a countess, say you?
FACE
A Spanish countess, sir.
PLIANT
Why? Is that better than an English countess?
FACE
Better? 'Slight, make you that a question, lady?
KASTRIL
Nay, she is a fool, Captain, you must pardon her.
FACE
Ask from your courtier, to your Inns of Court-man,
To your mere milliner: they will tell you all,
Your Spanish jennet is the best horse. Your Spanish
Stoop is the best garb. Your Spanish beard
Is the best cut. Your Spanish ruffs are the best
Wear. Your Spanish pavan the best dance.
Your Spanish titillation in a glove
The best perfume. And, for your Spanish pike,
And Spanish blade, let your poor Captain speak.
Here comes the Doctor.

[*Enter* SUBTLE]

SUBTLE
My most honoured lady,
(For so I am now to style you, having found
By this my scheme, you are to undergo
An honourable fortune, very shortly.)
What will you say now, if some—
FACE
I ha' told her all, sir.
And her right worshipful brother, here, that she shall be
A countess: do not delay 'em, sir. A Spanish countess.
SUBTLE
Still, my scarce worshipful Captain, you can keep
No secret. Well, since he has told you, madame,
Do you forgive him, and I do.
KASTRIL
She shall do that, sir.
I'll look to't, 'tis my charge.
SUBTLE
Well then. Nought rests
But that she fit her love, now, to her fortune.

10 *Stoop* bow; *garb* fashion 12 *pavan* a grave, stately dance
13 *Spanish titillation* a long, elaborate process of perfuming material
18 *scheme* some horoscope or figure
26 *rests* remains

9–15 *Your Spanish jennet* &c. In the reign of James I Spanish fashions were popular at Court, since James wished for closer relations between England and Spain, though the people did not.

PLIANT
Truly, I shall never brook a Spaniard.
SUBTLE
No?
PLIANT
Never, sin' eighty-eight could I abide 'em,
And that was some three year afore I was born, in truth.
SUBTLE
Come, you must love him, or be miserable:
Choose, which you will.
FACE
By this good rush, persuade her,
She will cry strawberries else, within this twelvemonth.
SUBTLE
Nay, shads, and mackerel, which is worse.
FACE
Indeed, sir?
KASTRIL
God's lid, you shall love him, or I'll kick you.
PLIANT
Why?
I'll do as you will ha' me, brother.
KASTRIL
Do,
Or by this hand, I'll maul you.
FACE
Nay, good sir,
Be not so fierce.
SUBTLE
No, my enraged child,
She will be ruled. What, when she come to taste
The pleasures of a countess! To be courted—
FACE
And kissed, and ruffled!
SUBTLE
Ay, behind the hangings.
FACE
And then come forth in pomp!
SUBTLE
And know her state!
FACE
Of keeping all th'idolators o' the chamber
Barer to her, than at their prayers!
SUBTLE
Is served
Upon the knee!
FACE
And has her pages, ushers,
Footmen, and coaches—

32 *rush* picked up from the floor, which was strewed with rushes
33 *cry strawberries* sink to the position of a market girl
34 *shads* a kind of herring–sinking from market girl to fishwife
41 *ruffled* touzled

---

29 *Never, sin' eighty-eight.* 1588, the year of the Armada; the allusion is a common one in seventeenth century poetry.

SUBTLE
Her six mares—

FACE
Nay, eight!

SUBTLE
To hurry her through London, to th' Exchange,
Bedlam, the China-houses—

FACE
Yes, and have
The citizens gape at her, and praise her tires!
And my lord's goose-turd bands, that rides with her!

KASTRIL
Most brave! By this hand, you are not my suster,
If you refuse.

PLIANT
I will not refuse, brother.

[*Enter* SURLY]

SURLY
Qué es esto, Señores, que no se venga?
Esta tradanza me mata!

FACE
It is the Count come!
The Doctor knew he would be here, by his art.

SUBTLE
En galanta madama, Don! Galantissima!

SURLY
Por todos los dioses, la más acabada
Hermosura, que he visto en my vida!

FACE
Is't not a gallant language, that they speak?

KASTRIL
An admirable language! Is't not French?

FACE
No, Spanish, sir.

KASTRIL
It goes like law-French,
And that, they say, is the courtliest language.

FACE
List, sir.

49 *tires* attires
50 *goose-turd* yellowish-green
53–4 How is it, gentlemen, that she does not come? This delay is killing me.
57–8 By all the gods, the most perfect beauty I have seen in my life.

47–8 *th'Exchange, Bedlam, the China-houses.* Centres of fashionable resort. The New Exchange in the Strand, known as 'Britain's Burse', was built in 1608–9; Bethlehem Hospital was a place where one could watch the madmen for amusement; the China-houses were private houses where porcelain, ivory, silks etc. were on view, and, since trade with the East had not long been opened, were objects of general interest and curiosity.

SURLY
El sol ha perdido su lumbre, con el
Resplandor, que trae esta dama. Válgame Dios!

FACE
He admires your sister.

KASTRIL
Must she not make curtsey?

SUBTLE
'Ods will, she must go to him, man; and kiss him!
It is the Spanish fashion, for the women
To make first court.

FACE
'Tis true he tells you, sir:
His art knows all.

SURLY
Porqué no se acude?

KASTRIL
He speaks to her, I think?

FACE
That he does sir.

SURLY
Por el amor de Dios, qué es esto, que se tarda?

KASTRIL
Nay, see: she will not understand him! Gull.
Noddy.

PLIANT What say you brother?

KASTRIL
Ass, my suster,
Go kuss him, as the cunning man would ha' you,
I'll thrust a pin i' your buttocks else.

FACE
O, no sir.

SURLY
Señora mía, mi persona muy indigna está
Á llegar á tanta hermosura.

FACE
Does he not use her bravely?

KASTRIL
Bravely, i' faith!

FACE
Nay, he will use her better.

KASTRIL
Do you think so?

SURLY
Señora, si sera servida, entremos.

[*Exeunt* SURLY, DAME PLIANT]

63–4 The sun has lost his light with the splendour this lady brings, so help me God
69 Why doesn't she come to me?
71 For the love of God, why does she delay?
76–7 My lady, my person is quite unworthy to come near such beauty
80 Lady, if it is convenient, we will go in

KASTRIL
Where does he carry her?
FACE
Into the garden, sir;
Take you no thought: I must interpret for her.
SUBTLE
Give Dol the word [*Exit* FACE] Come, my fierce child, advance,
We'll to our quarrelling lesson again.
KASTRIL
Agreed.
I love a Spanish boy, with all my heart.
SUBTLE
Nay, and by this means, sir, you shall be brother
To a great count.
KASTRIL
Ay, I knew that, at first.
This match will advance the house of the Kastrils.
SUBTLE
Pray God, your sister prove but pliant.
KASTRIL
Why,
Her name is so: by her other husband.
SUBTLE
How!
KASTRIL
The widow Pliant. Knew you not that?
SUBTLE
No faith, sir.
Yet, by erection of her figure, I guessed it.
Come, let's go practice.
KASTRIL
Yes, but do you think, Doctor,
I e'er shall quarrel well?
SUBTLE
I warrant you.
[*Exeunt* SUBTLE, KASTRIL]

Act IV, Scene v

[*Enter*] DOL, MAMMON

DOL
For, after Alexander's death— *In her fit of talking*
MAMMON
Good lady—
DOL
That Perdiccas, and Antigonus were slain,
The two that stood, Seleuc', and Ptolomee—
MAMMON
Madam.

83 *the word* i.e. to begin raving
92 *erection of her figure* casting her horoscope

DOL Made up the two legs, and the fourth Beast.
That was Gog-north, and Egypt-south: which after
Was called Gog-iron-leg, and South-iron-leg—

MAMMON Lady—

DOL
And then Gog-horned. So was Egypt, too.
Then Egypt-clay-leg, and Gog-clay-leg—

MAMMON Sweet madam.

DOL
And last Gog-dust, and Egypt-dust, which fall
In the last link of the fourth chain. And these
Be stars in story, which none see, or look at—

MAMMON
What shall I do?

DOL For, as he says, except
We call the Rabbins, and the heathen Greeks—

MAMMON
Dear lady.

DOL To come from Salem, and from Athens,
And teach the people of Great Britain—

[*Enter* FACE]

FACE What's the matter, sir?

DOL
To speak the tongue of Eber, and Javan—

MAMMON O,
She's in her fit.

DOL We shall know nothing—

FACE Death, sir,
We are undone.

DOL Where, then, a learned linguist
Shall see the ancient used communion
Of vowels, and consonants—

FACE My master will hear!

1–32 *For, after Alexander's death* &c. Dol's raving is made up of scraps and fragments quoted from Hugh Broughton's *A Concent of Scripture* (1590), an attempt to settle Biblical chronology. Broughton (1549–1612) was a theologian and rabbinical scholar, and he was a staunch Puritan. Jonson satirises him again in *Volpone*, II.ii, 119. It would be pedantry to explain every allusion which Dol makes in her 'fit of talking', but Togarmah (27) refers to *Ezekiel*, xxxviii, 6, the description of the 'habergeons' as 'Brimstony' comes from Wyclif's version of *Revelation*, xi,17, 'Abaddon, and the Beast of Cittim' are from Broughton's *A Revelation of the Holy Apocalyps* (1610), and refer to the Pope. David Kimchi, or Kimhi, was one of a family group of Jewish grammarians and Biblical scholars who worked at Narbonne in the twelfth century, Onkelos was a first century scholar and translator, and Abraham ben Meir Ibn Ezra (1092–1157) a Biblical critic and poet.

DOL
A wisdom, which Pythagoras held most high—
MAMMON
Sweet honourable lady.
DOL
To comprise
All sounds of voices, in few marks of letters—
FACE
Nay, you must never hope to lay her now.

They speak together

DOL
And so we may arrive by Talmud skill,
And profane Greek, to raise the building up
Of Heber's house, against the Ismaelite,
King of Togarmah, and his habergeons
Brimstony, blue, and fiery; and the force
Of King Abaddon, and the Beast of Cittim:
Which Rabbi David Kimchi, Onkelos,
And Aben-Ezra do interpret Rome.

FACE
How did you put her into't?
MAMMON
Alas I talked
Of a fifth monarchy I would erect,
With the philosopher's stone (by chance) and she
Falls on the other four, straight. FACE Out of Broughton!
I told you so. 'Slid stop her mouth. MAMMON Is't best?
FACE
She'll never leave else.
If the old man hear her,
We are but fæces, ashes.
SUBTLE [*within*] What's to do there?
FACE
O, we are lost. Now she hears him, she is quiet.

Upon SUBTLE'S *entry they disperse*

MAMMON
Where shall I hide me?
SUBTLE
How! What sight is here!
Close deeds of darkness, and that shun the light!
Bring him again. Who is he? What, my son!
O, I have lived too long.

28 *habergeons* sleeveless coats of mail (used here only for sound)
31 *fæces* dead matter

25 *a fifth monarchy*. The Fifth Monarchy Men were a millenarian sect in England during the seventeenth century.

MAMMON
Nay good, dear Father,
There was no unchaste purpose.

SUBTLE
Not? And flee me,
When I come in?

MAMMON
That was my error.

SUBTLE
Error?
Guilt, guilt, my son. Give it the right name. No marvel,
If I found check in our great work within,
When such affairs as these were managing!

MAMMON
Why, have you so?

SUBTLE
It has stood still this half hour:
And all the rest of our less works gone back.
Where is the instrument of wickedness,
My lewd false drudge?

MAMMON
Nay, good sir, blame not him.
Believe me, 'twas against his will, or knowledge.
I saw her by chance.

SUBTLE
Will you commit more sin,
T'excuse a varlet?

MAMMON
By my hope, 'tis true, sir.

SUBTLE
Nay, then I wonder less, if you, for whom
The blessing was prepared, would so tempt heaven:
And lose your fortunes.

MAMMON
Why, sir?

SUBTLE
This'll retard
The work, a month at least.

MAMMON
Why, if it do,
What remedy? But think it not, good Father:
Our purposes were honest.

SUBTLE
As they were,
So the reward will prove. How now! Ay me.

A great crack and noise within

God, and all saints be good to us. What's that?

[*Enter* FACE]

FACE
O sir, we are defeated! All the works
Are flown *in fumo*: every glass is burst.

41 *managing* going on
47 *more sin* i.e. perjure yourself
58 *in fumo* in smoke

---

55 s.d. *A great crack*. All the earlier instructions about 'luting' and hermetically sealing the vessels seem like a preparation for this dramatically apt explosion.

Furnace, and all rent down! As if a bolt
Of thunder had been driven through the house.
Retorts, receivers, pelicans, boltheads,
All struck in shivers! Help, good sir! Alas,

SUBTLE *falls down as in a swoon*

Coldness, and death invades him. Nay, sir Mammon,
Do the fair offices of a man! You stand,
As you were readier to depart, than he.
Who's there? My lord her brother is come.

One knocks

MAMMON
Ha, Lungs?

FACE
His coach is at the door. Avoid his sight,
For he's as furious, as his sister is mad.

MAMMON
Alas!

FACE
My brain is quite undone with the fume, sir,
I ne'er must hope to be mine own man again.

MAMMON
Is all lost, Lungs? Will nothing be preserved,
Of all our cost?

FACE
Faith, very little, sir.
A peck of coals, or so, which is cold comfort, sir.

MAMMON
O my voluptuous mind! I am justly punished.

FACE
And so am I, sir.

MAMMON
Cast from all my hopes—

FACE
Nay, certainties, sir.

MAMMON
By mine own base affections.

SUBTLE
O, the curst fruits of vice, and lust!

SUBTLE *seems to come to himself*

MAMMON
Good father,
It was my sin. Forgive it.

SUBTLE
Hangs my roof
Over us still, and will not fall, O justice,
Upon us, for this wicked man!

FACE
Nay, look, sir,
You grieve him, now, with staying in his sight:

62 *shivers* pieces
64 *fair* appropriate, kind
70 *mine own man* myself

Good sir, the nobleman will come too, and take you,
And that may breed a tragedy.

MAMMON I'll go.

FACE
Ay, and repent at home, sir. It may be,
For some good penance, you may ha' it, yet,
A hundred pound to the box at Bedlam—

MAMMON Yes.

FACE
For the restoring such as ha' their wits.

MAMMON I'll do't.

FACE
I'll send one to you to receive it.

MAMMON Do.
Is no projection left?

FACE All flown, or stinks, sir.

MAMMON
Will nought be saved, that's good for medicine, thinkst thou?

FACE
I cannot tell, sir. There will be, perhaps,
Something, about the scraping of the shards,
Will cure the itch: though not your itch of mind, sir.
It shall be saved for you, and sent home. Good sir,
This way: for fear the lord should meet you.

[*Exit* MAMMON]

SUBTLE Face.

FACE
Ay.

SUBTLE Is he gone?

FACE Yes, and as heavily
As all the gold he hoped for, were in his blood.
Let us be light, though.

SUBTLE Ay, as balls, and bound
And hit our heads against the roof for joy:
There's so much of our care now cast away.

FACE
Now to our Don.

SUBTLE Yes, your young widow, by this time
Is made a countess, Face: she's been in travail
Of a young heir for you.

FACE Good, sir.

SUBTLE Off with your case,

86 *Bedlam* Bethlehem hospital for the insane
92 *shards* pots
103 *case* his uniform as Lungs; to Dame Pliant he is Captain Face

And greet her kindly, as a bridegroom should,
After these common hazards.

FACE
Very well, sir.
Will you go fetch Don Diego off, the while?

SUBTLE
And fetch him over too, if you'll be pleased, sir:
Would Dol were in her place, to pick his pockets now.

FACE
Why, you can do it as well, if you would set to't.
I pray you prove your virtue.

SUBTLE
For your sake, sir.

[*Exeunt* SUBTLE *and* FACE]

Act IV, Scene vi

[*Enter*] SURLY, DAME PLIANT

SURLY
Lady, you see into what hands, you are fallen;
'Mongst what a nest of villains! And how near
Your honour was t'have catched a certain clap
(Through your credulity) had I but been
So punctually forward, as place, time,
And other circumstance would ha' made a man:
For you're a handsome woman: would you're wise, too.
I am a gentleman, come here disguised,
Only to find the knaveries of this citadel,
And where I might have wronged your honour, and have not,
I claim some interest in your love. You are,
They say, a widow, rich: and I am a bachelor,
Worth nought: your fortunes may make me a man,
As mine ha' preserved you a woman. Think upon it,
And whether, I have deserved you, or no.

PLIANT
I will, sir.

SURLY
And for these household-rogues, let me alone,
To treat with them.

[*Enter* SUBTLE]

SUBTLE
How doth my noble Diego?
And my dear madam, Countess? Hath the Count

107 *fetch him over* get the better of him
110 *prove your virtue* test your skill
5 *punctually forward* ready to take advantage
9 *Only* solely

Been courteous, lady? Liberal? And open?
Donzell, me thinks you look melancholic,
After your *coitum*, and scurvy! Truly,
I do not like the dulness of your eye:
It hath a heavy cast, 'tis upsee Dutch,
And says you are a lumpish whore-master.
Be lighter, I will make your pockets so.

He falls to picking of them

SURLY
Will you, Don bawd, and pickpurse? How now? Reel you?
Stand up sir, you shall find since I am so heavy,
I'll gi' you equal weight.

SUBTLE
Help, murder!

SURLY
No, sir.
There's no such thing intended. A good cart,
And a clean whip shall ease you of that fear.
I am the Spanish Don, that should be cozened,
Do you see? Cozened? Where's your Captain Face?
That parcel-broker, and whole-bawd, all rascal.

[*Enter* FACE]

FACE
How, Surly!

SURLY
O, make your approach, good Captain.
I have found, from whence your copper rings, and spoons
Come now, wherewith you cheat abroad in taverns.
'Twas here, you learned t'anoint your boot with brimstone,
Then rub men's gold on't, for a kind of touch,
And say 'twas naught, when you had changed the colour,
That you might ha't for nothing? And this Doctor,
Your sooty, smoky-bearded compeer, he
Will close you so much gold, in a bolt's head,
And, on a turn, convey (i' the stead) another
With sublimed mercury, that shall burst i' the heat,
And fly out all *in fumo*? Then weeps Mammon:

19 *courteous, Liberal, open* with sexual overtones, applied to the lady
23 *upsee Dutch* Dutch fashion, phlegmatic
41 *compeer* companion
43 *on a turn* i.e. by sleight of hand

---

21 *After your coitum*. Omne animal post coitum triste est. See *John Donne: The Elegies and The Songs and Sonnets*, ed. Gardner (Oxford 1956), p. 213.
33 *parcel-broker*. Part-time go-between. 'Broker' usually meant pawn-broker, but always referred to an agent, middleman, factor, and was a term of abuse. Cf. *Everyman in His Humour*, III.v, 32, 'One of the deuil's neere kinsmen, a broker'.

Then swoons his worship. Or, he is the Faustus,
[FACE *slips out*]
That casteth figures, and can conjure, cures
Plague, piles, and pox, by the ephemerides,
And holds intelligence with all the bawds,
And midwives of three shires? While you send in—
Captain, (what is he gone?) damsels with child,
Wives, that are barren, or, the waiting-maid
With the green sickness? [SUBTLE *attempts to leave*] Nay, sir, you must tarry
Though he be 'scaped; and answer, by the ears, sir.

Act IV, Scene vii

[*Enter*] FACE, KASTRIL, SURLY, SUBTLE

FACE
Why, now's the time, if ever you will quarrel
Well (as they say) and be a true-born child.
The Doctor, and your sister both are abused.

KASTRIL
Where is he? Which is he? He is a slave
Whate'er he is, and the son of a whore. Are you
The man, sir, I would know?

SURLY
I should be loath, sir,
To confess so much.

KASTRIL
Then you lie, i' your throat.

SURLY
How?

FACE
A very errant rogue, sir, and a cheater,
Employed here, by another conjurer,
That does not love the Doctor, and would cross him
If he knew how—

SURLY
Sir, you are abused.

KASTRIL
You lie:
And 'tis no matter.

FACE
Well said, sir. He is
The impudentest rascal—

SURLY
You are indeed. Will you hear me, sir?

FACE
By no means: bid him be gone.

46 *Faustus* familiar from Marlowe's play
47 *figures* horoscopes
48 *ephemerides* astronomical almanacs
53 *green sickness* chlorosis, a form of anaemia
54 *by the ears* in the pillory

KASTRIL
Be gone, sir, quickly.
SURLY
This's strange! Lady, do you inform your brother.
FACE
There is not such a foist, in all the town,
The Doctor had him, presently: and finds, yet,
The Spanish Count will come, here. Bear up, Subtle.
SUBTLE
Yes, sir, he must appear, within this hour.
FACE
And yet this rogue, would come, in a disguise,
By the temptation of another spirit,
To trouble our art, though he could not hurt it.
KASTRIL
Ay,
I know–away, you talk like a foolish mauther.
SURLY
Sir, all is truth, she says.
FACE
Do not believe him, sir:
He is the lyingest swabber! Come your ways, sir.
SURLY
You are valiant, out of company.
KASTRIL
Yes, how then, sir?

[*Enter* DRUGGER]

Nay, here's an honest fellow too, that knows him,
And all his tricks. (Make good what I say, Abel,)
This cheater would ha' cozened thee o' the widow.
He owes this honest Drugger, here, seven pound,
He has had on him, in two-penny 'orths of tobacco.
DRUGGER
Yes sir. And he's damned himself, three terms, to pay me.
FACE
And what does he owe for *lotium*?
DRUGGER
Thirty shillings, sir:
And for six syringes.
SURLY
Hydra of villany!

16 *foist* pickpocket, rogue
21 i.e. set on by another conjurer
23 *mauther* a great awkward girl
31 *on* from
33 *lotium* stale urine used by barbers as a 'lye' for the hair

34 *Hydra*. The seventh labour of Hercules was to kill the Hydra, the many-headed snake of the marsh of Lerna; its heads grew again twice as fast as he cut them off. Surly, here, sees himself losing through the multiplication of his enemies.

FACE
Nay, sir, you must quarrel him out o' the house.
KASTRIL I will.
Sir, if you get not out o' doors, you lie:
And you are a pimp.
SURLY Why, this is madness, sir,
Not valour in you: I must laugh at this.
KASTRIL
It is my humour: you are a pimp, and a trig,
And an Amadis de Gaul, or a Don Quixote.
DRUGGER
Or a knight o' the curious coxcomb. Do you see?

[*Enter* ANANIAS]

ANANIAS
Peace to the household.
KASTRIL I'll keep peace, for no man.
ANANIAS
Casting of dollars is concluded lawful.
KASTRIL
Is he the constable?
SUBTLE Peace, Ananias.
FACE No, sir.
KASTRIL
Then you are an otter, and a shad, a whit,
A very tim.
SURLY You'll hear me, sir?
KASTRIL I will not.
ANANIAS
What is the motive!
SURLY Zeal, in the young gentleman,
Against his Spanish slops—
ANANIAS They are profane,
Lewd, superstitious, and idolatrous breeches.

39 *trig* dandy, coxcomb
45 *whit* bawd (*cf.* Captain Whit in *Bartholomew Fair*)
46 *tim* meaning unknown

---

39 *It is my humour*. See *Every Man Out of his Humour*, Induction, 110–14.
40 *an Amadis de Gaul* &c. a Spanish or Portuguese romance, written in the form in which we have it by Garcia de Montalvo *circa* 1450–1500. It was early translated into French, and many continuations were written, relating to the son and nephew of Amadis. 'The introduction of his name here, coupled with that of the hero of the greatest satire on chivalry, fitly keeps up the bizarre nature of Kastril's conversation' (Hathaway). See Edwin B. Knowles, 'Allusions to "Don Quixote" before 1660', *Philological Quarterly*, XX, 4 (October 1941) 573–86.

SURLY

New rascals!

KASTRIL Will you be gone, sir?

ANANIAS Avoid Satan,

Thou art not of the light. That ruff of pride,
About thy neck, betrays thee: and is the same
With that, which the unclean birds, in seventy-seven,
Were seen to prank it with, on divers coasts.
Thou lookest like Antichrist, in that lewd hat.

SURLY

I must give way.

KASTRIL Be gone, sir.

SURLY But I'll take

A course with you—

(ANANIAS Depart, proud Spanish fiend)

SURLY

Captain, and Doctor—

ANANIAS Child of perdition.

KASTRIL Hence, sir.

[*Exit* SURLY]

Did I not quarrel bravely?

FACE Yes, indeed, sir.

KASTRIL

Nay, and I give my mind to't, I shall do't.

FACE

O, you must follow, sir, and threaten him tame.
He'll turn again else.

KASTRIL I'll re-turn him, then.

[*Exit* KASTRIL]

FACE

Drugger, this rogue prevented us, for thee:
We had determined, that thou shouldst ha' come,
In a Spanish suit, and ha' carried her so; and he
A brokerly slave, goes, puts it on himself.

53 *unclean birds* allusion to *Revelation* xviii,2: *cf.* V.iii, 47
56–7 *take a course* be revenged 60 *and* if
63 *prevented us, for thee* anticipated what we intended for you
64 *determined* decided 65 *carried* won
66 *brokerly* pettifogging

---

53 *the unclean birds, in seventy-seven.* This allusion has never been fully explained. Herford and Simpson suggest that the date is an error, and should read either 'sixty-seven' (the date of D'Alva's invasion of the Netherlands) or 'eighty-eight' (the year of the Armada). More convincing is Hathaway's conjecture that they are birds in some popular superstition, the details of which have not survived. The context supports the impression of a contemporary joke.

Hast brought the damask?

DRUGGER
Yes sir.

FACE
Thou must borrow,
A Spanish suit. Hast thou no credit with the players?

DRUGGER
Yes, sir, did you never see me play the fool?

FACE
I know not, Nab: thou shalt, if I can help it.
Hieronymo's old cloak, ruff, and hat will serve,
I'll tell thee more, when thou bring'st 'em.

[*Exit* DRUGGER]

ANANIAS
Sir, I know

SUBTLE *hath whispered with him this while*

The Spaniard hates the Brethren, and hath spies
Upon their actions: and that this was one
I make no scruple. But the holy Synod
Have been in prayer, and meditation, for it.
And 'tis revealed no less, to them, than me,
That casting of money is most lawful.

SUBTLE
True.
But here, I cannot do it; if the house
Should chance to be suspected, all would out,
And we be locked up, in the Tower, forever,
To make gold there (for th' state) never come out:
And, then, are you defeated.

ANANIAS
I will tell
This to the Elders, and the weaker Brethren,
That the whole company of the Separation
May join in humble prayer again.

(SUBTLE
And fasting.)

ANANIAS
Yea, for some fitter place. The peace of mind
Rest with these walls.

SUBTLE
Thanks, courteous Ananias.

[*Exit* ANANIAS]

FACE
What did he come for?

SUBTLE
About casting dollars,
Presently, out of hand. And so, I told him,
A Spanish minister came here to spy,
Against the faithful—

FACE
I conceive. Come Subtle,

70 *help* forward
71 *Hieronymo* hero of Kyd's *Spanish Tragedy*
75 *scruple* doubt 90 *Presently* now, at once

Thou art so down upon the least disaster!
How wouldst th' ha' done, if I had not helped thee out?

SUBTLE
I thank thee Face, for the angry boy, i' faith.

FACE
Who would ha' looked, it should ha' been that rascal?
Surly? He had dyed his beard, and all. Well, sir,
Here's damask come, to make you a suit.

SUBTLE
Where's Drugger?

FACE
He is gone to borrow me a Spanish habit,
I'll be the Count, now.

SUBTLE
But where's the widow?

FACE
Within, with my lord's sister: Madam Dol
Is entertaining her.

SUBTLE
By your favour, Face,
Now she is honest, I will stand again.

FACE
You will not offer it?

SUBTLE
Why?

FACE
Stand to your word,
Or–here comes Dol. She knows—

SUBTLE
You're tyrannous still.

[*Enter* DOL]

FACE
Strict for my right. How now, Dol? Hast told her,
The Spanish Count will come?

DOL
Yes, but another is come,
You little looked for!

FACE
Who's that?

DOL
Your master:
The master of the house.

SUBTLE
How, Dol!

FACE
She lies.
This is some trick. Come, leave your quiblins, Dorothy.

DOL
Look out, and see.

SUBTLE
Art thou in earnest?

DOL
'Slight,
Forty o' the neighbours are about him, talking.

93 *down* dejected 96 *looked* foreseen
103 *stand* make a bid for her 105 *still* always
110 *quiblins* tricks

FACE
'Tis he, by this good day.
DOL
'Twill prove ill day,
For some on us.
FACE
We are undone, and taken.
DOL
Lost, I am afraid.
SUBTLE
You said he would not come,
While there died one a week, within the liberties.
FACE
No: 'twas within the walls.
SUBTLE
Was't so? Cry you mercy:
I thought the liberties. What shall we do now, Face?
FACE
Be silent: not a word, if he call, or knock.
I'll into mine old shape again, and meet him,
Of Jeremy, the butler. I' the mean time,
Do you two pack up all the goods, and purchase,
That we can carry i' the two trunks. I'll keep him
Off for today, if I cannot longer: and then
At night, I'll ship you both away to Ratcliff,
Where we'll meet tomorrow, and there we'll share.
Let Mammon's brass, and pewter keep the cellar:
We'll have another time for that. But, Dol,
Pray thee, go heat a little water, quickly,
Subtle must shave me. All my Captain's beard
Must off, to make me appear smooth Jeremy.
You'll do't?
SUBTLE
Yes, I'll shave you, as well as I can.
FACE
And not cut my throat, but trim me?
SUBTLE
You shall see, sir.
[*Exeunt* SUBTLE, FACE, DOL]

116 *liberties* suburbs
117 see I.i, 182
122 *purchase* winnings

---

125 *Ratcliff*. In Stepney. It was an important place of resort at the time, because of the highway of the river.

Act V, Scene i

[*Enter*] LOVEWIT, NEIGHBOURS

LOVEWIT
Has there been such resort, say you?
NEIGHBOUR 1 Daily, sir.
NEIGHBOUR 2
And nightly, too.
NEIGHBOUR 3 Ay, some as brave as lords.
NEIGHBOUR 4
Ladies, and gentlewomen.
NEIGHBOUR 5 Citizens' wives.
NEIGHBOUR 1
And knights.
NEIGHBOUR 6 In coaches.
NEIGHBOUR 2 Yes, and oyster-women.
NEIGHBOUR 1
Beside other gallants.
NEIGHBOUR 3 Sailors' wives.
NEIGHBOUR 4 Tobacco-men.
NEIGHBOUR 5
Another Pimlico!
LOVEWIT What should my knave advance,
To draw this company? He hung out no banners
Of a strange calf, with five legs, to be seen?
Or a huge lobster, with six claws?
NEIGHBOUR 6 No, sir.
NEIGHBOUR 3
We had gone in then, sir.
LOVEWIT He has no gift
Of teaching i' the nose, that e'er I knew of!
You saw no bills set up, that promised cure
Of agues, or the toothache?

6 *advance* set forth, advertise
11 *teaching i' the nose* i.e. preaching like a Puritan

---

6 *Pimlico.* Not the district, but a house noted for cakes and 'Pimlico' ale at Hoxton. It is described in *Pimlico, Or Runne Red-Cap. Tis a mad world at Hogsdon*, 1609.

8 *a strange calf, with five legs.* See *Bartholomew Fair*, III.vi, 7, and V.iv, 84–5.

12–13 *cure of agues, or the toothache.* The idea of a fairground still plays behind Lovewit's questions. Mountebanks and itinerant tooth-drawers were part of every fair. For the latter see Chettle, *Kind-Harts Dreame*, 1592 (*Bodley Head Quartos*, IV, 1923, 31–4).

NEIGHBOUR 2 No such thing, sir.

LOVEWIT
Nor heard a drum struck, for baboons, or puppets?

NEIGHBOUR 5
Neither, sir.

LOVEWIT What device should he bring forth now!
I love a teeming wit, as I love my nourishment.
Pray God he ha' not kept such open house,
That he hath sold my hangings, and my bedding:
I left him nothing else. If he have eat 'em,
A plague o' the moth, say I. Sure he has got
Some bawdy pictures, to call all this ging;
The friar, and the nun; or the new motion
Of the knight's courser, covering the parson's mare;
The boy of six year old, with the great thing:
Or 't may be, he has the fleas that run at tilt,
Upon a table, or some dog to dance?
When saw you him?

NEIGHBOUR 1 Who sir, Jeremy?

NEIGHBOUR 2 Jeremy butler?
We saw him not this month.

LOVEWIT How!

NEIGHBOUR 4 Not these five weeks, sir.

NEIGHBOUR 1
These six weeks, at the least.

LOVEWIT Y' amaze me, neighbours!

NEIGHBOUR 5
Sure, if your worship know not where he is,
He's slipped away.

NEIGHBOUR 6 Pray God, he be not made away!

LOVEWIT
Ha? It's no time to question, then. *He knocks*

14 *baboons, or puppets* popular entertainments
15 *device* ingenious invention 21 *ging* company, gang
25 *run at tilt* joust 31 *made away* murdered

---

14 *puppets.* Herford and Simpson quote several instances in support of their statement that Jonson held puppets in contempt. This is true, but it should be noted that he uses them for brilliant satiric effects in the fifth act of *Bartholomew Fair.*

22–5 *The friar, and the nun* &c. These curiosities appear to have been actually exhibited in London at the time. See T. Heywood, *If You know not me*, part ii, 1606, sig. D3 ('her's the Fryer whipping the Nuns arse'); Beaumont and Fletcher, *The Knight of the Burning Pestle*, III.i ('the little child that was so faire growne about the members'); *The Devil is an Ass*, V.ii, 10–13 ('I would sooner Keepe fleas within a circle').

NEIGHBOUR 6 About
Some three weeks since, I heard a doleful cry,
As I sat up, a-mending my wife's stockings.

LOVEWIT
This's strange! That none will answer! Didst thou hear
A cry, saist thou?

NEIGHBOUR 6 Yes, sir, like unto a man
That had been strangled an hour, and could not speak.

NEIGHBOUR 2
I heard it too, just this day three weeks, at two o'clock
Next morning.

LOVEWIT These be miracles, or you make 'em so!
A man an hour strangled, and could not speak,
And both you heard him cry?

NEIGHBOUR 3 Yes, downward, sir.

LOVEWIT
Thou art a wise fellow: give me thy hand I pray thee.
What trade art thou on?

NEIGHBOUR 3 A smith, and't please your worship.

LOVEWIT
A smith? Then, lend me thy help, to get this door open.

NEIGHBOUR 3
That I will presently, sir, but fetch my tools—
[*Exit* NEIGHBOUR 3]

NEIGHBOUR 1
Sir, best to knock again, afore you break it.

Act V, Scene ii

LOVEWIT
I will.

[*Enter* FACE]

FACE What mean you, sir?

NEIGHBOURS 1, 2, 4 O, here's Jeremy!

FACE
Good sir, come from the door.

LOVEWIT Why! What's the matter?

37 *an hour* not meant literally, though Lovewit takes it so
41 *downward* indeed (probably)

V.ii. Most editors have noted that this scene seems to have been suggested by similar trickery in the *Mostellaria* ('Haunted House') of Plautus. There is considerable correspondence of incident, and in both plays the intelligence and wit of the cozeners is vindicated in the resolution.

FACE
Yet farther, you are too near, yet.
LOVEWIT I'the name of wonder!
What means the fellow?
FACE The house, sir, has been visited.
LOVEWIT
What? With the plague? Stand thou then farther.
FACE No, sir,
I had it not.
LOVEWIT Who had it then? I left
None else, but thee, i'the house!
FACE Yes, sir. My fellow,
The cat, that kept the buttery, had it on her
A week, before I spied it: but I got her
Conveyed away, i'the night. And so I shut
The house up for a month—
LOVEWIT How!
FACE Purposing then, sir,
T'have burnt rose-vinegar, treacle, and tar,
And, ha' made it sweet, that you should ne'er ha' known it:
Because I knew the news would but afflict you, sir.
LOVEWIT
Breathe less, and farther off. Why, this is stranger!
The neighbours tell me all, here, that the doors
Have still been open—
FACE How, sir!
LOVEWIT Gallants, men, and women,
And of all sorts, tag-rag, been seen to flock here
In threaves, these ten weeks, as to a second Hogsden,
In days of Pimlico, and Eye-bright!
FACE Sir,
Their wisdoms will not say so!
LOVEWIT Today, they speak

19 *threaves* droves

---

19 *Hogsden*. Now Hoxton, a place much favoured for holidays by the London citizens.

20 *Eye-bright*. See note to V.i, 6. 'Eye-bright' is quoted in *Pimlico, Or Runne Red-Cap*, sig. D3^{v}, and the passage is given by Herford and Simpson without comment:

> *Eye-bright*, (so fam'd of late for *Beere*)
> Although thy *Name* be numbred heere, – i.e. at Hoxton –
> Thine ancient *Honors* now runne low;
> Thou art struck blind by *Pimlyco*.

O.E.D. suggests that it might be 'A kind of ale in Elizabeth's time', but from the quotation above it seems more likely to be either the name of an inn, or the nickname of the innkeeper.

Of coaches, and gallants; one in a French hood,
Went in, they tell me: and another was seen
In a velvet gown, at the window! Divers more
Pass in and out!

FACE
They did pass through the doors then,
Or walls, I assure their eyesights, and their spectacles;
For here, sir, are the keys: and here have been,
In this my pocket, now, above twenty days!
And for before, I kept the fort alone, there.
But, that 'tis yet not deep i'the afternoon,
I should believe my neighbours had seen double
Through the black pot, and made these apparitions!
For, on my faith, to your worship, for these three weeks,
And upwards, the door has not been opened.

LOVEWIT
Strange!

NEIGHBOUR 1
Good faith, I think I saw a coach!

NEIGHBOUR 2
And I too,
I'd ha' been sworn!

LOVEWIT
Do you but think it now?
And but one coach?

NEIGHBOUR 4
We cannot tell, sir: Jeremy
Is a very honest fellow.

FACE
Did you see me at all?

NEIGHBOUR 1
No. That we are sure on.

NEIGHBOUR 2
I'll be sworn o' that.

LOVEWIT
Fine rogues, to have your testimonies built on!

[*Enter* NEIGHBOUR 3 *with his tools*]

NEIGHBOUR 3
Is Jeremy come?

NEIGHBOUR 1
O, yes, you may leave your tools,
We were deceived, he says.

NEIGHBOUR 2
He has had the keys:
And the door has been shut these three weeks.

NEIGHBOUR 3
Like enough.

LOVEWIT
Peace, and get hence, you changelings.

[*Enter* SURLY *and* MAMMON]

FACE
Surly come!
And Mammon made acquainted? They'll tell all.

22 *one in a French hood* Dame Pliant (II.vi, 33)
24 *In a velvet gown* Dol (V.iv, 134)

(How shall I beat them off? What shall I do?)
Nothing's more wretched, than a guilty conscience.

Act V, Scene iii

SURLY
No, sir, he was a great physician. This,
It was no bawdy-house: but a mere chancel.
You knew the lord, and his sister.
MAMMON Nay, good Surly—
SURLY
The happy word, 'be rich'—
MAMMON Play not the tyrant—
SURLY
Should be today pronounced, to all your friends.
And where be your andirons now? And your brass pots?
That should ha' been golden flagons, and great wedges?
MAMMON
Let me but breathe. What! They ha' shut their doors,
Me thinks! MAMMON *and* SURLY *knock*
SURLY Ay, now, 'tis holiday with them.
MAMMON Rogues,
Cozeners, imposters, bawds.
FACE What mean you, sir?
MAMMON
To enter if we can.
FACE Another man's house?
Here is the owner, sir. Turn you to him,
And speak your business.
MAMMON Are you, sir, the owner?
LOVEWIT
Yes, sir.
MAMMON And are those knaves, within, your cheaters?
LOVEWIT
What knaves? What cheaters?
MAMMON Subtle, and his Lungs.
FACE
The gentleman is distracted, sir! No lungs,
Nor lights ha' been seen here these three weeks, sir,
Within these doors, upon my word!
SURLY Your word,
Groom arrogant?
FACE Yes, sir, I am the housekeeper,
And know the keys ha' not been out o' my hands.

2 *mere* absolute

SURLY
This's a new Face?
FACE You do mistake the house, sir!
What sign was't at?
SURLY You rascal! This is one
O' the confederacy. Come, let's get officers,
And force the door.
LOVEWIT Pray you stay, gentlemen.
SURLY
No, sir, we'll come with warrant.
MAMMON Ay, and then,
We shall ha' your doors open.
[*Exeunt* SURLY, MAMMON]
LOVEWIT What means this?
FACE
I cannot tell, sir!
NEIGHBOUR 1 These are two o' the gallants,
That we do think we saw.
FACE Two o' the fools?
You talk as idly as they. Good faith, sir,
I think the moon has crazed 'em all!

[*Enter* KASTRIL]

(O me,
The angry boy come too? He'll make a noise,
And ne'er away till he have betrayed us all.)
KASTRIL
What rogues, bawds, slaves, you'll open the door anon,
KASTRIL *knocks*
Punk, cockatrice, my suster. By this light
I'll fetch the marshal to you. You are a whore,
To keep your castle—
FACE Who would you speak with, sir?
KASTRIL
The bawdy Doctor, and the cozening Captain,
And Puss my suster.
LOVEWIT This is something, sure!
FACE
Upon my trust, the doors were never open, sir.

21 *This's a new Face?* i.e. is this yet another trickster?
22 *sign* as of a tavern 35 *marshal cf.* I.i, 120

34 *cockatrice.* A mythical reptile, also called the basilisk, hatched by a serpent from a cock's egg, and fabled to kill by its mere glance. Hence, it was applied to persons in the sense of monster; and especially to a prostitute. Cf. *Poetaster*, IV.vii, 6.

KASTRIL
I have heard all their tricks, told me twice over,
By the fat knight, and the lean gentleman.

LOVEWIT
Here comes another.

[*Enter* ANANIAS, TRIBULATION]

FACE
Ananias too?
And his pastor?

TRIBULATION
The doors are shut against us.

ANANIAS
Come forth, you seed of sulphur, sons of fire,
They beat too, at the door
Your stench, it is broke forth: abomination
Is in the house.

KASTRIL
Ay, my suster's there.

ANANIAS
The place,
It is become a cage of unclean birds.

KASTRIL
Yes, I will fetch the scavenger, and the constable.

TRIBULATION
You shall do well.

ANANIAS
We'll join, to weed them out.

KASTRIL
You will not come then? Punk, device, my suster!

ANANIAS
Call her not sister. She is a harlot, verily.

KASTRIL
I'll raise the street.

LOVEWIT
Good gentlemen, a word.

ANANIAS
Satan, avoid, and hinder not our zeal.
[*Exeunt* ANANIAS, TRIBULATION, KASTRIL]

LOVEWIT
The world's turned Bedlam.

FACE
These are all broke loose,
Out of St. Katherine's, where they use to keep,
The better sort of mad folks.

NEIGHBOUR 1
All these persons
We saw go in, and out, here.

41 i.e. Mammon and Surly, whose Spanish dress made him appear fatter: *cf.* IV.iii, 28
50 *Punk, device* i.e. arrant whore: a play on 'point-device', faultlessly exact in dress
55 *St. Katherine's* a hospital founded by Queen Matilda in 1148

NEIGHBOUR 2
Yes, indeed, sir.

NEIGHBOUR 3
These were the parties.

FACE
Peace, you drunkards. Sir,
I wonder at it! Please you, to give me leave
To touch the door, I'll try, and the lock be changed.

LOVEWIT
It mazes me!

FACE
Good faith, sir, I believe,
There's no such thing. 'Tis all *deceptio visus*.
(Would I could get him away.) *Dapper cries out within*

DAPPER
Master Captain, master Doctor.

LOVEWIT
Who's that?

FACE
(Our clerk within, that I forgot!) I know not, sir.

DAPPER
For God's sake, when will her Grace be at leisure?

FACE
Ha!
Illusions, some spirit o' the air: (his gag is melted,
And now he sets out the throat.)

DAPPER
I am almost stifled—

FACE
(Would you were altogether.)

LOVEWIT
'Tis i' the house.
Ha! List.

FACE
Believe it, sir, i' the air!

LOVEWIT
Peace, you—

DAPPER
Mine aunt's Grace does not use me well.

SUBTLE [*within*]
You fool,
Peace, you'll mar all.

FACE
Or you will else, you rogue.

LOVEWIT
O, is it so? Then you converse with spirits!
Come sir. No more o' your tricks, good Jeremy,
The truth, the shortest way.

FACE
Dismiss this rabble, sir.
What shall I do? I am catched.

LOVEWIT
Good neighbours,
I thank you all. You may depart. [*Exeunt* NEIGHBOURS]
Come sir,
You know that I am an indulgent master:

62 *deceptio visus* an optical illusion
67 *sets out the throat* raises his voice

And therefore, conceal nothing. What's your medicine,
To draw so many several sorts of wild fowl?

FACE
Sir, you were wont to affect mirth, and wit:
(But here's no place to talk on't i' the street.)
Give me but leave, to make the best of my fortune,
And only pardon me th'abuse of your house:
It's all I beg. I'll help you to a widow,
In recompense, that you shall gi' me thanks for,
Will make you seven years younger, and a rich one.
'Tis but your putting on a Spanish cloak,
I have her within. You need not fear the house,
It was not visited.

LOVEWIT
But by me, who came
Sooner than you expected.

FACE
It is true, sir.
Pray you forgive me.

LOVEWIT
Well: let's see your widow.

[*Exeunt* LOVEWIT, FACE]

Act V, Scene iv

[*Enter* SUBTLE, DAPPER]

SUBTLE
How! Ha' you eaten your gag?

DAPPER
Yes faith, it crumbled
Away i' my mouth.

SUBTLE
You ha' spoiled all then.

DAPPER
No,
I hope my aunt of Fairy will forgive me.

SUBTLE
Your aunt's a gracious lady: but in troth
You were to blame.

DAPPER
The fume did overcome me,
And I did do't to stay my stomach. Pray you
So satisfy her Grace. Here comes the Captain.

[*Enter* FACE]

FACE
How now! Is his mouth down?

78 *medicine* charm, spell (see *O.E.D.*)
79 *draw* decoy

8 Hathaway notes that at the end of Act IV Face had his beard shaved to make him appear 'smooth Jeremy', and he has no time to procure a false one; the pace and economy of these final scenes make such things unnecessary.

SUBTLE
Ay! He has spoken!

FACE
(A pox, I heard him, and you too.) He's undone, then.
(I have been fain to say, the house is haunted
With spirits, to keep churl back.

SUBTLE
And hast thou done it?

FACE
Sure, for this night.

SUBTLE
Why, then triumph, and sing
Of Face so famous, the precious king
Of present wits.

FACE
Did you not hear the coil,
About the door?

SUBTLE
Yes, and I dwindled with it.)

FACE
Show him his aunt, and let him be dispatched:
I'll send her to you. [*Exit* FACE]

SUBTLE
Well sir, your aunt her Grace,
Will give you audience presently, on my suit,
And the Captain's word, that you did not eat your gag,
In any contempt of her Highness.

DAPPER
Not I, in troth, sir.

[*Enter*] DOL *like the Queen of Fairy*

SUBTLE
Here she is come. Down o' your knees, and wriggle:
She has a stately presence. Good. Yet nearer,
And bid, God save you.

DAPPER
Madam.

SUBTLE
And your aunt.

DAPPER
And my most gracious aunt, God save your Grace.

DOL
Nephew, we thought to have been angry with you:
But that sweet face of yours, hath turned the tide,
And made it flow with joy, that ebbed of love.
Arise, and touch our velvet gown.

SUBTLE
The skirts,
And kiss 'em. So.

11 *churl* countryman (because of his hop-yards I.i, 184)
12 *triumph* accented on the second syllable
14 *coil* fuss, disturbance
15 *dwindled* shrank (see quotation in *O.E.D.*)

---

12 *Why, then triumph, and sing* &c. This may perhaps be a quotation from, or parody of, a popular song.

DOL
Let me now stroke that head,
Much, nephew, shalt thou win; much shalt thou spend;
Much shalt thou give away: much shalt thou lend.

SUBTLE
(Ay, much, indeed.) Why do you not thank her Grace?

DAPPER
I cannot speak, for joy.

SUBTLE
See, the kind wretch!
Your Grace's kinsman right.

DOL
Give me the bird.
Here is your fly in a purse, about your neck, cousin,
Wear it, and feed it, about this day se'ennight,
On your right wrist—

SUBTLE
Open a vein, with a pin,
And let it suck but once a week: till then,
You must not look on't.

DOL
No. And, kinsman,
Bear yourself worthy of the blood you come on.

SUBTLE
Her Grace would ha' you eat no more Woolsack pies,
Nor Dagger frumety.

DOL
Nor break his fast,
In Heaven, and Hell.

SUBTLE
She's with you everywhere!
Nor play with costermongers, at mum-chance, tray-trip,
God make you rich, (whenas your aunt has done it:)
but keep
The gallantest company, and the best games—

DAPPER
Yes, sir.

SUBTLE
Gleek and primero: and what you get, be true to us.

DAPPER
By this hand, I will.

SUBTLE
You may bring's a thousand pound,
Before tomorrow night, (if but three thousand,
Be stirring) and you will.

41–2 *Woolsack . . . Dagger* famous taverns (see I.i, 191)
42 *frumety* a dish made of hulled wheat boiled in milk, and seasoned
43 *Heaven, and Hell* two taverns on the site of the present committee-rooms of the House of Commons (HS)
44 *mum-chance* a dice game;
tray-trip a dice game that depended on throwing threes
45 *God make you rich* a variety of backgammon

47 *Gleek and primero.* These were the 'best games' because they were the games played by the Court.

DAPPER I swear, I will then.

SUBTLE
Your fly will learn you all games.

FACE [*within*] Ha' you done there?

SUBTLE
Your grace will command him no more duties?

DOL No:
But come, and see me often. I may chance
To leave him three or four hundred chests of treasure,
And some twelve thousand acres of Fairyland:
If he game well, and comely, with good gamesters.

SUBTLE
There's a kind aunt! Kiss her departing part.
But you must sell your forty mark a year, now:

DAPPER
Ay, sir, I mean.

SUBTLE Or, gi't away: pox on't.

DAPPER
I'll gi't mine aunt. I'll go and fetch the writings.
[*Exit* DAPPER]

SUBTLE
'Tis well, away.

[*Enter* FACE]

FACE Where's Subtle?

SUBTLE Here. What news?

FACE
Drugger is at the door, go take his suit,
And bid him fetch a parson, presently:
Say, he shall marry the widow. Thou shalt spend
A hundred pound by the service! [*Exit* SUBTLE] Now, queen Dol,
Ha' you packed up all?

DOL Yes.

FACE And how do you like
The lady Pliant?

DOL A good dull innocent.

[*Enter* SUBTLE]

SUBTLE
Here's your Hieronimo's cloak, and hat.

FACE Give me 'em.

SUBTLE
And the ruff too?

FACE Yes, I'll come to you presently.
[*Exit* FACE]

SUBTLE
Now, he is gone about his project, Dol,
I told you of, for the widow.
DOL
'Tis direct
Against our articles.
SUBTLE
Well, we'll fit him, wench.
Hast thou gulled her of her jewels, or her bracelets?
DOL
No, but I will do't.
SUBTLE
Soon at night, my Dolly,
When we are shipped, and all our goods aboard,
Eastward for Ratcliff; we will turn our course
To Brainford, westward, if thou saist the word:
And take our leaves of this o'erweening rascal,
This peremptory Face.
DOL
Content, I am weary of him.
SUBTLE
Th' hast cause, when the slave will run a-wiving, Dol,
Against the instrument, that was drawn between us.
DOL
I'll pluck his bird as bare as I can.
SUBTLE
Yes, tell her,
She must by any means, address some present
To th' cunning man; make him amends, for wronging
His art with her suspicion; send a ring;
Or chain of pearl; she will be tortured else
Extremely in her sleep, say: and ha' strange things
Come to her. Wilt thou?
DOL
Yes.
SUBTLE
My fine flitter-mouse,
My bird o'the night; we'll tickle it at the Pigeons,
When we have all, and may unlock the trunks,
And say, this's mine, and thine, and thine, and mine—

They kiss

[*Enter* FACE]

FACE
What now, a-billing?
SUBTLE
Yes, a little exalted
In the good passage of our stock-affairs.

72 *we'll fit him* perhaps a glance at *The Spanish Tragedy*, IV.i, 70
77 *Brainford* Brentford, Middlesex
81 *instrument* agreement
88 *flitter-mouse* bat, term of endearment
89 *Pigeons* 'The Three Pigeons', an inn in Brentford market-place
93 *stock-affairs* joint venture

FACE
Drugger has brought his parson, take him in, Subtle,
And send Nab back again, to wash his face.

SUBTLE
I will: and shave himself?

FACE
If you can get him. [*Exit* SUBTLE]

DOL
You are hot upon it, Face, what e'er it is!

FACE
A trick, that Dol shall spend ten pound a month by.

[*Enter* SUBTLE]

Is he gone?

SUBTLE
The chaplain waits you i'the hall, sir.

FACE
I'll go bestow him. [*Exit* FACE]

DOL
He'll now marry her, instantly.

SUBTLE
He cannot, yet, he is not ready. Dear Dol,
Cozen her of all thou canst. To deceive him
Is no deceit, but justice, that would break
Such an inextricable tie as ours was.

DOL
Let me alone to fit him.

[*Enter* FACE]

FACE
Come, my venturers,
You ha' packed up all? Where be the trunks? Bring forth.

SUBTLE
Here.

FACE
Let's see 'em. Where's the money?

SUBTLE
Here,
In this.

FACE
Mammon's ten pound: eight score before.
The Brethren's money, this. Drugger's, and Dapper's.
What paper's that?

DOL
The jewel of the waiting maid's,
That stole it from her lady, to know certain—

FACE
If she should have precedence of her mistress?

DOL
Yes.

FACE
What box is that?

SUBTLE
The fish wives' rings, I think:

And th' ale wives' single money. Is't not Dol?

DOL
Yes: and the whistle, that the sailor's wife
Brought to you, to know, and her husband were with Ward.

FACE
We'll wet it tomorrow: and our silver beakers,
And tavern cups. Where be the French petticoats,
And girdles, and hangers?

SUBTLE
Here, i' the trunk,
And the bolts of lawn.

FACE
Is Drugger's damask, there?
And the tobacco?

SUBTLE
Yes.

FACE
Give me the keys.

DOL
Why you the keys!

SUBTLE
No matter, Dol: because
We shall not open 'em, before he comes.

FACE
'Tis true, you shall not open them, indeed:
Nor have 'em forth. Do you see? Not forth, Dol.

DOL
No!

FACE
No, my smock-rampant. The right is, my master
Knows all, has pardoned me, and he will keep 'em.
Doctor, 'tis true (you look) for all your figures:
I sent for him, indeed. Wherefore, good partners,
Both he, and she, be satisfied: for, here
Determines the indenture tripartite,
Twixt Subtle, Dol, and Face. All I can do
Is to help you over the wall, o' the back-side;
Or lend you a sheet, to save your velvet gown, Dol.
Here will be officers, presently; bethink you,
Of some course suddenly to scape the dock:
For thither you'll come else. *Some knock*
Hark you, thunder.

SUBTLE
You are a precious fiend!

OFFICER [*without*]
Open the door.

114 *single money* small change 120 *bolts* rolls of fabric
126 *right* truth of it 129 *I sent for him* not true, but a useful lie
131 *Determines* ends, is concluded

116 *Ward.* A famous Mediterranean pirate, whose base was at Tunis. He is mentioned in several plays of the period, and Daborne's *A Christian turned Turk*, 1612, is based, in part, on his exploits.

FACE
Dol, I am sorry for thee i' faith. But hearst thou?
It shall go hard, but I will place thee somewhere:
Thou shalt ha' my letter to mistress Amo.

DOL
Hang you—

FACE
Or madam Cæsarean.

DOL
Pox upon you, rogue,
Would I had but time to beat thee.

FACE
Subtle,
Let's know where you set up next; I'll send you
A customer, now and then, for old acquaintance:
What new course ha' you?

SUBTLE
Rogue, I'll hang myself:
That I may walk a greater devil, than thou,
And haunt thee i' the flock-bed, and the buttery.

[*Exeunt* SUBTLE, FACE, DOL]

Act V, Scene v

[*Enter*] LOVEWIT [, PARSON]

LOVEWIT
What do you mean, my masters?

MAMMON [*without*]
Open your door,
Cheaters, bawds, conjurers.

OFFICER [*without*]
Or we'll break it open.

LOVEWIT
What warrant have you?

OFFICER
Warrant enough, sir, doubt not:
If you'll not open it.

LOVEWIT
Is there an officer, there?

OFFICER
Yes, two, or three for failing.

LOVEWIT
Have but patience,
And I will open it straight.

[*Enter* FACE]

FACE
Sir, ha' you done?
Is it a marriage? Perfect?

LOVEWIT
Yes, my brain.

141–2 *mistress Amo . . . madam Cæsarean* two brothel-keepers (Q reads 'Imperiall' for 'Cæsarean')
148 i.e. while you sleep and eat
5 *for failing* as a precaution against failure

FACE
Off with your ruff, and cloak then, be yourself, sir.

SURLY [*without*]
Down with the door.

KASTRIL [*without*] 'Slight, ding it open.

LOVEWIT Hold.
Hold gentlemen, what means this violence?

[*Enter* MAMMON, SURLY, KASTRIL, ANANIAS, TRIBULATION, OFFICERS]

MAMMON
Where is this collier?

SURLY And my Captain Face?

MAMMON
These day-owls.

SURLY That are birding in men's purses.

MAMMON
Madam Suppository.

KASTRIL Doxy, my suster.

ANANIAS Locusts
Of the foul pit.

TRIBULATION Profane as Bel, and the dragon.

ANANIAS
Worse than the grasshoppers, or the lice of Egypt.

LOVEWIT
Good gentlemen, hear me. Are you officers,
And cannot stay this violence?

OFFICER Keep the peace.

LOVEWIT
Gentlemen, what is the matter? Whom do you seek?

MAMMON
The chemical cozener.

SURLY And the Captain pander.

KASTRIL
The nun my suster.

MAMMON Madam Rabbi.

ANANIAS Scorpions,
And caterpillars.

LOVEWIT Fewer at once, I pray you.

9 *ding* break 11 *collier* see I.i, 90 note
14 *Bel, and the dragon* from the book in the *Apocrypha*
17 *stay* control
20 *nun* facetious term for a prostitute

---

13 *Madam Suppository*. An apt word, since it not only refers to her study of medicine but was a cant term for 'prostitute'.

OFFICER
One after another, gentleman, I charge you,
By virtue of my staff—

ANANIAS
They are the vessels
Of pride, lust, and the cart.

LOVEWIT
Good zeal, lie still,
A little while.

TRIBULATION
Peace, deacon Ananias.

LOVEWIT
The house is mine here, and the doors are open:
If there be any such persons, as you seek for,
Use your authority, search on o' God's name.
I am but newly come to town, and finding
This tumult 'bout my door (to tell you true)
It somewhat mazed me; till my man, here, (fearing
My more displeasure) told me he had done
Somewhat an insolent part, let out my house
(Belike, presuming on my known aversion
From any air o' the town, while there was sickness)
To a Doctor, and a Captain: who, what they are,
Or where they be, he knows not.

MAMMON
Are they gone?

They enter

LOVEWIT
You may go in, and search, sir. Here, I find
The empty walls, worse than I left 'em, smoked,
A few cracked pots, and glasses, and a furnace,
The ceiling filled with poesies of the candle:
And madam, with a dildo, writ o' the walls.
Only, one gentlewoman, I met here,
That is within, that said she was a widow—

KASTRIL
Ay, that's my suster. I'll go thump her. Where is she?

LOVEWIT
And should ha' married a Spanish count, but he,
When he came to't, neglected her so grossly,
That I, a widower, am gone through with her.

SURLY
How! Have I lost her then?

LOVEWIT
Were you the Don, sir?
Good faith, now, she does blame y'extremely, and says

31 *mazed* amazed, puzzled
41 *poesies of the candle* marks made by candle smoke
42 *dildo* phallus

You swore, and told her, you had ta'en the pains,
To dye your beard, and umbre o'er your face,
Borrowed a suit, and ruff, all for her love;
And then did nothing. What an oversight,
And want of putting forward, sir, was this!
Well fare an old harquebuzier, yet,
Could prime his powder, and give fire, and hit,
All in a twinkling.

MAMMON
The whole nest are fled!

Mammon comes forth

LOVEWIT
What sort of birds were they?

MAMMON
A kind of choughs,
Or thievish daws, sir, that have picked my purse
Of eight score, and ten pounds, within these five weeks,
Beside my first materials; and my goods,
That lie i' the cellar: which I am glad they ha' left.
I may have home yet.

LOVEWIT
Think you so, sir?

MAMMON
Ay.

LOVEWIT
By order of law, sir, but not otherwise.

MAMMON
Not mine own stuff?

LOVEWIT
Sir, I can take no knowledge,
That they are yours, but by public means.
If you can bring certificate, that you were gulled of 'em,
Or any formal writ, out of a court,
That you did cozen yourself: I will not hold them.

MAMMON
I'll rather lose 'em.

LOVEWIT
That you shall not, sir,
By me, in troth. Upon these terms they are yours.
What should they ha' been, sir, turned into gold all?

MAMMON
No.
I cannot tell. It may be they should. What then?

LOVEWIT
What a great loss in hope have you sustained?

56 *harquebuzier* musketeer, armed with an 'harquebus', the forerunner of the rifle
59 *choughs* birds of the crow family
67 *public means* course of law

61 *these five weeks*. This agrees, more or less, with V.i, 28–9, but the experiments of II.i, 5 have taken ten months. See Herford and Simpson for a discussion of the play's time-scheme.

MAMMON
Not I, the Commonwealth has.
FACE
Ay, he would ha' built
The city new; and made a ditch about it
Of silver, should have run with cream from Hogsden:
That, every Sunday in Moorfields, the younkers,
And tits, and tomboys should have fed on, *gratis*.
MAMMON
I will go mount a turnip cart, and preach
The end o' the world, within these two months. Surly,
What! In a dream?
SURLY
Must I needs cheat myself,
With that same foolish vice of honesty!
Come let us go, and harken out the rogues.
That Face I'll mark for mine, if e'er I meet him.
FACE
If I can hear of him, sir, I'll bring you word,
Unto your lodging: for in troth, they were strangers
To me, I thought 'em honest, as myself, sir.
[*Exeunt* MAMMON, SURLY]
TRIBULATION
'Tis well, the Saints shall not lose all yet. Go,
They come forth
And get some carts—
LOVEWIT
For what, my zealous friends?
ANANIAS
To bear away the portion of the righteous,
Out of this den of thieves.
LOVEWIT
What is that portion?
ANANIAS
The goods, sometimes the orphan's, that the Brethren,
Bought with their silver pence.
LOVEWIT
What, those i' the cellar,
The knight Sir Mammon claims?
ANANIAS
I do defy
The wicked Mammon, so do all the Brethren,
Thou profane man. I ask thee, with what conscience
Thou canst advance that idol, against us,
That have the seal? Were not the shillings numbered,
That made the pounds? Were not the pounds told out,
Upon the second day of the fourth week,

79 *younkers* children
80 *tits, and tomboys* young girls
85 *harken out* find out by enquiry
100 *That have the seal?* see, for example, *Revelation* ix,4

In the eighth month, upon the table dormant,
The year, of the last patience of the Saints,
Six hundred and ten.

LOVEWIT Mine earnest vehement botcher,
And deacon also, I cannot dispute with you,
But, if you get you not away the sooner,
I shall confute you with a cudgel.

ANANIAS Sir.

TRIBULATION
Be patient Ananias.

ANANIAS I am strong,
And will stand up, well girt, against an host,
That threaten Gad in exile.

LOVEWIT I shall send you
To Amsterdam, to your cellar.

ANANIAS I will pray there,
Against thy house: may dogs defile thy walls,
And wasps, and hornets breed beneath thy roof,
This seat of falsehood, and this cave of cozenage.
[*Exeunt* ANANIAS, TRIBULATION]

Drugger enters, and he beats him away

LOVEWIT
Another too?

DRUGGER Not I sir, I am no Brother.

LOVEWIT
Away you Harry Nicholas, do you talk? [*Exit* DRUGGER]

FACE
No, this was Abel Drugger. Good sir, go,
To the Parson
And satisfy him; tell him, all is done:
He stayed too long a-washing of his face.
The Doctor, he shall hear of him at Westchester;
And of the Captain, tell him at Yarmouth: or
Some good port town else, lying for a wind. [*Exit Parson*]
If you get off the angry child, now, sir—

103 *table dormant* permanent side table, as distinct from the moveable 'board'
111 *Gad in exile* HS suggest an allusion to *Genesis* xlix,19
121 *Westchester* modern Chester

117 *Harry Nicholas*. Henrick Niclaes (fl. 1502–1580), a native of Munster, was an Anabaptist and the leader of the sect called 'The Family of Love' (see Mosheim, *Ecclesiastical History*, IV.vii). He came to England during the reign of Edward VI, and his pamphlets were translated into English by Christopher Vittel, a Southwark joiner. Queen Elizabeth issued a proclamation against the sect in 1580.

[*Enter* KASTRIL, DAME PLIANT]

KASTRIL
Come on, you ewe, you have matched most sweetly, ha'
you not?
To his sister
Did not I say, I would never ha' you tupped
But by a dubbed boy, to make you a lady tom?
'Slight, you are a mammet! O, I could touse you, now.
Death, mun' you marry with a pox?

LOVEWIT
You lie, boy;
As sound as you: and I am aforehand with you.

KASTRIL
Anon?

LOVEWIT
Come, will you quarrel? I will feeze you, sirrah.
Why do you not buckle to your tools?

KASTRIL
God's light!
This is a fine old boy, as e'er I saw!

LOVEWIT
What, do you change your copy, now? Proceed,
Here stands my dove: stoop at her, if you dare.

KASTRIL
'Slight I must love him! I cannot choose, i' faith!
And I should be hanged for't. Suster, I protest,
I honour thee, for this match.

LOVEWIT
O, do you so, sir?

KASTRIL
Yes, and thou canst take tobacco, and drink, old boy,
I'll give her five hundred pound more, to her marriage,
Than her own state.

LOVEWIT
Fill a pipe-full, Jeremy.

FACE
Yes, but go in, and take it, sir.

LOVEWIT
We will.
I will be ruled by thee in anything, Jeremy.

KASTRIL
'Slight, thou art not hidebound! Thou art a jovy boy!
Come let's in, I pray thee, and take our whiffs.

126 *tupped* mated, carrying on the 'farm' metaphor
128 *mammet* puppet; *touse* beat
131 *feeze you* frighten you off
132 *buckle to your tools* draw your weapon
134 *your copy* your style of behaviour
135 *stoop* swoop like a hawk (technical term in falconry)
144 *jovy* jovial

LOVEWIT

Whiff in with your sister, brother boy.
[*Exeunt* KASTRIL, DAME PLIANT]
That master
That had received such happiness by a servant,
In such a widow, and with so much wealth,
Were very ungrateful, if he would not be
A little indulgent to that servant's wit,
And help his fortune, though with some small strain
Of his own candour. Therefore, gentlemen,
And kind spectators, if I have outstripped
An old man's gravity, or strict canon, think
What a young wife, and a good brain may do:
Stretch age's truth sometimes, and crack it too.
Speak for thyself, knave.

FACE

So I will, sir. Gentlemen,
My part a little fell in this last scene,
Yet 'twas decorum. And though I am clean
Got off, from Subtle, Surly, Mammon, Dol,
Hot Ananias, Dapper, Drugger, all
With whom I traded; yet I put myself
On you, that are my country: and this pelf,
Which I have got, if you do quit me, rests
To feast you often, and invite new guests.

THE END

152 *candour* fair reputation
162–3 *I put myself . . . country* a reference to the legal description of a jury
164 *quit* acquit

TEXTUAL NOTES

Dedication

2–3 *DESERVING . . . BLOOD* most æquall with vertue, and her Blood: The Grace, and Glory of women Q

10–12 *Or, how . . . virtue?* Or how, yet, might a gratefull minde be furnish'd against the iniquitie of Fortune; except, when she fail'd it, it had power to impart it selfe? A way found out, to overcome euen those, whom Fortune hath enabled to returne most, since they, yet leaue themselues more. In this assurance am I planted; and stand with those affections at this Altar, as shall no more auoide the light and witnesse, then they doe the conscience of your vertue Q

14 *value of it, which* valew, that Q

15 *as the times are* in these times Q

17 *assiduity* daylinesse Q

18 *This, yet* But this Q

To the Reader

1 *To the Reader . . . than composed* Q; not in F

The Persons of the Play

1 *Play* Comœdie Q

14 **The Scene** *LONDON* F; not in Q

Prologue

10 *for* to Q

I.i

51 *you're* yo'were F (also I.ii, 128; I.iii, 51; IV.vi, 7) you were Q

69 *our state of grace* the high state of grace Q

114 *it* not in Q

149 *Death on me* Gods will Q

I.ii

45 *Dogs-meat* Dogges-mouth Q

56 *Xenophon* Testament Q

135 *Jove* Gad Q

I.iii

44 *metoposcopy* metaposcopie Q, F

67 *mercurial* Mercurian Q

I.iv

16 *possessed* possess'd on't Q

II.i

11 *the young* my yong Q

30 *thy* my Q, perh. correctly

II.ii

13 *Buy* Take Q

58 *They will . . . all others* not in Q

60 *pure* best Q

II.iii

18 *Now* No Q, F

25 SURLY SVB. Q

176 *metals* mettall Q

221–2 transposed in Q

249 *Eulen* Zephyrus Q

259 *her–wit– / Or so* her– / Wit? or so Q

260 SUBTLE *Eulen* not in Q SUBTLE not in F

272 SURLY SVB. Q, F

315 *Eulen* not in Q

II.iv

nil

II.v

10 *styptic* stipstick Q, F, (perh. intentionally to indicate Subtle's own error)

II.vi

25 FACE not in Q

III.i

2–4 *we of the . . . Sent forth* th'Elect must beare, with patience; / They are the exercises of the Spirit, / And sent Q

III.ii

36 *talc* Talek F

99 *glorious* holy Q

135 *you'll* you shall Q

142 *have a trick* F2; have trick Q, F

III.iii

22 *milk* feele Q

62 FACE F2; not in Q, F

79 *Let's* Lett's vs Q

III.iv
4 (*he says.*) not in Q
8 DRUGGER NAB. Q, E
9 *Nab* not in Q
75 *'Od's* God's Q
132 *go* go, sir Q

III.v
nil

IV.i
18 *Eulen* Lungs Q
101 *solecism* solæcisme Q, F
107 *the light* light Q
112 *in* of Q
171 *laboratory* labaratory F

IV.ii
nil

IV.iii
11 *'Slight* 'Sblood Q
21 ff. Surly's Spanish has been corrected and modernized throughout

IV.iv
3 FACE Q; not in F

IV.v
25, 29 MAMMON MAN. F
27 *Heber's* Helens Q, F
With the Which the Q
31 *fæces* fœces Q, F
42 *stood still* gone back Q
43 *gone back* stand still Q
51 *This'll retard* This will hinder Q
74 *voluptuous* voluptuouos F

IV.vi
16 SURLY SVB. F

IV.vii
32 *he's* he hath Q
104 SUBTLE SVR. F
126 *there* then Q

V.i
29 NEIGHBOUR 1 ed. Q, F omit 1

V.ii
nil

V.iii
44 *sulphur, sons of fire* Vipers, Sonnes of Belial Q
45 *stench, it* wickednesse Q
46 *Ay*, not in Q
48 *Yes*, I (*i.e.*, Ay) Q

V.iv
23 *you* her Q
50 *and* if Q
55 *twelve* fiue Q
58 *your* Q; you F
59 *pox* A pox Q
60 DAPPER FAC. Q, F
95 *Nab* him Q
138 SUBTLE SYB. F
142 *Cæsarean* Imperiall Q

V.v
13 *suster* Q; sister F
24 *pride, lust, and the cart* shame, and of dishonour Q
32 *he* ed.; not in Q, F
99 *idol* Nemrod Q
116 s.d. at 118 F
124 *get* can get Q
145 *I* not in Q

Printed in Great Britain by
Fletcher & Son Ltd, Norwich

The Physiotherapist's Pocket Guide to Exercise

Assessment, Prescription and Training

Angela Glynn PhD, PG Cert, MCSP

Helen Fiddler MSc, MCSP, PG Cert

CHURCHILL LIVINGSTONE

ELSEVIER

EDINBURGH LONDON NEW YORK OXFORD
PHILADELPHIA ST. LOUIS SYDNEY TORONTO 2009

CHURCHILL
LIVINGSTONE
ELSEVIER

An imprint of Elsevier Limited

ISBN: 978-0-443-10269-1

British Library Cataloguing in Publication Data
A catalogue record for this book is available from the British Library

Library of Congress Cataloging in Publication Data
A catalog record for this book is available from the Library of Congress

Notice
Neither the Publisher nor the Authors assume any responsibility for any loss or injury and/or damage to persons or property arising out of or related to any use of the material contained in this book. It is the responsibility of the treating practitioner, relying on independent expertise and knowledge of the patient, to determine the best treatment and method of application for the patient.

The Publisher's policy is to use paper manufactured from sustainable forests

Printed in China

CONTENTS

PREFACE

Therapeutic exercise is one of the core skills upon which the profession of physiotherapy is based. Although there are many different professionals involved in delivering advice on physical activity and exercise, physiotherapists are equipped to provide therapeutic exercise programmes in light of their knowledge of the impact of pathological processes on an individual. Physiotherapists prescribe exercise to manage both acute and chronic conditions and to maximize an individual's functional ability.

From our experience of working with pre- and post-registration physiotherapy students in this field we have identified a need for a quick reference guide to exercise prescription that can be used both in the classroom and in clinical practice. This book provides essential information to prescribe exercise safely and effectively in conditions commonly seen by physiotherapists. As such it will be useful for physiotherapists working in specialist areas and when prescribing exercise for patients who have co-morbidities which may affect their response to exercise. It is beyond the scope of this book to provide detailed information on all aspects of therapeutic exercise prescription; therefore reference and further reading lists are provided at the end of each chapter.

The early chapters of this book focus on important principles of exercise physiology, design and prescription. Later chapters apply these principles to exercise prescription in patient populations. The final chapter contains some examples of case studies to illustrate the application of exercise prescription.

There has recently been some controversy about who has the necessary skills to prescribe exercise. From our work in this area we firmly believe that physiotherapists should be taking a lead in exercise prescription. We hope that this book will help to provide a basis to support this role.

ACKNOWLEDGEMENTS

Our thanks go to everyone who has supported the writing of this book. We would particularly like to thank our students, who provided the initial inspiration for this text, and we hope that this will be a helpful tool in the challenges of exercise prescription.

Thank you to those at Elsevier for taking our ideas forward to become a reality and for their support when the going got tough.

Most importantly we would like to thank our families. To John and Thomas, for your support in giving Helen the time to work on the book, and to Phil, Emily and Jasper for letting Angela monopolize the computer. Thank you for being so patient.

Introduction to Exercise Physiology

This chapter provides a broad introduction to exercise physiology. Physiology of muscle, the cardiovascular system and energy supply are considered here. This chapter is not intended to be an in-depth study of this area but contains the underpinning knowledge with which physiotherapist who prescribes exercise in practice should be familiar. More details of any of the topics covered can be found in other exercise physiology texts and there are some suggestions of these at the end of the chapter.

MUSCLE

Skeletal muscle accounts for 40–50% of total body weight. It has three main functions:

- force generation for movement
- postural support
- heat production during periods of cold stress.

Structure

Skeletal muscle is made up of fascicles or bundles of muscle fibres and is surrounded by and held together with connective tissue. This connective tissue forms three layers, the epimysium which surrounds whole muscles, the perymysium which surrounds fascicles or bundles of 10–100 muscle fibres and the endomysium which surrounds individual muscle fibres. The connective tissue layers hold the muscle together, connect muscle to other structures in the body and form tendons to connect muscle to bone. When a muscle contracts, tension is

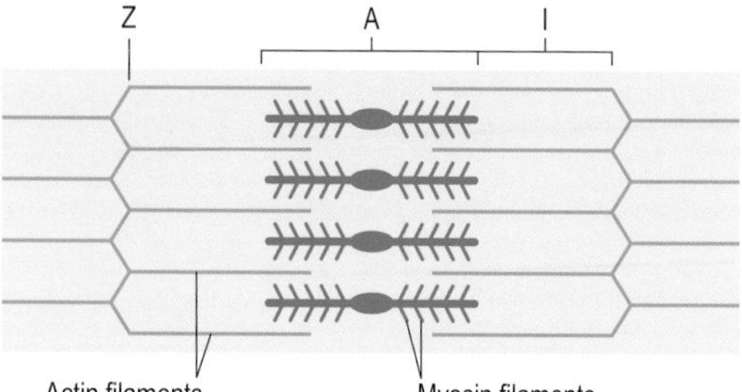

Figure 1.1 The components of a sarcomere showing Z lines, the A band and the I band. From Borell D, Nimmo M and Wood L (1996) Principles of Physiology. London: WB Saunders Ltd, p. 105

transmitted through the connective tissue which pulls on the muscle insertion and produces movement.

Muscle fibres are long cylindrical cells which lie parallel to one another. The plasma membrane of the muscle cell (sarcolemma) contains many myofibrils lying lengthways, within which are the contractile elements of the muscle. The myofibrils are composed of filaments, which are arranged in compartments called sarcomeres. These filaments are both thick and thin and overlap by differing amounts depending on whether the muscle is relaxed, contracting or stretched. This causes the striated (alternate light and dark bands) appearance of skeletal muscle at microscopic level. The component parts of a sarcomere are illustrated in Figure 1.1. Each sarcomere lies between Z lines. The A band is mostly made of myosin and does not change in length with contraction. The I band is mostly made of actin but there is also overlap of myosin here. This band alters in length with contraction.

Contraction

Muscles contract according to the sliding filament theory first described by Huxley in the 1960s. The thick filaments made up of the protein myosin have crossbridges which extend towards the thin filaments. These are formed mainly of the protein actin but also contain troponin and tropomyosin. Tropomyosin is attached to troponin. These are regulatory proteins to stop myosin and actin from making contact (Figure 1.2a). At the start of a muscle contraction, calcium attaches to troponin, changes its shape and moves the tropomyosin. The myosin heads (crossbridges) can then attach to the actin and pull on the thin filaments to generate force (Figure 1.2b). When a muscle relaxes tropomyosin again covers the myosin binding site.

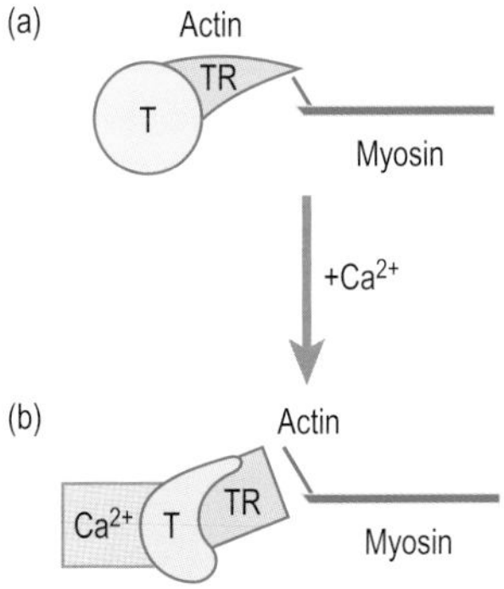

Figure 1.2 Protein crossbridges during muscle contraction and relaxation. T, troponin; TR, tropomyosin; Ca, calcium. Adapted from Borell D, Nimmo M and Wood L (1996) Principles of Physiology. London: WB Saunders Ltd, p. 106

Nerve supply

Motor neurones stimulate muscles to contract. Each motor neurone supplies a group of muscle fibres within a muscle; this is called a motor unit. As all the muscle fibres contract together in a motor unit, the number of fibres in a unit depends on the quality of the movement being produced by a muscle, i.e. few fibres for a precise movement and vice versa.

Blood supply

Muscles are well supplied with blood vessels. There are many capillaries in the endomysium to deliver oxygen and other nutrients and to remove waste products. These capillary beds are under local and central control to allow adequate blood supply as a muscle starts to contract.

Skeletal muscle fibre types

Different types of muscle fibres have been described and there are many ways of classifying these according to functional characteristics. In Table 1.1 muscle fibre types are classified according to speed of contraction.

Most muscle groups within the body have an equal amount of type 1 and type 2 muscle fibres. Fifty per cent of the type 2 muscle fibres are 2a and 50% 2b. Some muscles have higher proportions of type 1 or type 2 fibres depending on the type of activity which they usually perform, e.g. postural muscles have a high proportion of type 1 fibres as they are used almost continuously throughout waking hours.

Table 1.1 Characteristics of human skeletal muscle fibres

Characteristic	Slow twitch type 1 fibre	Intermediate type 2A fibre	Fast twitch type 2X fibre
Diameter	Small	Intermediate	Large
Motor neurone size	Small	Large	Large
Nerve conduction	Slow	Fast	Fast
Contractile speed	Slow	Fast	Fast
Fatigue resistance	High	Moderately high	Low
Motor unit strength	Low	High	High
Oxidative capacity	High	Moderately high	Low
Glycolytic capacity	Low	High	High
Capillarity	Dense	Dense	Sparse
Myoglobin content	High	Intermediate	Low

Adapted from Bruton A (2002) Muscle plasticity: Response to training and detraining. Physiotherapy, 88(7): 399.

DETERMINANTS OF MUSCLE STRENGTH

There is a large individual variation in the amount of force that muscle can generate. This is largely determined by genetics but can also be attributed to the following.

Nerve supply

The number of motor units recruited. Slow twitch motor units are recruited more easily but fast twitch motor units contain more muscle fibres and so generate more force.

Muscle length

Muscles generate most force when working in mid-range. This is the position where there is optimal overlap of thick and thin filaments at sarcomere level and is usually the resting length of most muscles in the body.

Speed of shortening

The slower the movement, the more force is generated. More force is generated when a muscle produces movement than with an isometric contraction of the same muscle where no movement is produced.

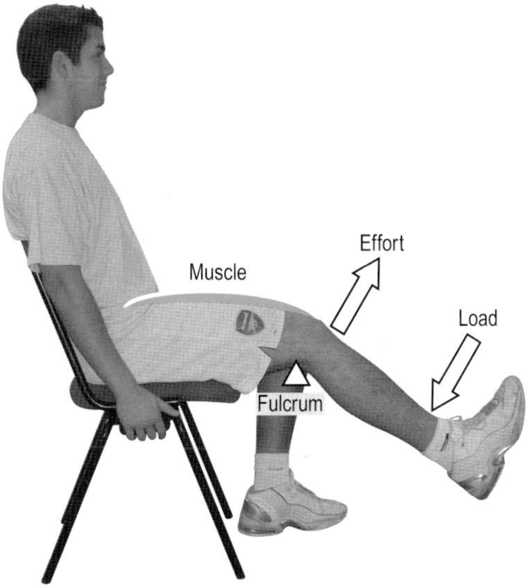

Figure 1.3 To illustrate how quadriceps works across the bone levers of the femur and tibia as a third-class lever

Mechanical advantage

Most muscles work at a considerable mechanical disadvantage owing to the position of their point of insertion in relation to the portion of the limb being moved. This is illustrated in Figure 1.3, which shows how quadriceps acts across the bone levers of the femur and tibia, the knee joint being the fulcrum and inserts into the upper end of the tibia. Small changes in how quadriceps inserts into the tibial tubercle can lead to big changes in force generation when measured at the ankle.

Muscle fibre pennation

Muscles have different shapes and the fascicles are arranged accordingly. Those muscles where the fascicles are parallel with the longitudinal axis of the muscle will produce force more effectively.

Connective tissue

The connective tissue matrix within and around a muscle offers support to the muscle and increases the muscle's ability to generate force. Following a strength training programme, increased collagen synthesis has been found in animal muscle. After training human muscles have been found to be denser radiologically and this could be due to increased connective tissue.

ENERGY SYSTEMS

The source of energy used for muscle contraction is adenosine triphosphate (ATP). When ATP breaks down into adenosine diphosphate (ADP) and inorganic phosphate (Pi) energy is released that can be used for muscle contraction. Only limited amounts of ATP are stored in muscle cells. For exercise, muscles require a continuous source of energy and muscle cells can produce energy by one or any combination of three ways.

1. **ATP-CP system or direct phosphorylation** – As ATP is broken down into ADP + Pi at the start of exercise, ATP is reformed by the creatine phosphate (CP) reaction. A phosphate is donated to the ADP from CP and ATP is reformed. This is the fastest and simplest method of producing energy for muscle contraction. Muscle cells store only a small amount of ATP and CP so this energy source lasts for only about 5 seconds, producing energy for the start of exercise and for short-term high-intensity exercise. This is an anaerobic method of energy production, i.e. without oxygen.

2. **Glycolysis** – This is the mobilization and breakdown of glucose or glycogen which transfers energy to rejoin Pi to ADP resulting in ATP production. This process also results in the production of pyruvic acid and lactic acid. Although this is an anaerobic process, i.e. without oxygen, the pyruvic acid can be utilized in the production of ATP aerobically if oxygen is present in the mitochondria and so is the first step towards aerobic ATP production. This is the predominant source of energy for exercise lasting up to about a minute and a half.

3. **Oxidative phosphorylation** – This is the aerobic production of ATP, i.e. with oxygen, and occurs in the mitochondria of the cell. Two metabolic pathways, the Krebs cycle and electron transport chain, work together to remove hydrogen from food substances (carbohydrates, fats and proteins) so that the potential energy in the hydrogen can be used to produce ATP. This pathway is used for longer-term, aerobic exercise.

These three methods of energy production work together when an individual is exercising to produce ATP. Figure 1.4 illustrates this at the start of exercise.

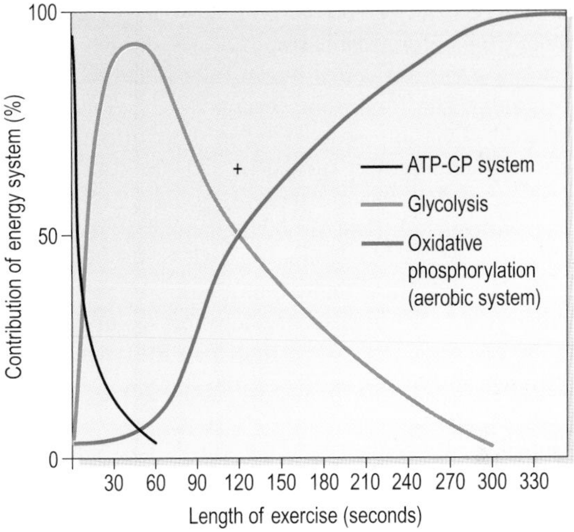

Figure 1.4 Contribution of energy systems during initial phase of exercise

A certain energy pathway will usually predominate in a particular type of exercise. For instance, short-term, intense exercise, such as weightlifting or resistance training for increasing muscle strength, will utilize the ATP-CP system whilst a steady-state, sub-maximal exercise such as a 30-minute brisk walk will use the aerobic energy pathways. Most types of exercise however will require the energy systems to work together. A person playing a game of rugby will use the aerobic pathways to sustain low-intensity movements around the pitch and the anaerobic pathways for short intense activities such as sprints or tackles. In general anaerobic energy systems are used for short high-intensity exercise and aerobic pathways for longer bouts of exercise.

Lactate threshold

During near-maximal, high-intensity exercise the aerobic energy pathways do not supply sufficient energy and the reliance shifts back towards the anaerobic pathways. This leads to an increased production of lactic acid. The point at which the amount of lactate in the blood rises above the pre-exercise level is termed the lactate threshold (LT). The point at which the systemic level of lactic acid in the blood reaches 4 nM is termed the **onset of blood lactate accumulation (OBLA)**.

THE CARDIORESPIRATORY SYSTEM

The supply of oxygen for aerobic respiration and the removal of metabolic waste products are dependent on the integrity of the cardiorespiratory system. During **aerobic exercise** the oxygen required for oxidative phosphorylation is delivered to the working muscle combined with the haemoglobin carried by red blood cells. The blood is carried to the muscle in an extensive capillary network that is in close contact with each muscle fibre. The increase in temperature and acidity at the site of exercising muscle causes the oxyhaemoglobin dissociation curve to shift so that haemoglobin releases oxygen more readily at the muscle. During exercise additional blood is brought to the muscle by diverting blood flow into the capillary network of the exercising muscle and by increasing cardiac output.

Oxygen uptake

Oxygen uptake (VO_2) is the amount of oxygen that the body takes up and utilizes. This is an outcome used in exercise physiology as it is reflective of the oxygen uptake at the exercising muscle. Oxygen is taken up in the lungs and is carried around the body by the blood until it is released at the exercising tissues. Oxygen uptake can be measured by gas analysis of the oxygen content of inspired air vs. the oxygen content of expired air. During exercise at a constant workload, VO_2 increases exponentially at the start of exercise until it reaches the point at which oxygen supply matches oxygen demand and then it plateaus, this plateau is termed **steady-state** (Figure 1.5).

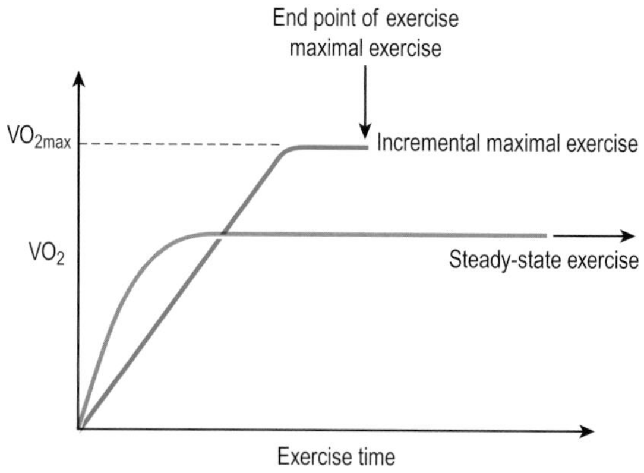

Figure 1.5 Oxygen uptake over time during steady-state and incremental maximal exercise

Maximal oxygen uptake

Maximal oxygen uptake (VO_{2max}) is the maximal amount of oxygen that the body can uptake and utilize and is the gold standard measure of exercise capacity. VO_{2max} is the point at which oxygen uptake plateaus and shows no further increase in response to additional workload (Figure 1.5). VO_{2max} is dependent on a person's gender, height, weight, lung function and fitness level and also on the activity they are performing. VO_{2max} is exercise-specific and is greater for activities involving large muscle groups. VO_{2max} increases with aerobic training.

Arteriovenous oxygen difference

The arteriovenous oxygen difference is a measure of the amount of oxygen taken up from the blood by the tissues. The greater the amount of oxygen extracted by the tissues, the greater the arteriovenous oxygen difference. Cardiac output and arteriovenous oxygen difference are the two factors that determine the overall oxygen uptake. At rest 5 ml of the 20 ml of oxygen in every 100 ml of blood is extracted, producing an arteriovenous oxygen difference of 5 ml. During exercise blood flow to the tissues increases, and haemoglobin dissociates more easily; therefore the arteriovenous oxygen difference widens during exercise. With aerobic training the tissues become more efficient at taking up oxygen; therefore the arteriovenous oxygen difference is still greater in trained individuals.

Heart rate

Heart rate (HR) increases alongside oxygen uptake during exercise to reach steady-state HR during constant workload sub-maximal exercise, and up to maximal HR (HR_{max}) in incremental maximal exercise. Cardiac output during exercise increases initially due to an increase in stroke volume and then, with increasing workload, further increase becomes dependent on HR. In healthy people maximal exercise is limited by HR_{max}, which can be estimated using the equation 220 – age. In trained subjects the stroke volume is increased, therefore allowing a greater cardiac output for a given HR. The linear relationship between HR and VO_2 can be used to predict VO_{2max} from incremental exercise without requiring the person to work up to maximum exercise intensity. By plotting HR vs. VO_2 through a range of workloads the linear relationship can be extended to reach the predicted HR_{max}. The corresponding VO_{2max} can then be estimated from the graph (Figure 1.6).

Ventilation

Ventilation increases linearly with oxygen uptake and carbon dioxide production during light- to moderate-intensity exercise in order

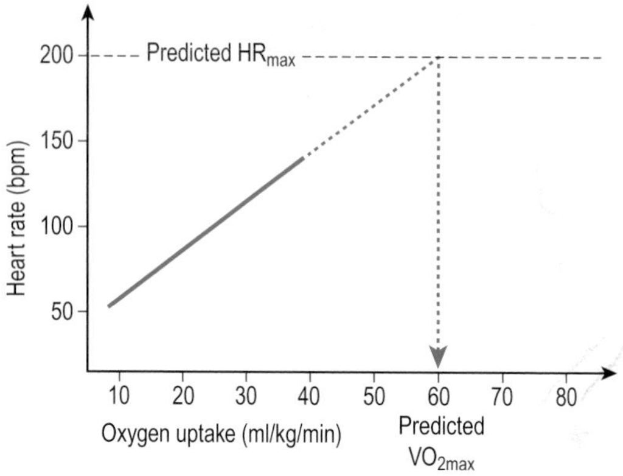

Figure 1.6 Estimation of VO_{2max} by extrapolation of linear relationship between HR and VO_2

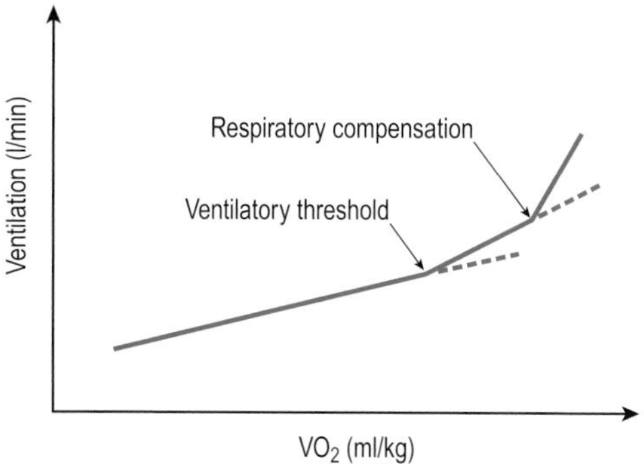

Figure 1.7 Ventilation over oxygen uptake during incremental exercise

to meet the oxygen requirements and expire the additional carbon dioxide produced. The increase in ventilation is initially achieved by increasing tidal volume, and with increasing demand by increasing respiratory rate. A rise in ventilation is seen during heavy to maximal exercise in response to the lactate threshold, this is called the **ventilatory threshold**. With continued exercise a further rise in ventilation is seen at the OBLA in order to expel more carbon dioxide in an effort to reduce the acidity in the blood. This rise is called **respiratory compensation** (Figure 1.7).

Blood flow and pressure during exercise

Local factors in exercising muscle, such as an increase in temperature, decrease in oxygenation and metabolic products, cause vasodilation and opening of dormant capillaries. This produces a significant increase in blood flow to the muscle. Systemically vasoconstriction causes blood to move from the periphery into the central circulation in order to maintain a sufficient blood pressure. This balance of vasodilation and vasoconstriction ensures that, apart from a slight initial increase in systolic pressure, there is little change in blood pressure during steady-state exercise. During incremental exercise the systolic pressure may increase up to around 200 mmHg due to the large increase in cardiac output required at high levels of exercise; diastolic pressure remains relatively stable.

Thermoregulation during exercise

The increase in metabolism during muscular activity produces heat which must be dissipated to prevent a dangerous increase in core temperature. This is achieved by vasodilatation of the blood vessels in the skin causing the heated blood to pass close to the body surface, losing heat through radiation and conduction. The heated blood also stimulates the sweat glands, which increase sweat production to lose more heat through evaporation. The evaporation of sweat leads to fluid and electrolyte loss, which may lead to dehydration. Dehydration may impair cognitive and exercise performance and predispose the person to heat stroke. Vasoconstriction occurs at the viscera to maintain blood pressure in response to the fluid loss and the redirection of blood to the skin. The effects of fluid loss are magnified when exercising at high ambient temperatures; therefore the room temperature should be considered before exercising patients. Patients should be advised to drink some fluid before exercising and small amounts of fluid during and after exercise rather than drinking large amounts of fluid, which stimulates urine production.

Further reading

Borell D, Nimmo M, Wood L (1996) Principles of Physiology. London: WB Saunders Ltd.

Bruton A (2002) Muscle plasticity: Response to training and detraining. Physiotherapy 88(7): 398–408.

McArdle W, Katch F, Katch V (1994) Essentials of Exercise Physiology. Philadelphia, PA: Lea and Febiger.

Powers S, Howley E (2004) Exercise Physiology: Theory and Application to Fitness and Performance: 5th edition. New York: McGraw Hill.

Tortora G, Derrickson B (2005) Principles of Physiology and Anatomy: 11th edition. New York: Wiley International.

Principles of Therapeutic Exercise Design

This chapter describes the underlying principles for designing a therapeutic exercise programme. Treatment goals, adherence, safety and training principles are addressed. Specific considerations such as motor learning, physical principles and starting positions are discussed.

THERAPEUTIC EXERCISE

Therapeutic exercise is one of the core skills upon which the profession of physiotherapy is based. By considering definitions of therapeutic exercise, physical activity and exercise, it is possible to see that, although therapeutic exercise contains the components of both physical activity and exercise, it also provides a systematic exercise programme for remediation of impairments and improvement of function.

'**Physical activity** is any bodily movement produced by skeletal muscles that results in an expenditure of energy' (www.cdc.gov/nccdphp/dnpa/physical/terms/). Examples of physical activity could include housework, walking, dancing, gardening or exercise.

'**Exercise** is physical activity that is planned or structured. It involves repetitive bodily movement done to improve or maintain one or more of the components of physical fitness – cardiorespiratory endurance, muscular strength, muscular endurance, flexibility and bodily composition' (www.cdc.gov/nccdphp/dnpa/physical/terms/).

'**Therapeutic exercise** is the systematic implementation of planned physical movements, postures, or activities designed to:

- remediate or prevent impairments
- enhance function
- enhance fitness and well-being' (APTA 2001).

DESIGNING A THERAPEUTIC EXERCISE PROGRAMME

A programme may include a range of different types of exercise such as those for improving or preventing deterioration in aerobic capacity, muscle strength, power and endurance, flexibility or range of movement, balance, coordination and agility. Although there are many different professionals involved in delivering advice on physical activity and exercise to various population groups, physiotherapists are equipped with special skills to provide therapeutic exercise programmes. To be able to do this, a physiotherapist requires an understanding of the underlying disease process or pathology, exercise physiology, biomechanics, physical principles and the evidence base supporting the area as well as an awareness of psychological and safety issues. The physiotherapist must also be able to identify appropriate treatment goals in conjunction with the patient. This section discusses the general principles to be considered when designing a therapeutic exercise programme.

Identifying treatment goals

To identify suitable treatment goals for a person, the physiotherapist needs to carry out a thorough assessment which covers general information about the patient such as age, pathology, health status and how accustomed to activity the person is. Specific information about the presenting condition, for which the patient is being prescribed the exercise, will also need to be gathered, along with the patient's perception of the problem and how it affects them. Appropriate clinical and exercise tests should be carried out so that an individualized exercise prescription can be made. Some information about the patient's lifestyle may be gathered so that the exercise prescription can be tailored to fit in with this if possible.

Once this information has been obtained, the main problems to be addressed can be identified. Treatment goals should be set with the patient. The range of appropriate exercise options should be discussed with the patient so that they can make an informed decision in collaboration with the physiotherapist about what would be the best treatment for them. Any treatment goals which are set should be SMART – specific, measurable, achievable, realistic and timely – for the patient concerned. Setting agreed goals with patients will improve their adherence to the exercises.

Table 2.1 shows some examples of treatment goals.

Adherence

Many people who begin an exercise programme drop out once their initial enthusiasm dies or they have achieved enough improvement from the programme so that they are fit enough for their current lifestyle. This usually means that they can carry out everyday activities without undue feelings of strain. It should be noted that there may be differences in how well people adhere to an exercise programme. A person who has sustained an injury which limits their ability to walk because of weak leg muscles may adhere strictly to their strengthening programme, so that they are able to walk normally again. If a person is very weak or unfit before starting an exercise programme, the effort involved in carrying out the simplest programme may be unsustainable. Each individual's experiences and beliefs will affect their subsequent behaviours and influence their adherence to an exercise programme. It is therefore important to consider psychosocial factors that relate to individual patients to try to find the best approach to help the person adhere to their exercise programme. Certain factors have been shown to improve adherence to an exercise programme.

Treatment goals

It is important to identify individual treatment goals and make these realistic and achievable. Breaking down the main goal into achievable steps may make adherence easier.

Exercise programme

This should be enjoyable and varied, carried out in regular sessions and supervised by a pleasant, enthusiastic physiotherapist. The physiotherapist should be encouraging and praise any improvements. Using moderate exercise intensities which are also effective will help to avoid injury and muscle soreness. Progress charts and periodic re-assessment to illustrate improvement from carrying out the exercise programme will all encourage the participant. The exercise programme should be adapted to the available environment so that it is easy to carry out. Some people prefer to participate in group exercise programmes, as the social benefits of these will help with adherence.

Support from others

Research into patient adherence to cardiac rehabilitation programmes has shown that patients adhere more if their doctor has emphasized

Table 2.1 **Example treatment goals**

Patient's presenting condition	Patient's treatment goal	Example of a treatment aim	Example of a prescribed treatment
60-year-old woman following right total knee replacement for osteoarthritis	To be able to climb the stairs leading with either leg	Increase strength of right knee extensors	Functional resistance training programme for right knee extensors
25-year-old footballer following fractured right tibia now full weight-bearing	To return to playing football	Increase strength of large muscle groups around the knee	Resistance training programme for right knee extensors and flexors
50-year-old man 4 weeks following coronary artery bypass grafting	To return to playing golf	Increase aerobic capacity	30 min brisk walking daily
75-year-old woman following a prolonged hospitalization for chest infection	To catch bus into town	Increase cardiorespiratory and muscular fitness	Repeated sit to stand Progressive walking programme

the importance of exercise in their recovery. People also tend to stick to exercise programmes when their family and friends offer support.

Stages of rehabilitation

As a patient progresses through their exercise programme, they may pass through early, intermediate and late stages of rehabilitation. This will most commonly be true of patients who have had an acute illness or injury from which they are expected to recover. These stages of rehabilitation correspond to the healing process and the common symptoms with which the patient may present. Therefore there will be common features as to the type of exercises which are most suitable for the patient at a particular stage of rehabilitation. Moving through the stages of rehabilitation can signify important steps in progress for the patient; for example a patient who has fractured their tibia may be able to move from non-weight-bearing in the early stage of rehabilitation to partial weight-bearing in the intermediate stage. More detail about the stages of rehabilitation can be found in Chapter 11.

Common training principles

There are four common principles which apply to any training programme that is prescribed for an individual.

Overload

A system must be exercised at a level beyond which it is presently accustomed for a training effect to occur. The system being exercised will gradually adapt to the overload or training stimulus being applied, and this will go on happening as long as the training stimulus continues to be increased until the tissue can no longer adapt. The training stimulus applied consists of different variables such as intensity, duration and frequency of exercise. It is important to give the system being exercised enough time to recover and only apply a training stimulus again when the system is no longer fatigued. Loading a fatigued system will not result in a training effect. This is illustrated in Figure 2.1.

Specificity

Any exercise will train a system for the particular task being carried out as the training stimulus. This means that, for example, a training programme including muscle strengthening will train the muscle in the range that it is working and the way that the muscle is being used, i.e. isometrically, concentrically or eccentrically. It is important that any exercise to strengthen muscle targets the muscle range and type of muscle work specific to the task required. For example, riding

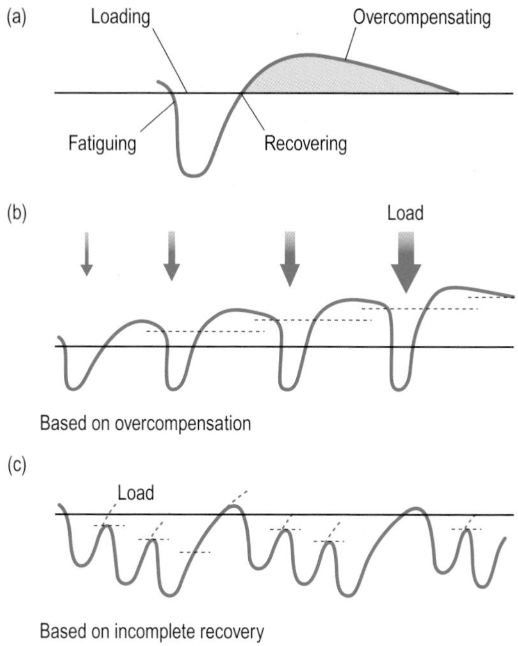

Figure 2.1 Application of a training stimulus. Adapted from Borell D, Nimmo M and Wood L (1996) Principles of Physiology. WB Saunders Ltd, p. 196

a bicycle requires concentric knee extension from mid- to inner range, as the pedal is pushed down to propel the bicycle along. A cyclist wishing to increase the strength of his quadriceps will need to train concentrically in mid- to inner range. Depending on the presenting problem, the required task should become part of the training programme at an appropriate stage.

Reversibility

The beneficial effects of training begin to be lost as soon as training stops. This happens in a similar timeframe as it takes to train the system.

Individuality

Variation in response to a training programme will occur in a population as people respond differently to the same training programme. This response can be explained by the initial fitness level of the individual, their health status and their genetic makeup. Training programmes should be designed to take this into account.

Some individuals will have a predisposition to endurance training and some to strength training. Some will respond well to a training programme and others much more slowly. Those individuals with a lower fitness level before starting an exercise programme show improvement in fitness more quickly than those who are relatively fit before training begins. Some individuals with health conditions may not be able to work at the same kind of intensity as a healthy individual and so will take longer to achieve a training goal.

Motor learning

To be able to teach and supervise an exercise programme effectively, the physiotherapist needs an understanding of how people learn motor skills. Motor learning is not just concerned with the acquisition of motor skills but also with how the individual interacts with the task to be learnt and the environment. This uses perception or sensing, cognition and motor processes. Learning a skill is a relatively permanent change in an individual and there are several stages that the person will go through before the skill is retained.

Initially a person may be unable to perform a task. With practice, they will achieve the task but it will not be carried out efficiently. With further practice and feedback the person will be able to carry out the task to a reasonable standard but they may forget how to do it if they do not do the task regularly. In the final stage the person will carry out the task efficiently, in a skilled manner and will not forget how to do the task.

When teaching a patient an exercise, the physiotherapist should explain or demonstrate how to carry out the exercise, doing this as a whole if the exercise is simple or breaking a complex exercise into parts. When the patient is able to carry out the component parts, the exercise should be practised as a whole. The patient needs to think about and practise the exercise. Both the physiotherapist and the patient should evaluate how well the exercise was performed and if the exercise task was completed. The physiotherapist should allow the patient a short time to evaluate their own performance, before providing feedback prior to subsequent practice. Practising a skill (or exercise) in a varied manner, for example at different speeds or in different environments, will help with learning.

Safety

Whenever an individual exercises there is a risk that they may injure themselves. Safety factors are considered here in relation to the physiotherapist, the environment and the patient or person carrying out the exercise.

The **physiotherapist** should:

- have a knowledge and understanding of pathology, physiology, psychology and the evidence base relating to exercise prescription
- carry out a thorough assessment of the patient to identify factors that will affect the exercise prescription, such as age, health status and how much activity the person is normally accustomed to
- be able to assess the risk involved with a person doing a particular exercise and adapt the exercise appropriately, e.g. provide support for an unsteady person carrying out an exercise that involves challenging their balance
- be able to teach the patient how to carry out the exercise correctly; this may involve breaking down the activity into parts initially and then allowing the patient time to practise, with adequate supervision and feedback, until they can perform the activity
- monitor intensity of the activity to make sure that the patient is carrying out the exercise at the appropriate level
- follow guidelines for specific patient groups
- have up-to-date skills in basic life support and other relevant policies and procedures that relate to the area that the patient is exercising in.

The **patient** should:

- be suitably dressed for the activity to be carried out
- begin slowly and build up the intensity if not used to exercising; generally there is less risk involved in increasing the duration of an activity before increasing the intensity
- be adequately hydrated before, after and throughout the exercise session and have enough nutrition on board to provide energy before exercising
- work at a level appropriate to their level of fitness, how much exercise they are accustomed to and understand how this should feel; usually the risk of injury increases in relation to the intensity of an exercise versus the initial level of fitness of the individual and how accustomed they are to doing the exercise
- be aware of signs that they are working too hard or need to stop such as chest pain, excessive shortness of breath or dizziness
- have appropriate medication such as drugs for the management of angina or asthma inhalers or dextrose tablets nearby if they suffer from pathologies which may be affected by exercising
- be aware of times when it is not appropriate to exercise, for example immediately after a meal.

The **environment**:

- The space being used should be large enough for the activity with a non-slip floor and any obstacles or trip hazards removed.

- The temperature of the room should be considered. People respond differently doing the same exercise programme in different temperatures. When it is hot, the intensity of the activity may need to be reduced if the temperature of the room cannot be adjusted.
- Any equipment should be checked, cleaned and maintained properly. Risk assessments and guidelines for equipment use must be in place. People should be taught to use equipment safely and utilize safety straps or be aware of emergency stop buttons where appropriate.
- First aid and resuscitation equipment, including an automatic defibrillator, should be in place with trained personnel available.

DESIGNING A SPECIFIC EXERCISE

This section will discuss principles that should be considered when designing the specific exercises that make up an exercise programme.

An understanding of the following physical principles is needed so that the influences of these factors on the body can be considered, and exercises can be designed to produce the desired effect:

- centre of gravity
- base of support
- levers
- momentum
- inertia
- friction.

Centre of gravity (COG)

The centre of gravity is the point in the body where the body mass is centred. In the anatomical position the COG is thought to be in the midsagittal plane, several centimetres anterior to the second sacral vertebra inside the pelvis (Figure 2.2). As the body changes position the centre of gravity will move towards the greater concentration of mass.

If a person is carrying a load, the load also becomes part of their total mass and influences the position of the centre of gravity. For example lifting a load with both arms to a position of 90° of shoulder flexion will move the centre of gravity forwards and upwards. In this situation the centre of gravity may be located outside of the body.

Considerations for exercise design

The most stable positions are those in which the centre of gravity is closest to the supporting surface, and well within the base of support (see below).

The centre of gravity will change throughout an exercise as movement is performed, and even small alterations to the position

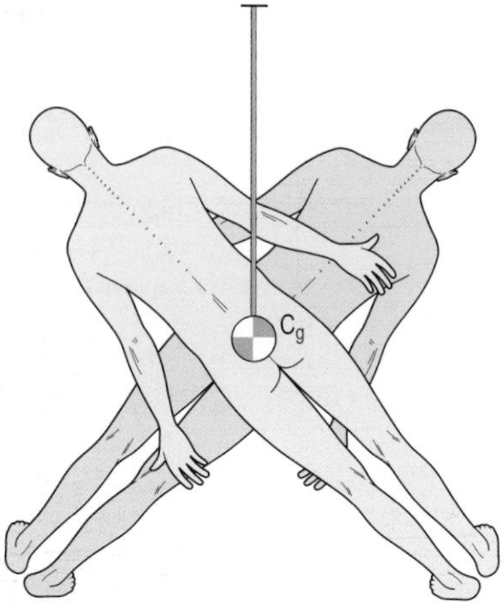

Figure 2.2 Centre of gravity. Adapted from Panjabi M, White A (2001) Biomechanics in the Musculoskeletal System. Philadelphia, PA: Churchill Livingstone, p. 35

of a person, such as raising their arms, may cause sufficient change in centre of gravity to challenge their balance. Therefore the starting position of an exercise may be stable, but the person may become unstable as the centre of gravity moves during the activity.

The use of equipment, such as a dumbbell, may also cause balance disturbances as the weight becomes part of the person's total mass and shifts their centre of gravity.

Base of support

Base of support (BOS) is the supporting area of a body or object (Figure 2.3a, b). When more than one part of the body is in contact with the supporting surface the BOS includes the area in between the contact surfaces (Figure 2.4a, b). If a walking aid is being used, the base of support is the feet, the part(s) of the walking aid in contact with the ground and the area in between (Figure 2.5a, b).

The greater the area of the BOS, the more stable the object. Standing on the tiptoe of one foot is the most unstable modification of standing, as the BOS is only the surface area of the toes; close standing is more stable as the BOS is the surface area of both feet. Stride standing is more stable still, as the BOS is increased to the surface area of both feet and the area in between.

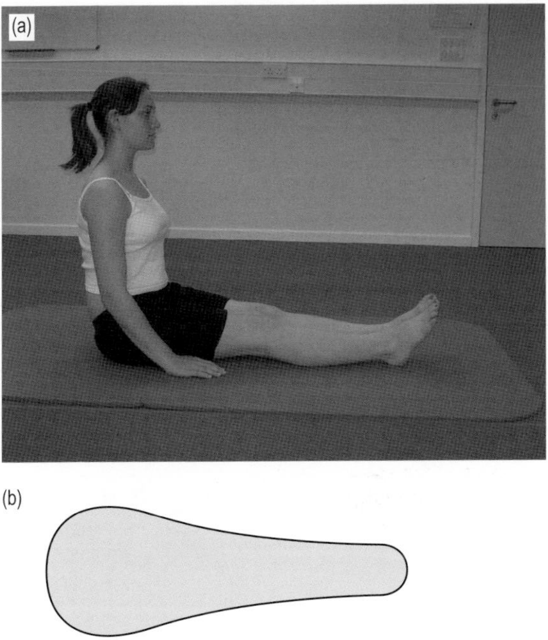

Figure 2.3 (a) Base of support, long sitting. (b) Base of support aerial view, long sitting

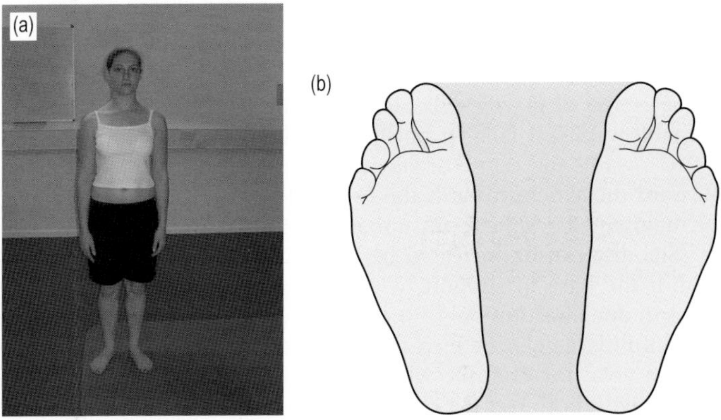

Figure 2.4 (a) Base of support, standing. (b) Base of support aerial view, standing

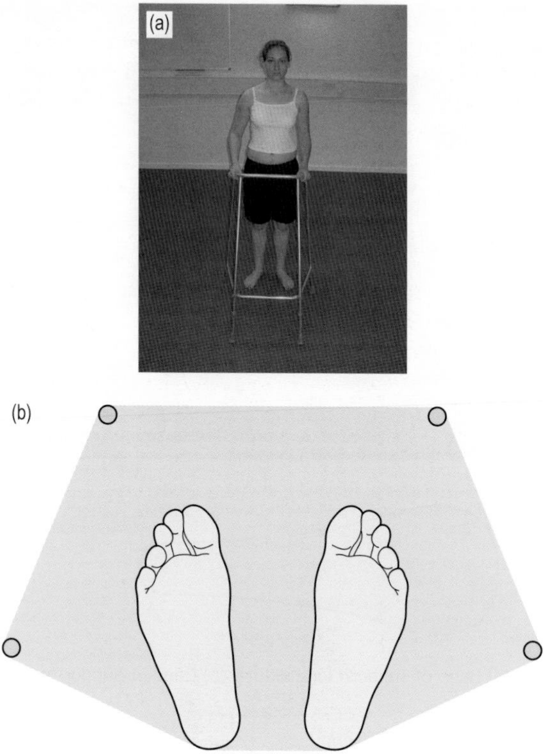

Figure 2.5 (a) Base of support, standing with a frame. (b) Base of support aerial view, standing with a frame

Considerations for exercise design

If the centre of gravity falls outside of the BOS the person will be unstable, and if it falls far outside the BOS some movement of the body towards the centre of gravity is required. During walking, the forward movement towards the COG allows an upright position to be maintained despite the disturbance to stability.

Stability can be increased by keeping the centre of gravity well within the base of support by avoiding movements that shift the mass in one direction only, for example reaching to one side.

Stability can also be increased by making the BOS cover a greater surface area; for example when sitting on the edge of a plinth a patient with both feet flat on the floor is more stable than one with their legs dangling from the plinth (high sitting) as the BOS incorporates a wider area.

Levers

A lever is a rigid bar pivoted around a fixed point or fulcrum. In the body the lever is the bone, which moves about the articular surface, which is the fulcrum. The effort required to move the lever is produced by the muscles in the body.

The different relative positions of the fulcrum, the distance from the fulcrum to the weight or resistance (the resistance arm) and the distance from the fulcrum to the effort or muscle (effort arm) provide the characteristics of different types of lever.

- ***First-class levers.*** First-class levers have the fulcrum positioned in between the effort and the resistance. The length of the effort and weight arms may or may not be equal. There are very few first-class levers in the body, and the feature of these levers in the body is stability and equilibrium. An example of a first-class lever in the body is neck extension. The anterior part of the skull, with gravity acting upon it, is the resistance, the atlas and occipital bone form the fulcrum and the neck extensors are the effort (Figure 2.6).

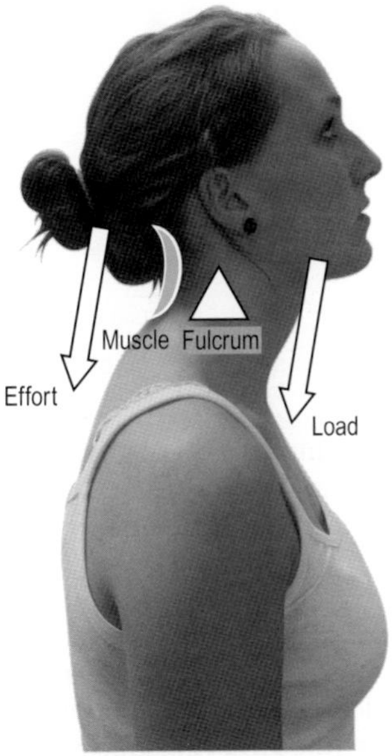

Figure 2.6 First class lever: neck extension

- ***Second-class levers.*** Second-class levers have the resistance positioned in between the fulcrum and the effort. This means that the effort arm is always longer than the resistance arm. There are few second-class levers in the body; a commonly quoted example is the action of standing on tiptoe in which the ball of the foot is the fulcrum, the body weight acts in a line falling between the ankle and the toes and is the resistance, and the calf muscles, which act behind the ankle, are the effort (Figure 2.7).

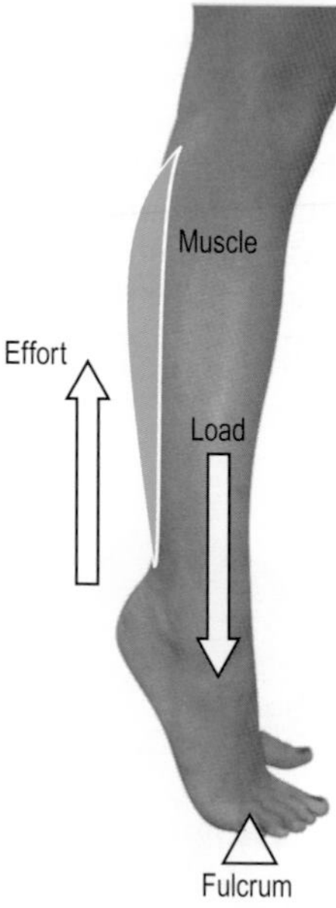

Figure 2.7 Second class lever: standing on tiptoe

- ***Third-class levers.*** Third-class levers have the effort positioned between the fulcrum and the resistance; therefore the effort arm is always smaller than the lever arm. This is the most common type of lever found in the body as the attachments of most muscles are nearer to the joint than to the external resistance of gravity on the limb. This lever is related to speed and range of movement. An example of a third-class lever in the body is adduction of the leg, where the fulcrum is the hip, the resistance is the weight of the whole leg with gravity acting upon it, and the effort is the adductor muscles (Figure 2.8).

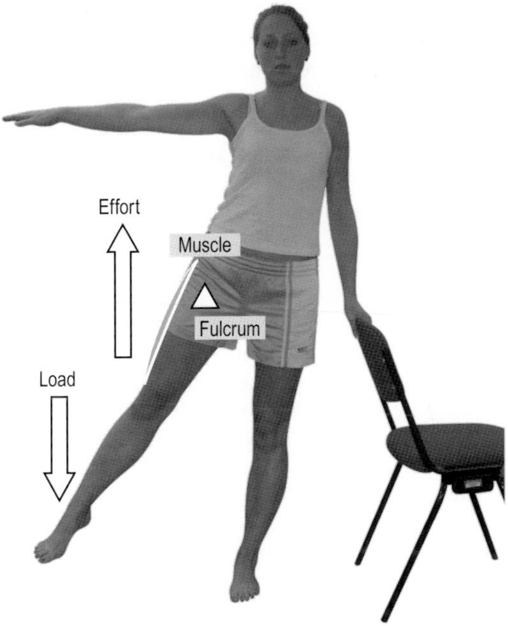

Figure 2.8 Third class lever: hip abduction in standing

Considerations for exercise design

- A long resistance arm will make movement more difficult; therefore this is a way of progressing exercise. This should also be considered when applying manual resistance, as if the physiotherapist uses a long resistance arm they will have to use less effort to resist the patient's movement.
- A shorter resistance arm will make the production of movement easier, i.e. performing shoulder flexion and abduction in the upright position with the elbow flexed requires less effort than with an extended arm. This is a useful way of facilitating movement in a joint.

Inertia

Inertia relates to Newton's first law of motion. It describes the resistance of a body to a change in velocity, which is its speed in a certain direction. This means that, once a certain speed of movement is achieved, the body will require application of a force to either increase or decrease the speed.

Momentum

Momentum also relates to Newton's first law of motion, which states that a body in motion will remain in motion unless acted on by an outside force. The amount of momentum a body possesses is the product of its mass and velocity and is related to its inertia. The more the mass and the greater the speed of the body, the more momentum the body has. This means that a body possesses more momentum to keep it moving and requires a greater force to overcome the inertia and stop movement.

Considerations for exercise design

A very weak person may require some assistance to overcome the inertia to initiate movement, but once movement is started and they possess some momentum they may have sufficient muscle force to continue. It may be helpful to start movement with the muscle in its strongest position and ask the person to move into their weaker range.

Pendular exercises of the shoulder are a common example of using momentum to facilitate movement, the whole mass of the arm is used to develop momentum to facilitate shoulder movement, as the greater the mass the more momentum the arm will have, and the easier movement will be.

It is also important to consider whether a person is able to generate sufficient muscle force to decrease the speed of movement as this could become a safety risk; for example a limb moving into a painful range due to poor muscle control.

Friction

The movement of two surfaces over one another is opposed by the force of friction. When the two surfaces move the force of friction converts the movement (kinetic) energy to thermal energy, which is released as heat; this is why rubbing hands together when cold warms them. Friction converts the kinetic energy of the moving hands to thermal energy. Conversion of kinetic energy to thermal energy creates a resistance to movement known as 'drag'. The amount of drag produced will vary according to the properties of the two surfaces moving over one another.

Considerations for exercise design

Drag can make it more difficult to perform an exercise that requires movement of a body part across a surface. To allow easy movement a low friction interface should be provided. For example there can be considerable drag on the leg when performing hip abduction in long sitting on a plinth; however provision of a sliding sheet reduces friction.

It is possible that a person may get a burn when performing an exercise in which an area of skin is repeatedly moved across a surface that produces heat due to friction.

Starting positions

It is important to consider the position of the body at the start of an exercise, as a change in the starting posture may change the effect of the exercise. There are five fundamental 'starting positions', these are the postures from which the movement can take place and are illustrated in Figure 2.9.

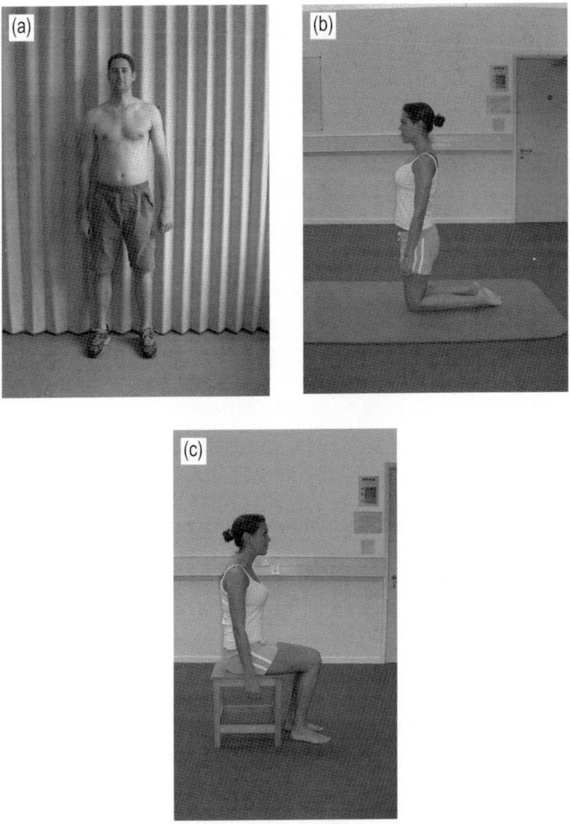

Figure 2.9 (a) Standing. (b) Kneeling. (c) Sitting.

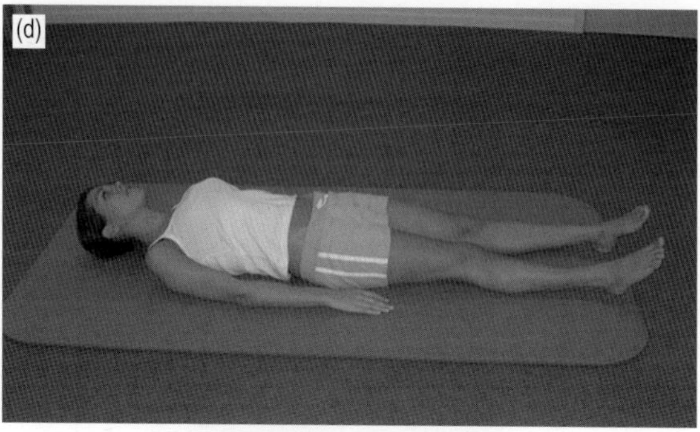

Figure 2.9 *Continued* (d) Lying or supine. (e) Hanging

All other positions are derived from these fundamental starting positions and are illustrated in Figures 2.10–2.15.

Considerations when selecting a starting position

Safety of the position

- The position should be stable so that the patient is not in danger of falling.
- If the patient requires assistance to get into or out of the position, for example on or off the floor, then someone should stay with them.
- Consideration should be given to ensure that there is adequate space around the patient for them to perform the exercise; for example that chair arms or other equipment is not in the way.
- Contraindications to the position should be borne in mind; for example is the patient able to weight bear through the affected limb if standing is selected?

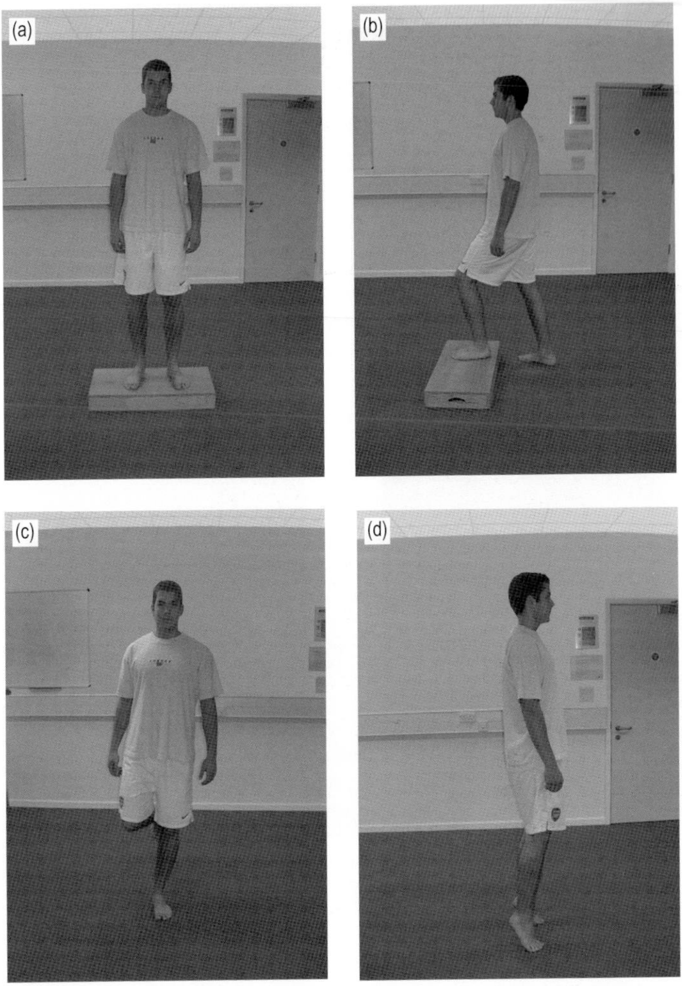

Figure 2.10 Positions derived from standing. (a) High standing (High St). (b) Step standing (Step St). (c) Half standing (1/2 St). (d) Toe standing (T. St)

Comfort and accessibility of the position

Some patients will find certain positions uncomfortable; for example a patient with breathing problems may find supine lying makes them more breathless, a pregnant woman will not be able to adopt prone lying and a patient with knee pain may not tolerate kneeling. Some patients may also have limitations to range of movement

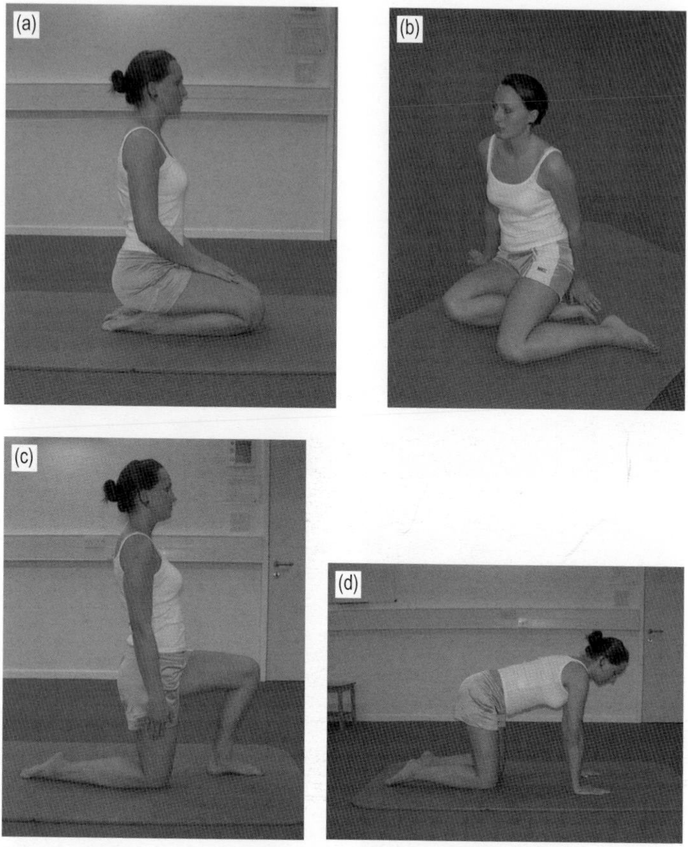

Figure 2.11 Positions derived from kneeling. (a) Kneel sitting (Kn. Sitt). (b) Side sitting (Side Sitt). (c) Half kneeling (1/2 Kn). (d) Prone kneeling (Pr Kn)

that prevent them from actually getting into a starting position; for example a fixed flexion deformity at the hip would make it very difficult to adopt prone lying.

Range of movement

The starting position should allow full access to the desired range of movement. For example in supine lying the supporting surface will prevent hip extension beyond neutral, whereas side lying allows access to full range.

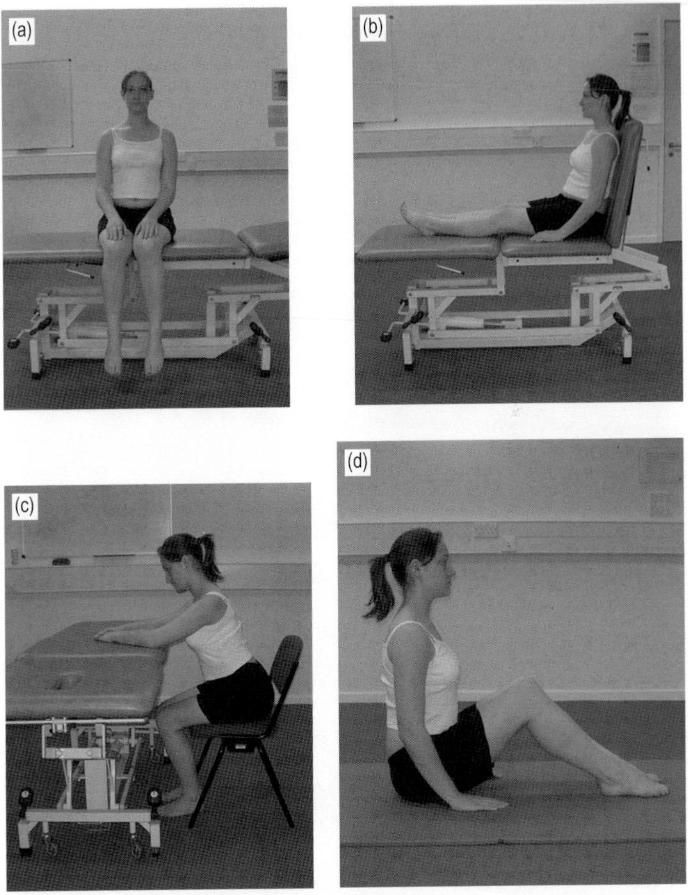

Figure 2.12 Positions derived from sitting. (a) High sitting (High sitt). (b) Long sitting (supported) (Supp Long Sitt). (c) Forward lean sitting (Fwd Ln Sitt). (d) Crook sitting (Crk Sitt)

Stability of the position

If an unstable starting position is selected then patient effort is required to maintain this position. Unless balance retraining is the aim of the exercise this will detract from performance of the exercise. A stable posture can help to localize muscle activity and provide a solid base from which to produce movement. For example a person

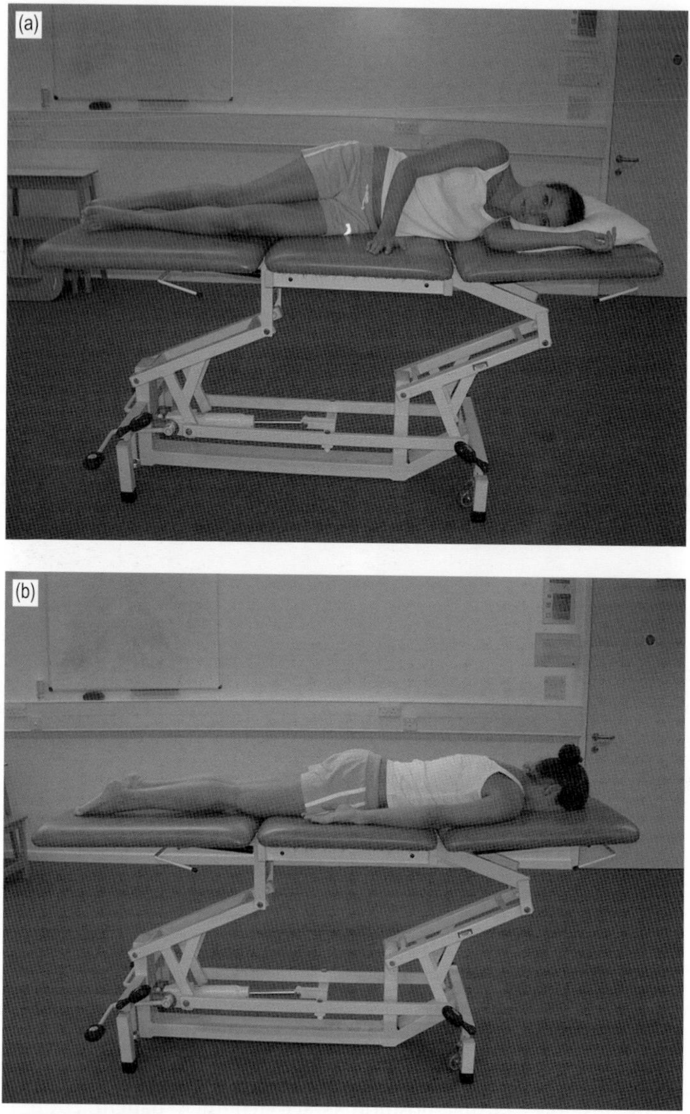

Figure 2.13 Positions derived from lying. (a) Side lying (S Ly). (b) Prone lying (Pr Ly).

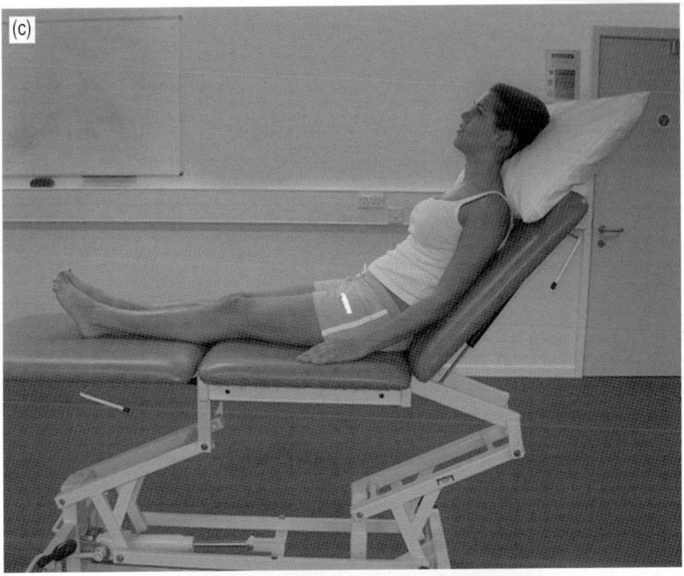

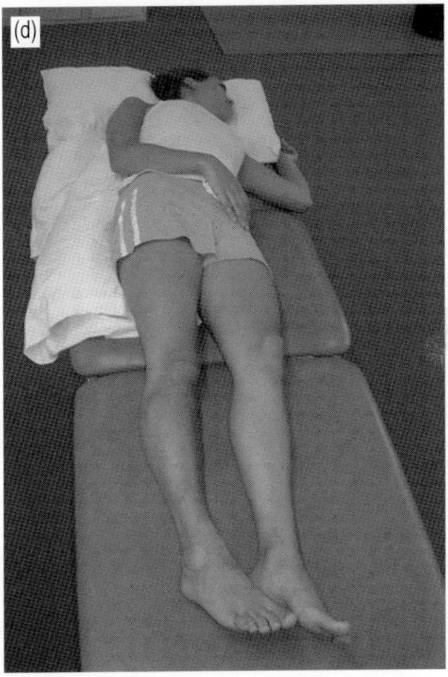

Figure 2.13 *Continued* (c) Half lying (1/2 Ly). (d) Quarter turn lying (from supine) (1/4 Ly).

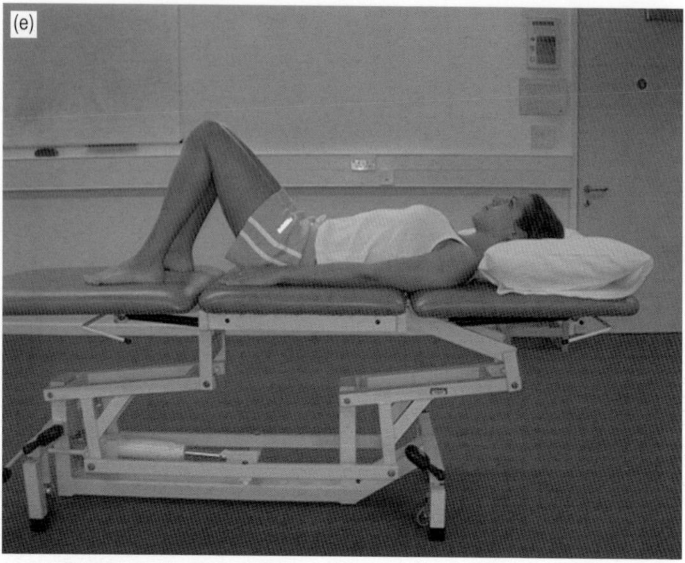

Figure 2.13 *Continued* (e) Crook lying (Crk Ly)

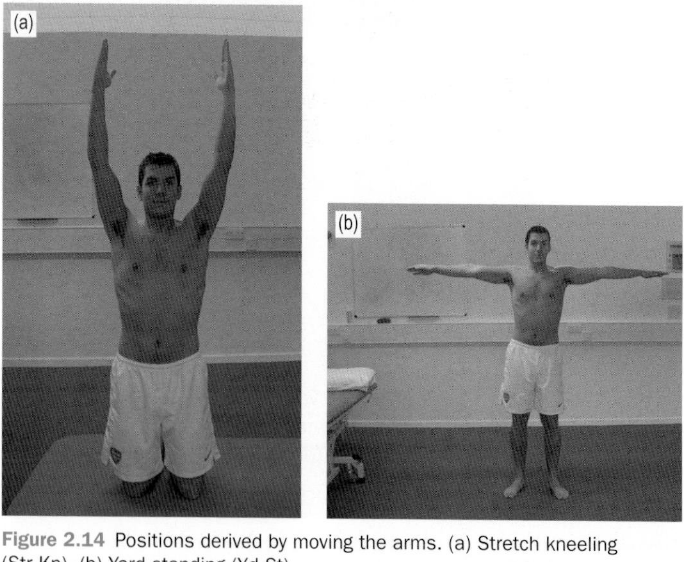

Figure 2.14 Positions derived by moving the arms. (a) Stretch kneeling (Str Kn). (b) Yard standing (Yd St).

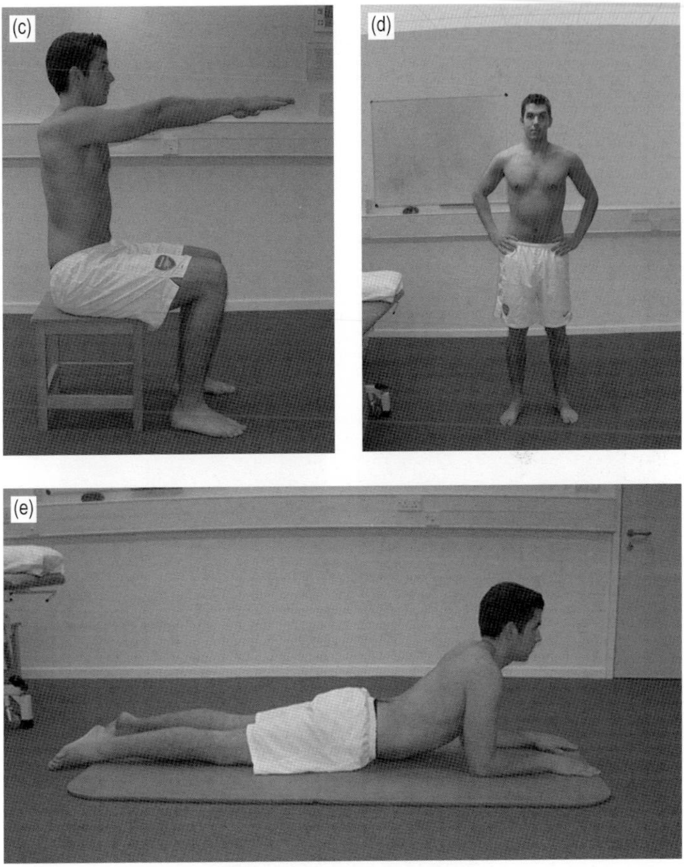

Figure 2.14 *Continued* (c) Reach sitting (Rch Sitt). (d) Wing standing (Wg St). (e) Prone lying with forearm support (Pr Ly fore A supp)

carrying out strength training of the external rotators of the shoulder in standing (Figure 2.16a) is relatively unstable and the movement of the arm is not localized to focus on shoulder rotation, whereas the desired movement can be achieved from the more stable position of sitting with the arm positioned on a table to allow more focused movement into external rotation (Figure 2.16b).

Effect of gravity

The effect of gravity on the part or parts of the body to be moved should be considered. The starting position of an exercise can be

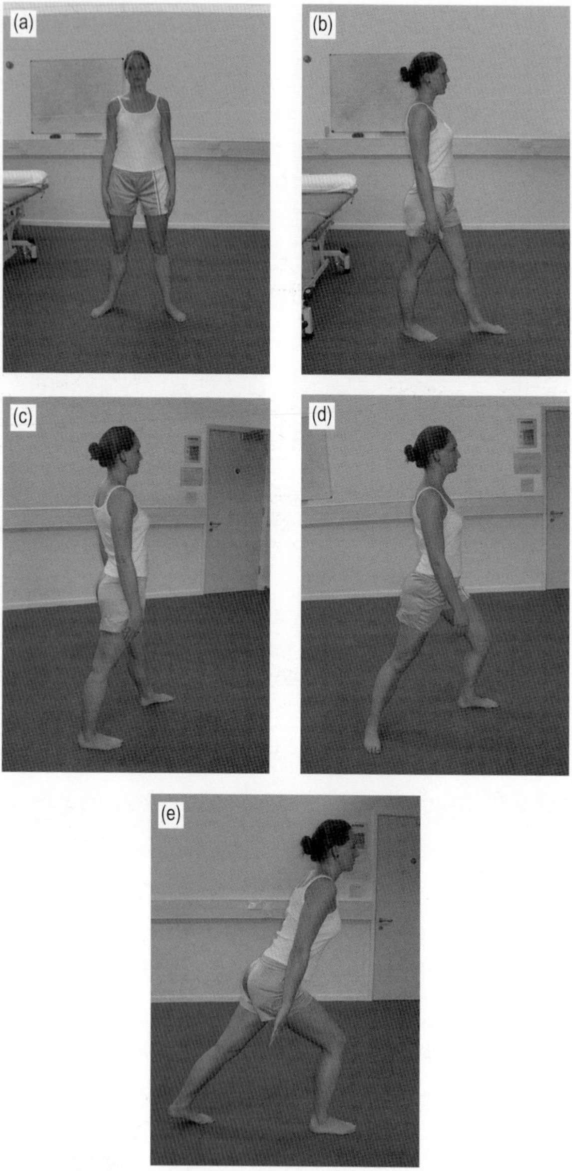

Figure 2.15 Positions derived by moving the legs. (a) Stride standing (Std. st.). (b) Walk standing (Wk. st.). (c) Oblique stride standing (Obl. st.). (d) Forward lunge standing (Fwd. Lunge st.) (e) Fallout standing (fallout st.)

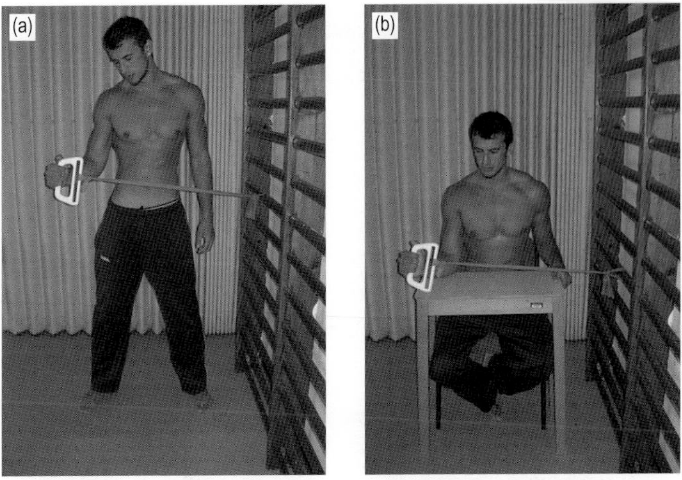

Figure 2.16 Strength training of the external rotators of the shoulder. (a) In standing (movement not localized). (b) In sitting with arm supported

adjusted so that movement is performed with gravity, against gravity or with gravity counterbalanced. Gravity can be used to make the production of movement easier by positioning the patient so that the limb moves downwards with gravity; for example in prone lying knee extension from 90° flexion to full extension is assisted by gravity (Figure 2.17a). Knee extension performed in side lying is done with

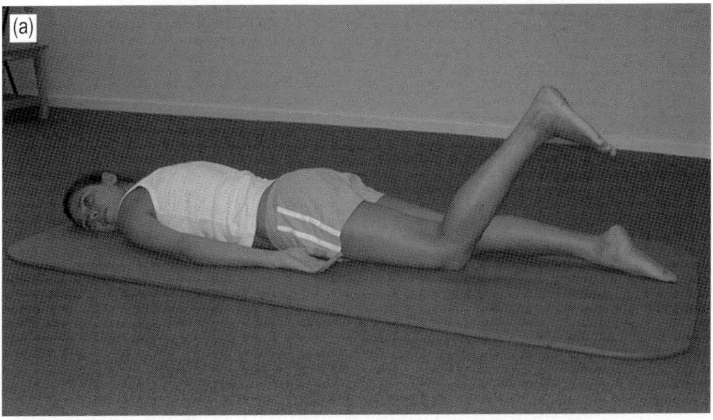

Figure 2.17 The effect of gravity on knee extension exercises. (a) Pr Ly, with gravity.

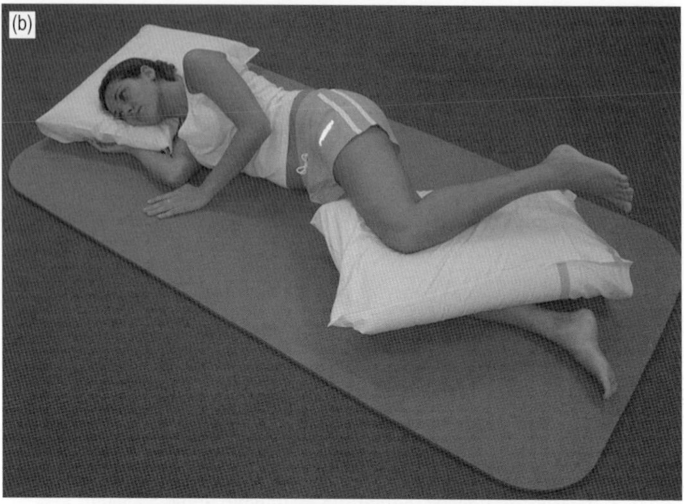

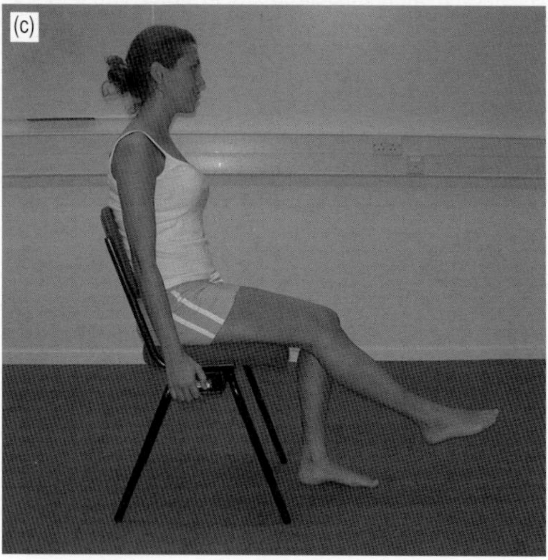

Figure 2.17 *Continued* (b) S Ly, kn ext, gravity counterbalanced. (c) Sitt, kn ext, against gravity

gravity counterbalanced (Figure 2.17b). In sitting the same movement is again performed upward against gravity (Figure 2.17c).

- When performing movements with gravity, eccentric muscle activity is required to control and regulate the movement, the muscle group performing this action should have sufficient available strength. Movements with gravity are useful during exercise to increase range of motion as little effort is needed to access the range.

- Movements against gravity are used in strength training to allow resistance to be applied. The effect of gravity will change during movement, and those movements with a wide arc, such as shoulder flexion, require several starting positions in order to move through the complete range against gravity (Figure 2.18a–c).

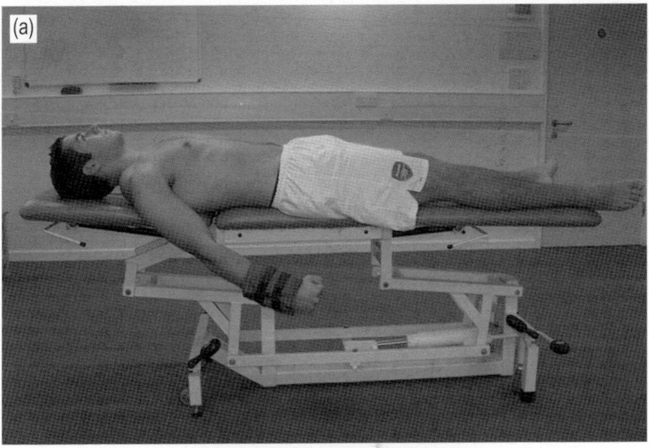

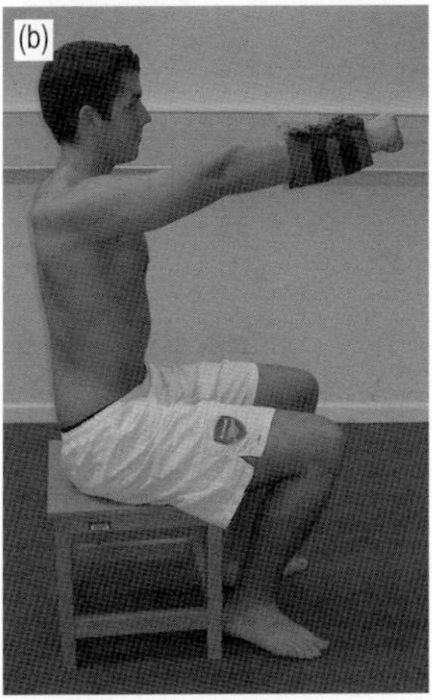

Figure 2.18 Shoulder flexion against gravity. (a) Ly. Outer range shoulder flexion. (b) Sitt. Mid-range shoulder flexion.

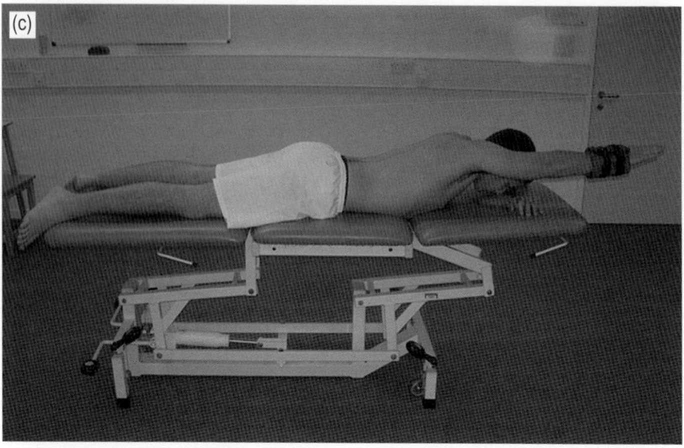

Figure 2.18 *Continued* (c) Pr Ly. Inner range shoulder flexion

- Movements in the horizontal plane, with gravity counterbalanced, are often useful in weaker patients who do not have sufficient concentric or eccentric muscle strength to maintain control in the vertical plane. It is desirable to provide support for the limb during the horizontal movement, such as a sliding board on a bed to allow hip abduction in supine, or placing the arm on a plinth to allow supported elbow flexion and extension in sitting. If it is not possible to place the patient in such a supported position it should be remembered that the stabilizing muscles of the proximal joints are working to maintain a stable base for the movement and the patient may tire; for example if performing hip flexion and extension in side lying the hip abductors will be working isometrically to support the leg.

Specificity

It is desirable where possible to use functional starting positions related to the patient's goals, as this will ensure that training effects are specific to the task required. If lower limb strength training is being carried out to help with stair climbing, early training may be carried out in sitting or lying positions but should progress to a starting position of step standing.

Reference

American Physical Therapy Association (APTA) (2001) Guide to physical therapist practice: 2nd edition. Physical Therapy 81(1): 9–74.

Further reading

Ades PA, Waldmann ML, McCann WJ, et al (1992) Predictors of cardiac rehabilitation participation in older coronary patients. Arch Intern Med 152: 1033–1035.

Borell D, Nimmo M, Wood L (1996) Principles of Physiology. London: WB Saunders Ltd.

Gardiner M (1983) The Principles of Exercise Therapy: 4th edition. London: Bell and Hyman.

Pail Y, Patton J (1997) Centre of mass velocity position predictions for balance control. Journal of Biomechanics 30(4): 347–354.

Panjabi M, White A (2001) Biomechanics in the Musculoskeletal System. Philadelphia, PA: Churchill Livingstone.

Shumway-Cook A, Woollacott M (2001) Motor Control – Theory and Practical Applications: 2nd edition. Baltimore, MA: Lippincott Williams & Wilkins.

Trew M, Everett T (2005) Human Movement: An Introductory Text: 5th edition. Edinburgh, UK: Churchill Livingstone.

Whaley MH (ed.) (2005) ACSM's Guidelines for Exercise Testing and Prescription: 7th edition. Baltimore, MA: Lippincott Williams & Wilkins.

Further reading

Exercise to Increase Cardiovascular Fitness

This chapter gives an overview of cardiovascular fitness. Training adaptations seen following a successful cardiovascular training programme are outlined, along with the principles of assessment and prescription and example exercises for increasing cardiovascular fitness. These principles are related to current guidelines for cardiovascular training.

DEFINITION

Cardiovascular fitness, aerobic capacity and endurance are all terms used to describe the body's ability to sustain exercise over a period of time. Exercise designed to increase cardiovascular fitness is often termed 'aerobic exercise' as sustained exercise uses the aerobic pathways of oxidative phosphorylation for energy supply and training adaptations result in a more efficient aerobic energy pathway. Such exercise generally targets large muscle groups and aims to overload the cardiovascular system, thus increasing heart rate and respiratory rate during exercise.

FACTORS DETERMINING CARDIOVASCULAR FITNESS

An individual's cardiovascular fitness is dependent on a number of factors, which combine to form the oxygen uptake chain. Oxygen must be delivered to the lungs by adequate ventilation, and then

Table 3.1 Factors determining cardiovascular fitness

Determining factor	Influencing factors	Effect
Ability of the respiratory system to supply oxygen to blood	Respiratory pathology	Limits gas exchange and ventilation
	Neuromuscular pathology	Limits muscles of ventilation
	Altitude	Fraction of inspired O_2 available
Ability of the blood to carry the oxygen	Anaemia	Reduced carrying capacity
	Circulatory disorders	Restricts delivery of oxygenated blood to working muscle
	Aerobic training – volume of circulating plasma	Oxygen-carrying capacity
Ability of the heart to pump the blood to the working muscle	Cardiac pathology	Reduced cardiac output
	Aerobic training – left ventricular hypertrophy	Increased cardiac output
Ability of the muscles to uptake and utilize the oxygen from the blood	Aerobic training – increased capilliarization of trained muscle	Increased oxygen delivery to muscle
	Aerobic training – number and size of mitochondria	Increased ability to uptake and utilize oxygen
	Oxyhaemoglobin dissociation curve	Ease of transfer of oxygen from blood to working muscle

must pass into the blood at the alveolar level. The circulatory system carries the oxygenated blood to the working muscle where the oxygen is taken up by the mitochondria (Table 3.1).

TRAINING ADAPTATIONS

The physiological training adaptations that take place following aerobic training can be divided into local adaptations, seen in the muscles used during the training exercises, and systemic adaptations. These physiological adaptations are seen approximately 6 weeks into a training programme. Performance in exercise tests may improve before physiological adaptations are detectable, and this may be due to other factors such as improved skill in task performance and increased confidence during exercise.

Local training adaptations

Local adaptations occur in trained skeletal muscles which enable them to uptake and utilize oxygen more efficiently. These adaptations are as follows.

Capillaries

An increase in the number and size of capillaries within the trained muscle, providing a greater surface area for delivery of oxygen and removal of waste products by the blood.

Mitochondria

An increase in both the size and number of mitochondria in all skeletal muscle fibre types within the trained muscle. This increase in mitochondrial material also results in a doubling of the oxidative enzymes, thus increasing the capacity to produce adenosine triphosphate (ATP) using the aerobic pathways.

Lipolysis

An increase in lipolysis, resulting in a greater use of fatty acid for energy supply.

Muscle fibre type

There is some evidence to suggest that aerobic training leads to conversion from type 2 to type 1 muscle fibres.

Hypertrophy

Selective hypertrophy of the type 1 fibres occurs, resulting in a greater surface area of slow-twitch fibres.

Systemic training adaptations

Systemic training adaptations increase the body's ability to deliver oxygen to the exercising muscle. These adaptations are as follows.

Cardiac hypertrophy

The left ventricle increases in size and thickness. This results in greater end-diastolic volume and stroke volume. The increase in stroke volume leads to a decrease in resting heart rate and heart rate during sub-maximal exercise.

Plasma volume

An increase in plasma volume leads to a greater circulatory reserve. This allows blood to be redistributed for increased delivery to exercising muscle and temperature regulation.

Blood pressure

A decrease in both systolic and diastolic blood pressure is seen in both normotensive and hypertensive subjects at rest and during exercise.

PRINCIPLES OF CARDIOVASCULAR EXERCISE DESIGN

When designing an exercise programme to increase cardiovascular fitness the following principles should be considered.

Energy source

The exercise duration should be long enough for the aerobic pathways to become the main source of energy production, which occurs after approximately 5 minutes of exercise.

Rhythmical

Cardiovascular exercises use large muscle groups and are often rhythmical in nature.

Specificity

Although cardiovascular training has systemic effects that contribute to an overall increase in exercise capacity, it is also muscle- and task-specific. Therefore the exercises should be designed with individual patient goals in mind.

Range of exercises

For the greatest training effect both upper and lower limb activities should be included in the programme of exercise. If using a variety of exercises it is desirable to alternate the emphasis on particular muscle groups when sequencing the exercises to avoid local muscle fatigue; for example adding a 'throwing and catching' exercise in between 'sit to stand' and 'stair climbing' allows the quadriceps to recover.

The exercise programme may be one continuous activity, such as jogging, or comprise a combination of exercises such as circuit training.

Intensity level

When designing a circuit, care should be taken to ensure that the heart rate is maintained within the required parameters for training during all activities, although there may be a combination of high- and lower-intensity activity throughout the circuit. Using a range of exercises at different training intensities allows recovery periods in between bursts of higher-intensity activity. A baseline level of activity should be maintained to prevent rapid decreases in heart rate (see Cool down).

Safety

Before prescribing a cardiovascular exercise programme the person's cardiovascular system should be assessed and safe limits of exercise clearly set. Healthy individuals can exercise within the normal guidelines, but individuals with respiratory, cardiac or circulatory disorders could become severely compromised by the stress placed on their cardiovascular system, and they should be carefully assessed and specific levels of activity applied. It is good practice to monitor the heart rate during the exercises whilst under supervision of the physiotherapist to check for any unexpected response to exercise, before instructing the person to carry out the exercises in an unsupervised environment.

Activities that include a jumping, running or bouncing component are classed as high impact and will be of higher intensity. There is an increased risk of injury with high-impact exercise and it may not be appropriate for some people, in which case the activity should be modified to remove the jump component.

WARM UP AND COOL DOWN

A warm up and cool down should always be incorporated into a cardiovascular training routine.

Warm up

A warm up may comprise exercises that are included in the exercise programme itself, but should start at a low intensity and gradually build up to the required training intensity over a period of 10 minutes. This is to allow a gradual redistribution of blood to the exercising muscles, in particular the cardiac muscle.

Cool down

A period of around 10 minutes, during which the intensity of exercise is gradually reduced, is important immediately following exercise. This cool-down period maintains muscle contraction of the exercised muscles, which aids the redistribution of blood after exercise and prevents blood pooling in the peripheral muscles, which can lead to fainting.

Therefore the main purpose of the warm up and cool down is the gradual change in heart rate and the redistribution of blood. Warm up is often seen as essential for injury prevention, and there is some evidence in the literature to suggest that warm muscles are less vulnerable to injury as they have increased extensibility.

Stretching is often incorporated into the warm up and cool down; however stretching before exercise can reduce performance and has little effect on injury (Stone 2006).

Example exercises

- Walking
- Skipping
- Jogging
- Rowing
- Cycling
- Aerobic dance

- Trampette (Figure 3.1)
- Rapid throw and catch
- Stair climbing
- 'Jumping jack' (Figure 3.2)
- Arm ergometry (Figure 3.3)
- Step-ups
- Repeated sit to stand.

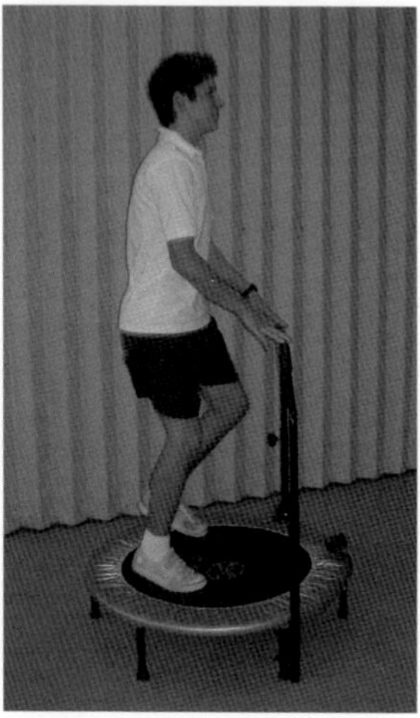

Figure 3.1 Trampette

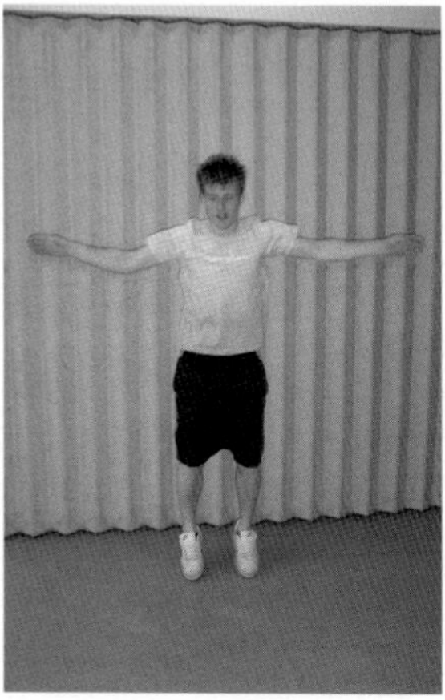

Figure 3.2 'Jumping jack'

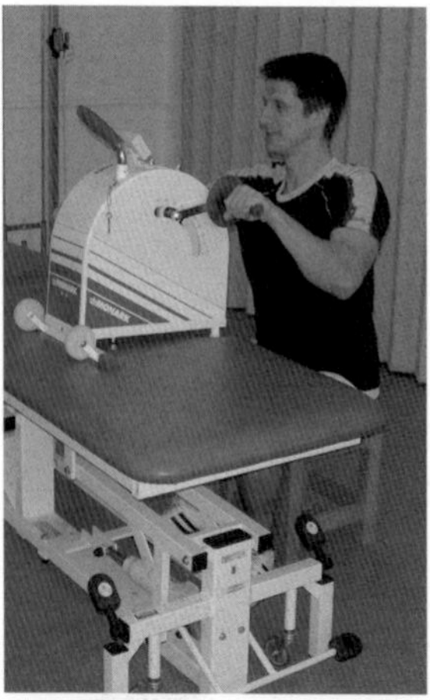

Figure 3.3 Arm ergometry

ASSESSMENT OF CARDIOVASCULAR FITNESS

Principles of assessment

Cardiovascular training is exercise-specific; therefore the mode of assessment is best linked to the type of training and the desired outcomes. The most common modes of assessing cardiovascular fitness are walking, running and cycling. The testing activity can also be modified to suit the person being tested; a timed swim for a swimmer in training, or a more functional repeated sit to stand test for a deconditioned patient.

Walking and running can be assessed using overground or treadmill walking. A treadmill allows control of the work rate; however it should be remembered that overground walking is more functional when considering a patient population.

Cycle ergometers are commonly used for exercise testing; however cycling is often limited by local muscle fatigue in people who are not regular cyclists, so unless cycle training has been included in the exercise programme it may not be so sensitive to changes following training.

The test protocol, which is how high the work rate should be set or how much and how quickly the workload should be increased, should be selected to suit the person being tested. Ideally a cardiovascular exercise test should last 10–12 minutes. If the workload is increased too slowly during an incremental test the person may terminate the test due to boredom or general fatigue before maximum exercise parameters are reached. If the initial workload is set too high the test will be terminated before sufficient data have been collected.

Encouragement has been shown to have a significant effect on the outcome of exercise testing; therefore any encouragement given should be standardized as much as possible.

Safety should be considered when selecting the appropriate exercise test. It may not be desirable to exercise some patients to maximum capacity; in these cases a steady-state test may be preferable. Also, the general ability of the person to be tested should be considered; for example treadmill testing would be inappropriate for a person who is very frail, and overground walking may be more suitable.

All people involved with the exercise test should be familiar with the end points of the test. This includes the person being tested, who should be instructed how to signal that they wish to terminate the test.

Emergency equipment should be available when exercise testing is taking place, and staff should be appropriately trained to deal with an emergency.

Cardiovascular fitness can be assessed by testing incremental maximum exercise capacity or steady-state exercise capacity.

Maximum incremental exercise testing

During incremental maximal exercise testing the work rate is gradually increased, either at regular intervals or at a continuous gradual rate, until the person being tested can no longer sustain the exercise. The outcomes of the test are the length of time the test was sustained and the level of work rate reached during the test.

The increase in work rate may be achieved by an increase in the required speed, resistance or gradient.

If one of the physiological parameters reaches a maximal value the test is terminated and the end point of the test is termed 'maximum exercise'. This would be determined by reaching the predicted maximal heart rate (HR_{max}), or a plateau in oxygen uptake despite an increase in workload (VO_{2max}).

If exercise is terminated before one of the physiological parameters reaches a maximum then the end point is termed 'peak exercise'. In this case the exercise test is often stopped by the person being tested due to factors such as general fatigue, local muscle fatigue, pain, shortness of breath or boredom.

For some patients, such as those in the 'relative contraindications' column in Table 3.2, the end point of the test may be set at a lower level for safety reasons. For example if 85% of predicted maximal HR is reached, or oxygen levels drop below a desired level.

After cardiovascular training an increase in work rate at maximal/peak exercise is often seen along with an increase in maximal oxygen uptake. The maximal HR does not increase, but HR will be less for a given work rate.

The safety aspect of incremental maximal testing should also be considered as it puts a significant stress on the person being tested; in some patients it may be preferable to use steady-state testing.

Steady-state (endurance) exercise capacity

During steady-state exercise testing a constant work rate is maintained, and the outcomes of the test are the length of time the test was sustained or the distance covered during the test. Other outcomes may be HR and VO_2 during the steady-state exercise.

The work rate is set at a pre-determined level, often at between 40% and 60% of the person's maximum ability. This may be done by initially performing a maximal incremental test and selecting the work rate that produces 40–60% of maximal HR, or by estimating the 40–60% of maximal HR (See Monitoring exercise intensity below) and determining the correct work rate by trial and error.

The alternative to setting a constant work rate is to use a set time, and record the distance covered. This does not necessarily ensure that the person is in true steady state as their work rate may vary

Table 3.2 Contraindications to maximal exercise testing

Absolute contraindications	Relative contraindications
Recent acute cardiac event (within 2 days) or unstable angina	Severe arterial hypertension (systolic BP of >200 mmHg and/or diastolic BP of >120 mmHg)
Uncontrolled symptomatic dysrhythmias	Moderate stenotic valvular disease
Uncontrolled symptomatic heart failure	Electrolyte or metabolic abnormalities
Complete heart block	Tachydysrhythmia or bradydysrhythmia
Symptomatic severe aortic stenosis	Left main coronary stenosis
Acute pulmonary embolus or pulmonary infarction	Hypertrophic cardiomyopathy and other forms of outflow tract obstruction
Acute myocarditis or pericarditis	Neuromuscular, musculoskeletal or rheumatoid disorders that are exacerbated by exercise
Suspected or known dissecting aneurysm	High degree atrioventricular block
Known intracardiac thrombi	Ventricular aneurysm
Acute systemic infection	Chronic infectious disease
Mental or physical impairment leading to inability to exercise safely	Advanced/complicated pregnancy

throughout the test as their speed changes. Whether this kind of test is sub-maximal or maximal depends on how hard the person exerts themselves, and whether they correctly judge the pace to ensure that they have exercised maximally at the end of the test time period.

Exercise testing may take the form of a formal laboratory-based test or, more commonly in clinical practice, a field-based test.

Laboratory testing

Integrated cardiopulmonary exercise testing, such as that described here, gives much information, including oxygen uptake, and is regarded as the gold standard of exercise testing.

Multiple physiological parameters are monitored during formal laboratory cardiopulmonary exercise testing. A gas analyser is used to measure oxygen and carbon dioxide levels. This equipment also measures gas volumes, giving information on ventilation parameters during exercise. Heart rate and rhythm are monitored using ECG. Exercise testing staff may also take blood at the start and end of exercise to measure blood gas values and/or lactate levels. From these basic measurements other values, such as respiratory quotient and oxygen pulse, can be derived.

Laboratory tests use either treadmill or cycle ergometry to enable control of the work rate during the test and because it is easier to record data when a stationary exercise task is used.

This degree of monitoring of the physiological parameters allows exercise testing to be used for diagnostic purposes as it is possible to identify the body system that is the limiting factor to exercise by studying the results to see which system reaches its maximum capacity first.

The physiological information gained can also identify physiological training effects following an exercise intervention; therefore these tests may also be used when researching the effectiveness and mechanism of action of exercise programmes.

Laboratory testing is also advantageous as it allows exercise to take place in a controlled environment with close monitoring, which may be safer for some patients.

Laboratory testing is relatively expensive, as it requires laboratory time, a minimum of two staff per test, and the use of sophisticated equipment. These tests can also be quite daunting for the patient due to the array of equipment and the invasive nature of blood testing.

An example of a commonly used protocol for incremental treadmill testing is the Balke protocol. During this test the treadmill speed is set at 3.3 mph and the gradient is set at 0% for the first minute and 2% for the second minute; thereafter the gradient is increased by 1% every minute.

Field-based exercise testing

Field-based exercise tests are widely used in clinical practice as they require little equipment and use simple activities that are familiar to patients.

These tests most often use walking, running or step-ups, but may be made up of more functional tasks such as sit to stand.

Field-based exercise tests may be internally paced, that is the patient determines how fast they walk or step, or they may be externally paced, that is when the patient is required to pace their activity in time with a signal, such as the bleep test or a metronome.

Externally paced tests allow a standardized protocol, and may be less influenced by encouragement. The use of pace setting also allows an incremental test to be carried out, as pacing can produce a gradual increase in speed up to maximal exercise.

The Multistage Fitness Test, commonly known as the 'bleep test', is a standardized, externally paced, incremental field running test. It is based on a series of recorded timed signals (bleeps). The signals indicate the time allowed to run a 20 m course between two markers. Every minute a triple signal indicates that the bleeps are getting closer together; therefore the person under testing must increase their speed in order to reach the marker before the next timed bleep sounds. The end points of the test are the second time the person fails to reach the marker before the bleep sounds, the person terminating the test voluntarily or the tester halting the test due to safety factors, e.g. excessively high HR.

The Incremental Shuttle Walking Test (ISWT) was developed from the Multistage Fitness Test to provide a standardized, externally paced exercise test suitable for a more limited population. The pace of the test is initially very slow, which allows testing of severely compromised subjects. The person being tested is required to walk a distance of 10 m between the timed bleeps. The Modified Shuttle Walking test contains additional increments to allow testing of fitter patients.

The outcome of these shuttle tests is the number of completed shuttles, i.e. the distance covered. A relationship between the number of shuttles completed and maximum oxygen uptake has been demonstrated; therefore it is possible to estimate maximal oxygen uptake from the distance covered during the ISWT and the Multistage Fitness Test.

The ISWT was developed for exercise testing in patients with chronic obstructive pulmonary disease (COPD), but has been validated in other patient groups such as those with cardiac failure and low back pain.

The Endurance Shuttle Walking test had been developed to allow sub-maximal steady-state exercise testing. The test has a series of recorded bleeps the same distance apart to allow a set pace to be maintained in between the cones. There are a range of set walking speeds provided in the test, from 1.8 to 6 km/h. The appropriate walking speed can be selected based on the patient's performance in the incremental shuttle walking test, or by estimating the correct speed for the individual.

Cooper's 12-minute running test is an example of an internally paced test in which the subject is asked to cover the greatest distance possible in the set time of 12 minutes. When performed with maximal effort by fit subjects the distance covered in the 12-minute run has been shown to correlate with maximum oxygen uptake.

The 6- and 12-minute walking tests are widely used field tests that have been developed from the Cooper's test to allow testing of a patient population. The person being tested is instructed to walk as far as possible during the time allowed, but they may not run or jog during the test. They should ideally pace themselves to maintain walking throughout the test and reach maximum exercise at the end of the test; however, they may stop and rest throughout the test as required. The 6-minute walk test (6MWT) should be carried out in a straight corridor which has a hard, flat surface and allows a 30 m walking area to be marked out. The corridor should not be in general use during the performance of the test, as this may affect the results. The American Thoracic Society (2002) has published guidelines for the performance of the 6MWT, and these guidelines include very precise wording to give the instructions to the participant, and also exact wording for feedback regarding the time elapsed during the test.

As the 6MWT more closely mimics functional activity than the externally paced tests it has been suggested that it is more reflective of functional ability.

For both the 6MWT and the ISWT one practice test is recommended for repeatability.

The Harvard Step Test uses an externally controlled pace of 30 step-ups per minute onto a 50 cm high bench which is maintained for 5 minutes. The heart rate recovery time is used as the main outcome measure. Modifications of a step test can be used in clinical practice; for example how many step-ups can the patient complete in a set time, or how long can they maintain a set rate of steps. Step testing can be a useful alternative to walking tests when space is limited.

Interpretation of exercise test results

Following cardiovascular training the following changes may be seen on exercise testing as the training adaptations make the uptake and distribution of oxygen more efficient.

- Heart rate and oxygen uptake for a given work rate will decrease.
- Maximal oxygen uptake will increase.
- The subject will cover a greater distance or achieve more repetitions in a given time or sustain a set work rate for longer during a steady-state test.
- The subject will reach a higher maximum work rate and longer testing time in an incremental test.

GUIDELINES FOR PRESCRIPTION OF AEROBIC EXERCISE

These guidelines are for a healthy population; guidelines for specific patient groups are given in the relevant chapters.

Intensity

Intensity can be monitored by heart rate in most patients, although some patients may have pathology or be on drug treatment that affects their HR response to exercise in which case HR cannot be used to monitor exercise intensity.

The recommended training HR zone is from 55–65% to 90% of maximum heart rate. Maximum HR can be estimated by 220 – age.

The Karvonen method, which takes into account resting HR, can also be used to calculate an individual's training HR band using the following calculation.

1. Maximum heart rate (MHR) is estimated by 220 – age in years, and resting heat rate (RHR) measured.
2. Heart rate reserve (HRR) is calculated as: MHR – RHR = HRR
3. 60% and 80% of HRR are calculated and added onto RHR to give the parameters of the 60–80% training band.

Heart rate can be monitored using heart rate monitors during supervised sessions, and some patients purchase their own monitors so they can continue to accurately monitor HR at home.

In the absence of a heart rate monitor people can monitor their own pulse to ensure that they are working at the correct intensity. Patients should be taught how to take their carotid pulse within the first 10 or 15 seconds of terminating exercise and multiplying up the beats counted by 6 or 4 respectively to provide beats per minute.

Oxygen uptake can also be used to set exercise intensity, and an intensity of 40–50% to 85% of the oxygen uptake reserve is recommended. This is not often used in clinical practice as VO_2 is not commonly measured in the patient population.

For HR or VO_2 reserve the lower part of the recommended training band should be used in individuals who are quite unfit. Greater training effects are seen following higher-intensity training; however there is more injury risk associated with high-intensity work.

The Borg Rating of Perceived Exertion (RPE) scale (1998) (Figure 3.4) can also be used to set exercise intensity (production protocol) or it can be used to measure exercise intensity (estimation protocol). It has been shown to correlate well with blood lactate, heart rate, pulmonary ventilation and oxygen uptake during exercise. The RPE is a useful tool in clinical practice, as patients can continue to monitor their exercise easily at home.

The Borg scale is an interval ratio scale and is numbered from 6 to 20. The numbers run from 6 to 20 owing to the relationship between exercise intensity and heart rate, 60 being an average resting HR, and 200 being the upper end of maximal heart rate. The rating numbers are anchored with descriptions of how the person should feel at that particular exercise intensity to increase the validity of the scale. The numbers at either end of the scale are anchored, along with a selection of the numbers throughout the scale.

6	No exertion
7	Extremely light
8	
9	Very light
10	
11	Light
12	
13	Somewhat hard
14	
15	Hard (heavy)
16	
17	
18	
19	Extremely hard
20	Maximal exertion

Figure 3.4 The Borg Rating of Perceived Exertion scale (1998)

Using the RPE as a production protocol the person is introduced to the Borg scale and asked to exercise to a certain level on the scale, for example level 13 'somewhat hard'. The scale should be visible throughout the exercise to allow the person to modify their exercise intensity as needed. In patient groups that require specific monitoring of HR for safety reasons, such as some cardiac patients, the Borg scale is not sufficient. Familiarization with the Borg scale is needed before it can be accurately used for setting exercise intensity.

If using the Borg scale in an estimation protocol the scale is shown to the person whilst they are exercising and they are asked to rate how hard they are working; in this case the scale is used as an outcome measure.

Frequency

Exercise should be carried out 3–5 days a week. Training three times a week produces significant training effects; however training 5 days a week at a lower-intensity exercise may be more manageable for some people.

Little additional benefit is seen with more than five training sessions a week, and the risk of injury is increased. Training twice a week does not produce increases in VO_{2max}; however it may produce some functional changes and it is probably better than no exercise at all.

Duration

A total of 20–60 minutes of continuous or intermittent aerobic activity a day should be performed. The activity can be divided into a minimum of 10-minute bouts throughout the day.

The duration of training is dependent on the intensity. Unfit individuals starting at the lower end of the training band need to sustain exercise longer (30–60 minutes) to achieve training effects.

PROGRESSION AND REGRESSION OF AEROBIC EXERCISE

Aerobic activities can be progressed by increasing the intensity of training to a higher point in the training band and by increasing the duration of the activity.

Intensity can be increased by using both upper and lower limbs, using the upper limbs above shoulder height, increasing step size and speed of activity.

A regression activity using lower-impact activities, without upper limbs and at a slower pace, should also be offered to patients (Table 3.3, Figures 3.5–3.7).

Table 3.3 Examples of progression of aerobic exercise

Low intensity	→		**High intensity**
Step on spot	March on spot with high knees	March on spot with high knees and upper limbs	Step-ups
Sit to stand from perch sitting	Sit to stand from lower seat	Sit to stand more rapidly	Sit to stand rapidly with arms
Seated throw and catch ball	Standing throw and catch ball with some stepping and reaching required	Rapid throw and catch requiring running to reach ball	Add in additional activity, e.g. clapping or touching ground before catching ball
Walking	Increased pace of walking	Walking up hill	Increase speed and length of walk
Alternate side steps	Add arms with side steps to form 'half jacks'	Increase to full 'jumping jack'	Increase intensity by adding larger jump, increase speed
Walking on trampette	Light jog on trampette	Light bounce on trampette with arms to shoulder height	Bigger bounce on trampette with arms above shoulder height

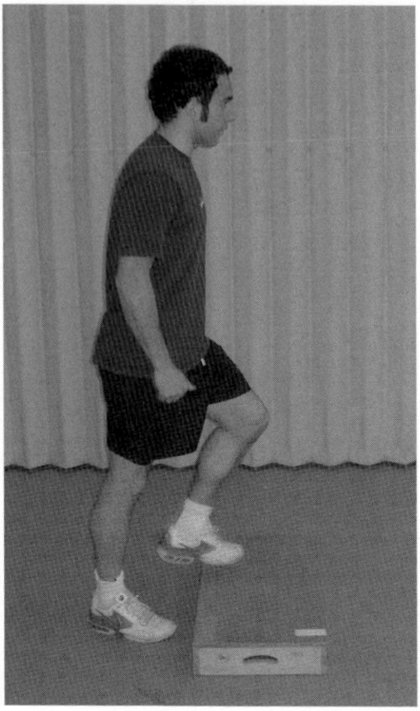

Figure 3.5 Step-up

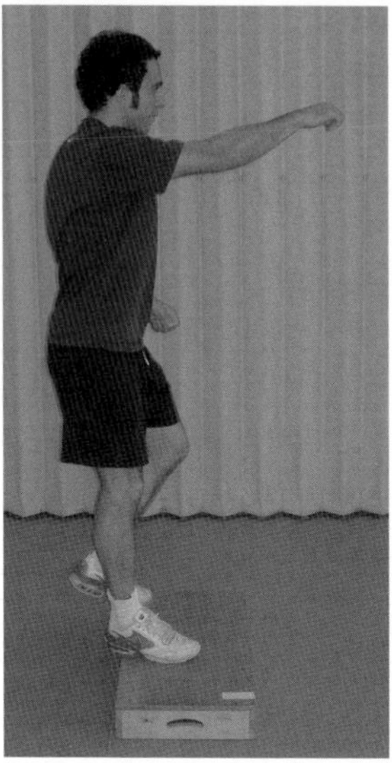

Figure 3.6 Step-up with arms

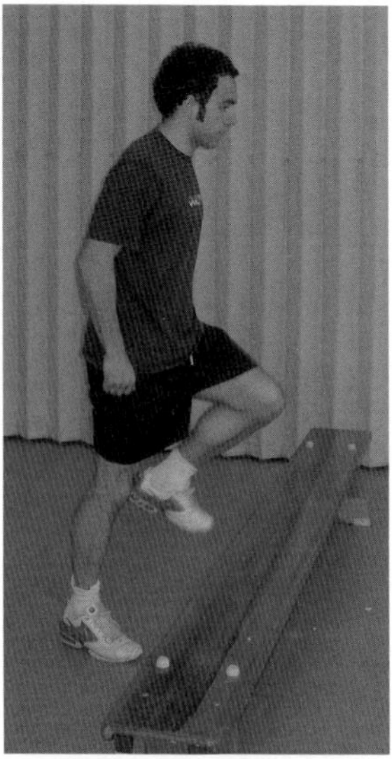

Figure 3.7 Bench step

Reference

American Thoracic Society (ATS) (2002) Statement: Guidelines for the six minute walk test. American Journal Respiratory Critical Care Medicine 166: 111–117.

Borg G (1998) Borg's Perceived Exertion and Pain Scales. Champaign, IL: Human Kinetics.

Stone M, Ramsey MW, Kinser AM, et al (2006) Stretching: Acute and chronic? The potential consequences. Strength and Conditioning Journal 28(6): 66–74.

Further reading

American College of Sports Medicine (ACSM) (2006) Guidelines for Exercise Testing and Prescription: 7th edition. Philadelphia, PA: Lippincott Williams & Wilkins.

Holloszy J, Coyle E (1984) Adaptations of skeletal muscle to endurance exercise and their metabolic consequences. Journal of Applied Physiology 56(4): 831–838.

McArdle W, Katch F, Katch V (1994) Essentials of Exercise Physiology. Philadelphia, PA: Lea & Febiger.

Pollock M, Gaesser G, Butcher J, et al (1998) The recommended quantity and quality of exercise for developing and maintaining cardiorespiratory and muscular fitness, and flexibility in healthy adults. Medicine and Science in Sports and Exercise 30(6): 371–378.

Singh S, Morgan M, Scott S, Walters D, Hardman A (1992) Development of a shuttle walking test of disability in patients with chronic airways obstruction. Thorax 47: 1019–1024.

Thacker S (2004) The impact of stretching on sports injury risk: a systematic review of the literature. Medicine and Science in Sports and Exercise 36(3): 371–378.

Thayer R, Collins J, Noble EG, Taylor AW (2000) A decade of aerobic endurance training: histological evidence for fibre type transformation. Journal of Sports Medicine and Physical Fitness 40(4): 284–289.

Wasserman K, Hansen JE, Sue DY, Casaburi R, Wipp BJ (1999) Principles of Exercise Testing and Interpretation: 3rd edition. Philadelphia, PA: Lippincott Williams & Wilkins.

Whaley MH (ed.) (2005) ACSM's Guidelines for Exercise Testing and Prescription: 7th edition. Philadelphia, PA: Lippincott Williams & Wilkins.

Exercise to Increase Muscle Strength

An overview of muscle strength is provided in this chapter. Assessment of muscle strength and training adaptations following a successful resistance training programme are considered. Exercise design, based on current guidelines for increasing muscle strength, is discussed and example exercises given.

DEFINITION

Muscle strength is the ability of a muscle to generate force. This may be by isometric or static muscle contraction, concentric muscle contraction, where the muscle shortens as it contracts, or eccentric muscle contraction, where the muscle lengthens as it contracts.

FACTORS DETERMINING MUSCLE STRENGTH

An individual's muscle strength is determined by several factors. These are considered in Table 4.1.

TRAINING ADAPTATIONS

Following a properly designed strength training regime various adaptations will be seen. Systemically a muscle-strengthening programme, which targets several muscle groups, may result in a more

Table 4.1 Factors determining muscle strength

Determining factor	Influencing factors	Effect
Muscle tissue	Pathology of muscle, e.g. muscular dystrophy	Muscle's ability to generate force reduced
Nerve supply	Pathology of the nervous system, both upper and lower motor neurone problems	Limited ability to recruit motor units
Muscle length	Range in which muscle is working Muscle injury Joint pathology	Muscle will not be able to generate maximal force
Connective tissue	Connective tissue disease	Supporting matrix weak so reduces muscle's ability to generate force
Muscle insertion	Fractures Tendinopathies	Alteration in force generation in relation to the portion of limb being moved
Muscle fibre pennation	Type of muscle being used	Most force generated when muscle fibres are parallel to the longitudinal axis of the muscle

positive body image and increased self-confidence as body composition changes and muscle mass increases. Local adaptations within the muscle or muscle group being trained include the following.

Local adaptations

Neural

There is an increased ability to recruit motor units and the recruitment of motor units is better synchronized. Co-ordination may be improved along with decreased activity in antagonist muscles to those being trained. This is an early change demonstrated by an increase in muscle strength over baseline measurement and is usually seen after about 2 weeks of a strength training programme.

Muscular hypertrophy

The cross-sectional area of muscle fibres will enlarge. For a strength training programme, this will be seen in both type 1 and type 2 muscle fibres but mostly in type 2. This is a late change seen after 8–12 weeks of an appropriate training programme.

Muscular hyperplasia

This refers to an increase in the number of muscle fibres. Although this has been shown in animal studies following strength training, the results of these studies have not been definitively reproduced in humans.

Changes in capillary density and mitochondria

As muscle fibres enlarge following a high-resistance, strength training programme, the densities of both capillaries and mitochondria decrease in proportion to muscular hypertrophy. With moderate-intensity resistance training programmes, capillary density may in fact increase. These changes may become important when training for specific sports and occur 8–12 weeks after the start of a strength training programme.

Changes in metabolic activity

There is an increase in enzymes and stored nutrients following a training programme.

PRINCIPLES OF EXERCISE DESIGN TO INCREASE MUSCLE STRENGTH

The training principles of overload, specificity, reversibility and individuality, which have been covered in Chapter 2, should always be considered when developing a strength training programme. Other principles which are also important in exercise design to increase muscle strength include the following.

Energy source

The adenosine triphosphate (ATP) – creatine phosphate (CP) and glycolysis energy pathways are utilized during strength training programmes. Exercise duration is short, usually less than a minute per muscle or muscle group being trained.

Starting position

This must be considered before beginning a programme to increase muscle strength. The person must be stable in whichever position is chosen. It may be appropriate to fix the joints above or below the muscles to be exercised to isolate the work being performed. At the same time the person should be able to work the muscle group freely in the desired manner. If an individual has very weak muscles a larger base of support is usually appropriate at the start of the programme, e.g. side lying for weak hip flexors and extensors. Starting position also needs to be considered as it may be appropriate to use gravity alone as the training stimulus or to position an individual in such a way that they do not have to lift their limb against gravity (cf. previous example).

Range of exercises

A strength training programme may target a particular muscle or muscle group or several muscle groups. It is important to think about the needs of the individual when designing a strength training programme, particularly in terms of incorporating functional activity into a training programme in its latter stages.

Rest intervals

To avoid training a fatigued muscle, adequate rest time is needed between training sessions. For strength training 24–48 hours are recommended between sessions training the same muscle group. In general, the higher the intensity of the training, the longer the rest period required between sessions.

Safety

Safety factors which are especially important to consider when prescribing and supervising strength training programmes are:

- ***Cardiovascular stress***. When a person is lifting a weight, their blood pressure will increase in proportion to the effort involved in lifting the weight. As the effort intensity is highest as the person reaches fatigue, people with increased cardiovascular risk should avoid high-intensity training.
- ***Breathing***. To avoid breath holding or Valsalva manoeuvre, it is recommended that the person carrying out a resistance training programme should breathe out during the concentric phase of the weight lift.
- ***Injury***. If individuals are using large weights, they should work with a training partner or a supervisor particularly if using techniques where there is a risk of dropping the weight on themselves. Certain patient populations, for example those who are frail, may also need constant assistance and supervision. If weights have not been properly secured to a limb there is also the risk of these dropping onto feet. Muscle strains may occur if a weight is too heavy for an individual or if they are using a poor movement technique.
- ***Delayed-onset muscle soreness***. This usually occurs 24–48 hours after excessive unaccustomed physical activity and is thought to be due to damage to the connective tissue supporting the muscle.

There is a higher risk of delayed-onset muscle soreness with eccentric training. This may discourage people from continuing with their training programme. Progressive training regimes should minimize this problem.

EQUIPMENT

One of the main differences in equipment used for weight training is that it can provide a constant or variable resistance.

Constant resistance equipment

This provides a resistance which does not change through range of motion. Examples of constant resistance equipment are free weights and the Westminster Pulley System.

Variable resistance equipment

This allows the muscle to work maximally through its entire range by varying the resistance offered to the muscle and so accommodates to muscle strength through range. Variable resistance machines are designed to isolate muscle work and are associated with a lower risk of injury than free weights because they control body position and speed of movement. They can be expensive and take up a lot of space. Examples of variable resistance equipment include isokinetic machines and Nautilus equipment. At the opposite end of the spectrum elastic resistance bands offer variable resistance and have the advantages of being cheap and portable.

Not everyone will have access to or need the complete range of different strength training equipment. Cost, available space or the situation in which somebody works is more likely to dictate the type of equipment available. It is important to be able to adapt a strength training programme to different situations. Equipment which is more commonly available to physiotherapists is discussed below.

Free weights

This is probably one of the commonest methods used in clinical practice to strengthen muscle. Free weights can easily be used in many settings such as the ward, the gym and the home. To be able to carry out resistance training programmes effectively, a variety of different weights are needed as well as different methods of attaching them to the body. Commonly used weights include dumbbells, barbells and wrist and ankle weights, which are all most useful when adjustable. The appropriate training load can then be applied and increased gradually (see Figure 4.1). If there is not an adequate range of weights available the training programme may become ineffective or dangerous.

Figure 4.1 A range of different free weight equipment

Using free weights is a very effective way of increasing muscle strength but the muscle being exercised needs to be relatively strong to benefit from this kind of training, i.e. able to work against gravity with a resistance. The person carrying out the exercise also needs to be able to safely lift and attach the weight they are going to use. There is a higher risk of possible injury with this type of activity than with some other kinds of resistance training. The added benefit of using free weights is that other muscles are recruited during the programme to stabilize the body and maintain posture. The activity of attaching a weight will generate a training stimulus for the other muscles which assist in this.

The type of muscle work carried out using free weights will be a hybrid concentric/eccentric programme. The muscle will shorten as it works to lift the weight against gravity and then lengthen as the weight is lowered in a controlled manner. Figure 4.2 shows a dumbbell being used to strengthen the elbow flexors.

Westminster Pulley System

This is a wall-mounted frame with a weight carrier and more than one pulley in circuit to allow loading of muscle to occur. Muscle loading can occur in different muscle ranges and planes of movement whilst the person exercising is lifting a known weight which is often visible. It is a much neglected piece of therapeutic equipment, probably because it takes a little time to develop the skill necessary to set up the pulley system quickly and effectively. To be able to use a pulley system for resistance training, a set of different weights which fit on the weight holder are needed along with devices to attach the pulley system to

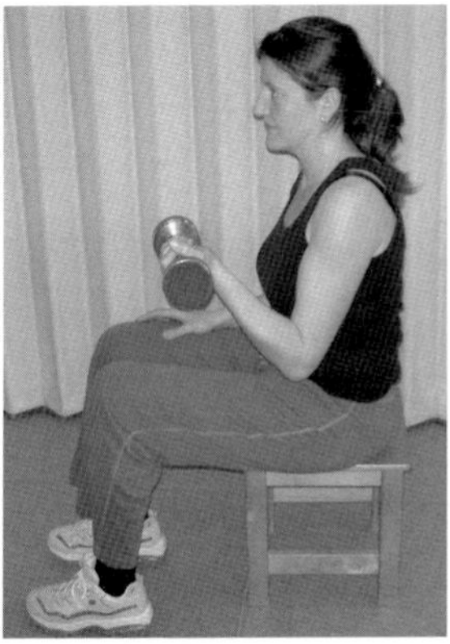

Figure 4.2 A dumbbell being used to strengthen the elbow flexors

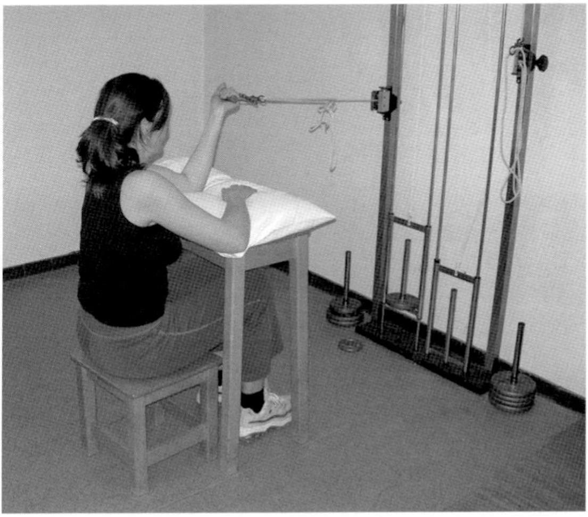

Figure 4.3 The Westminster Pulley System being used to strengthen elbow flexors

the person, such as handles or three-ringed loops. Figure 4.3 shows the Westminster Pulley System being used to strengthen the elbow flexors.

The process for setting up the Westminster pulley is as follows:

1. position patient in appropriate starting position
2. localize muscle to be strengthened
3. check targeted range of movement is available
4. ensure that there is no weight on the pulley
5. attach the pulley to the patient

6. ask the patient to move through the range to be strengthened and identify the mid-point of the movement
7. set the angle of the pulley rope to 90° at the mid-point of the range
8. ask the patient to move the limb so that the muscle to be strengthened is in the outer part of the range to be worked (this is where the rope will be most slack); tighten up the rope so that there is no slack and the weight will be applied as soon as the patient begins the movement
9. ensure there are no dangling ropes
10. ask the patient to perform the movement and check the set up
11. apply appropriate weight and begin the exercise.

Elastic resistance bands

There are several types of elastic resistance bands available on the market. Most manufacturers produce a range of bands which offer different resistances to movement. This resistance is generally determined by the percentage elongation of the band. If these are to be used clinically, it is therefore important to have a range of bands available. There is a growing body of evidence to support the use of elastic resistance bands as a useful tool for increasing muscle strength, and the gains in muscle strength, physiological responses and patterns of muscle activation are similar to those produced by other strengthening methods. One big advantage of elastic resistance bands is that they are easily portable and, as long as the person exercising has been taught how to use the band correctly, they can continue to exercise at home using the same equipment. When using elastic resistance bands, attention should be paid to the following.

- If the person who is to use the band has a latex allergy, an alternative strengthening method should be sought unless a latex-free elastic resistance band is available.
- Bands should be checked for nicks and tears before each use.
- Bands should be anchored securely to a sturdy object or attachment before use.
- Bands should not be tied tightly around extremities so that circulation is impaired.
- Avoid using very short pieces of band – the user will have more control when exercising with a longer piece.
- The correct resistance band for strengthening a muscle group would allow the person exercising to complete 8–12 repetitions with mild fatigue on completion.

Figure 4.4 shows an elastic resistance band being used to strengthen the knee flexors.

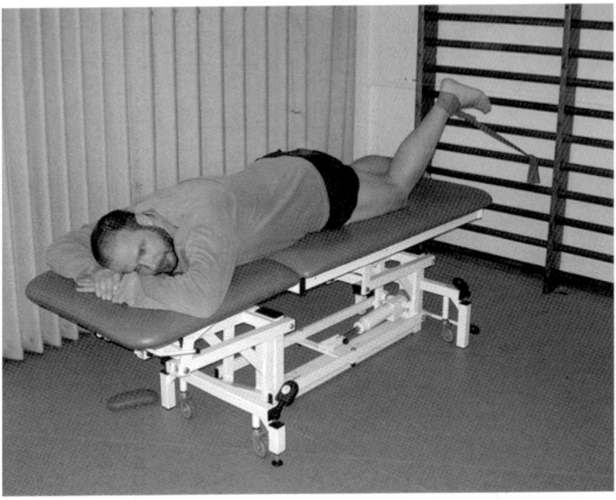

Figure 4.4 Elastic resistance band being used to strengthen the knee flexors

Isokinetics

Isokinetic machines are expensive pieces of equipment and may not be available to all clinical physiotherapists. Although these machines may be used for muscle strengthening, where they have been shown to be effective in producing strength gains, they are more often used for assessment, research and measurement as they can provide detailed information such as peak torque during a muscle contraction. These machines became popular in an effort to maximize the gains of a strengthening programme over the entire range that a muscle works and so are a type of variable resistance machine. Isokinetic machines allow a person to exert force against a resistance that moves at a pre-set constant speed. In practice muscles do not work like this and other more specific training may also be required.

OTHER METHODS TO INCREASE MUSCLE STRENGTH

Free exercise

This type of exercise is a valuable clinical tool. It is suitable for people with very weak muscles and easily transferable to the home situation as no equipment is required. Body position and gravity can be used to alter the amount of resistance applied to a particular muscle group. For example, the person doing the exercise may be positioned in such a way that gravity is 'neutral' – it offers neither resistance nor assistance to the working muscle (see Figure 2.17). Body weight may also be used as the resistance in a strength training programme. For instance moving from sitting to standing could be used as a resistance training exercise for the knee or hip extensor muscles. It would be particularly suitable if the person doing the exercise could only manage this 8–10 times. Lowering the height of the chair or weighting the individual around the waist would be ways of progressing the exercise. It is important to incorporate functional activities into a strength training programme. The activity chosen would depend on the needs of the individual.

Manual resistance

This technique may also be particularly useful when working with people with very weak muscles. The therapist may apply resistance to a single muscle or muscle group and placing their hands carefully on the person gives instant feedback about how a muscle should work to produce a movement. The therapist can alter resistance through range in response to the varying muscle strength. Resistance may also be given to whole patterns of movement in specific ways to help strengthen muscle groups. This is called proprioceptive neuromuscular facilitation (PNF) and there are several techniques within PNF which can be used to strengthen muscle. For instance the technique of 'slow reversals' aims to stimulate as many motor neurones as possible in a normal pattern of movement so that the maximum number of motor units are utilized as a muscle contracts.

ASSESSMENT OF MUSCLE STRENGTH

An initial assessment of muscle strength should be made before a resistance training programme is commenced. This assessment will produce a baseline value for an appropriate exercise prescription. This value can be monitored to show where progression of a programme is needed and also demonstrate the effectiveness of a strengthening regime at its conclusion. If muscle strength is the ability of a muscle to generate force, the appropriate unit for measuring muscle strength is Newtons. However, strength is usually expressed in terms of the weight being moved, i.e. kilograms.

Principles of assessment

Measurements of muscle strength repeated over the time span of a strengthening programme should be carried out in a standardized manner using:

- the same starting position
- the same assessment test
- the same type of muscle work (isometric, concentric or eccentric) in the same range at the same speed.

Muscle strength can be assessed either statically or dynamically.

Static muscle strength

This type of testing only gives information about the strength of a static or isometric muscle contraction at the point in the muscle range where the static strength is assessed. It can be measured using:

Dynamometry

This type of myometer consists of a digital display, an electrical amplifier and transducer. It can usually be attached to a handle, which can measure hand or finger grip strength, or a tensiometer, used to measure static strength of other muscle groups. The strength of the muscle being tested can be read directly from the digital display.

Manual muscle testing

Therapists may use manual muscle testing as a quick means of assessing whether muscle strength is normal by comparing muscle strength of a certain muscle group on the right with the left. If abnormalities are found, more detailed testing is usually necessary. It is not usually appropriate to prescribe a resistance training programme from this type of assessment.

Dynamic muscle strength

This is measured when movement of an external load or body part takes place and the muscle changes length. The type of muscle work and range that the muscle moves through during the test is important here as the test result will be specific to these variables. Dynamic muscle strength can be measured using one of the following means.

Medical Research Council (MRC) scale

This scale is commonly used in clinical practice and provides a subjective view of muscle strength. If applied in a standardized manner, it has the advantage of being easy to use without the need for expensive equipment. The disadvantages of the MRC scale are that it is subjective, huge strength gains may be needed to change grade and the person being tested may need to change position several times to record the grade accurately. The scale is:

- 0 – no muscle contraction
- 1 – a flicker of muscle contraction
- 2 – the muscle contracts through full range with gravity neutral
- 3 – the muscle contracts through full range against gravity
- 4 – the muscle contracts through full range against gravity and a load
- 5 – normal muscle contraction.

The value recorded should only be in whole numbers and the person being tested must be able to contract their muscle through the whole available range to achieve a specific grade. This scale is particularly useful for weak muscles.

Isokinetic muscle testing

As described above, an isokinetic dynamometer may be used for assessing muscle strength through range at a pre-set constant speed.

Repetition maximum (RM)

This is the standard measure for assessing muscle strength. As training regimes are usually described in terms of nRM, it is probably the simplest test to use clinically for people who can lift a load against gravity. The 1 RM is the greatest resistance that can be moved through a defined muscle range in a controlled manner with good posture. There is skill required in identifying a RM without overly fatiguing the person being tested and so the technique requires practice. Rather than identifying a 1 RM for measurement of muscle strength a 4 or 6 RM may be just as useful for tracking changes in muscle strength over time and reduce the risk of injury involved in performing a 1 RM test. There are different equations available with varying amounts of error to convert nRM to 1 RM. Other nRMs can then be identified as a percentage of the 1 RM, for example 10 RM is about 75% of 1 RM. This may not always be completely accurate but is an accepted method of calculating the required RM. One example of such an equation (Brzycki 1993) is shown here:

$$\text{Predicted 1 RM} = \text{Weight lifted}/1.0278 - 0.0278n$$

where n = the number of repetitions performed.

This formula is valid only for predicting a 1 RM where the number of repetitions to fatigue is less than 10. If the repetitions (x) exceed 10, the prediction of 1 RM becomes much less accurate.

The following steps should be taken to test for 1 RM or nRM.

1. Decide on starting position and muscle range then ask the person to warm up by doing some sub-maximal contractions at a slow speed and through the required range.
2. Choose an initial weight which is a reasonable estimate of 50–75% of the person's maximal capacity. Take into account the age of the person, the muscle group being tested, the gender of the person and whether the person is accustomed to weight lifting.
3. Count how many times (n) the person can lift the weight before the onset of muscular fatigue. This weight will be the nRM for the muscle work that has been assessed. Signs of fatigue include

being unable to maintain a strict posture, the muscle quivering and a slower or lesser range of movement.

4. If a 10 RM has been identified and a smaller RM, i.e. 1 RM, is required then the muscle can be loaded incrementally and the test repeated to directly measure this value. Alternatively an estimation equation may also be used to calculate this.

The RM should be identified within four trials with 3–5-minute rest periods between trials. If this has not been achieved the person will be excessively fatigued and the testing will need to be carried out at another time when the person has fully recovered.

GUIDELINES FOR PRESCRIPTION OF EXERCISE TO INCREASE MUSCLE STRENGTH

Exercises to increase muscle strength are specific to the muscle group used, the type of muscle contraction, the muscle range, the velocity of movement and the type of equipment being used. It is therefore important to assess the person carefully so that a suitable resistance training programme can be devised. This will include considering the age of the individual, their health status and fitness level, the rationale for increasing muscle strength and their personal goals. The variables which can be manipulated in a resistance training programme are the resistance, the number of repetitions and the speed of movement.

Type of muscle work

The strength training programme may include muscle work which is concentric, eccentric or isometric and should mimic the muscle work required for function. The speed and range of movement also need to be considered.

Intensity, duration and frequency

Research evidence would suggest that a programme of one set of 6–8 RM, practised 2–3 days a week to allow time for recovery, at a slow speed (allowing about 3 seconds for concentric then 3 seconds for eccentric work), would provide the best training stimulus for increasing strength in muscles which are able to work against gravity.

For a very weak muscle, one able to produce a flicker of contraction it is important to:

- position the person so that the muscle/muscle group to be re-educated is in mid-range
- give clear instructions and a demonstration of the muscle work expected
- try to work the muscle as it normally would, i.e. isometrically or isotonically

- consider using sliding boards or other devices which reduce the friction generated by the movement produced by the muscle; this may help to increase the range through which the muscle works.

Standard guidelines and position statements exist for general resistance training. These have been developed for both healthy individuals and other groups and are based on the best evidence available. For healthy individuals unaccustomed to resistance training the recommended training prescription would be:

- **Frequency** – 2–3 days a week.
- **Intensity** – one set of 8–10 RM to volitional fatigue.
- **Duration** – 3 seconds for the concentric phase and 3 seconds for the eccentric phase of the activity (about 1 minute in total).

A general strengthening programme would include 8–10 exercises which target all the major muscle groups in the body. Other patient groups such as those with cardiac disease are considered in more detail in other relevant chapters.

Progression and regression

For a very weak muscle, graded at 2 on the MRC scale, a muscle-strengthening regime can be progressed in several ways:

- if the person is unable to work the muscle through full range, the muscle range can be gradually increased
- increasing the number of repetitions
- working the muscle against gravity.

The therapist may start to offer some manual resistance to the movement being produced by the muscle, using a short lever arm at first, then gradually increasing the length of the lever arm.

Once the person can work their muscle against gravity the normal recommendations for training should be followed. The intensity of the resistance training programme can be progressed by increasing the weight, the number of repetitions or reducing the speed of movement. Improvements in muscle strength normally occur within 2 weeks of starting a programme and this will mean that the person can carry out their exercise prescription with ease. The training intensity should be increased.

Exercises would need to be regressed if the person experienced untoward pain with the exercise programme. Training may need to be stopped in the unlikely case of muscle injury. When the person re-starts the programme, it should be at a lower intensity than when the injury occurred. A new assessment of muscle strength should be carried out.

Figures 4.5–4.8 show a progressive muscle-strengthening programme for the elbow extensors.

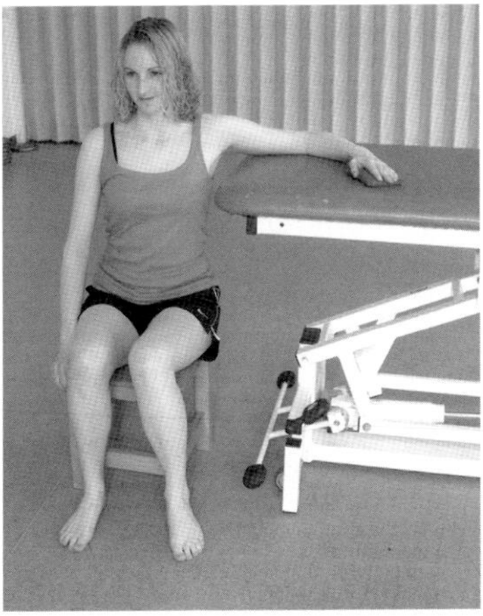

Figure 4.5 Elbow extension with gravity counterbalanced

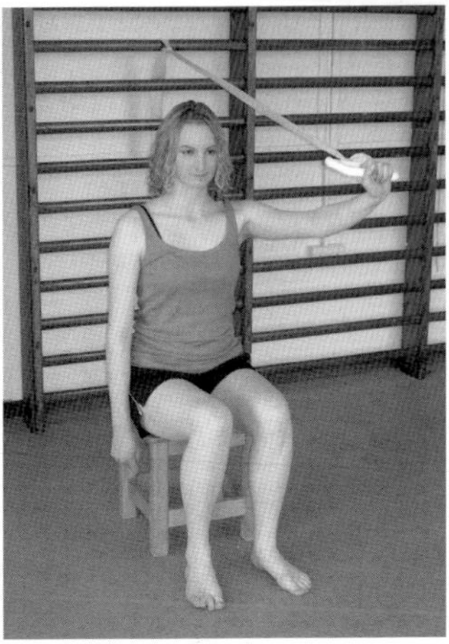

Figure 4.6 Elbow extension with elastic resistance band

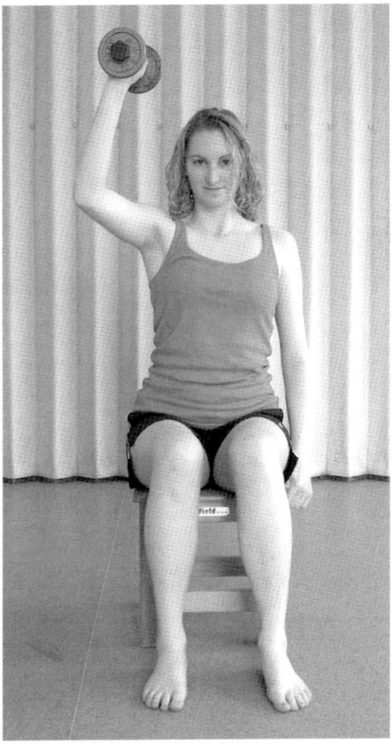

Figure 4.7 Elbow extension with a free weight

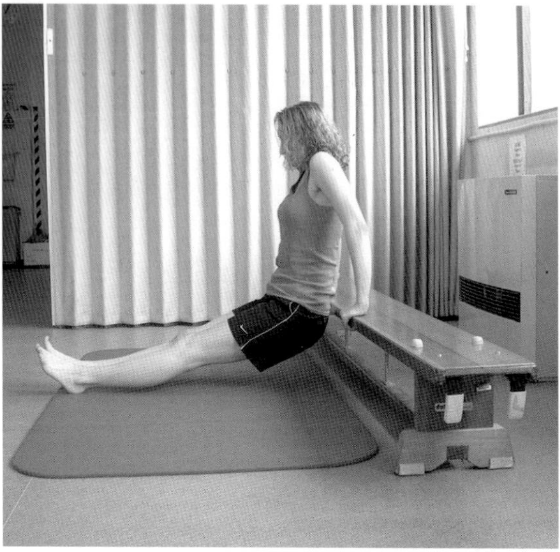

Figure 4.8 Strengthening the elbow extensors using tricep dips. Here body weight acts as the training stimulus

Reference

Brzycki M (1993) Strength testing – predicting a one rep max from reps to fatigue (measuring muscular strength). The Journal of Physical Education, Recreation and Dance 64(1): 88–91.

Further reading

Atha J (1981) Strengthening muscle. Exercise and Sports Science Review 9: 1–73.

Feigenbaum M, Pollock ML (1999) Prescription of resistance training for health and disease. Medicine and Science in Sports and Exercise 31: 38–45.

Thera-Band Instruction Manual available at www.Thera-BandAcademy.com

Whaley MH (ed.) (2005) ACSM's Guidelines for Exercise Testing and Prescription: 7th edition. Philadelphia, PA: Lippincott Williams & Wilkins.

CHAPTER FIVE

Exercise to Increase Muscle Endurance

This chapter defines muscle endurance. It also explains how to assess muscle endurance and produce a suitable exercise prescription for increasing local muscle endurance.

DEFINITION

Muscle endurance is the ability of a muscle to carry out repeated contractions over a period of time. The term 'endurance' implies prolonged use and the ability to avoid fatigue. In any individual there is a relationship between muscle strength and muscle endurance and both are important for everyday life. People need adequate muscle strength to be able to complete functional activities, such as picking up a reasonably heavy object, and muscle endurance so that they are able to do this repeatedly throughout the day or sustain the activity. In the healthy population muscle strength and endurance can be considered together as muscular fitness. There is an association between muscular fitness and quality of life.

Local muscle endurance can be trained in a similar manner to muscle strength by altering the exercise prescription. General muscle endurance may be trained by using the principles of aerobic exercise design, which have been considered in Chapter 3. This chapter will concentrate on local muscle endurance.

FACTORS DETERMINING MUSCULAR ENDURANCE

Factors determining muscle endurance are a combination of those which determine cardiovascular fitness and muscle strength. Tables illustrating these factors can be found in Chapters 3 and 4 respectively.

TRAINING ADAPTATIONS

Many training adaptations will be similar to those for strength training, for example neural changes in terms of motor unit recruitment. The training adaptations will depend on the exercise programme being followed. For an individual muscle group, local muscle endurance exercises will take only slightly longer to complete than strength training exercises. This will mean that the energy pathways being utilized are similar, that is the adenosine triphosphate (ATP) – creatine phosphate (CP) and glycolysis systems.

If aerobic activity is being used to improve muscle endurance, the training adaptations will be similar to those described in Chapter 3, as the person exercising becomes reliant on aerobic metabolism as the method of producing energy for the exercising muscles.

PRINCIPLES OF EXERCISE DESIGN TO INCREASE MUSCLE ENDURANCE

Local muscle endurance may be improved by utilizing a progressive resistance training programme similar to that for muscle strengthening except that the prescription will use a lower weight and larger number of repetitions (15 RM) than that for pure strength training (8 RM). For people with low muscular fitness, one set of exercises will produce training gains and is time efficient. For those with good initial muscular fitness, for example athletes, more sets (up to five or six) may be needed to produce training gains. If multiple sets are used, rest intervals should be incorporated into the programme between sets. These should be long enough to allow the next exercise to be performed in good form.

Considerations such as starting position, safety and equipment are similar to those for strength training.

General muscle endurance may also be improved by using aerobic exercise. Many exercise programmes for improving muscle endurance may start with an exercise programme for specific local muscle endurance and progress to a programme which incorporates this into a functional, general endurance training programme.

ASSESSMENT OF MUSCLE ENDURANCE

As with strength training, accurate assessment of muscle endurance is important to provide an appropriate exercise prescription. Assessment of muscle endurance relies on looking at a person's ability to carry out repeated contractions of a muscle or muscle group to fatigue. For this reason muscle endurance testing is usually dynamic. There are various methods to measure muscle endurance.

The absolute method

Count the number of repetitions that an individual can perform at a given amount of resistance over time; for example, count how many times an individual can lift a 5 kg weight with their knee extensors in a minute.

Repetition maximum method

Assess muscle strength and then with a fixed percentage of the 1 RM, normally 70%, count how many times the person can successfully lift this weight. This is usually 12–15 times. Any gains in the number of times the person can lift the weight will show an increase in muscular endurance.

Callisthenic exercises

These can be used when other muscle-testing equipment is not available. Whaley (2005) recommends using a press-up test to assess upper body strength but there are test protocols and normal values for other commonly performed muscle endurance tests such as abdominal curls and pull-ups (Johnson and Nelson, 1986). To perform a press-up test count how many consecutive press-ups the person can do without resting and compare with published age and gender normal values. Starting position for men is the standard press-up position and for women the starting position is modified by allowing the person to kneel with knees flexed to 90°, ankles crossed and hands placed shoulder width apart on the floor as illustrated in Figure 5.1.

Figure 5.1 The press-up test carried out by a woman

Isokinetic dynamometer

Do an initial trial to find the peak torque of the muscle group being tested, at a speed setting of 120–180° a second and then count the number of repetitions that the person can do until the torque reaches 50% of the peak value.

PRINCIPLES OF ASSESSMENT

Measurements of muscle endurance repeated over the time span of an exercise programme should be carried out in a standardized manner using:

- the same starting position
- the same assessment test
- the same type of muscle work (dynamic, concentric or eccentric) in the same range.

The amount of encouragement provided as well as the motivation level of the person being tested and time of day should also be considered.

GUIDELINES FOR EXERCISE TO INCREASE MUSCLE ENDURANCE

The principles of overload, specificity and reversibility apply to muscle endurance training as they do to strength training programmes. Exercises to increase muscle endurance are specific to the muscle group used, the type of muscle contraction, the muscle range, the velocity of movement and the type of equipment being used. It is therefore important to assess the person carefully so that a suitable training programme can be devised. This will include considering the age of the individual, their health status and fitness level, the rationale for increasing muscle endurance and their personal goals. The variables which can be manipulated in an endurance training programme are the resistance, the number of repetitions, the number of sets and the speed of movement.

Type of muscle work

An endurance training programme usually includes dynamic, concentric or eccentric muscle work and should be translated into the muscle work required for function as the training programme progresses. The speed and range of movement also need to be considered.

Intensity, frequency and duration

To train local muscle endurance rather than strength, evidence would suggest that a lower resistance and more repetitions than that used for strength training should be used. Gains in muscle endurance are made when the training load is less than 60% of 1 RM (15–20 RM) and one set of the training is carried out 3 days a week. A rest day is important for muscle groups being trained to allow the muscle to recover from fatigue.

Progression and regression

Progression and regression of a muscle endurance training programme is carried out in a similar manner to that for strength training, as described in Chapter 4. The regime can be progressed by increasing the number of repetitions, sets or the resistance being used. The regime can be regressed by decreasing the intensity and by reducing the resistance being used.

Figures 5.2–5.4 show a progressive muscle endurance training programme for the hip extensors.

Figure 5.2 The hip extensors working against gravity. Excessive lumbar extension should be avoided

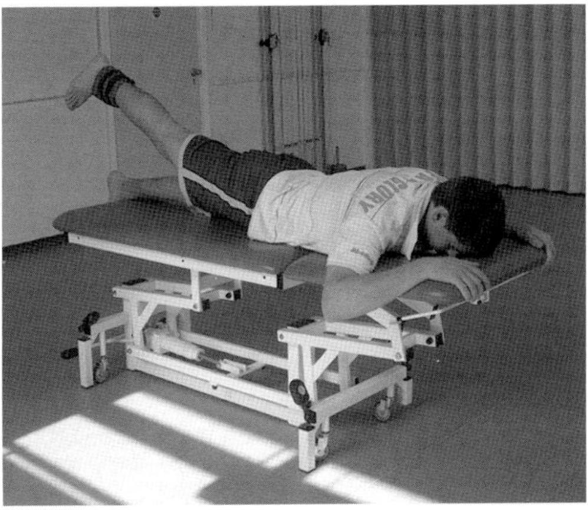

Figure 5.3 The hip extensors working against gravity and resistance

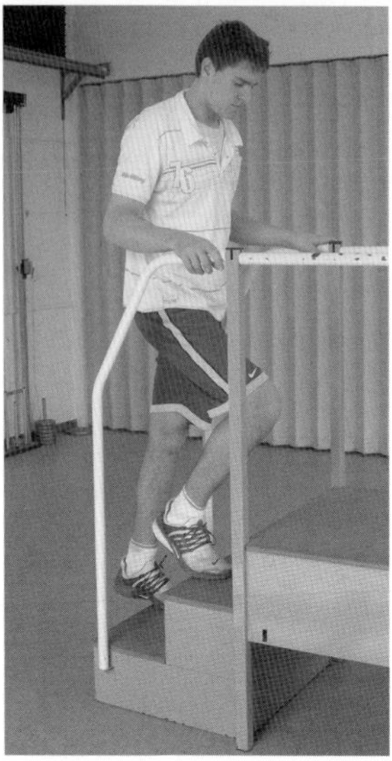

Figure 5.4 The hip extensors working functionally during stair climbing

Further reading

Heyward V (1997) Advanced Fitness Assessment and Exercise Prescription: 3rd edition. Champaign, IL: Human Kinetics.

Johnson B, Nelson J (1986) Practical Measurements for Evaluation of Physical Fitness. New York: Macmillan Publishing Company.

Whaley MH (ed.) (2005) ACSM's Guidelines for Exercise Testing and Prescription: 7th edition. Philadelphia, PA: Lippincott Williams & Wilkins.

Exercise to Improve Power

This chapter defines muscle power and the factors which determine this. It explains how to assess power output and the principles of exercise prescription for improving power.

DEFINITION

Power is the rate of doing work and may be referred to as anaerobic power or muscle power. The concept of power is important as it relates to exercise. When exercising the work rate or power output describes the intensity of the exercise, that is how quickly an individual can complete an exercise. Two individuals may both be able to carry out a similar amount of work but a highly trained individual will be able to carry out the work in a shorter time and so have a higher power output than the individual who is less highly trained. Power may need to be considered most commonly for athletes competing in events such as sprinting and jumping. However it may be just as important for ordinary functional activities. An example of this is that of somebody being able to cross a road at a fast enough pace whilst the green light is showing at a pedestrian crossing. For many older people or those with other mobility problems this can be extremely difficult.

FACTORS DETERMINING ANAEROBIC OR MUSCLE POWER

Several factors determine an individual's ability to do work. These include the velocity of shortening and the overall size and strength of the muscle as well as the ability of the person to carry out a specific task.

Velocity of shortening

It is possible for a muscle to generate most force when it contracts slowly. As the speed of contraction becomes faster, force generated by the muscle becomes less until a point is reached, the maximum velocity of shortening, where no force is generated. This is illustrated in Figure 6.1. Speed of shortening largely depends on the different types of muscle fibre, I, IIa and IIb, within a muscle and this is genetically programmed. There is no real evidence to suggest that speed of shortening can be improved with training.

Muscle strength

Muscle strength is an important contributing factor to muscle power as a basis for power development. Factors determining muscle strength have been considered in detail in Chapter 4. Traditional resistance training programmes have been found to increase muscle strength and therefore power at slow movement velocities. More recent research has shown that strength training with light to moderate loads (30–60% of 1 RM) at high velocities may produce larger increases in maximal power by increasing fast force production.

Task specificity

If a person is skilled at doing a task, they will be able to complete the task quickly and efficiently. Development of maximal power for

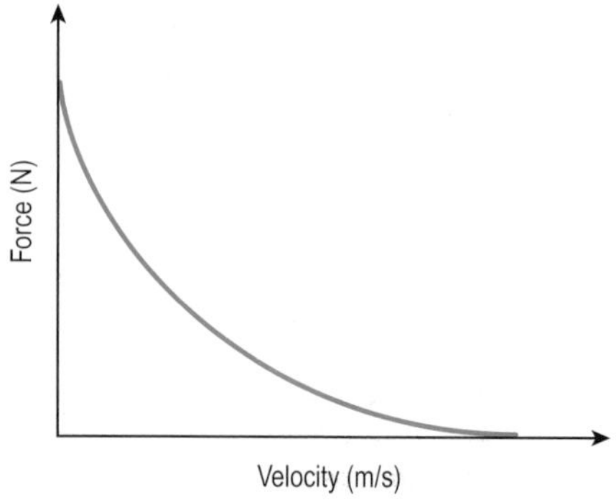

Figure 6.1 Graph to show the force–velocity relationship in muscle

a task is the combination of muscle strength required for the task and the skill and ability of the person to coordinate the movement pattern required to carry out the task. There are many factors which contribute to a person's ability to perform a task. However practice of the specific task for which power is required will improve the neural mechanisms used for muscles to work together to achieve the task.

Energy pathways

Anaerobic energy pathways are used for the short explosive activities that require power. Activities lasting less than 10 seconds will utilize the adenosine triphosphate (ATP) – creatine phosphate (CP) system and those lasting about a minute will use energy derived from glycolysis.

Fatigue

The ability to resist fatigue is important in determining muscle power especially in tasks when the glycolysis energy pathway is utilized. Certain assessments for muscle power utilize fatigue as a marker of fitness.

Motivation

A high level of arousal is required for a person to achieve their maximal power output. Improved motivation for a task will increase the recruitment of motor units required for the task.

TRAINING ADAPTATIONS

If an appropriate training programme is used to increase power, there will first be an improvement in the ability of the person to carry out the training task. This will be as a result of learning the motor process required for the task with no associated increase in the size or strength of the muscle carrying out the task. This process is specific to the task being carried out. The muscle being used for the task then shows an increase in strength without an associated increase in cross-sectional area either because of improved neural activation or because of changes in connective tissue in the muscle. Finally the muscle used for the task will start to increase in cross-sectional area.

PRINCIPLES OF EXERCISE DESIGN TO INCREASE POWER

Power output is dependent on muscle strength, the ability of a person to carry out a particular task in a coordinated manner and the energy supply for the task; therefore, an exercise programme to increase power should take these factors into consideration.

Muscle strength should be improved with a resistance training programme as described in Chapter 4, tailored to the needs of the individual and based on the principles of overload, specificity and reversibility. For athletes this may involve multiple sets of 4–8 RM. For those with lower initial muscular fitness one set of 8–10 RM may be suitable. The exercise should be carried out at the specific speed and in the range of the required muscle work if possible. Considerations such as safety, starting position and equipment are similar to those for strength training.

Once a good base of muscle strength has been developed, fast force development exercises can be added to the training regime.

The task required should be practised as part of the training programme and can be utilized within it. For example a sprinter may practise sprinting using a tyre to drag along behind them to increase the intensity of the task.

Energy pathways can be stressed using short, high-intensity activities which use the muscles required for the task in a repeated manner. This is a type of interval training.

There may be a higher level of risk of injury when training for performance as the exercises used may require heavier loads, the exercise task may need to be carried out quickly and the person may be exercising repeatedly to a point of maximal effort. These factors should be taken into account when supervising this type of training.

ASSESSMENT OF POWER

To assess power the test used should involve the muscle groups used in the performance of the activity for which the person is being trained and the energy systems used in the performance of these tasks. There are standard anaerobic power tests but task-specific tests have also been devised. For patients this type of test may be more suitable. Certain functional tests such as the timed up and go test or the timed 10-metre walk will also test the work rate of the patient. There are various tests to measure the power output.

The Margaria power test

This is a test of the ATP – CP energy system. To carry out this test the subject has to run up a flight of nine steps as quickly as possible. Timing switches are placed on the third and ninth steps to start and stop the clock. The power output can be calculated by multiplying the weight of the person carrying out the test by their vertical displacement, divided by the time they took to do the test.

The Wingate test

This test has been developed to assess power output in cycling. There have been modifications to this test since it was first developed as a

30-second maximal effort test. Depending on the protocol, it can be used to assess the ATP – CP system or glycolysis for energy production. Details of how to carry out the test can be found in the further reading list at the end of this chapter.

Timed running or walking power tests

Short-distance, timed walks or sprints of maximal effort have been used to assess power output. These can be used for patients or athletes and the distance covered in the test can be related to the task for which the person is training. The person may perform two or three tests with full recovery between efforts and the fastest completion time is recorded. Other functional activities such as sit to stand can be used in a similar timed test to assess performance.

PRINCIPLES FOR ASSESSMENT

As with other types of testing, power tests should be carried out in a standardized manner using the same:

- activity or test
- type of muscle work at the same range in the same speed
- level of encouragement.

GUIDELINES FOR EXERCISE TO INCREASE POWER

The principles of overload, specificity and reversibility apply to muscle power training as they do to strength training programmes. Exercises to increase muscle power are specific to the muscle group used, the type of muscle contraction, the muscle range and the velocity of movement. It is therefore important to assess the person carefully so that a suitable training programme can be devised. This will include considering the age of the individual, their health status and fitness level, the rationale for increasing muscle power and their personal goals. The variables which can be manipulated in a muscle power training programme are the resistance, the number of repetitions, the number of sets and the speed of movement.

Type of muscle work

A power training programme usually includes dynamic, concentric or eccentric muscle work at slow and high velocity. The activity for which the person is training should be used within the training programme.

Intensity, frequency and duration

To improve muscle power a muscle-strengthening programme, as described in Chapter 4, should be used. Once a good base of muscle strength has been developed, a power component or fast force development exercises can be introduced as well. This requires one to three sets of three to six repetitions performed at 30–60% of 1 RM to be carried out at high velocity in the muscle group being trained but not to fatigue. If power needs to be improved in a specific activity, this can be incorporated into the training programme by using the activity to do interval training. The frequency of training should be similar to that for a strength training regime.

Progression and regression

Progression and regression of a muscle power training programme is carried out initially in a similar manner to that for strength training as described in Chapter 4. The regime can be progressed by increasing the number of repetitions, sets or the resistance being used. The fast force development component of the programme can be progressed by increasing the number of repetitions or sets. To regress the activity load, repetitions or sets can all be reduced. Figures 6.2–6.4 show a progressive training regime to improve muscle power for sit to stand. The final exercise in Figure 6.4 may then be carried out at speed.

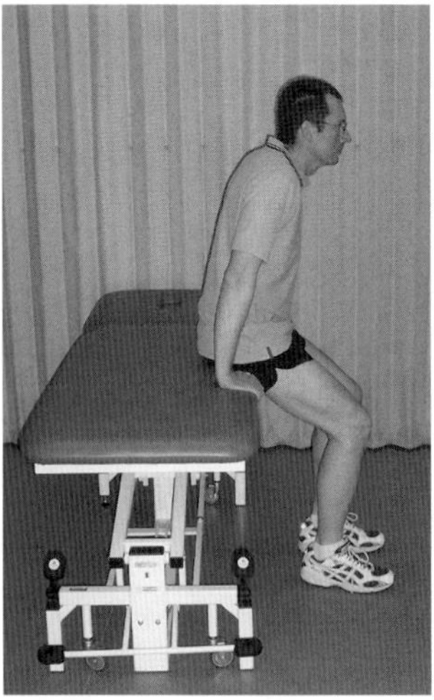

Figure 6.2 Sit to stand from a high plinth using arms

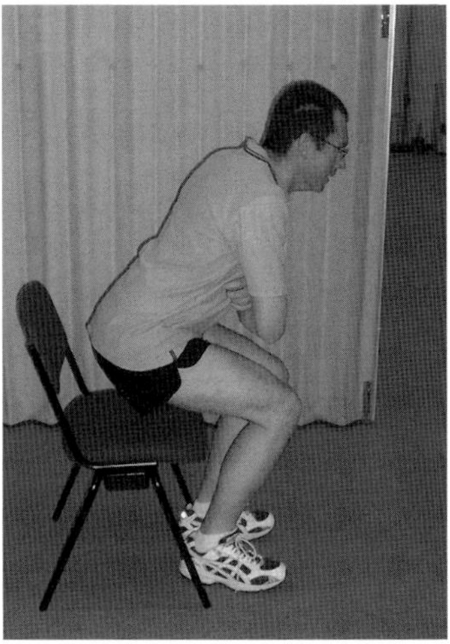

Figure 6.3 Sit to stand from a chair

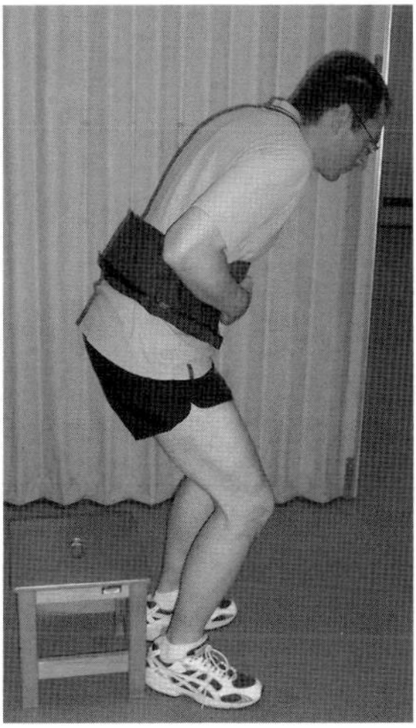

Figure 6.4 Sit to stand weighted from a stool

Further reading

ACSM Position Stand (2002) Progression models in resistance training for healthy adults. http//www.acsm-msse.org

Jones D, Round J (1990) Skeletal Muscle in Health and Disease. Manchester, UK: Manchester University Press.

Powers S, Howley E (1994) Exercise Physiology – Theory and Application to Fitness and Performance: 2nd edition. Madison, WI: WCB Brown and Benchmark.

CHAPTER SEVEN

Exercise to Increase Range of Movement and Flexibility

This chapter discusses factors affecting normal and limited range of movement. Methods of assessing range of movement are considered. Principles of exercise design, exercise prescription for increasing range of movement and the training adaptations seen in response to a successful exercise programme are addressed.

DEFINITION

Range of movement (ROM) refers to the range through which the bones of a joint can be moved.

Active ROM refers to the range of joint movement produced by a voluntary muscle contraction. Passive ROM is the range through which the joint can be moved by the application of an external force, such as that produced by a physiotherapist. For some joints active and passive ROM may be different.

Range can also be described in terms of the excursion of the muscle producing the movement; the position when the muscle is in its shortest position is termed 'inner range' (Figure 7.1), and the position when the muscle is at its longest is termed 'outer range' (Figure 7.3), with 'mid-range' falling in between the two (Figure 7.2).

Flexibility can be defined as the ROM of a joint or joints, or alternatively the freedom to move.

It is important that joints have a balance between stability, which limits abnormal direction and range of movement, and flexibility, for ease of movement. The type and position of a joint will determine the amount of movement available at the joint, along with some of the other specific factors listed below.

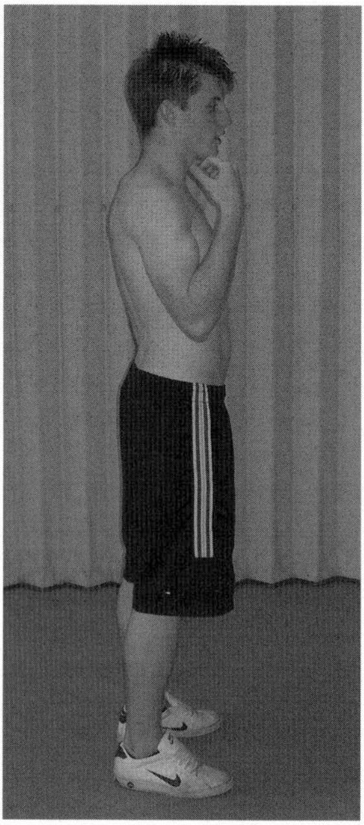

Figure 7.1 Elbow flexors in inner range

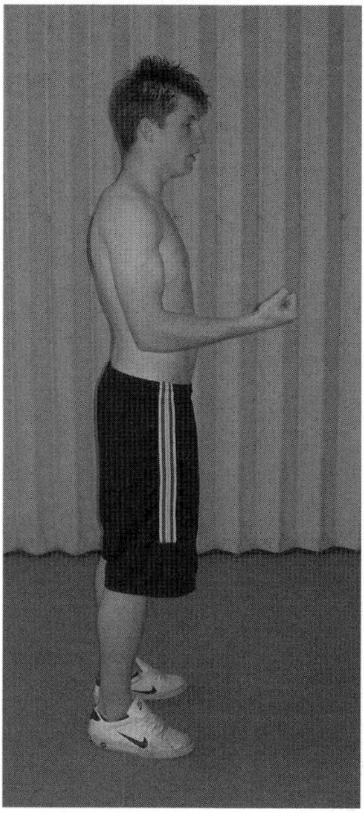

Figure 7.2 Elbow flexors in mid-range

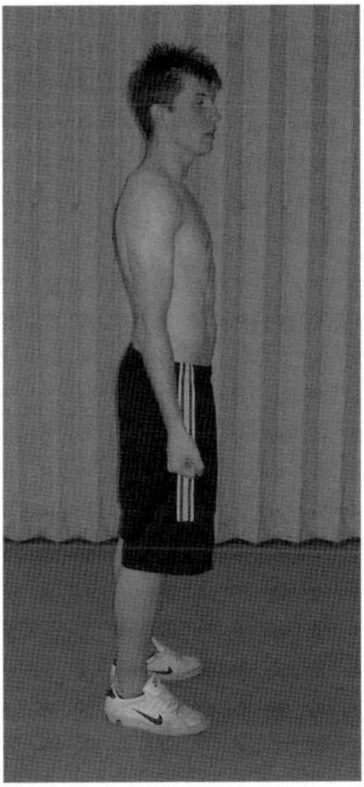

Figure 7.3 Elbow flexors in outer range

FACTORS LIMITING NORMAL RANGE OF MOVEMENT

Joint articular surfaces

The structure and shape of the articulating surfaces provide a complementary surface area over which the two bone ends can move. The specific bony shape determines the direction of movement available at the joint. The end of normal ROM may occur when the contact of the bony surfaces prevents further movement; for example, apposition of the posterior talus and the posterior tibia limit plantarflexion.

Ligaments around a joint

The length and tension of the ligaments limit joint movement as most ligaments are inelastic because they are made up of white fibrous collagen. When a ligament or tendon is at its full length no further movement in that direction is possible. In this way ligaments both restrict movement and direct the movement of the articulating surfaces over one another. An example of normal ROM, limited by ligaments, is the limitation of knee extension by the anterior cruciate ligament which prevents anterior sliding of the tibia on the femur.

Muscles

The position and tension of muscles can limit joint movement. Muscles are able to lengthen and allow movement; however they may restrict normal movement when they reach the limit of their extensibility, for example the length of the hip adductors limits the range of hip abduction. This is particularly seen in muscles that cross two joints. If a muscle is already approaching full length due to the position of one joint, there will be little extensibility remaining to allow movement of the second joint crossed by that muscle. For example when gastrocnemius is lengthened during knee extension, there may be insufficient extensibility remaining in the muscle to allow full dorsiflexion to take place.

Soft tissue

Apposition of soft tissue, or the point at which two surfaces touch each other, can also limit ROM; for example elbow flexion is normally limited by the forearm coming into contact with the biceps brachii in the upper arm.

FACTORS CAUSING ABNORMAL RANGE OF MOVEMENT

Mechanical disruption

Articular surfaces

Changes in the articular surfaces may restrict the movement of the joint. Deterioration of cartilage and formation of osteophytes on the joint surface in osteoarthritis limits ROM.

Loose body

A loose body within the joint can block the movement of the articular surfaces; the degree of limitation may vary as the loose body moves within the joint.

Bone

Fracture of a bone is likely to limit movement due to the altered mechanics of the fractured bone providing an unstable surface and disrupting the muscle action.

Ligaments

Damage to the joint ligaments can disrupt movement by failing to limit movement, hence producing an abnormal increase in ROM. They may also limit the movement through the loss of the ability to direct the movement of the articular surfaces.

Immobility

Imposed restriction of movement

Immobility may be due to an imposed restriction at a specific joint or joints secondary to injury or surgery. For example a period in plaster following a fracture, or deliberate restriction of movement following skin grafting.

Muscle

Immobility may also be due to the inability of the patient to access full ROM actively due to muscle weakness. This may be due to specific muscle weakness following local injury. Muscle weakness may also be the result of general deconditioning, as seen in some long-term intensive-care patients.

Tear or rupture of a muscle will disrupt the muscle filaments and the ability of the muscle to contract.

Neurological disorders

Absence of or change in neural control, due to upper or lower motor neurone disorders or brain injury or pathology, may cause a muscle to become denervated or have altered muscle innervation and therefore restrict the ROM available actively. An example of this is the loss of range of dorsiflexion secondary to foot drop.

Imbalance of muscle activity secondary to neurological disorders, such as that seen in spasticity, may also limit the ability to move through range resulting in the loss of range.

Decreased functional range

Immobility may also be due to a person not using the full normal ROM during their daily activities and therefore losing the extremes of movement; for example an older person who may spend a lot of time sitting and walks with a stooped posture is likely to lose some range of hip extension.

Articular structures

After prolonged immobilization, 32 weeks, the articular structures become the main limiting factor to movement (Trudel and Uhthoff 2000). The mechanism of intra-articular limitation is not clear, although the proliferation of intra-articular connective tissue, increase in collagen cross-linking and adaptive shortening of the capsule have all been suggested (Trudel and Uhthoff 2000).

Muscle

The lack of longitudinal force through a muscle during immobilization leads to tissue remodelling to accommodate the new shortened resting length. Muscles immobilized in a shortened position over a period of time demonstrate a reduction in sarcomeres (Goldspink et al 1974), and an increase in the proportion of connective tissue which results in a decrease in joint ROM and compliance of the muscle (Williams 1988). These changes in sarcomeres can be seen as early as 24 hours after immobilization (McLachlan 1983). There is evidence from animal studies demonstrating that after a period of 2 weeks of immobilization the main factor limiting movement is muscle shortening.

Collagen

After a period of immobilization there is a change to the organization of the collagen within the muscle, leading to an increase in the number of perpendicularly orientated collagen fibres, which connect two adjacent muscle fibres (Jarvinen et al 2002). Chains of collagen molecules contain cross-links which weld them into a strong unit. It has been suggested that during immobilization there is a change in chemical structure and loss of water within the collagen which leads to the fibres coming into close contact with one another. This close contact is thought to lead to the formation of abnormal crossbridges, leading to an increase in tissue stiffness (Alter 2004).

Scar tissue and adhesions

Following soft-tissue injury fibrous adhesions form between structures, and the healing process of the damaged structures produces fibrous scar tissue in place of the original tissue. This fibrous tissue is not very extensible, and therefore may limit ROM. In active scar tissue the production of collagen exceeds the breakdown of collagen and more cross-links are formed, which causes the tissue to become more resistant to stretching. This may occur following trauma to the joint itself, such as following an anterior cruciate ligament tear, or trauma unrelated to the joint, for example a burn to the anterior aspect of the lower limb may limit knee flexion due to the tight scar tissue.

Abnormal apposition of soft tissue

The movement of a joint may be prematurely blocked by apposition of soft tissue, for example in obesity or extreme muscle hypertrophy. Swelling of, or around, a joint may also physically restrict movement, although pain may limit movement before a physical restriction.

Pain

In the acute stages of injury or inflammation pain may often be the limiting factor to movement; however pain may also limit movement in chronic conditions such as arthritis.

Psychological factors

Movement may also be limited by psychological factors such as fear of movement, for example fear of pain or injury.

TRAINING ADAPTATIONS SEEN FOLLOWING EXERCISE TO INCREASE RANGE OF MOVEMENT

Exercise is able to increase ROM that is limited by soft-tissue shortening, adhesions, scar tissue or muscle weakness. Exercise may also decrease pain and oedema, and allow a subsequent increase in ROM. Exercise cannot influence ROM which is limited due to mechanical problems such as a loose body.

Soft tissues

Stretching increases the extensibility of soft tissues and can therefore increase ROM. Stretching produces viscous deformation that is a mechanical response to a stretch.

Muscles

Muscles adapt to their habitual length by the addition or removal of sarcomeres in series. The muscle can be lengthened by sustained stretching with casts or serial splinting which produce sustainable structural changes (Harvey et al 2002). It is thought that the isometric tension produced by a passive stretch stimulates protein synthesis and increases growth of muscle when it is in a lengthened state (Goldspink 1977). Decreases in muscle tension of 30% have been demonstrated after a 90-second stretch; however this adaptation is reversed within minutes of removing the stretch, suggesting that short-duration stretching may not be effective in increasing muscle length (Harvey et al 2002). The studies investigating the effects of stretching on muscle length have mainly been carried out with subjects without clinically significant contractures; therefore further research to underpin clinical practice is required.

Connective tissue

Changes that occur in the connective tissue within immobilized muscle can be prevented by a regimen of regular passive stretching; however this is not sufficient to prevent the loss of muscle length (Williams 1988).

Collagen

Exercise has been shown to decrease the number of cross-links and decrease passive stiffness, although this work was undertaken in rats (Gosselin et al 1998).

PRINCIPLES OF RANGE OF MOVEMENT AND FLEXIBILITY EXERCISE DESIGN

Exercise to maintain ROM

These exercises may be used in the healthy population to maintain normal flexibility and joint range, or by people at risk of losing ROM, for example a person confined to bed or a person with an area of denervated muscle.

End of available range

Exercises to maintain ROM should take the movements to the end of the available range. The purpose of these exercises is to maintain the strength and soft-tissue length required to access the full range.

Exercise to increase ROM

These exercises may be used in the healthy population to increase a normal range, for example in ballet dancers or gymnasts, or by people with abnormally limited ROM in an attempt to regain normal movement.

Cause of limitation

The cause of limitation and the effect on the structures involved should always be considered when prescribing the exercises. In some people full ROM may not be desirable due to the possibility of causing damage, for example in the early stages following a tendon repair, in which case activity within the permitted range would be encouraged. In other cases the person should aim to gain full ROM with the help of pain relief, for example following a burn injury.

Free active exercise

Starting position

Starting position should be selected to place the person in the optimal position for accessing the desired range. It is likely that the person will also have decreased muscle strength; therefore it is helpful to use a position in which gravity assists movement, or is counterbalanced. For example when working into the last third of shoulder flexion supine lying allows gravity to assist the movement (Figure 7.4), rather than working against gravity (Figure 7.5) in the upright position. In order to use eccentric muscle activity the person should have sufficient control over the movement.

Access range as it becomes available

If ROM is limited by pain or oedema then ROM exercises aim to access range as it becomes available. Exercise can reduce pain and oedema by increasing blood flow and lymphatic drainage to the area;

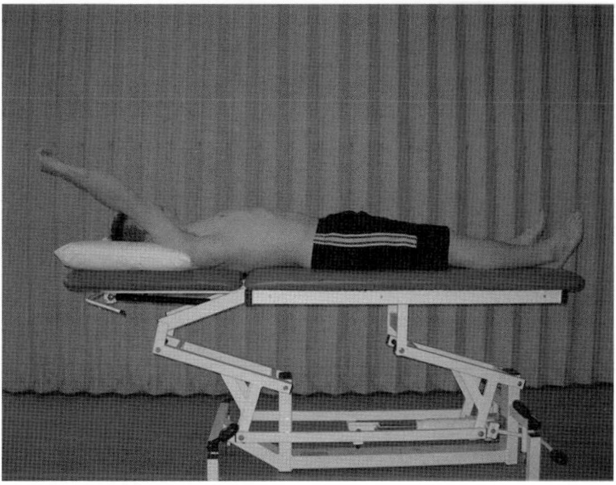

Figure 7.4 Shoulder flexion with gravity assisting

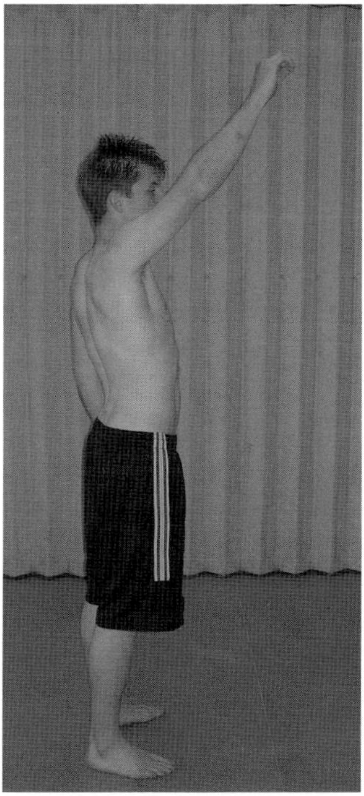

Figure 7.5 Shoulder flexion with gravity resisting

therefore gentle movement to the end of the available range may increase ROM.

Muscle strength and endurance

If muscle weakness is the primary cause of limitation then a muscle-strengthening programme will be the main exercise intervention. In addition for all people with restricted ROM as an increase in range is achieved the exercise regimen should be adapted to include strengthening and local muscle endurance into the new range to ensure that the person is able use the new range in daily activities.

Facilitate the movement

It may be useful to provide some kind of assistance to help the person reach the end ROM. This may be achieved by using support to counter the effects of gravity, for example 'walking the arm up a wall' for shoulder flexion (Figure 7.6) or resting the arm over a small gymball and reaching to the side for shoulder abduction (Figure 7.7). Reducing friction makes the production of movement easier, for example this can be achieved by placing the foot on a sliding board or sheet for lower limb movements (Figure 7.8). Auto-assisted exercises are also useful, whereby the unaffected limb can support the other limb through range; for example shoulder flexion can be assisted by clasping the hands together and moving the unaffected arm with the affected side (Figure 7.9). Stretch at the end of range can be applied in the absence of pain and where no further injury

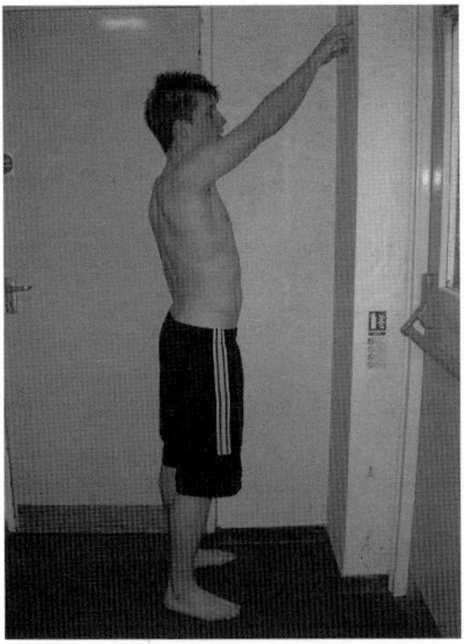

Figure 7.6 Shoulder flexion with support of wall

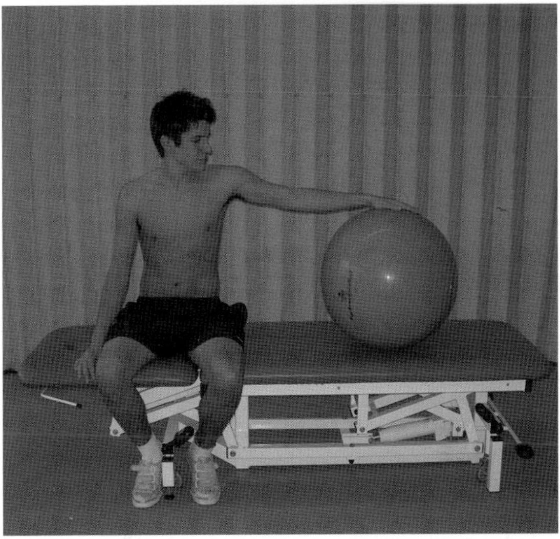

Figure 7.7 Shoulder abduction with assistance of ball

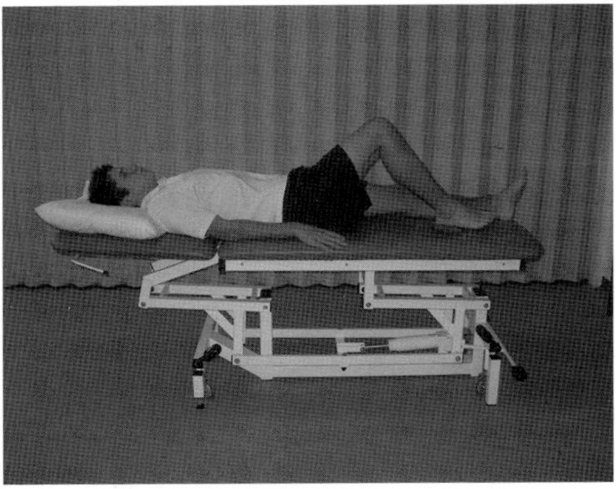

Figure 7.8 Knee flexion with reduced friction

would be caused, for example in late-stage rehabilitation. Body weight is often used to provide the stretching force (Figure 7.10).

Targets

It is important that the movements are performed to the end of the available range, and setting targets can help people achieve this

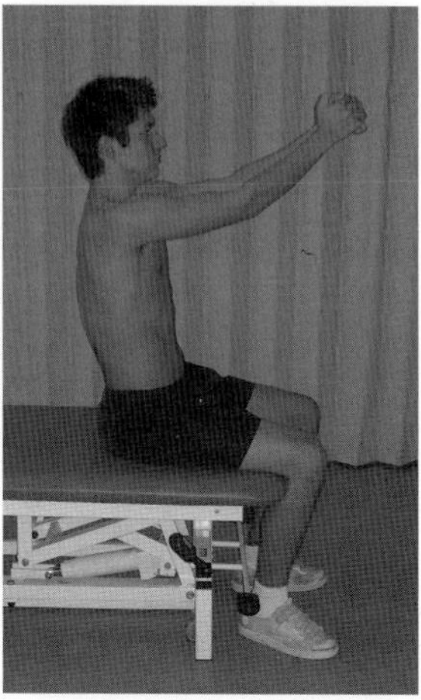

Figure 7.9 Shoulder flexion with autoassistance

Figure 7.10 Dorsiflexion with assistance of body weight

consistently; for example if a person is reaching up a wall to increase shoulder flexion, the wall can be marked at the highest point they can reach, they can then aim to reach further than that mark.

Static stretching exercises

When aiming to increase normal ROM or ROM limited by soft-tissue shortening, the exercises often take the soft tissues to the absolute limit of their available length and are also termed stretching exercises. In order to produce change in length the soft tissues must be taken to their elastic limit. It is recommended that stretching should be to the point of 'discomfort' or 'tension' but not into 'pain'. Alter (2004) suggests that the 'pain threshold', which is the lowest point of pain that the subject can recognize, can be used. This approach is not appropriate for people in the early or intermediate stages of rehabilitation following an injury or surgery, as damage may occur to healing tissues before the person reaches their pain threshold.

Ballistic stretching exercises

Ballistic stretching uses the momentum of the activity to move into the end of range and the elastic recoil of the muscle under stretch to move back away from the end of range. At one time ballistic stretches were thought to cause injury due to their rather uncontrolled nature, and also to cause increased tension in the muscle under stretch due to repeated activation of the tendon stretch reflex. However these concerns do not seem to be supported by the literature, and ballistic stretches form part of the American College of Sports Medicine's recommendation for activities to increase flexibility.

Proprioceptive neuromuscular facilitation (PNF)

The PNF techniques of 'hold–relax' and 'contract–relax' are specifically used to increase the range of movement. The principle of hold–relax is to achieve maximal relaxation in the tight muscle group that is limiting the movement by using the maximal relaxation achieved after a maximal contraction. During the technique the limb is taken to the end of available ROM and the patient is instructed to 'hold' the position whilst the physiotherapist applies measured resistance to build up a maximal isometric contraction in the muscle group that requires lengthening. Following this maximal contraction the instruction to relax is given whilst the limb is fully supported to allow maximal relaxation. The limb is then taken to the new end of ROM and the technique repeated.

Contract–relax works on the principle of reciprocal inhibition, whereby a maximal contraction is built up in the antagonistic muscle group to produce relaxation in the tight muscle group.

Other PNF techniques are also useful to increase ROM, the facilitatory nature of PNF can help to move into new ROM and PNF is also effective in muscle strengthening.

EXAMPLE EXERCISES

These are some example exercises to illustrate the points above.

- To increase knee flexion sitting with the foot on a ball, moving into flexion (Figure 7.11)
- To increase hip extension standing on a step holding onto a wall bar, swing leg back into extension (Figure 7.12)
- To increase external rotation of the shoulder, sitting with the arm supported on a plinth, moving to pick up beanbags (Figure 7.13).

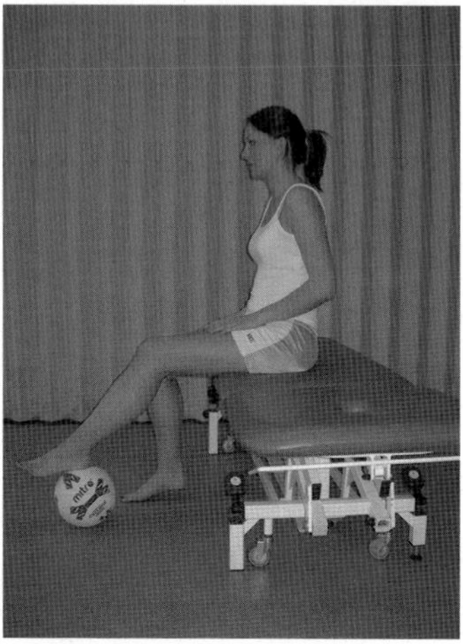

Figure 7.11 Knee flexion with assistance of ball

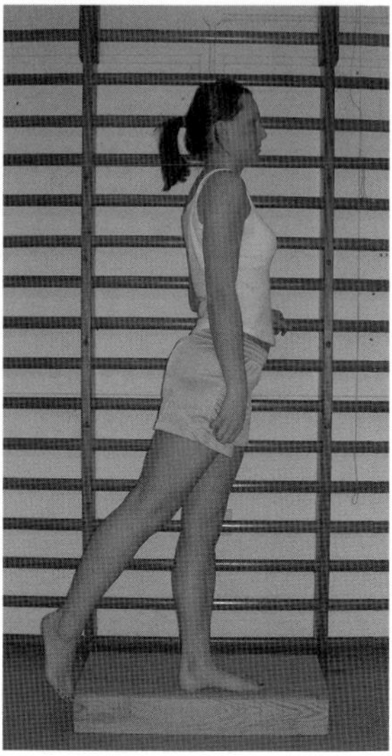

Figure 7.12 Hip flexion with assistance of momentum

Figure 7.13 External rotation of shoulder with targets

ASSESSMENT OF RANGE OF MOVEMENT

Joint ROM is often assessed clinically by visual estimation or goniometry. Both of these methods are subject to error, although they are often sufficient in practice. Healthcare professionals have been shown to be more accurate in visual estimation of ROM than the general public. The accuracy of goniometry varies by as much as 45% according to the joint movement being assessed, and also the part of the range being measured. Intrarater reliability has been shown to be moderate for goniometry; therefore it may be an acceptable means of assessment if used by the same physiotherapist. However as there is poor interrater reliability it may be less suitable for use if different physiotherapists are assessing the same person.

A tape measure is also used in clinical practice to measure range of movement; for example in the thoracic spine the increase in distance between C7 and T12 can be used to measure flexion. More specific tools are also available to measure spinal curves and ROM, such as the Flexicurve, which is a flexible tape measure.

If a high degree of accuracy is required in the assessment of range of movement then computerized electronic motion analysers may be more useful; however these are not used in day-to-day clinical practice.

Functional goals and markers can also be used to monitor progress; for example whether a person can reach to brush their hair, or reach a target during an exercise.

The sit and reach test is a standardized test to assess flexibility of the back and hamstrings. The person undergoing testing sits on the floor with shoes off, knees against the floor and feet against a 'sit and reach table' or bench. After three practice attempts they reach their hands as far along the tabletop in front of them as possible and the distance is recorded. The table has a 15-cm overhang, so reaching 15 cm along the table top would bring them in line with their toes.

PRINCIPLES OF ASSESSMENT

- A standard starting position should be used and measurements taken from the same place each time.
- It should be clear whether the recorded ROM is active or passive.
- The limiting factor to movement should be noted.
- Normal ROM varies; therefore movement should be compared with the other limb where relevant.
- The position of adjacent joints should be considered to account for passive insufficiency.

GUIDELINES FOR PRESCRIPTION OF EXERCISE TO INCREASE OR MAINTAIN RANGE OF MOVEMENT

Owing to the conflicting published research the guidelines below are general recommendations; however if pain or inflammation are experienced following ROM exercises, or ROM is reduced following exercise, then the intensity and frequency of exercise should be reduced.

Intensity

- For increasing soft-tissue length, the movement should be taken to the point of discomfort, provided this is not causing damage to healing tissues.

Frequency

- Exercises to maintain flexibility should be performed 2–3 days a week on all major muscle groups.
- There should be at least four repetitions per muscle group.
- In healthy groups wishing to increase ROM beyond the normal ROM then stretching up to twice daily may be desired.
- Research seems to suggest that the more often the movement is undertaken the more improvement is seen.

Duration

- Stretch should be maintained at the end of ROM for 10–30 seconds.
- For long-term structural changes in shortened tissues longer-term casting or serial splinting is required.

PROGRESSION AND REGRESSION FOR EXERCISES TO INCREASE RANGE OF MOVEMENT

Movement should be facilitated by using gravity, but well controlled in the early stages to prevent further injury (Figures 7.14 and 7.15).

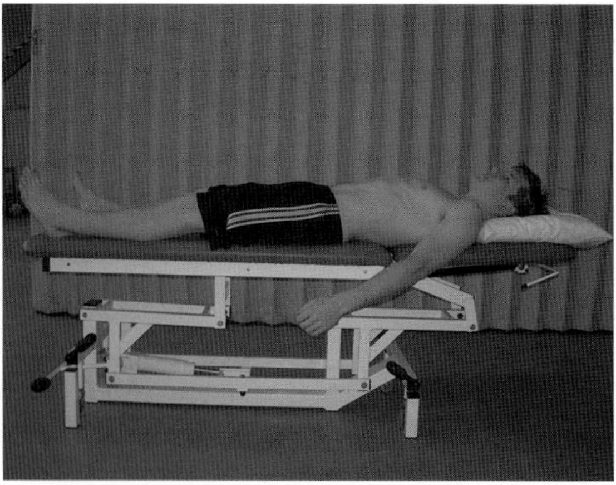

Figure 7.14 Shoulder extension with gravity assisting

As range increases the target should be moved to ensure that end ROM is reached in order to gain further improvement. If there is no danger of causing further damage or pain, stretch can be applied to the end of range of movement (Figure 7.16). As range is gained more functional tasks should be introduced along with muscle-strengthening activities (Figure 7.17).

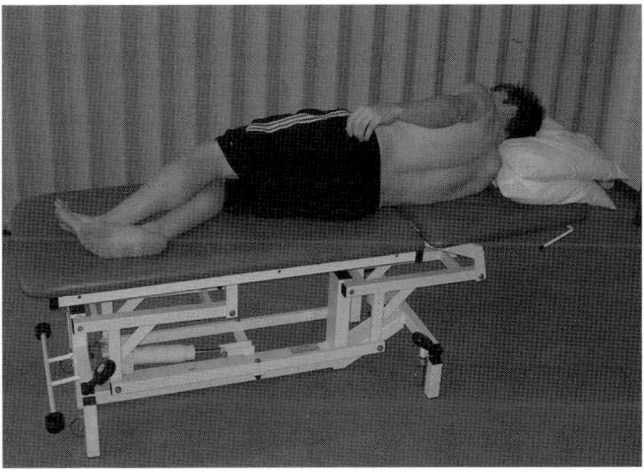

Figure 7.15 Shoulder extension in side lying with gravity counterbalanced

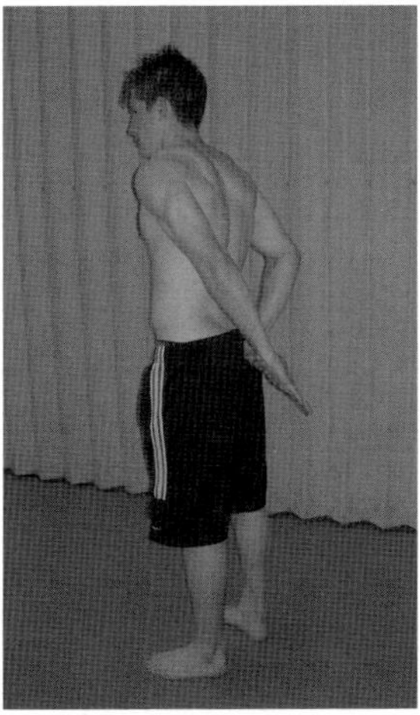

Figure 7.16 Shoulder extension with stretch

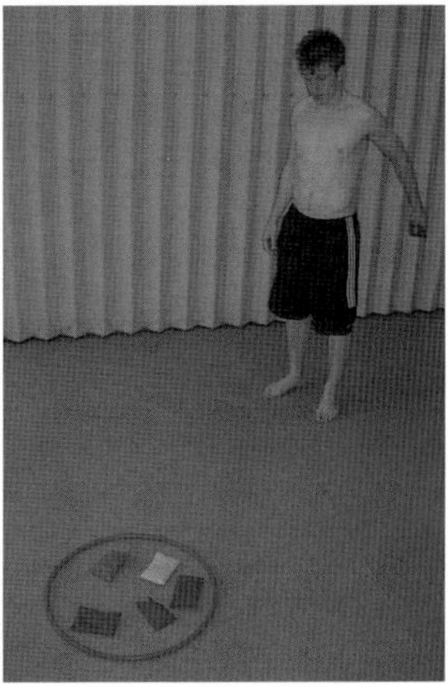

Figure 7.17 Shoulder extension during functional activity

References

Alter M (2004) Science of Flexibility: 3rd edition. Champaign, IL: Human Kinetics.

Goldspink DF (1977) The influence of immobilization and stretch on protein turnover of rat skeletal muscle. Journal of Physiology 264(1): 267–282.

Goldspink G, Tabary C, Tabary JC, et al (1974) Effect of denervation on the adaptation of sarcomere number and muscle extensibility to the functional length of the muscle. Journal of Physiology 236(3): 733–742.

Gosselin L, Adams C, Cotter TA, McCormick RJ, Thomas DP (1998) Effect of exercise training on passive stiffness in locomotor skeletal muscle: role of extracellular matrix. Journal of Applied Physiology 85: 1011–1016.

Harvey L, Herbert R, Crosbie J (2002) Does stretching induce lasting changes in joint ROM? A systematic review. Physiotherapy Research International 7(1): 1–13.

Jarvinen TA, Jozsa L, Kannus P, Jarvinen TA, Jarvinen M (2002) Organization and distribution of intramuscular connective tissue in normal and immobilized skeletal muscles. An immohistochemical, polarization and scanning electron microscope study. Journal of Muscle Research and Cell Motility 23: 245–254.

McLachlan EM (1983) Rapid adjustment of sarcomere length in tenotomized muscles depends on an intact innervation. Neuroscience Letters 35: 127–133.

Trudle G, Uhthoff HK (2000) Contractures secondary to immobility: Is the restriction articular or muscular? An experimental longitudinal study in the rat knee. Archives of Physical Medicine and Rehabilatation 81: 6–13.

Williams PE (1988) Effect of intermittent stretch on immobilised muscle. Annals of the Rheumatic Diseases 47: 1014–1016.

Further reading

Pollock M, Gaesser G, Butcher JD, et al (1998) The recommended quantity and quality of exercise for developing and maintaining cardiorespiratory and muscular fitness, and flexibility in healthy adults. Medicine and Science in Sports and Exercise 30(6): 371–378.

Thacker S (2004) The impact of stretching on sports injury risk: a systematic review of the literature. Medicine and Science in Sports and Exercise 36(3): 371–378.

Tortora J (2005) Principles of Human Anatomy: 10th edition. Hoboken, NJ: Wiley & Sons.

Williams PE, Goldspink G (1978) Changes in sarcomere length and physiological properties in immobilised muscle. Journal of Anatomy 127: 459–468.

Prescription of Home Exercise Programmes

This chapter discusses the prescription of exercises to be carried out at home, and the importance of home exercise programmes in producing and maintaining change in exercise ability. Considerations specific to home exercise design, including equipment and safety, are highlighted. The challenges of monitoring and progression of home exercises are addressed, and some examples of exercises suitable for the home are given.

THE IMPORTANCE OF HOME EXERCISES

In order to achieve optimal training effects, cardiovascular exercise should be performed 3–5 times a week, and muscle strength and power training should be performed 2–3 times a week. To achieve this it will usually be necessary for a patient to carry out some exercises independently in between visits to the physiotherapist. When designing an exercise programme it is essential to consider which exercises will be carried out at home, as it may be necessary to make modifications to some exercises in order to adapt them for the home environment.

In many cases it will be necessary to continue the exercise programme after discharge from the supervision of a physiotherapist, in order to maintain and build on the training effects achieved. Implementing independent, home-based exercise early in the treatment programme may help to develop new exercise habits and increase long-term exercise adherence.

PRINCIPLES OF HOME EXERCISE DESIGN

Clear instruction

It is important that home exercises are performed correctly, and sufficient time should be allocated during the treatment session to ensure that the exercises are understood. Most physiotherapists provide a handout of the home exercise programme with a written explanation and pictures, and computer packages are available to help produce these. Although these handouts are a useful 'aide-memoire' they should never be given in place of an explanation and demonstration, and should be individually tailored to the patient's requirements. This is particularly important if the exercises to be carried out independently are not the same as the exercises that have been carried out during the supervised treatment with the physiotherapist.

When teaching exercises the principles of motor learning (Chapter 2) should be considered, and the exercise should be explained, demonstrated and the patient asked to carry it out for themself as part of the learning process. Breaking down the exercise into its component parts, by teaching the starting position and then the activity required, may make it easier for the patient to remember the exercise correctly. It is advisable to be specific about the starting position for each exercise, as a change in starting position may change the effect of an exercise. For example, if using 'sitting' as the starting position, the type of chair to be used should be specified; sitting in an old armchair which may be quite low will produce more hip and knee flexion than sitting on a firm dining chair (Figure 8.1).

Once the patient is clear how to perform the exercise, the specific frequency, intensity and duration required should be prescribed.

The home exercises should be reviewed at the next visit. This is best done by asking the patient to demonstrate the exercises

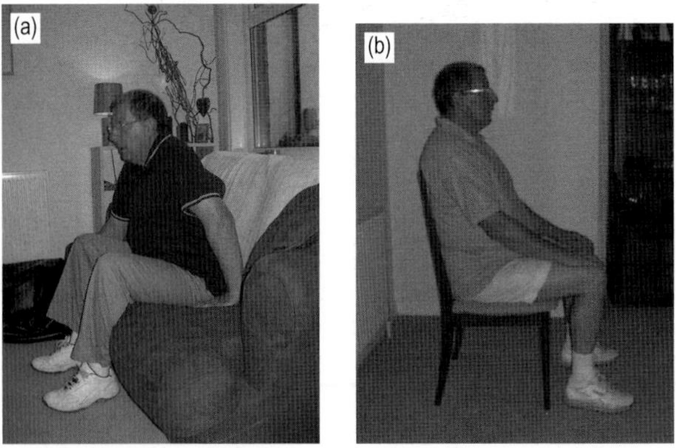

Figure 8.1 (a) Low chair leading to increased hip flexion in starting position. (b) Correct starting position in firm chair

that they have been performing independently. It is not sufficient to ask *if* they are doing the exercises, as what is important is *how* they are doing the exercises. It is quite possible that a patient may be performing the exercises regularly but they may be ineffective (Figure 8.2), or more importantly unsafe (Figure 8.3), due to a small alteration in the way that the patient is carrying out the exercise.

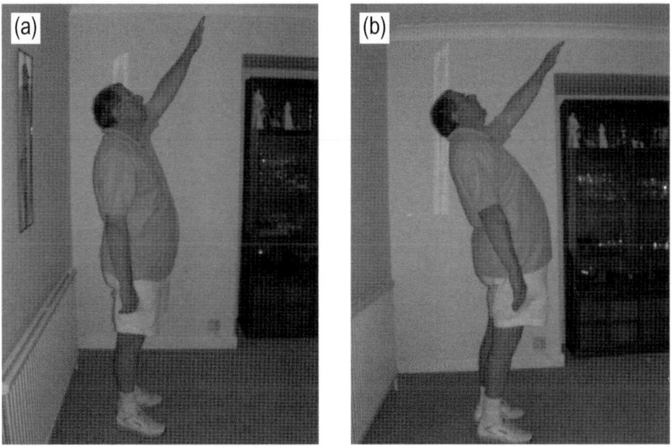

Figure 8.2 (a) Correct performance of exercise to increase range of movement (ROM) shoulder flexion. (b) Ineffective performance of the exercise due to back extension compensating for poor shoulder flexion

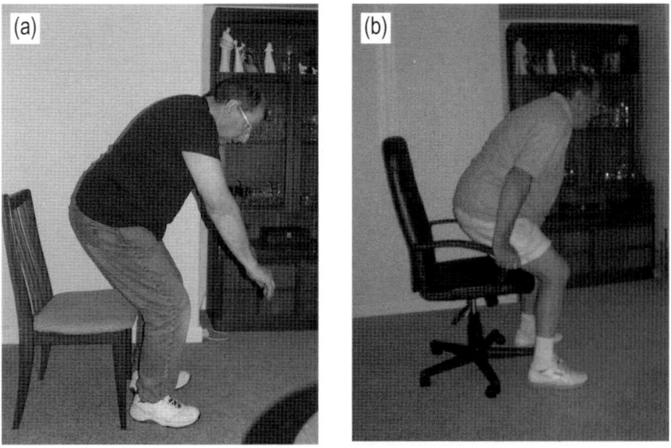

Figure 8.3 (a) Safe performance of repeated sit to stand exercise. (b) Unsafe performance of repeated sit to stand exercise using a chair with wheels

Practicality

A home exercise programme is unlikely to be followed if it is impractical for the person to carry out; therefore the physiotherapist should discuss with the patient how their exercise programme will fit into their daily life. This should address where they will do the exercises, what equipment is available to them and when they can identify time to do the exercises.

Environment

It should not be assumed that home exercises will be carried out in the home – the person may attend a gym, or may prefer to do the exercises in their lunch break at work; therefore the exercises must be adapted to the setting used.

The exercises may need to be tailored to fit the space available; for example walking could be adapted to marching on the spot to achieve the same result. In addition to modifying the exercise, the physiotherapist can also make recommendations about changing the environment, for example walking outside. Changing the environment can also be used to modify exercises; for example changing a walking route to incorporate a gradient can be used to increase exercise intensity.

The physiotherapist needs to ensure that the home exercises will be carried out in a safe manner, as they may not be in a position to carry out a home visit. Highlighting common safety issues for low-risk patients is sufficient. For example, if a bar is needed for stability during an exercise the physiotherapist should check what will be used at home: a kitchen sideboard or stair rail would be suitable alternatives; a high-backed chair which may be unstable would not be suitable. Trip hazards are another common issue when exercising in the home.

Equipment

Many exercise goals can be achieved without specific exercise equipment; however it is always useful to ask the patient if they have access to any equipment that can be incorporated into the programme.

Cardiovascular exercise is relatively easy to perform without specialized equipment. If a treadmill or an exercise bicycle is available then the patient should be advised how to use it safely and effectively. Some people attend a local gym and it is useful to discuss with them which pieces of gym equipment would be most appropriate for them to use. In the absence of equipment, activities such as walking, stair climbing, step ups and repeated sit to stand are some examples of exercises that can be used to increase cardiovascular fitness without specialist equipment.

Providing resistance for muscle strength, power and endurance training can be more challenging as once the appropriate weight has been prescribed it needs to be reproduced at home. Some people will have access to weights through local gyms, or may prefer to invest in their own set of weights. However it is usually possible to produce home-made weights which are just as effective. Resistance can be added to the upper limbs by lifting everyday items such as cans of food of the appropriate weight. Home-made weights can be made by filling small water bottles with rice, sand or water to produce the required weight. Adding resistance to the lower limb is a little more challenging due to the difficulty of fixing the weight to the ankle. A pair of tights can be weighted with rice and then secured (not too tightly) around the ankle to produce an ankle weight (Figure 8.4).

Elastic resistance bands can easily be provided for home use once the correct level of resistance has been determined. If these are used it is vital that the correct use of the band is clearly demonstrated as simple alterations, such as doubling up the band or attaching the band at a different angle, will significantly change the exercise by altering the resistance applied or the range through which it is applied. The bands should be checked for wear and tear prior to every use and it should not be forgotten that resistance bands become stretched through repeated use and do not last forever. If it is necessary to attach the elastic resistance band to something to carry out the exercise, this should be done in a secure and stable manner. More details on using elastic resistance bands safely can be found in Chapter 4.

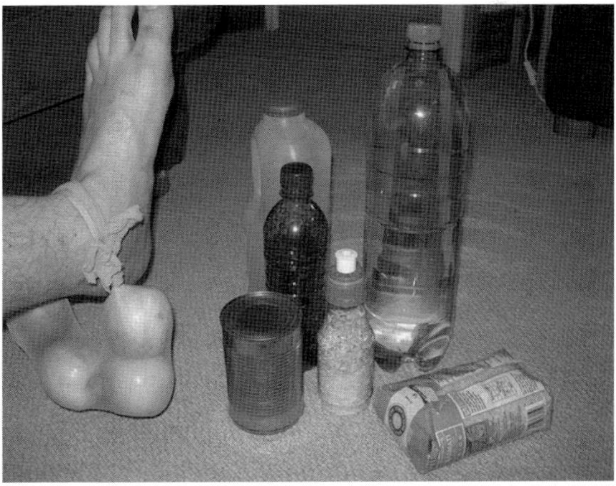

Figure 8.4 Selection of home-made weights

Prescription

The recommended prescription for home exercise programmes is, of course, no different from any supervised programme. It is very important to give the person specific guidance as to the amount of exercise required in order to achieve training effects whilst avoiding over-training.

Frequency

How often people are asked to carry out their home exercise programme should be related to the total amount of exercise that the person will carry out in a week. For example if a patient is attending physiotherapy twice a week to carry out strengthening exercises in the department, then, according to guidelines, they should carry out their exercises only once a week at home. This is in contrast to a patient who has been discharged from a cardiac rehabilitation programme who should be advised to continue their cardiovascular exercise 3–5 times a week at home.

Intensity

Anecdotal evidence suggests that intensity is the hardest parameter to target correctly at home. It is vital to get intensity right, as exercise performed at too low intensity will be less effective, and if the intensity is too high there is a danger of injury or untoward cardiovascular event.

Intensity of local muscle exercise is set by the weight prescribed, and the number of repetitions; therefore if the physiotherapist has been specific, and the weight has been accurately reproduced at home, the exercise should fall within the target intensity.

Intensity of cardiovascular exercise is more difficult to control, as it is more easily affected by motivation and needs to be sustained over longer periods of time.

Studies that have found home exercise programmes to be less effective than supervised hospital-based programmes have suggested that differences seen were because the unsupervised home programmes were carried out at a lower intensity. Education regarding the importance of training intensity, a realistic target intensity, reinforcement and reassurance when working with the patient should all help them continue to work at the correct intensity. Some patients monitor their intensity by checking heart rate, using either their own heart rate monitor or by checking their pulse. Borg (1998) can also be used to monitor exercise intensity; however general guidance explaining to the patient how they should feel whilst exercising, for example 'warm and sweaty' or 'short of breath but still able to hold a conversation', is often used in the home setting for determining exercise intensity.

Duration

If the exercise programme requires a large variety of exercises to be performed they may be split up to make smaller, more manageable, daily exercise sessions to fit in with the person's lifestyle. For example it may be desirable to alternate cardiovascular exercises one day with strengthening exercises the next. It may also be more manageable for a person to chunk their exercise into three sets of 10 minutes of cardiovascular exercise than to identify a 30-minute period in the day when they can do the whole programme.

Progression/regression

Unless the person is attending for regular review by the physiotherapist progression of home exercise programmes can be difficult to manage without specific instruction at the time of providing the programme.

Muscle strength, power and endurance

An example of the challenges when progressing resistance training is the use of an elastic resistance band for a strengthening programme; over time the training effects will allow the patient to perform the exercise more easily and the tendency is to continue to perform more and more repetitions of the exercise. Whilst this may have some local muscle endurance benefits, it is not progressing strength gains. If they remain under the supervision of a physiotherapist the patient should be reviewed and progressed to the next resistance band. If the patient is expected to progress their own exercise they should be told that when they are able to do 10–15 repetitions easily they should move on to a heavier resistance, bringing them back into the range of 6–10 repetitions.

Cardiovascular exercise

Cardiovascular exercise can also be challenging to progress. As training effects occur, the person will be able to sustain the activity for longer, and although this increase in duration will continue to produce beneficial effects, the exercise programme can become impractical due to the time commitment required. It is often useful to advise patients that once they can carry out 30 minutes of exercise and still feel quite comfortable then they should perform the exercise harder or faster, rather than continue to increase the exercise time indefinitely.

If patients are correctly monitoring their heart rate or perceived exertion they will automatically increase the work rate with which they perform the exercise, because as the benefits of the training effects start to show a higher work rate will be required to produce the same heart rate or Borg rating. However people often get accustomed to performing the exercise at a certain speed, or for a set time period. It is important to teach patients how to progress their programme by increasing the intensity or the duration to continue to gain further benefits.

Safety

It is essential that the patient is able to carry out the exercise programme safely when following their programme independently.

Some key safety considerations are as follows.

Accurate performance of the exercise

It is vital that the exercise is performed correctly to avoid undue stress or risk of injury. The actual movements being carried out and the intensity with which they are being performed should be checked at each review appointment.

Correct prescription

Some patients may push themselves beyond the safe limits that have been recommended for the exercise. It is a common belief that 'the more the better' applies to exercise, and patients may be performing far more than the recommended amount of exercise, which may be detrimental in terms of overtraining or cause specific irritation to their condition. The amount of exercise that people are doing should be regularly reviewed.

Effect of exercise/change in condition

As it is impossible to predict the effect that a particular exercise will have on an individual it is also important to check for any adverse responses to the exercises. It is important to ask how the person feels during and after performing the exercise, and to check that they are not experiencing pain or other undesirable symptoms during or after the exercises.

When instructing the patient in the exercise programme in the first instance they should be given the appropriate cautions and warnings about when to stop performing the exercises. They should clearly understand the limits of the exercise in relation to their stage of rehabilitation, for example 'do not move into pain'. Patients should be aware of adverse changes in their signs and symptoms, such as increased pain and swelling, and be advised to cease exercising until they have been reviewed by their physiotherapist. Patients should also be advised when and how to seek urgent help in case of a serious untoward event.

Equipment

The physiotherapist is responsible for any equipment that they provide or advice given to the patient regarding exercising at home. Equipment should regularly be checked for safety, for example elastic resistance bands should be checked for tears. How patients are adapting and carrying out exercises at home should be checked regularly and noted. General advice can be given about the use of existing home equipment and equipment in the local gym, but without a home visit it is impossible to check the safety of this equipment; therefore it is advisable to tell patients to seek induction from the exercise advisors in the gyms and to ensure their own equipment is well maintained in line with the manufacturer's guidelines.

EXAMPLES OF EXERCISES ADAPTED FOR HOME

A stable item, at a suitable height, should be used to help the patient balance when performing exercises in standing, for example to increase range of movement at the hip (Figure 8.5).

Home-made weights can be used to provide resistance for endurance training of the elbow flexors (Figure 8.6).

Cardiovascular training at home may be carried out by stair climbing in restricted space (Figure 8.7) or outdoors through walking programmes which can also provide a variety of gradients and more interest (Figure 8.8).

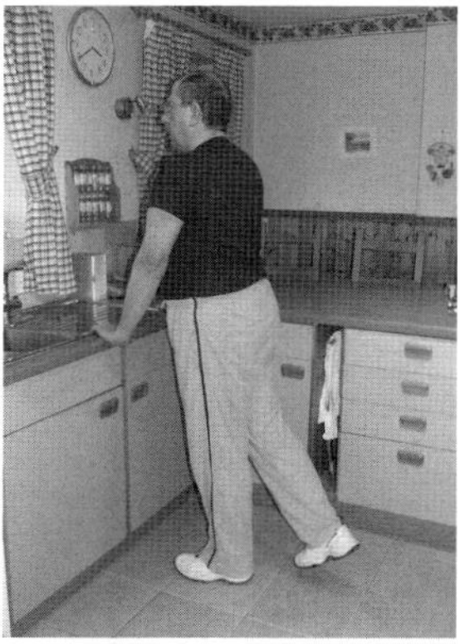

Figure 8.5 Exercise to increase hip extension

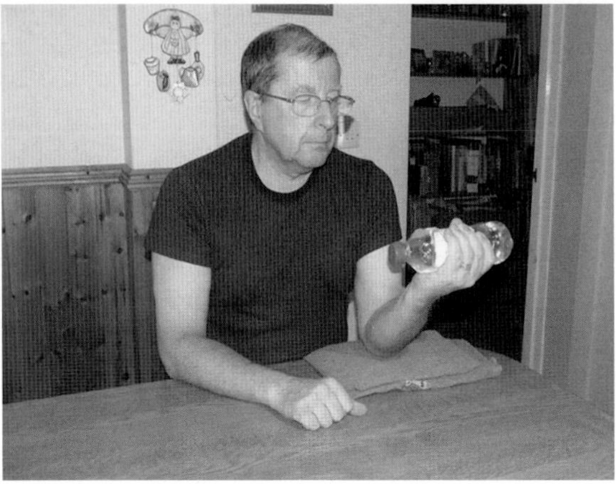

Figure 8.6 Resistance training of the elbow flexors with weight

Figure 8.7 Cardiovascular training using stairs

Figure 8.8 Cardiovascular training using outdoor walking

Reference

Borg G (1998) Borg's Perceived Exertion and Pain Scales. Champaign, IL: Human Kinetics.

Group Exercise

This chapter gives an overview of group exercise. It explains the points to consider when deciding whether a group exercise programme is suitable in relation to the patient, the physiotherapist and the available space. The chapter also discusses how to plan and set up an appropriate exercise programme for a group of patients.

THE VALUE OF GROUP EXERCISE

Group exercise is widely used by physiotherapists for a variety of reasons. It may be used for:

- people with a specific condition, for example a cardiac rehabilitation class for patients following myocardial infarction or for those with heart failure
- patients at a similar stage of rehabilitation such as a group of patients who are now able to weight bear fully following knee injury
- people who require a particular treatment approach, for example a group of people learning to manage chronic back pain whilst exercising.

There are many advantages to exercising in a group for both patients and the people taking the group. The transition into a group may mark an important step in the patient's recovery and show that progress is being made. For these patients and those who start their rehabilitation in a group, there are both psychological and social benefits to exercising in a group such as the opportunity to mix with people who are in a similar situation to themselves, to share experiences and to offer mutual support and encouragement. These benefits may enhance the overall improvement that may be made by an individual patient during the rehabilitation process. Patients may also be more likely to attend for a group exercise class because of the social support offered by the other members of the group and the feeling of 'letting the others down' if they do not attend.

For the people taking the group, it is usually an enjoyable, rewarding experience. There is also the obvious benefit of treating several patients together; however patients should be treated in the group situation only if they will benefit from this type of treatment. Groups should not be used for purely economical reasons.

CONSIDERATIONS FOR GROUP EXERCISE

When planning to set up a group exercise class, considerations fall into three broad areas: the patient, the physiotherapist and the environment. Safety considerations encompass all of these.

The patient

Assessment

Some patients will join a class as their primary treatment intervention and others will transfer into the class after a period of individual treatment or even continue to have some individual treatments alongside their attendance at the class. Prior to joining an exercise class, an individual patient assessment should take place. The assessment should include consideration of whether the patient is suitable to join the class.

For a patient who has been receiving individual treatment, the stage of rehabilitation and ability must be appropriate for the exercise group that they will join. Relevant past medical history or co-morbidities which could make the group exercise class unsuitable for the patient may become apparent at the assessment. If a patient with chronic obstructive pulmonary disease who was to join a pulmonary rehabilitation class also had osteoarthritis in their right knee and used a walking aid, it would usually be possible to safely adapt the exercises in the class for the patient without disrupting the class for other individuals. However certain other co-morbidities such as cardiac disease may make it impossible or unsafe for the patient to exercise in a group environment.

The person running the class would need to be aware of the patient's other relevant co-morbidities which may be affected by participating in the exercise class, for example diabetes or asthma, and should make sure that the patient has appropriate medication for the management of these conditions with them.

A full assessment also allows identification of appropriate outcome measures and baseline measurement so that the patient's progress can be monitored and the correct intensity of exercise can be prescribed. Finally the assessment is an opportunity to explore whether the group exercise class is the appropriate environment for the patient to continue their rehabilitation.

Ability/suitability to join the group exercise class

Other factors that should be considered before placing a patient in a group exercise class include:

- **Supervision.** The patient moving into a group should be able to work effectively in a situation with less supervision than that which they would receive during an individual treatment.
- **Physical ability.** The patient should be fit enough to effectively participate in the exercise programme for the duration of the class. The patient's ability to balance should allow them to participate safely in the class.
- **Ability to work with others.** The patient should have the ability to work with others and understand and carry out instructions.
- **Functional ability.** The patient's functional ability should allow them to do any functional activities related to participating in the class, for example taking shoes and socks off. It may also be important for the patient to be able to get up and down from the floor independently depending on the type of class they are joining.
- **Timing of exercise class.** As group exercise classes take place at a regular time in the same place, it is important to consider whether the patient is able to attend the class regularly in terms of their other commitments.

Preparation to join the group exercise class

If the patient is moving from an individual treatment situation to a group exercise class, they should have this explained to them as early as possible in the rehabilitation process so that there is the opportunity to discuss any worries or queries. The transition to the group exercise class will be smoother if the patient is familiar with any equipment used in the class and if some of the exercises used in the class have been introduced into their individual rehabilitation programme. Any patient joining a group exercise class should ideally be introduced to the physiotherapist who takes the class and also have an opportunity to see some or all of the class, so that they are aware of how the class runs and what they will be required to do in the class.

The patient should be given a full explanation about the intensity at which they will be working and how they can monitor that intensity, the exercises that they will do and how to use any equipment involved safely. The patient should also be given an explanation about what to do if they experience any untoward symptoms in the class, such as a sudden onset of pain in a joint or muscle, severe breathlessness or dizziness.

Clothing

The patient must wear appropriate clothing and footwear for the type of class that they are going to participate in. A minimum requirement would usually be sports shoes and tracksuit bottoms with a T shirt. For a knee class, it would be preferable for the patient to wear shorts. Any items that the patient is wearing that could stop the patient exercising safely should be removed. Long hair should be tied back. People who are not used to exercising will need specific advice about this so that they wear appropriate dress.

The physiotherapist

The physiotherapist leading the exercise class is responsible for the patients in the class and anyone else who may be helping with the delivery of the class. They are responsible for making sure that the class starts on time, that any equipment to be used has been set up and that they have an appropriate set of exercises for the patients in the class. It is useful for the physiotherapist to know the names of the patients who are in the class so that if anyone starts to exercise in an unsafe manner the problem can be quickly addressed.

Other staff involved in the class

The physiotherapist may be taking the class alone or with the help of one or more physiotherapy or rehabilitation assistants or colleagues from other professions. There needs to be enough staff present to supervise the patients properly. For classes for patients with certain conditions there are guidelines in place for the recommended staff–patient ratio. The physiotherapist leading the class should be aware of these and adhere to them. The other staff involved in the class should be introduced to the patients in the class and an explanation given to the patients about their role. This means that the other staff involved in the exercise class need to be clear about their role. They may be involved in helping patients use certain pieces of equipment safely or giving extra guidance to patients so that they are able to monitor exercise intensity. Evaluating how a patient carries out the prescribed exercises, progressing the prescription and adapting exercises to make them easier for the patient to carry out should be the responsibility of the physiotherapist leading the class.

Presentation

The way in which the physiotherapist leading the class presents themself to the patients in the class is important. Presentation should be professional and also appropriate to the participants in the class. The way a physiotherapist addresses a group of children will be different from the approach that they take with a class of older people. It is important not to be 'over casual' or too formal. Patients will be more likely to attend the class if the physiotherapist is enthusiastic in presenting the exercises. The physiotherapist should be dressed in a manner appropriate to the class in case they need to demonstrate an exercise to the group.

Voice

The physiotherapist must speak clearly when running an exercise class. If patients cannot hear what the physiotherapist is saying, there is the danger that they may carry out an exercise in an unsafe manner. The physiotherapist needs to be sure that all participants can hear them properly. Patients will hear best if the physiotherapist stands at their front or side. Instructions should be given in a firm, assertive manner.

The physiotherapist should use simple language in short sentences to instruct the class and avoid the use of jargon. For example, rather than ask a class to 'extend' their knee, it is much clearer for the patient if they are asked to 'straighten their leg'.

Voice can be used to indicate to patients how they should move by varying speed and tone. If the physiotherapist wants to emphasize that an exercise is carried out slowly, they can slow the delivery of their instructions a little. If they want the patients to lift a limb, then the command 'up' at the end of the instruction can be given in a higher tone.

Teaching the exercises

It is important that the physiotherapist considers their position in the room where the exercise class takes place in relation to that of the patients. The patients need to be able to see the physiotherapist so that they can hear him or her clearly and see any demonstration of an activity. The physiotherapist needs to be able to see the patients so that they can make sure that the patients are managing

Figure 9.1 An example of a suitable room layout for a hand class. Note that the physiotherapist can sit at their table to demonstrate exercises but also has room to walk between the tables to observe and give individual feedback

to carry out the exercises effectively and safely. A suitable room layout for a hand class is shown in Figure 9.1.

If there is an individual patient who is unable to carry out an exercise, the physiotherapist may need to adapt the exercise so that the patient can do it or provide feedback on the steps that the patient needs to take to improve their performance of the exercise. If there are new patients in a class or patients who may require a little more help and feedback with the exercise class, these should be positioned within the class so that the physiotherapist can reach them easily. The front or sides of the class are good positions for these patients so that any assistance can be easily given.

The physiotherapist should continually evaluate how effectively all the patients in the class are carrying out the exercises and provide praise, feedback and encouragement both when the exercises are going well and when the patients need more explanation or help. Feedback on performance should be given in a suitable manner. Where more explanation and help are required with an individual exercise, the physiotherapist should direct this at the whole group first of all. It is important to remember to correct one problem at a time. Patients will feel uncomfortable if they are singled out for performing an exercise incorrectly.

Each exercise within the class should be taught with a clear start and end. It is important that the patient begins the exercise from the appropriate starting position. The exercise can be explained or demonstrated or taught by using a combination of both explanation and demonstration. Whichever method is chosen, the physiotherapist should demonstrate the exercise and then return to a position in the class where they can observe how the patients are continuing to carry out the exercise to give feedback on performance. This should continue whilst the exercise is in progress and then a clear instruction should be given to terminate the activity. This may be after a particular time interval or at the point where performance of the activity would reduce if the patients were to continue.

At the end of the class it is important for the physiotherapist to praise the patients' efforts and remind them of any exercises that they should continue with at home until the next class.

Environment

A physiotherapist may take group exercise classes in different places such as the gymnasium or treatment room in a physiotherapy outpatient department, at a community or leisure centre or in a residential home for older people. Wherever the class takes place, careful consideration should be given to the environment.

Space

Space is very often at a premium in many places where an exercise class could be carried out. The space is often shared and only available for the period of time that the exercise class is being carried out. It is important that the space is big enough to accommodate the people in the group comfortably. The patients in the group should be able to carry out the exercises in the class without bumping into each other or into the equipment that may be used.

The room should have adequate ventilation and heating so that the room temperature can be controlled and kept within a suitable range for exercising. There should be adequate lighting and the floor should be smooth and covered in a non-slip surface.

The room should be free from any unnecessary furniture or objects which may obstruct the patients as they are exercising. The walls should be as free as possible from pictures or other decorations so that wall space is available to use for exercises in the class if required.

In some group exercise situations, it is important that partners or carers of the patients in the class can observe what the patient is doing, for example the partner of a patient who is coming to a cardiac rehabilitation class following a myocardial infarction. By involving the patient's partner in the rehabilitation class they can see how much the patient can do, and there is a higher probability that the partner will support the patient to achieve this level of activity at home. Adequate space needs to be allowed within the class for observers to be present.

Waiting and changing areas

If group exercise classes are running one after the other in a particular venue, it is important that there is an appropriate area in which patients may wait prior to their class. They may also wish to use this space after the class to talk to other patients in the class to offer advice and support. Adequate seating should be available here and the area may be suitable for providing some refreshments for patients. As a minimum, drinking water should be available for patients participating in the exercise class.

There should be a changing area and toilets available for patients to use. The changing area is particularly important if the physiotherapist is expecting patients to wear appropriate clothing. People who are participating in a class and then going on to work afterwards will need somewhere suitable to change.

Equipment

Any equipment to be used in the exercise class should have regular maintenance checks, and appropriate risk assessments in relation to its use should be in place. The equipment should be cleaned thoroughly and regularly. Patients should be taught how to use equipment that will be used in the class in a safe manner. There should be adequate space around equipment so that it can be accessed and used safely.

Small equipment should be stored in a suitable area or container close to the exercise space. It should be put away when not in use so that it does not become a trip hazard.

Any equipment to be used in the class should be collected together or put into position beforehand so that it is available when needed.

For certain types of classes and depending on where a class is taking place there will normally be some emergency resuscitation equipment available in case of an untoward medical emergency. This type of equipment should be clearly marked and stored securely in or adjacent to the exercise area. The physiotherapist and other staff involved in the class should be trained in its use where it is available.

Timing

The timing of an exercise class should be considered in relation to the type of class it is and the type of patients who may need to access the class. For example, patients participating in a late-stage knee rehabilitation class may already be back at work and may prefer to come to the exercise class first thing in the morning or late in the afternoon so that the timing of the class causes minimal disruption to their working day. For patients with moderate to severe lung disease who are participating in a pulmonary rehabilitation programme, their exercise class may be better timed in the middle of the morning or afternoon. It may not always be possible to choose the time of the exercise class due to space limitations. However attendance at the class will be better when the timing of the class suits the needs of the majority of participants.

Punctuality

The consideration of punctuality spans the patient, the physiotherapist and the environment. It is important for exercise classes to run in a timely manner for several reasons. The space where the exercise class is taking place may be used for many other purposes on the same day as the exercise class. An exercise class cannot begin until the person leading the class arrives. If the physiotherapist arrives late the patients in the class may not have time to carry out the whole exercise programme. If patients arrive late for a class, they will not benefit from the whole exercise programme and may need to do some separate warm-up exercises prior to joining in with the exercise class at the point it has reached. This can be disruptive for other patients in the group.

Patients should be advised not to start exercising or using any equipment until the person leading the class arrives.

DESIGN OF THE EXERCISE PROGRAMME

The design of an exercise programme for an exercise class should be given careful thought. The physiotherapist needs to put together a suitable exercise programme for the patients in the class in terms of the reason they are attending the class and the group's other characteristics such as age and level of mobility. The exercise should maintain the interest of the group, use the allotted class time effectively and be based on the best evidence for the particular type of exercise programme being used. Areas for consideration when designing a group exercise programme are discussed below.

Fixed or rolling programme

The physiotherapist designing the exercise programme should decide whether the exercise class will be for a fixed time where all the patients start and finish the programme together or whether the patient will join an ongoing, rolling exercise programme. Most group exercise classes will fall into the latter category. Choosing which type of programme to design will depend largely on the number of patients who are being referred to the exercise group. A rolling exercise programme also offers the advantage of patients being able to join the programme at any time and attend for as long as they need to achieve treatment goals. This may not always be possible for financial reasons, in which case fixed programmes offer an advantage. If there are only small numbers of a particular type of patient who would benefit from group treatment, it may be better to use a fixed programme and start the class when enough patients have been recruited.

Exercise circuit or exercise class

Another major consideration for the physiotherapist running the class is whether to carry out the exercise programme as a circuit training programme where patients will be doing different activities at the same time for a fixed period of time or as an exercise class where patients will all be doing the same exercise at the same time. There are advantages and disadvantages to both types of programme. A circuit training programme is well suited to a rolling programme. It is possible to have similar exercises of differing intensity at each exercise station which will suit individual patients in terms of working at the correct intensity for their stage of rehabilitation. An example of this would be one station for training the shoulder flexors with three exercises of differing intensity, as shown in Figure 9.2. The first exercise could be auto-assisted shoulder flexion with a walking stick (Figure 9.2a), the second exercise would be throwing a ball overarm against a wall (Figure 9.2b) and the third

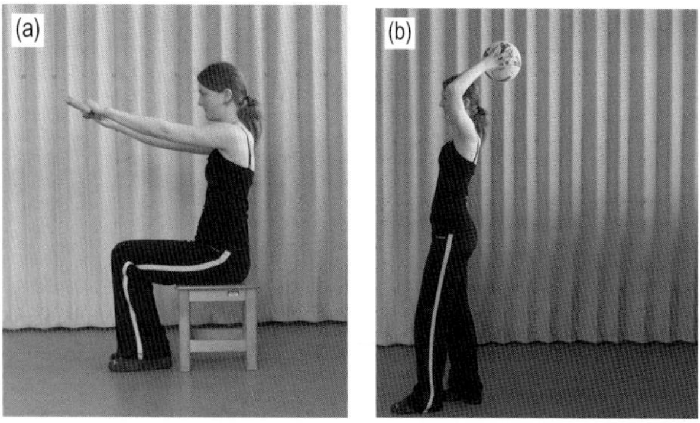

Figure 9.2 (a) Auto-assisted shoulder flexion with a walking stick. (b) Throwing a ball overarm against a wall.

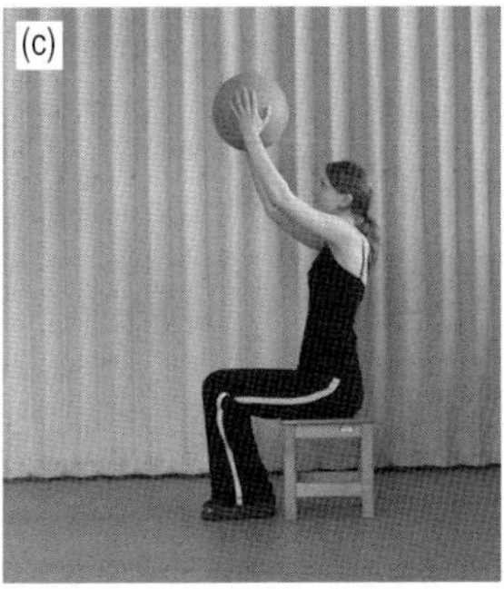

Figure 9.2 *Continued* (c) Shoulder flexion against resistance using a medicine ball

exercise would be shoulder flexion against resistance using a medicine ball (Figure 9.2c).

Patients can progress through the differing work intensities as appropriate for their needs and combine different intensities of exercise at different stations so that the exercise programme is suitable for their stage of rehabilitation. Patients would need to record the number of exercises that they completed at each point in the circuit so that progress can be monitored.

Circuit training is a type of interval training and so the physiotherapist needs to consider how long each training interval should be at each station and how long each rest interval should be between stations.

The other advantage of circuit training is that it can normally be carried out with less equipment than would be needed if patients were all doing the same exercise at once.

An exercise class may be more suitable for people with certain types of conditions and those at an earlier stage in the rehabilitation process. For example an exercise class for people who have just come out of plaster following a wrist or Colles fracture is a good way of providing effective treatment for several patients together. Some examples of the kind of exercises that might be suitable for this group are shown in Figures 9.3–9.5. An exercise class may be more appropriate for patients who would have difficulty moving from one exercise station to another; for example for those people who have a problem with balance. If patients are to do the same exercise at the same time in a class, there needs to be enough equipment for this to happen. The physiotherapist also needs each patient in the group to recognize the intensity at which they should be working as some patients will need to work harder than others at the same exercise to achieve training effects.

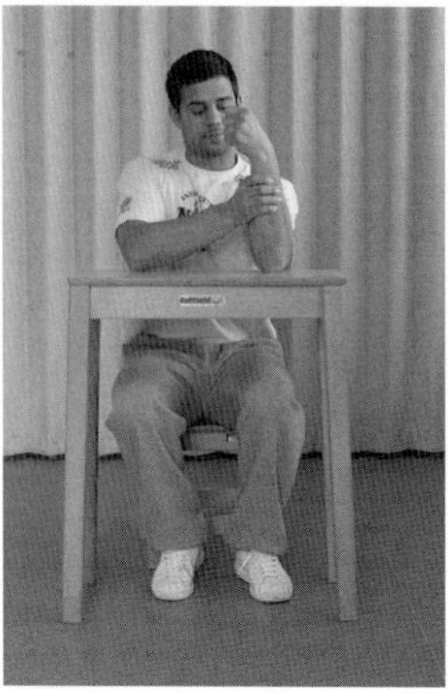

Figure 9.3 Wrist circumduction to increase range of movement

Figure 9.4 Resistance training for wrist extensors

Figure 9.5 Twisting a towel, which is held firmly using the unaffected hand, using the affected arm

Competition

Whenever a group of people start to exercise together, particularly those with similar conditions or at a similar stage of rehabilitation, they will start to compare how well they think they are doing with others in the group. Depending on the personalities of those in the group, some patients will inevitably start to try to see if they can do more repetitions of an exercise or lift more weight than the person next to them. The physiotherapist leading the group needs to monitor this carefully and either encourage competition where it would help achieve the aims of rehabilitation or discourage where it would be unhelpful or even prove dangerous. Competition can be used to motivate patients who may not be working as hard as necessary in a group situation. It is also useful in the later stages of rehabilitation, particularly when patients may be returning to competitive sport. Competition must always be carefully monitored and controlled so that patients do not overtrain or injure themselves in the excitement of the activity. In certain situations competition needs to be avoided and patients need to be reminded to think about the individual intensity at which they should be working.

Competition should usually be avoided in the earlier stages of rehabilitation where there is a greater risk of damage to healing tissues. Another area where competition should be avoided is during a cardiac rehabilitation class, because exercise intensity should be carefully controlled.

Music

Music is very often played during exercise classes for healthy individuals, and physiotherapists may also choose to play music during their exercise classes. Careful consideration should be given to the possible effects of playing music during an exercise class. There are many studies which have looked into the effect of exercising with music. In general, the evidence would suggest that exercising whilst music with a fast beat is playing increases the intensity at which people work, although the person feels that they are not actually working as hard as if they performed the same exercise without the music playing. This may seem a beneficial effect for patients in an exercise class; however it may be an unhelpful or even dangerous effect in some situations. Examples of this type of situation would be classes for patients in the early stages of rehabilitation where there is a risk of damaging healing tissue by working harder than the prescribed intensity. Music may also be distracting for patients in an exercise class. Not all the people in the class will enjoy the same type of music and so it can also have the adverse effect of removing a patient's concentration from the activity they are performing and reduce their performance. The physiotherapist has to work much harder to make themself heard if they choose to play music during an exercise class.

Aims of exercise class

The aims of any exercise class depend on the patients in the group. For each exercise class that a physiotherapist leads, they should spend time planning the class. This involves thinking about the common goals of the patients who will be participating, relating these to the aims of the exercise class and then devising a suitable exercise programme to achieve the aims. Some common examples of treatment aims would be to increase range of movement, to increase cardiorespiratory fitness and to increase muscle strength. Table 9.1 shows some specific aims for a class for patients who have just had their plaster removed following wrist or Colles fracture and the exercises chosen to achieve these aims.

The number of repetitions of each exercise will depend on how many the patient can do whilst maintaining good form. The exercises chosen must be suited to the patients in the class. For a person who has sustained a Colles fracture the exercises chosen for treatment will focus on general function such as those required for self-care. Individuals may also have specific goals, such as a person who is also interested in sewing; emphasis must then also be placed on regaining fine hand movements.

Phases of the exercise programme

The physiotherapist needs to consider how the exercise programme will progress during the planning stage. This means thinking about

Table 9.1 To show some specific aims for a class for patients who have just had their plaster removed following wrist or Colles fracture and the prescribed exercises

Aim of exercise class	Exercise
1. To improve range of movement of wrist extension	Sitt forearm in supination resting on arm table with hand over far edge of table. Extend wrist × 10
2. To improve hand mobility	Sitt Elbow resting on arm table flex and extend fingers × 10
3. To improve hand function	a. Sitt Wringing towel with both hands × 10 into wrist flexion, × 10 into wrist extension b. Sitt Taking the lid off and putting it back on a jar × 10

how the aims of the exercise programme can be achieved safely in the allotted time.

An exercise class normally starts with a warm-up phase to increase cardiac output so that blood flow to the heart and exercising muscles increases and to start to mobilize joints gently. A warm-up period will vary depending on the type of class that is being carried out.

The exercise class will then move into the next phase of the programme, which will contain the exercises which meet the main aims of the class. These will be specific training or conditioning exercises. It is important to consider the order of the exercises in this phase so that an individual muscle group or part of the body is not targeted for several exercises in a row. This will lead to fatigue and poor performance. Exercises should be given to the group in an order which targets different muscle groups or parts of the body in different ways during subsequent exercises. This will contribute to the exercises feeling varied but the physiotherapist also needs to plan the exercises that they will use in a class so that they are varied and interesting. This will encourage good performance and adherence.

The class should end with a period of gentler or cool-down exercise designed to prevent blood pooling and allow the cardiovascular system to gradually return to normal.

Further reading

Beauchamp MR, Carron AV, McCutcheon S, et al (2007) Older adults preferences for exercising alone versus in groups: Considering contextual congruence. Annals of Behavioural Medicine 33(2): 200–206.

Grindrod D, Paton C, Knez WL, et al (2004) Six minute walking distance is greater when performed in a group than alone. British Journal of Sports Medicine 40: 876–877.

Hollis M (1976) Practical Exercise Therapy. Oxford, UK: Blackwell Scientific Publications.

Nykanen M, Koivisto K (2004) Individual or group rehabilitation for people with low back pain: A comparative study with 6 month follow up. Journal of Rehabilitation Medicine 36: 262–266.

Potteiger JA, Schroeder JM, Goff KL (2000) Influence of music on ratings of perceived exertion during 20 minutes of moderate intensity exercise. Perceptual and Motor Skills 91(3): 848–854.

Uziel L (2006) Individual differences in the social facilitation effect: A review and meta-analysis. Journal of Research in Personality 41(3): 579–601.

Yamashita S, Twai K, Aktmoto T, et al (2006) Effects of music during exercise on RPE, heart rate and the autonomic nervous system. Journal of Sports Medicine and Physical Fitness 46(3): 425–430.

CHAPTER TEN

Exercise Through the Life Span

Previous chapters of this book have discussed exercise guidelines and prescription for adults. This chapter considers how exercise should be tailored for the specific life stages of childhood, pregnancy and older age. Physiotherapists need to have an understanding of exercise in relation to life stage for three main reasons:

- to understand the normal activity levels of children, pregnant women and older people
- to understand how to safely treat children, pregnant women and older people with an exercise programme
- to understand how children, pregnant women and older people may respond to treatment with an exercise programme.

EXERCISE AND CHILDREN

Healthy children are usually active by nature; some activities are aerobic but many others are short-term bouts of intense activity interspersed with short periods of rest. Children's physiology is different from that of adults and children respond to exercise differently from adults. As children develop at different rates, it is important to consider each child as an individual. There are several factors which will determine an individual child's response to exercise. These factors include the chronological age of the child, the size of the child in relation to this and their stage of biological and sexual maturation.

PHYSIOLOGICAL DIFFERENCES AND RESPONSES TO EXERCISE IN CHILDREN

This section considers some of the physiological differences and responses to exercise in children compared with adults.

Differences in the ventilatory system

Many markers of ventilatory capacity such as forced expiratory volume in one second (FEV_1) and vital capacity are related to the size of the child. There is little difference in these values between the sexes before puberty although some studies have shown a small increase in these values in favour of boys when comparing boys with girls. Small children have to work harder to breathe for each litre of oxygen consumed compared with adults so this means that they may not be able to sustain long periods of activity. As the child grows, breathing rate at rest falls and maximal breathing rate progressively declines. Resting tidal volume increases with age but also declines slowly relative to body size. Maximal exercise ventilation increases in proportion to height as the child gets older and their ability to sustain activity increases.

Differences in the cardiovascular system

Ventricular size and stroke volume increase in relation to the size of the child. Young children have a small heart and so have a higher heart rate and a comparatively small stroke volume. At maximal and sub-maximal exercise levels cardiac output is lower in children than in adults. To compensate for this the arteriovenous oxygen difference in children is larger so that the required amount of oxygen can reach exercising muscles during aerobic work. As the sinus node matures, resting heart rate falls in children. Myocardial contractility remains fairly constant between adults and children. Maximal changes in cardiac output parallel those of maximal oxygen uptake as the child grows. This again leads to an increased ability to sustain activity as the child grows.

Differences in oxygen uptake

Resting metabolic rate in children decreases relative to body size as children grow. Also as children grow, maximal oxygen uptake increases in relation to body size with little difference between the sexes in young children. As children go through puberty differences between boys and girls in maximal oxygen uptake of as much as 50% less in girls become apparent, particularly with boys in training. These differences between the sexes are related to body composition and size. Girls tend to be smaller and have more body fat than boys, and these differences persist into adulthood.

Differences in skeletal muscle

Muscle strength improves throughout childhood due to an increase in muscle size as the child grows and due to neural adaptation. At puberty, hormones play a large role in muscle development and result in much greater increases in lean body mass in boys than in girls.

Differences in other factors

Blood haemoglobin concentration and so the oxygen-carrying capacity of blood rises with age in boys more than in girls. Walking and running economy improve during childhood and so percentage of maximal oxygen uptake used at a given exercise intensity declines as the child gets older. Endurance performance improves as the child grows. Anaerobic performance also improves as the child grows – anaerobic power in children is smaller relative to size than that in adults.

THE EFFECTS OF EXERCISE TRAINING IN CHILDREN

Cardiovascular training

If an endurance programme is applied to young healthy children, any gains in maximal oxygen uptake will be less than those seen where an endurance training programme is applied to young adolescents or adults. The reasons for this are not clear and may be linked to the fact that children are usually active by nature so training programmes are not as effective or because of the hormonal changes which happen at puberty. Where children are hypoactive, for example those with chronic diseases, cardiovascular training may produce improvements in the child's ability to carry out functional activities.

Resistance training

More recent evidence suggests that it is possible to increase the strength of muscles in pre-pubertal children with resistance training programmes. Muscle hypertrophy is not seen in these children to the same degree as that in an older child or adult following a resistance training programme, suggesting that neural adaptations are largely responsible for strength gains. Larger strength gains, which may have a positive effect on function, have been seen when resistance training programmes have been applied to hypoactive children.

BENEFITS OF EXERCISE IN CHILDREN

Children may benefit from exercise in many different ways depending upon their reason for doing the exercise.

Healthy children

As has already been stated, healthy children are usually active by nature, although in the last 10–15 years there has been increasing concern that children are becoming less active than they were previously. Children are often driven to school now when previously they may have walked or cycled. Many of the activities which children now enjoy such as playing computer games or watching the television may have replaced more active pastimes. This has prompted consideration of how being a less active child may track into adulthood in terms of developing conditions such as obesity, osteoporosis, coronary artery disease or hypertension. All of these diseases are linked to physical inactivity as a risk factor. A definitive study looking into this area has not been carried out but the available evidence supports the notion that a child's activity pattern tracks into adulthood. If a child is very active, they are more likely to be active as an adult. The child's parents have also been shown to be important in acting as a role-model in developing their child's activity patterns. Children's fitness has been studied over the last 50 years and there appears to be no trend in decreasing maximal oxygen uptake in children over this period. Neither does there appear to be a strong relationship between activity levels and fitness in children. However it is important to encourage children to be active so that they are more likely to maintain higher levels of activity as an adult.

Children participating in sport

More younger people are now participating in elite sport or regular training. Training of this type should be carefully monitored, particularly in terms of intensity to avoid injury.

Children with chronic conditions

For children who have a condition such as juvenile rheumatoid arthritis, cerebral palsy or cystic fibrosis it is important that exercise is encouraged in their daily life. Many of these children are hypoactive compared with healthy children of a similar age. They may also have to work at near maximal intensity to carry out simple functional tasks. Some evidence is starting to emerge which is showing the benefits of resistance training and fitness training on function in these children. This may be related to their ability to propel a wheelchair or in economy of function in terms of carrying out activities of daily living.

SPECIAL CONSIDERATIONS WHEN EXERCISING CHILDREN

To prescribe exercise safely for children the physiotherapist should be aware of the expected outcome of training for both cardiovascular fitness and resistance training.

Activities should be chosen that are easy and interesting for the child to carry out. Active play should be encouraged in younger children and older children may be involved in selecting activities which they would like to do and are possible for them to carry out. Special consideration should be given to the specificity of the activity or game being used in relation to the training programme.

RECOMMENDED EXERCISE PRESCRIPTION

Cardiovascular training

Current recommendations suggest that healthy children should do at least 60 minutes of moderate activity with some vigorous activity, which is intermittent in nature, on most days of the week.

Resistance training

Where resistance training programmes are applied to children, for example in specific conditions such as cystic fibrosis or for sports training, the following guidelines should apply:

- maximal (1 RM) or high-intensity programmes should not be used
- young children should not lift a heavier weight than 8 RM and up to 15 RM for each exercise, intensity being increased only when the child can easily perform the required number of repetitions in good form
- training should be carried out under supervision with focus on good technique
- activities should be varied to maintain interest.

EXERCISE AND PREGNANCY

For healthy women, pregnancy is a normal part of life. Exercise and physical activity may also play an important role in the lives of healthy women. However pregnant women who are normally physically active may wonder whether continuing with physical activity during their pregnancy will adversely affect their baby or themselves. Physiotherapists working in all kinds of fields may come across pregnant women and so require some knowledge about exercise during pregnancy to answer questions and prescribe exercise safely.

PHYSIOLOGICAL DIFFERENCES AND RESPONSES TO EXERCISE DURING PREGNANCY

In early pregnancy response to moderate activity is similar to that of normal healthy women. As pregnancy progresses blood volume, uterine size and metabolic rate start to increase. Fatigue is often a feature of early pregnancy and if the pregnant woman finds that fatigue is coming on more quickly than usual during exercise, she should moderate her level of activity accordingly. Early pregnancy is an important time for foetal development and so rest, hydration and nutrition are particularly important at this time.

During the later stages of pregnancy blood volume and weight increase significantly. As the weight gain is centred around the abdomen, posture and centre of gravity will alter, affecting balance. Circulating hormones will relax ligaments around joints in preparation for the birth, so some consideration should be given to joint protection. It can take 4–6 weeks after giving birth for the physiology of the mother to return to normal.

Foetal response to maternal exercise has been studied and an increase in foetal heart rate has been shown in response to short bouts of maternal activity.

BENEFITS OF EXERCISE DURING PREGNANCY

Studies have shown that regular aerobic exercise during pregnancy can improve or maintain maternal fitness, prevent excess weight gain and speed recovery from giving birth. There is currently insufficient information available to be certain about other risks or benefits to the mother or foetus.

As the benefits of exercise in the management of hypertension have become recognized, consideration has been given to whether exercise during pregnancy could be useful in the prevention of pre-eclampsia. At present there is no clear evidence to support this suggestion.

SPECIAL CONSIDERATIONS WHEN EXERCISING DURING PREGNANCY

The main consideration for exercising during pregnancy is that no harm should come to the mother or foetus as a result of doing this.

Absolute contraindications to exercise during pregnancy include pre-eclampsia or pregnancy-induced hypertension, premature labour, ruptured membranes, persistent bleeding during the second or third trimesters, incompetent cervix, placenta praevia after 26 weeks' gestation, heart disease and restrictive lung disease. Relative contra-indications include severe anaemia, poorly controlled diabetes, hyperthyroidism, seizure disorder and hypertension, extreme over- or underweight, lung disease or heavy smoker and orthopaedic problems. It is advisable for a pregnant women who is not used to exercising to seek medical advice before commencing an exercise programme.

At all times the mother should monitor exercise intensity; the Rating of Perceived Exertion (RPE) is particularly useful for this during pregnancy. If any untoward symptoms such as vaginal bleeding, contractions, reduced foetal movement, unexplained breathlessness, undue fatigue, headache, dizziness, calf pain or muscle weakness occur, exercise should be discontinued and medical advice sought. Most women reduce their activity level naturally in the third trimester of pregnancy.

Women should avoid sports where there is a risk of contact, tripping, falling or excessive joint stress during pregnancy and also those that are very vigorous during the third trimester. Walking and swimming are both activities that could be recommended.

To allow adequate heat dissipation and avoid risk to the foetus, pregnant women should wear loose clothing and drink plenty of water to avoid dehydration during exercise. They should avoid exercising in hot humid weather.

Exercises that include periods of standing still should be avoided to prevent blood pooling and those which require supine lying should be avoided after the first trimester to prevent any obstruction of venous return.

RECOMMENDED EXERCISE PRESCRIPTION

Recommendations for exercise during pregnancy are similar to those for otherwise healthy individuals if the mother is accustomed to exercise, i.e. 30–40 minutes of moderate activity on most days of the week. If the mother is beginning to exercise during the pregnancy, provided there are no contraindications, a light exercise intensity is recommended to begin with.

There is very limited information available about strength training in relation to pregnancy. In non-pregnant adults blood pressure increases when a heavy weight is lifted. If technique is poor, there is the possibility of performing a Valsalva manoeuvre as the weight is lifted. Large increases in blood pressure and straining manoeuvres should be avoided in pregnant women.

EXERCISE AND OLDER PEOPLE

It is a cultural expectation in today's society that older adults will reduce their physical activity levels and enjoy a rest after retirement. Although some older people do maintain or even increase their activity levels, many people reduce their activity levels in older age. This leads to a detraining effect, just as in a younger person; however the resulting decrease in exercise ability is often accepted as part of the ageing process. Loss of muscle mass is seen in older people and is thought to be a key risk factor in the development of dependence and disability in the older population.

Co-morbidities, such as osteoarthritis, and balance problems can make it difficult for older people to maintain a healthy level of activity.

This section considers the impact of the physiological changes that occur with ageing on exercise ability and discusses the benefits of resistance and cardiovascular training in older people alongside the special considerations for exercise prescription in this group.

PHYSIOLOGICAL DIFFERENCES AND RESPONSES TO EXERCISE IN OLDER PEOPLE

Muscle strength

Loss of muscle mass, known as sarcopenia, is associated with ageing and is thought to occur at a rate of 1–2% a year after the age of 50 years. This muscle atrophy may be attributable to a loss of muscle fibres, in particular the type II fibres. Imaging of muscles shows a decrease in cross-sectional area, decreased muscle density and an increase in intramuscular fat. This loss of muscle mass is reflected by a decrease in muscle strength of 30% between the ages of 50 and 70 years, and more rapidly than that in older adults. The loss of muscle mass is related to a decline in muscle strength, and is seen alongside decreases in activity levels and health scores.

Muscle power

Contractile velocity also decreases with age. Muscle power is the product of muscle strength and the velocity of contraction and, as both of these factors decline with ageing, muscle power shows a more marked decline than strength at a rate of 3–4% per year. When investigating local muscle endurance in older people, fatigue has been demonstrated in the form of reduced contractile velocity during repeated contractions.

This loss of muscle power can lead to functional limitations, as lower-limb muscle power is required for normal gait and activities such as stair climbing and standing from sitting. Loss of muscle power is also a risk factor for falls due to the inability to produce a force quickly enough to counteract a loss of balance. This suggests the need for the inclusion of power training modalities in an exercise programme for older people.

Muscle endurance

There is generally thought to be no reduction in local muscle endurance in older people.

Cardiovascular exercise

Although there are physiological changes that occur with ageing that affect the capacity of the cardiovascular system for exercise, many older people decrease their activity levels for other reasons. Maximum oxygen uptake decreases by 9–15% per year in sedentary adults after the age of 25 years. This decrease in oxygen uptake is due to a decline in maximum cardiac output and also a decrease in the maximum exercise arteriovenous oxygen difference. The decrease in cardiac output is largely due to an age-related decrease in maximum heart rate, which occurs at a rate of around 6–10 bpm per decade. Cardiac output is also decreased due to difficulty in maintaining a high central blood volume; this is due to age-related elastic changes causing distention and increased flow to the peripheral blood vessels. The arteriovenous oxygen difference is in part due to a change in the distribution of the blood flow in older people, in which relatively less blood flows to the exercising muscle and more blood is delivered to the skin and viscera. The increase in blood flow to the skin is to aid in temperature regulation, as older people have decreased sweating and a thicker layer of subcutaneous fat.

Older adults have a lower oxygen uptake, lower cardiac output, lower stroke volume, greater arteriovenous oxygen difference and higher blood pressure than a younger person at the same relative workload. During sub-maximal exercise the arteriovenous gap is maintained at a normal or even higher value as the older person is able to adequately perfuse the exercising muscle. Higher systolic and diastolic blood pressures than those seen in younger adults are needed in order to perfuse the muscle; this is due to the increased muscle contraction required to produce force in a muscle with fewer fibres and also the circulatory system which has an increase in resistance due to the connective tissue changes seen with ageing.

These differences highlight the limitation of the cardiovascular system, rather than the oxygen uptake at the tissues, as the main limiting factor.

Flexibility

Age-related decrease in the extensibility of collagen, joint destruction secondary to arthritis and decline in muscle strength all contribute to a decrease in range of movement. In addition many people no longer perform activities that access the extremes of joint range, which leads to loss of movement through disuse. It has been demonstrated that loss of range of movement is associated with increasing age.

THE BENEFITS OF EXERCISE TRAINING IN OLDER ADULTS

Resistance training

Resistance training is recommended to maintain muscular fitness in the face of age-related muscle loss and a decrease in activity levels. Muscle-strengthening activities are often neglected by this population, with one study identifying that only 12% of people over the age of 65 years currently participate in such activity.

Resistance training programmes in older people have been shown to produce increases in strength that are similar to, or possibly greater than, those in the younger population suggesting that such an intervention is effective in this group.

Training programmes have also produced gains in muscle power. Interestingly these gains in power were attributable to an early increase in both peak velocity and strength, which is in contrast to the younger population, in whom initial power gains are largely due to increases in strength alone. Heavier loading during resistance training produces greater increases in strength and endurance; however loading does not appear to have a dose effect when power training, which reinforces the importance of the velocity component in the muscle power of older people.

An important benefit of resistance training, aside from local muscle adaptation, is the maintenance and improvement of bone mineral density.

Cardiovascular training

Cardiovascular training programmes in older populations have been shown to produce similar increases in VO_{2max} as those seen in younger adults. As with younger people the amount of increase in VO_{2max} is related to the training intensity.

In older women this increase seems to be due to an increase in the arteriovenous oxygen difference, rather than cardiovascular adaptations. There have been some cardiovascular adaptations demonstrated in older men in the form of an increased stroke volume secondary to an increase in end-diastolic pressure.

Older adults also exhibit similar improvements to younger people in glucose tolerance, reductions in body fat and reduced blood pressure after cardiovascular training.

High-intensity training may reduce the age-related changes in oxygen-uptake capacity, although general benefits in terms of function and reduction in cardiovascular risk factors are seen following low- to moderate-intensity training.

Flexibility training

Exercise programmes including a range of active exercises to access the full available range of movement of several joints have demonstrated positive benefits. There is a body of evidence demonstrating improvements in flexibility following activities such as yoga and Tai Chi, which also involve moving through full range in a controlled and often sustained manner. There is, however, very little evidence to support specific increases in range of movement following exercise programmes, but, owing due to the relationship between decreased range of movement and falls, flexibility is a recommended component of an exercise programme for older people.

SPECIAL CONSIDERATIONS FOR EXERCISE IN OLDER ADULTS

There are no contraindications to exercise specific to older people, but all exercise programmes should be individually prescribed bearing in mind the full medical history, functional level and goals of the person. Physiological changes associated with ageing place additional risk in even the healthy older person. In addition many older people will have several co-morbidities that need to be taken into consideration when designing an exercise programme. Overall it is thought that the risks of inactivity are far greater than any risk associated with exercise.

Balance and falls

Age-related changes in posture along with decreased muscle power, strength and visual problems all place the older person at higher risk of falling. As many older people have decreased bone density they are at a higher risk of sustaining a fracture in the event of a fall; therefore careful consideration needs to be given to balance when implementing an exercise programme. Unless the aim of the exercise is to specifically challenge balance, the most stable starting position should be selected and the physiotherapist should ensure that the person is able to perform the required movement without loss of balance.

It may be necessary to design a seated exercise programme to increase the cardiovascular fitness of a person with insufficient balance to perform the more common walking and stepping activities.

It should also be remembered that due to the changes in blood vessels and baroreceptors older adults may be affected by postural hypotension; therefore particular care should be taken with position changes during the exercise programme to prevent falls secondary to fainting.

Mobility and flexibility

The physiotherapist should assess the patient's mobility to ensure that they can move sufficiently well to get into and out of the starting position; for example the use of floor exercises is often inappropriate in the very elderly as they may be unable to get up from the floor.

Vision

Many older people function well in their own environment despite limited vision; however particular attention should be given to safety of the environment when carrying out exercise programmes to ensure that equipment is not left in a position that could lead to a trip or slip. Limited vision should also be taken into consideration when producing written instructions by using large font.

Cognition and memory

As with any patient the physiotherapist should be clear and specific when explaining the exercise programme; however this is particularly important in patients who may have some cognitive impairment or short-term memory loss. The use of written information and pictures is vital here, and exercise diaries may help people to remember when to do their exercises.

Heat tolerance

Owing to poor thermoregulation older adults are less tolerant to heat during exercise and careful attention should be paid to the temperature of the environment.

Co-morbidities

All patients should have a full screening to identify any other medical conditions and the effects of each condition considered in relation to exercise. Contraindications to exercise are the same as in any adult and include uncontrolled cardiac failure or angina, uncontrolled diabetes, acute illness and pyrexia. Many older people will have some degree of cardiovascular disease, chronic respiratory disease, osteoarthritis or osteoporosis. These conditions should not preclude exercise, and the physiotherapist should prescribe exercise bearing in mind the specific exercise guidelines for patients with such conditions.

RECOMMENDED EXERCISE PRESCRIPTION FOR OLDER ADULTS

For muscular strength

- ***Frequency:*** 2 or 3 non-consecutive days a week
- ***Repetitions:*** 1–3 sets of 10–15 repetitions for 8–10 of the major muscle groups, one and two joint muscles
- ***Intensity:*** 60–80% of 1 RM
- ***Duration:*** Lift at slow to moderate pace, with 1–2 min in between sets.

For muscular power

Training as recommended to increase muscular strength and

- ***Frequency:*** 2 or 3 non-consecutive days a week
- ***Repetitions:*** 1–3 sets of 6–10 repetitions for 8–10 of the major muscle groups, one and two joint muscles
- ***Intensity:*** 40–60% of 1 RM
- ***Duration:*** Lift at fast pace.

For local muscle endurance

Guidelines are as for younger adults.

For cardiovascular fitness

A baseline level of muscular fitness and balance is required in order to perform many of the activities used in cardiovascular training. It is recommended that aerobic training is introduced after strength and balance training when rehabilitating the frail older person.

- ***Frequency:*** 2 or 3 non-consecutive days a week
- ***Intensity:*** 40–60% of heart rate reserve or Borg rating 11–13. Start at low intensity and build up gradually. In previously active individuals higher-intensity exercise may be used. Increase intensity by increasing load, e.g. slopes rather than by increasing the speed in the first instance
- ***Duration:*** Build up to 20 minutes, or 3 × 10 minutes per day.

For flexibility

Owing to the lack of evidence to date there are no specific guidelines for flexibility. It is recommended that activities such as walking, aerobic dance, Tai Chi and stretching should be included in the general activity programmes for older people. It should be ensured that all joints are put through their full available range at least three times a week.

Further reading

American College of Obstetricians and Gynaecologists (2002) Exercise during pregnancy and the postpartum period. ACOG Committee Opinion No 267. Obstetrics and Gynecology 99: 171–173.

Armstrong N (1995) The challenge of promoting physical activity. Journal of the Royal Society on Health Conference Paper 115: 187–192.

Bale P (1992) The functional performance of children in relation to growth, maturation and exercise. Sports Medicine 13(3): 151–159.

Bar-Or O (1986) Pathological factors which limit the capacity of the sick child. Medicine and Science in Sports and Exercise 18(3): 276–282.

Bar-Or O (1989) Trainability of the pre-pubescent child. Physician Sports Medicine 17: 65–81.

Bassey EJ, Harries UJ (1993) Normal values for handgrip strength in 920 men and women aged over 65 years, and longitudinal changes over 4 years in 620 survivors. Clinical Science 84: 331–337.

De Vos NJ, Singh NA, Ross DA, et al (2005) Optimal loads for increasing muscle power during explosive resistance training in older adults. Journal of Gerontology, Series A Biological Sciences and Medical Sciences 60(5): 638–647.

Galvão DA, Taaffe DR (2005) Resistance exercise dosage in older adults: single- versus multiset effects on physical performance and body composition. Journal of the American Geriatrics Society 53(12): 2090–2097.

Kohrt WM, Bloomfield SA, Little KD, et al (2004) American College of Sports Medicine position stand: Physical activity and bone health. Medicine and Science in Sports and Exercise 36(11): 1985–1996.

Kramer M, McDonald S (2006) Aerobic exercise for women during pregnancy. Cochrane Database of Systematic Reviews(4): CD003226.

Maxxeo R, Cavanagh P, Evans W, et al (1998) American College of Sports Medicine position stand: Exercise and physical activity for older adults. Medicine and Science in Sports and Exercise 30(6).

Meher S, Duley L (2006) Exercise or other physical activity for preventing pre-eclampsia and its complications. Cochrane Database of Systematic Reviews(4): CD005942.

Nelson M, Rejeski WJ, Blair SN, et al (2007) Physical activity and public health in older adults: Recommendation from the American College of Sports Medicine and the American Heart Association. Medicine and Science in Sports and Exercise Special Communication (http:acsm-msse.org accessed: 26/11/07).

O'Connell D, Barnhart R (1995) Improvement in wheelchair propulsion in paediatric wheelchair users through resistance training: a pilot study. Archives of Physical Medicine and Rehabilitation 76(4): 368–372.

Petrella JK, Kim JS, Tuggle SC, Hall SR, Bamman MM (2005) Age differences in knee extension power, contractile velocity, and fatigability. Journal of Applied Physiology 98(1): 211–220.

Petrella JK, Kim J, Tuggle S (2007) Contributions of force and velocity to improved power with progressive resistance training in young and older adults. European Journal of Applied Physiology 99: 343–351.

Rowland TW (1996) Developmental Exercise Physiology. Champaign, IL: Human Kinetics.

Shephard R (1997) Physical Activity and Ageing. Philadelphia, PA: Human Kinetics.

Whaley MH (ed.) (2005) ACSM's Guidelines for Exercise Testing and Prescription: 7th edition. Philadelphia, PA: Lippincott Williams & Wilkins.

Exercise in Acute Conditions

This chapter will consider how exercise can be used through the stages of rehabilitation following an acute injury or illness. The chapter will define acute conditions, the importance of exercise in the rehabilitation process, the stages of rehabilitation and how suitable exercises may be prescribed and progressed during the recovery process.

ACUTE CONDITIONS

An acute condition is one which comes on suddenly and may be severe in onset. Acute conditions usually last for a limited time span as they have the capacity to improve and recover with the correct treatment. Much of the recovery from an acute condition may be due to the natural healing process but correct treatment will hasten, and help to ensure, a full recovery. This is in contrast to chronic conditions which last over long periods, may have no cure, are often progressive and are characterized by exacerbations and remissions. Exercise may be used to aid recovery in a wide range of acute conditions and illnesses. Some examples of where exercise may be used to help ensure a full recovery include fractures, muscle sprains and tears, ligamentous injuries, following surgical intervention for joint replacement, plastic surgery or skin grafting, coronary artery bypass grafting, and following a severe illness which required treatment in the intensive care unit.

THE IMPACT OF ACUTE CONDITIONS ON EXERCISE ABILITY

When a person is subject to an acute injury or illness, a non-specific inflammatory response is triggered. The extent and severity of the injury or illness will determine the magnitude of the inflammatory response. Normally acute inflammation is localized to the tissue around the site of injury, for example the foot and ankle may swell in response to a lateral sprain of the ankle. In response to a severe injury, such as a large surface area burn, or a severe illness, such as septicaemia, a whole-body inflammatory response may be triggered. The inflammatory process will act as a trigger for healing to occur in most cases. However in some situations, for example where the injury is too great or other factors such as infection are involved, healing may not occur and the condition may become chronic. In extreme cases of whole-body inflammation, multiple organ failure and death may result.

In the acute inflammatory process, tissue injury or infection occurs and cells are damaged. Various chemicals such as kinin and histamine are released, blood vessels dilate, capillaries become leaky and white blood cells move into the area. This results in increased blood flow to the affected tissues. Tissue oedema develops and damaged cells and pathogens are removed from the site. Clotting occurs, the metabolic rate of the tissue cells increases and healing begins usually resulting in tissue repair. The common signs of an inflammatory process are redness, heat, swelling and pain.

It is not the purpose of this text to examine inflammation and wound healing in detail – there are many other texts on this subject, examples of which can be found in the further reading section at the end of the chapter. However it is important for the physiotherapist to understand how these processes impact on exercise ability.

Acute conditions will impact on exercise ability in different ways depending on the nature and severity of the acute injury or illness. If a person suffers a lower limb muscle sprain, there will be swelling and pain in the affected area and this may lead to associated muscle inhibition and loss of joint range of movement. The person may be unable to weight bear or may require a walking aid. If the person has problems weight-bearing and their normal activity pattern is interrupted, this may result in loss of cardiovascular fitness and local muscle atrophy.

Following more severe injuries or illnesses, the patient may require a period of bed rest or limb immobilization. The changes in cardiorespiratory function and muscle function following imposed periods of bed rest have been researched and are well documented.

Maximal oxygen uptake has been shown to decrease by between 20% and 30% following 4 weeks of bed rest. The loss in cardiovascular fitness depends on the duration of the bed rest and how fit the individual was before the period of bed rest. Those with a higher maximal oxygen uptake prior to the period of bed rest tend to show a bigger reduction in VO_{2max} than those who are sedentary.

When a person is confined to bed and muscles are inactive, major changes in muscle function can be detected after a few hours. Protein synthesis starts to decrease and this results in muscle atrophy and loss of muscle strength. There is general agreement that muscle atrophy occurs at a rapid rate initially and then slows, and also that lower limb muscles atrophy at a faster rate than those of the upper limb. When a limb is immobilized, for example following a fracture, this causes absorption of sarcomeres, particularly when the muscle is held in a shortened position, and this results in loss of muscle strength. Other types of acute injuries or illnesses will impact on exercise ability in different ways. Some examples of the main ways that acute injuries and their symptoms can affect exercise ability are summarized in Table 11.1.

BENEFITS OF EXERCISE IN ACUTE CONDITIONS

It is important to begin an exercise programme as soon as practically possible, to minimize muscle atrophy and loss of cardiovascular fitness. Unaffected joints and limbs should be exercised to maintain range of movement and cardiovascular and muscular fitness. Pain and swelling can inhibit muscle function and cause loss of range of movement during the initial stages of the inflammatory process; therefore it may be impossible to exercise the injured area through range at this stage. As soon as swelling and bleeding start to subside and the healing process starts, an exercise programme can be prescribed for the injured area. Exercise at this stage may help to reduce swelling and pain, as well as increase range of movement and muscle function. The exercise programme should be progressed throughout the healing process to minimize adverse effects from the injury or illness and to enable the person to return to normal function as soon as possible.

STAGES OF REHABILITATION

The exercises prescribed for the patient will be determined by the stage of healing of the acute condition; in general the exercises will become more strenuous as healing progresses. Stages of rehabilitation are referred to as early, intermediate and late. Each stage of rehabilitation can be described by the stage of healing of the patient which relates to their presenting symptoms. The stages of rehabilitation

Table 11.1 Examples of how acute injuries and their symptoms can affect exercise ability

Acute condition or injury	Possible symptoms	Impact on exercise ability
Lateral ankle sprain with loss of ability to weight bear	Pain Swelling Redness/ bruising	Decreased range of movement at ankle and subtalar joints Loss of muscle strength in plantar flexors, dorsiflexors, invertors and evertors Loss of cardiovascular fitness because of physical inactivity Reduced proprioception at ankle joint
Fractured humerus immobilized in a collar and cuff	Pain Swelling	Decreased range of movement at shoulder, elbow and wrist Decreased muscle strength shoulder flexors, extensors, abductors, adductors and lateral and medial rotators
Hip replacement	Pain Swelling Redness/ bruising	Decreased range of movement at hip and knee Decreased muscle strength and endurance hip flexors, extensors, abductors, adductors and lateral and medial rotators and knee flexors and extensors Reduced proprioception at hip joint Decreased cardiovascular fitness due to reduced activity following joint replacement
Severe pneumonia which required intensive care admission and ventilation	Limited functional ability Fatigue and shortness of breath	Global decrease in muscle strength and endurance Decreased cardiovascular fitness

and their relation to the current presentation of the acute condition are described in Table 11.2.

At any point in the rehabilitation process, a patient may need to be regressed to an earlier stage of rehabilitation; for example if they develop swelling or pain in a joint associated with prescribed exercises, the exercises will need to be regressed and adapted to avoid the unwanted symptoms.

Table 11.2 Stages of rehabilitation related to typical patient presentation and exercise prescription

Stage of rehabilitation	Presentation	Exercises
Early stage – from the injury to almost full pain-free activities	Non-weight-bearing Pain Swelling Limited ROM	Carried out in stable starting positions, e.g. long sitting Within the limit of pain Should not disrupt the inflammatory or healing process Maintain available ROM at injury site as able Muscle work usually static around injury site Maintain ROM and muscle strength in unaffected areas Maintain cardiorespiratory fitness as able
Intermediate stage – activities become pain-free, with full range of movement and muscular control	Less swelling Almost pain-free Almost full range of movement Partial or full weight-bearing	If partial weight-bearing standing may not be a suitable starting position Exercises work into a larger/full ROM More focus on building muscle strength and endurance Start to work towards functional activities Avoid excessive resistance or stress that could disrupt the healing process Continue to maintain ROM and muscle strength in unaffected areas Continue to maintain cardiorespiratory fitness as able
Late stage – the injured area will gradually be exercised as in the patient's normal activities	Pain-free Full range of movement Full weight-bearing	Work towards regaining maximal levels of strength, endurance and cardiorespiratory fitness Exercises based on functional/occupational/recreational activities Re-educate proprioceptive function More stressful activities, e.g. twisting, jumping are incorporated where appropriate Exercises are normally dynamic and energetic incorporating the whole body

ROM, range of movement

The end point of rehabilitation will be different for each individual depending on their age, occupation, functional ability and normal activities. The final aim of treatment for a patient following an acute injury or illness would be to return them to their normal levels of function and fitness. Prior to discharge the physiotherapist should be certain that the patient has the necessary skills to undertake their normal activities confidently. The injury should have recovered with no residual swelling or pain on activity and movements should be through the full range. Cardiovascular fitness and muscle strength should be similar to that before the injury. For those returning to sport or strenuous occupations, it may be necessary for the physiotherapist to liaise with sports coaches or occupational health staff to ensure a safe and successful return to sport or work.

SPECIAL CONSIDERATIONS FOR EXERCISE IN ACUTE CONDITIONS

- Exercises should be appropriate for the stage of healing of the acute condition. If untoward pain or swelling occurs during or following exercise, the exercises should be regressed.
- Exercises will normally start in static positions or move through small ranges of movement following an acute injury. They will become dynamic and the intensity will increase as the patient progresses to the late stage of rehabilitation.
- Exercises should be prescribed in suitable and stable starting positions, taking into account the weight-bearing status of the patient to avoid inadvertent weight-bearing through the affected limb.
- At the end of the rehabilitation process the patient should have the necessary skills and fitness to carry out their activities confidently and without pain.
- Besides losses in muscle strength, cardiovascular fitness and range of movement, other changes associated with bed rest and decreased activity can occur such as a decrease in bone density, a decrease in visual acuity and changes in blood pressure responses. These factors should be considered when designing an appropriate exercise programme for individual patients.

RECOMMENDED EXERCISE PRESCRIPTION

There are no specific exercise prescriptions for people with acute conditions; therefore training should be adapted from the recommendations for cardiovascular and muscular fitness training for healthy people. However each patient should be thoroughly assessed to ensure that the exercises prescribed are suitable for the stage of rehabilitation and the stage of healing of the injury.

Further reading

Appell HJ (1990) Muscular atrophy following immobilisation: a review. Sports Medicine 10: 42–58.
Bruton A (2002) Muscle plasticity: response to training and detraining. Physiotherapy 88(7): 398–408.
Convertino A (1997) Cardiovascular consequences of bedrest: effect on maximal oxygen uptake. Medicine and Science in Sports and Exercise 29(2): 191–196.
Marieb E (2009) Essentials of Human Anatomy and Physiology: 9th edition. San Francisco, CA: Pearson Benjamin Cummings.
Shamley D (ed.) (2005) Pathophysiology: An Essential Text for the Allied Health Professions. Edinburgh, UK: Elsevier.
Smith G (1998) Orthopaedic Physiotherapy. London, UK: Mosby.

Exercise for People with Chronic Conditions

This chapter considers common chronic conditions which will be encountered by the physiotherapist. Physiotherapists should be aware of the impact of these conditions on exercise ability, the benefits of exercise and special considerations for prescribing exercise in these conditions. Patients with one of these chronic conditions may present for physiotherapy treatment to manage the condition itself, or the chronic condition may be a co-morbidity which requires consideration when prescribing exercise.

In view of the current healthcare priorities this chapter also considers exercise prescription for patients who are referred for exercise programmes to reduce the risk factors associated with the development and progression of some chronic conditions.

EXERCISE FOR PEOPLE WITH OBESITY

Obesity is defined as an accumulation of excess fat to the extent that it has a negative effect on health and is often quantified using the measurement of body mass index (BMI). The World Health Organization defines a BMI of >25 as overweight, and a BMI of >30 as obese.

This section will discuss the role of exercise in the prevention and management of obesity, as well as considerations for exercise in the obese population.

Benefits of exercise for obesity prevention and management

Obesity is caused when more energy is consumed than expended. There are many factors contributing to the cause of obesity; however obesity tends to occur after several years of inactivity as physical activity plays an important part in maintaining the amount of energy expended. Physical activity levels often decline from childhood to adult life; however there is not usually an accompanying decline in energy intake through the diet – this leads to a gradual increase in body weight.

Obesity can lead to many other health problems, most notably non-insulin-dependent (type 2) diabetes, cardiovascular disease and some types of cancer; therefore any intervention that can manage obesity is important for health.

In terms of exercise, the management of obesity can be approached from two perspectives: exercise for health and exercise for weight loss.

Regular physical activity reduces many of the health risks associated with obesity regardless of weight loss. Active obese individuals have lower morbidity and mortality than normal weight individuals who are sedentary; it appears that cardiorespiratory fitness is an important predictor of morbidity in obese individuals. Therefore it is important to educate people that regular exercise has health benefits in the absence of weight loss.

The management of weight loss tends to focus primarily on diet, and exercise is often recommended as a secondary activity. This may be due to the fact that exercise alone produces a somewhat modest weight loss of 0.5–1.0 kg per month; however implementation of an exercise programme and dietary intervention together have been demonstrated to produce greater weight loss than either intervention alone. Exercise in combination with diet affects the body composition by producing a greater loss of body fat and conservation of muscle. The inclusion of exercise is important for long-term weight loss, as diet in combination with exercise has been shown to produce long-term weight loss in comparison with diet alone.

When prescribing an exercise programme it should be remembered that individuals have differing responses to exercise for weight loss. This is thought to be due to genetic make up and gender – whereby men lose more weight in response to exercise than women.

In the guidelines below 'physical activity' can be exchanged for 'exercise,' as exercise to prevent obesity and/or to maintain long-term weight loss needs to be incorporated into the person's lifestyle and carried out on an ongoing basis. Although some people do get into the habit of attending a gym on a regular basis many people will not, and adapting their daily routine to include such activities as walking to work or taking the stairs may be more effective than a formal exercise programme.

Special considerations for exercise in people with obesity

- If the person has been sedentary for some time the exercise programme will need to be staged to produce a gentle increase in duration.
- Before embarking on an exercise programme the person should be screened for co-morbidities that may have an influence on the exercise prescription, such as diabetes or cardiac conditions.
- High-impact activities such as jogging should be avoided due to the excessive strain that is placed through the joints.
- Before using exercise equipment with morbidly obese people the individual's weight should be checked against the maximum weight limit of the equipment to ensure safe use.
- Fluid balance is not well regulated in people who are overweight and they are more susceptible to dehydration; therefore they should be advised to drink regularly.
- Temperature regulation is also affected in obesity, and people should be advised to wear light clothing and exercise in a cool environment.

Recommended exercise prescription

For prevention of obesity

- Intensity: Moderate intensity.
- Frequency: Split to 30 minutes, 5 times a week.
- Duration: 150 minutes of physical activity a week.

An alternative target is 10 000 steps a day, as people achieving this are likely to be sufficiently physically active.

Exercise in the management of obesity

Exercise for health

- Intensity: Moderate.
- Frequency: 30 minutes, 5 times a week – however this may not be achievable for a previously sedentary individual. When initiating an exercise programme several 10–15-minute activity sessions can be carried out over the course of a day to gradually build up the exercise programme to the required amount.
- Duration: A gradual build up to 150 minutes of physical activity a week.

- Mode: Predominantly cardiovascular exercise. Resistance exercise for muscular strength and endurance is also recommended to improve function, such as sit to stand.

Exercise for weight loss

- Intensity: Moderate.
- Frequency and duration: In order to achieve long-term weight loss 200–300 minutes of exercise a week is recommended.
- Mode: Cardiovascular exercise. There is no conclusive evidence to support the use of resistance training for weight loss.

EXERCISE FOR PEOPLE WITH DIABETES

This section will discuss the role of exercise in the prevention and management of types 1 and 2 diabetes and consider the effect of exercise on the control of diabetes.

The impact of non-insulin-dependent (type 2) diabetes on exercise ability

Exercise increases insulin sensitivity and helps with glycaemic control. Glucose levels drop during moderate-intensity exercise, as during activity there is a decrease in glucose production at the liver. The amount of change in glucose level varies with the intensity and duration of exercise. When people with obesity perform a period of short-term intense exercise, glucose levels often rise during the exercise and remain raised for an hour afterwards. The increases in insulin sensitivity following a single bout of exercise are relatively short-lived; therefore regular exercise is recommended.

The benefits of exercise in non-insulin-dependent (type 2) diabetes

Type 2 diabetes is defined as a combination of insulin resistance and insulin deficiency and is caused by a combination of factors. Insulin resistance is manifested as a decreased amount of glycogen stored in the liver and muscle, and decreased insulin transport and receptor substrate in the muscle restricting the amount of phosphorylation that can occur. The insulin deficiency is due to abnormal secretion of insulin and reduced secretion of insulin due to hyperglycaemia.

Type 2 diabetes can lead to the development of many co-morbid conditions, such as cardiovascular disease, neuropathy, cerebrovascular disease and susceptibility to infection. There appears to be a genetic tendency to develop the disease and other factors such as older age, ethnicity and obesity are also linked to developing diabetes.

If normal blood glucose levels can be maintained, then the onset of these conditions can be delayed.

Special considerations for exercise in people with type 2 diabetes

- Regular exercise at low to moderate intensity is recommended to increase insulin sensitivity and lower glucose levels.
- If insulin dependent, it may be preferable to exercise on a daily basis to allow a regular and stable insulin dosage to be established.
- Although additional cardiovascular fitness may be achieved by working at higher intensity, the low to moderate level recommended optimizes the risk/benefit balance for people with type 2 diabetes.
- Heart rate may not be a suitable means of monitoring exercise intensity in this group as development of autonomic neuropathy will affect the heart rate (HR) response to exercise.
- Patients with complications such as peripheral neuropathy may require modified exercises so that they can be safely performed without causing themselves injury.
- In people with advanced stages of cardiovascular or retinal complications resistance exercises should be modified to reduce the weight lifted, reduce the number of repetitions to avoid exhaustion and limit the amount of sustained grip time to prevent an untoward increase in systemic blood pressure.

Recommended exercise prescription

Cardiovascular exercise

Activities for which it is easy to control the intensity and that are easily maintained are recommended for this patient group. Low-impact activities are preferable in the presence of some complications, such as peripheral neuropathy.

- Intensity: Low- to moderate-intensity activity is recommended. It is suggested that at the start of the exercise programme exercise intensity is very low, and is increased to moderate throughout the programme.
- Frequency: Exercise should be spread over at least 3 non-consecutive days.

- Duration: A minimum of 100 minutes a week. Exercise periods of 15 minutes at the start of the exercise programme are advised, building up to the desired 30 minutes per session.

Resistance training

Although there is little direct evidence for the use of resistance training in type 2 diabetes it is thought to produce similar benefits in maintaining fat-free mass, increasing muscle strength and endurance and reducing glucose levels and insulin resistance as seen in the non-diabetic population. It is recommended that a minimum of 8–10 resistance exercises involving the major muscle groups should be performed as part of an exercise programme.

- Frequency: At least 2 days a week.
- Repetitions: A minimum of one set of 10–15 repetitions to near fatigue.

The impact of type 1 diabetes on exercise ability

In type 1 diabetes the pancreas does not produce insulin, which must be replaced by injections of insulin to regulate blood glucose levels. The response to exercise in people with type 1 diabetes needs to be understood so that a physiotherapist prescribing exercise to manage a co-morbid condition can take them into consideration. In addition people with type 1 diabetes may wish to take part in sports and exercise for pleasure or at a competitive level.

Blood glucose levels tend to decrease during and after aerobic exercise in people with type 1 diabetes; there are several factors which contribute to this. During aerobic activity there is an increase in the rate of absorption of subcutaneously injected insulin due to the increase in circulation. In addition the increase in body temperature produced during exercise leads to an increase in the rate of insulin absorption. Plasma levels of insulin do not decrease during exercise; therefore any insulin injected prior to exercise will remain present and impair glucose production. Exercise produces an increase in the insulin sensitivity of skeletal muscles, which may be sustained for several hours. Finally there is an increase in glucose uptake through non-insulin-mediated pathways, which leads to a decrease in insulin requirement. This produces an imbalance between glucose depletion and insulin levels, resulting in low blood glucose levels. If a person has repeated hypoglycaemic episodes, then the counter-regulation of insulin response becomes dampened, which makes a person who has been experiencing hypoglycaemia more prone to further episodes.

The combination of the factors above may lead the person to become hypoglycaemic both during and for several hours after the exercise. As hypoglycaemia can be fatal in extreme cases it is vital that both the physiotherapist and the person with diabetes are aware of the signs and symptoms of hypoglycaemia.

High-intensity, short-burst, anaerobic exercise in people with type 1 diabetes tends to cause blood glucose levels to rise, as it stimulates over-production of glucose from the liver and impairs glucose utilization. Blood glucose levels often stay raised for some time. The resulting hyperglycaemia and ketoacidosis leads to dehydration and an increase in the acidity of the blood, both of which can impair exercise performance.

These effects are seen at an exercise intensity of over 75% of maximum heart rate.

The benefits of exercise in people with type 1 (insulin-dependent) diabetes

There is no evidence to support the recommendation of exercise to improve the control of blood glucose levels in people with type 1 diabetes. People with type 1 diabetes are, however, at a much increased risk of cardiovascular disease, and regular exercise can reduce the risk of developing cardiovascular disease in this group as in any other population.

Consideration for exercise prescription in type 1 diabetes

- As with type 2 diabetes.
- Prevention and management of hypoglycaemia: particular attention to monitoring blood glucose before, during and for several hours after exercising should be given when establishing an exercise programme. It may be necessary to reduce the insulin dose or increase the intake of carbohydrates before exercise, which should be done in proportion to the intensity of the exercise to be undertaken.
- Ensure that there is an immediate source of sugar to hand. Fruit juice or glucose tablets are recommended, and anyone with type 1 diabetes should carry these sugar sources with them when exercising.
- Be aware of the signs and symptoms of hypoglycaemia in the early stages of diabetes:
  - shakiness
  - palpitations

  - excessive sweating
  - hunger.
- Be aware of the signs and symptoms of hypoglycaemia in the later stages of diabetes:
  - slow speech/movement
  - confusion
  - irritability
  - irrationality
  - blurred vision
  - pallor
  - headache
  - fatigue.
- Prevention and management of hyperglycaemia: blood glucose should be monitored before and for some period after high-intensity exercise.
- If blood glucose levels are found to be high then supplementary insulin may be required.
- Be aware of the high incidence of cardiovascular disease in this population and ensure that any cardiac conditions are stable before exercising.

Recommended exercise prescription

For guidelines for exercise for health see type 2 diabetes.

EXERCISE FOR PEOPLE WITH CARDIOVASCULAR DISEASE

Cardiovascular diseases are the most common type of diseases which affect the population of the United Kingdom. These diseases include coronary heart disease, angina and myocardial infarction, heart failure and hypertension. As these diseases are so common, physiotherapists will come across patients suffering from these types of disorder either as a primary reason for referral for treatment, for example to a cardiac rehabilitation class, or as a co-morbidity when a patient has been referred for treatment for another condition, for example back pain. Much has been written about exercise in relation to people with cardiovascular disease and so this section of the chapter will give only a broad overview of this area to allow the physiotherapist to safely prescribe exercise to patients with cardiovascular disease.

The impact of cardiovascular disease on exercise ability

People with cardiovascular disease may suffer from a variety of symptoms depending on the nature and severity of their disease.

Symptoms can include angina, dyspnoea and fatigue, all of which can cause discomfort whilst exercising and so reduce the patient's activity levels. Patients can become fearful of exercising because of bringing on symptoms and this can lead to a decrease in activity and further reduction in exercise tolerance. If this process is left unchecked, the reduction in exercise tolerance will start to affect the patient's ability to carry out normal daily activities. Physical inactivity is also a major risk factor in the development of coronary heart disease.

Benefits of exercise in cardiovascular disease

There is a large evidence base to support the therapeutic benefits of exercise in those with cardiovascular disease. These include reductions in symptoms and cardiovascular mortality and improvements in exercise tolerance and well-being. Most research in this group has been carried out using aerobic or endurance training. As a result, cardiac rehabilitation programmes are offered to those with coronary heart disease and controlled, chronic heart failure. Exercise is the cornerstone of these programmes but they also include an education component.

There is a large amount of evidence which supports using exercise to reduce the risk of onset of cardiovascular disease. Those who participate in exercise regularly reduce their risk of suffering from coronary heart disease and hypertension.

Cardiovascular training

This has been specifically shown to affect both central and peripheral physiology. Centrally an increase in myocardial perfusion and a decrease in myocardial oxygen consumption at a sub-maximal workload have been shown. This will lead to a reduction in heart rate and systolic blood pressure at sub-maximal workload. An increase in end diastolic volume and subsequent increase in stroke volume have also been shown. VO_2 peak improves during exercise and there is a reduction in resting blood pressure. Peripherally an increase in capillary beds and mitochondrial enzymes in muscles allows more efficient use of oxygen during exercise. The changes seen will be subject to the frequency, intensity and duration of exercise. This in turn will be affected by the severity of the patient's symptoms, due to their cardiovascular disease. These patients will be limited maximally by their cardiovascular symptoms.

Cardiovascular training also confers benefit on blood cholesterol levels. Raised blood cholesterol is another risk factor for the development of coronary artery disease. Regular exercise has been shown to increase levels of high-density lipo protein (HDL) cholesterol and reduce triglycerides and low-density lipo protein (LDL) cholesterol.

Coronary artery disease is associated with raised levels of triglyceride and LDL cholesterol, which deposits on the endothelial wall of the arteries. HDL cholesterol is thought to move cholesterol away from the arterial wall to the liver, where it is catabolized.

Psychological benefits including an enhanced sense of well-being, reduced anxiety and improvement in self-confidence have been shown in people with cardiovascular disease who have undergone a cardiac rehabilitation programme.

Resistance training

As resistance training is associated with increases in blood pressure and the possibility of straining manoeuvres if an incorrect technique is used, it has not been used as widely as aerobic training for those with cardiovascular disease. More recently resistance training, using moderate loads, has been used safely in cardiac rehabilitation programmes for those with normal left ventricular function and good cardiorespiratory fitness. Improvements in muscle strength will help with functional activities such as carrying shopping. Resistance training should not be used for high-risk patients with coronary artery disease or those with severe hypertension. Resistance training to fatigue is not recommended for high-risk patients. Fatigue should be kept to a moderate level (Borg scale < 15). Little research has been carried out to support the use of resistance training in those with chronic heart failure and current recommendations suggest using aerobic exercise only in this group.

Special considerations for exercise in cardiovascular disease

Exercise prescription for people with cardiovascular disease should be of adequate intensity to produce a training effect. Although this may not be the optimum intensity for the individual, the initiation of symptoms should be avoided. A mild to moderate exercise intensity is usually more suitable and exercise intensity should be monitored using the Borg scale or heart rate. For progression, frequency and duration of exercise should be increased before intensity.

Warm up and cool down should be given special attention. Warm up should be progressive in intensity so that the conditioning period of exercise is at the same intensity as the end of the warm-up period. The period of warm up should also be extended to allow the blood flow to the myocardium to adapt to the required exercise intensity. Cool down should be the opposite of warm up with a gradual reduction in exercise intensity.

Excessive upper body work increases blood pressure and this should be avoided. If upper body work is required, leg movements, for example walking on the spot, should be carried out at the same time. This helps to avoid large increases in blood pressure. Abrupt changes in position should be avoided to allow time for the cardiovascular system to adjust to the position change. Exercise intensity should be adapted to the environment. In hot weather exercise intensity may need to be reduced.

Contraindications to exercise training in people with cardiovascular disease are uncontrolled arrythmias, heart failure and hypertension, unstable angina, complete heart block and certain other systemic disorders such as a recent or acute infection.

Further guidelines for cardiac rehabilitation classes or exercising people with cardiovascular disease in a group environment include:

- All staff working with the class should be trained in basic life support, and one person present should be trained in advanced life support.
- Resuscitation equipment, especially a defibrillator, should be to hand.
- Alert the cardiac arrest team if the class is taking place in a hospital or have a procedure in place for contacting the ambulance service in case of emergency.
- A staff/patient ratio of 1:5 is recommended.
- High-risk patients should be monitored with an ECG.
- Appropriate risk assessments should be completed for tasks carried out in the class.
- Competition should be minimized within the exercises prescribed in the class.
- Participants should be observed for 30 minutes after they have finished exercising.

Recommended exercise prescription

Cardiorespiratory training

Current guidelines for those with cardiovascular disease are:

- Frequency: 1 or 2 times per week at rehabilitation class and exercise at home 1 or 2 times per week. Walking other days.
- Intensity: 60–75% HR_{max}, 12–13 Borg scale, 40–60% VO_2 peak.
- Time: 20–30 min conditioning with 15–20 min warm up and 10 min cool down.
- Type: Aerobic endurance involving large muscle groups and dynamic movement.

Resistance training

A low-resistance, high-repetition programme is recommended for strength training. Eight to ten large muscle groups should be exercised with one set of 10–15 RM, 2 or 3 days a week.

EXERCISE FOR PEOPLE WITH CHRONIC RESPIRATORY DISEASE

Chronic respiratory diseases such as asthma, chronic obstructive pulmonary disease (COPD), cystic fibrosis and interstitial lung disease can all impact on the patient's exercise ability as the disease progresses. The effects of respiratory disease are due to both the disease pathology and the secondary effects of deconditioning as a result of activity avoidance.

The impact of chronic respiratory disease on exercise ability

All respiratory conditions produce breathlessness in the patient as the disease progresses, although the pathological changes that occur to produce this breathlessness may be different. Initially the patient tends to feel breathless only on exertion, when there is an increased demand on the respiratory system due to the need for more oxygen to support aerobic energy production. As the sensation of breathlessness is unpleasant, patients often start to avoid the sensation by reducing the amount of physical activity undertaken. This leads to general decline in cardiovascular and muscular fitness due to inactivity. The decrease in fitness then completes the vicious cycle, as the patient then feels breathless at lower activity levels due to the body's less efficient response to exercise. This leads to a further reduction in activity levels.

The symptom of breathlessness is very complex, and its causes are multifactorial, being both physical and psychological. From a physical point of view, the ventilatory demand, or requirement to breathe in and out, is increased in patients with respiratory disease due to inefficient ventilation and gas exchange. This increase in ventilatory demand is paired with a decreased ventilatory capacity, and this mismatch leads to ventilation being the limiting factor to maximal exercise in this group of patients.

Although ventilation is the limiting factor to maximal exercise in this patient population, many patients stop exercising before reaching maximum capacity due to breathlessness or muscle fatigue. Fatigue in the leg muscles is commonly cited as a reason for the termination of exercise. This muscle fatigue may be due to a combination of the decrease in muscle strength, power and endurance seen in this population. In addition COPD is known to affect the muscles directly, with a decrease in fat-free body mass seen in this group.

Benefits of exercise in chronic respiratory disease

Exercise training has been used as part of the management of chronic respiratory disease for many years. There is now a strong body of evidence to support the inclusion of pulmonary rehabilitation in standards of care for chronic respiratory disease. Pulmonary rehabilitation is a comprehensive, multidisciplinary intervention for patients with limited exercise ability secondary to respiratory disease. The aim of pulmonary rehabilitation is to reduce symptoms, maximize function, increase participation and reduce healthcare burden. Exercise training is an essential component of pulmonary rehabilitation, the other components being an education programme and psychosocial support.

Cardiovascular training

Cardiovascular training modalities, such as walking, stair climbing and cycling, have been shown to produce increases in exercise ability and health-related quality of life in patients with respiratory conditions. Increases in walking distance and exercise endurance time and lower oxygen uptake and breathlessness for a given workload have all been demonstrated following a cardiovascular training programme in this patient group. Increases in maximal exercise parameters have been demonstrated, but these findings are not consistent and it appears that high-intensity training (>60% VO_{2max}) is needed to produce physiological changes. Improvements in functional performance are seen after lower-intensity training in the absence of physiological adaptations. These functional improvements are thought to be due to improvements in confidence, desensitization to breathlessness and improved co-ordination of task performance.

Resistance training

Strength training is also recommended for patients with respiratory disease due to the peripheral muscle weakness present in this group. Lower limb strength training has been demonstrated to increase walking distance and quality of life as well as muscle strength.

In addition to the direct training effects, patients become better able to manage their breathlessness and are more confident when exercising. These changes lead to an increase in activity levels and increased quality of life.

Special considerations for exercise in chronic respiratory disease

Contraindications to exercise training

In addition to the normal contraindications to exercise the conditions listed below need to be considered in this patient group:

- uncontrolled heart failure
- uncontrolled pulmonary hypertension
- acute chest infection.

Precautions for exercise training

In addition to the normal precautions to exercise the conditions listed below need to be considered in this patient group:

- Current or recent haemoptysis, as the increase in blood flow may exacerbate any bleed.
- Significant oxygen desaturation on exercise, >5% desaturation, or desaturates to <90%. These patients should exercise with supplementary oxygen.
- Cross-infection. Patients are more likely to cough when exercising and this may spread infection. If the patients are attending exercise groups, as is common in pulmonary rehabilitation, they should only exercise with other patients who are culturing similar bacteria. A common example of this would be that patients with and without *Pseudomonas* should not exercise together.
- Particular attention should be given to the patient's pattern of breathing during exercise training, as they may tend to hold their breath on exertion which will exacerbate their breathlessness. Advice regarding expiration on lifting a weight, and pacing of breathing during cardiovascular training, is often useful.

Recommended exercise prescription

Cardiovascular training

- Intensity: It is recommended that an exercise intensity of 60–70% VO_{2max} is used for cardiovascular training in patients with chronic respiratory disease. In practice this intensity may be too high for many patients, and good results are obtained from exercise training at lower intensities in the initial stages of the programme.
  - In COPD the heart rate does not increase linearly with increasing work rate; therefore it is unreliable for monitoring or setting exercise intensity. The Borg scale is most commonly used in this patient population.
- Frequency: Training is recommended 3–5 times a week.
- Duration: As with the healthy population the recommended exercise session duration is 20–30 minutes. As patients require time to recover their breath in between activities the training is in reality a form of interval training and usually takes up to an hour a session.
  - Patients with COPD show training response after 6–12 weeks of training.
- Mode: Patients with COPD report particular breathlessness when performing functional tasks with their upper limbs. This is because when the upper limbs are being used the shoulder girdle

cannot also be used to fix the accessory muscles of breathing. It is recommended that endurance and strength training of the upper limbs is included in the exercise programme.

Resistance training

- Resistance training is in accordance with guidelines for healthy subjects, with particular recommendation for training the muscles of ambulation.

EXERCISE FOR PEOPLE WITH CHRONIC NEUROLOGICAL CONDITIONS

Chronic neurological conditions often limit a person's ability to produce controlled movement, and this movement limitation has an impact on their exercise capacity. Historically neurological rehabilitation has focused very much on neurological impairment and activity-based problems; however there is now a move to specifically address cardiovascular fitness and muscle strength in this population.

This section will specifically consider stroke, multiple sclerosis (MS) and spinal cord injury as common neurological conditions seen by physiotherapists; however some of the principles discussed may also be applicable to other neurological conditions.

The impact of chronic neurological conditions on exercise ability

Cardiovascular exercise

In patients who have altered patterns of movement secondary to impairment of movement and balance, the performance of functional tasks often has a higher energy cost than in healthy people, as the task is not performed with optimum efficiency; for example oxygen uptake during walking in people with hemiplegia has been shown to be increased to as much as double that of an unaffected person. This increase in oxygen uptake during activity places an additional demand on the cardiovascular system. The additional demand is coupled with decreased cardiovascular fitness due to decreased activity levels, thus markedly limiting exercise capacity.

It is likely that some degree of deconditioning is present in patients with neurological disorders due to a decrease in habitual activity levels or enforced periods of decreased activity such as bed rest. Direct effects of the neurological disorder, such as altered muscle tone and decreased sensation, will also limit the person's ability to perform exercise.

Left ventricular dysfunction has been identified in some people following stroke, and this will contribute towards a limitation in cardiovascular performance. People who have had a stroke are likely to have artherosclerotic lesions throughout their vascular system and are at increased risk of cardiovascular disease.

Fatigue is a prominent feature of MS, and people with MS usually terminate a maximal incremental exercise test due to peripheral fatigue before reaching maximal predicted exercise, thus indicating that fatigue is a major limiting factor to exercise in this group. Exercise responses during sub-maximal exercise in people with MS are normal, with HR and VO_2 showing a linear increase with increasing workload; however VO_{2max} is reduced.

Maximum work capacity and cardiovascular fitness are reduced in people following spinal cord injury. This is in part due to a decrease in functional muscle mass and sympathetic control and, in many people, also secondary to a sedentary lifestyle.

During cardiovascular exercise in healthy people blood is diverted to the exercising muscle from the inactive muscle; however in people with spinal cord injury this vasoregulatory response is wholly or partially absent. In addition the inactive muscle in the lower limbs is not able to contribute to the muscle pump, thus reducing the venous return to the heart and the end-diastolic volume. These abnormal central responses to cardiovascular exercise limit stroke volume, blunt the heart rate response and reduce the myocardial contractility during exercise. The maximum HR is usually less than 130 bpm in this group. Although some people with spinal cord injury are very active, literature reports that activity levels are generally low in this group, and that activities of daily living do not cause people to work within the training zone required to increase cardiovascular fitness.

Muscle strength

Muscle strength is decreased in people following stroke and in those with MS. Muscle strength of the affected limb following stroke has been shown to be 20–34% of age-matched controls. This may not be surprising; however the strength of the unaffected limb has also been shown to be reduced to only 60–89% of normal muscle strength. Muscle strength in MS is extremely variable, depending on the stage of the disease. Lower limb muscle strength has been shown to be particularly affected in people with MS.

Increased muscle tone has long been thought to be the main cause of muscle weakness in people with neurological conditions; however research in people following stroke has found that both the agonist and antagonist muscle groups are weak, and it has been suggested that weakness may be more attributable to lack of motor recruitment and inco-ordination rather than muscle tone.

Muscle strength will vary in people with spinal cord injury depending on the level and pattern of innervation below their lesion.

Causes of muscle weakness in these groups are atrophy of type 2 muscle fibres and loss of motor units. In MS there is also decreased recruitment due to conduction block from the demyelinated fibres.

Flexibility

Neurological conditions affecting the ability to produce controlled movement through full range potentially lead to a decrease in range of movement due to adaptive tissue shortening and decreased muscle strength. In addition sustained postures, for example sustained sitting in a wheelchair or increased muscle tone maintaining a limb in position, also lead to adaptive shortening.

Benefits of exercise in chronic neurological conditions

Cardiovascular training

Cardiovascular training is important in people with neurological problems, as they are often performing with decreased efficiency due to their neurological impairments.

It has been demonstrated that cardiovascular exercise training following a stroke can produce similar training effects to those seen in healthy people.

Functional activity is often used as part of the exercise rehabilitation programme for people following stroke. It has been shown that performing these functional tasks in the early stages of rehabilitation brings people into their target HR for aerobic training; therefore if sustained for sufficient time this will increase cardiovascular fitness.

It is difficult to distinguish how much of the limitation to activity is caused directly by the disease pathology in MS, and what proportion is secondary to a decrease in activity levels. The secondary decline in exercise ability should be reversible, and indeed cardiovascular training programmes have demonstrated increases in exercise endurance time and a decrease in submaximal VO_2. In addition to these changes following cardiovascular exercise, a new body of emerging literature suggests that physical activity may have a direct influence on brain health in MS which is associated with cytokine activity, and a relationship between physical activity levels and cognitive function has been described.

A decrease in cardiovascular fitness is particularly significant in people with spinal cord injury, as cardiovascular disease is a common cause of mortality in this group. There appears to be an increase in the risk factors for cardiovascular disease in people with spinal cord injury, specifically glucose metabolism, lipid profile and obesity. As these factors are known to be modifiable by cardiovascular exercise it is recommended that cardiovascular exercise should be included in an exercise programme for spinal-cord-injured patients not only to increase exercise ability but also to reduce these risk factors. Cardiovascular exercise training has been demonstrated to increase VO_{2max} in this patient group and has also been associated with improved quality of life.

Resistance training

Strength training is important to maximize function following a stroke, in particular for those muscles that play a key role in gait. Contrary to historical concerns, research has demonstrated that resistance training in people with increased tone following stroke does not cause a further increase in muscle tone.

Resistance training programmes in people with MS, lifting 10–15 repetitions maximum, twice a week, have been shown to increase muscle performance and overall physical function with no adverse effects. Fatigue is an important consideration when carrying out exercise with people who have MS. It has been demonstrated that people with mild to moderate MS are able to perform repetitive exercises involving the same muscle group; however they show a significantly greater loss of strength in the exercised muscle group after exercise than that seen in healthy people.

The unaffected muscle groups should be optimized in people following spinal cord injury, and a programme of strength training twice a week has been demonstrated to produce significant increases in strength. The magnitude of the increases in strength was directly related to the length of time that the person had been participating in the training programme, with continued increases in strength being seen after a year of training. Functional electrical stimulation (FES) may also be used to train some of the muscle groups affected by the spinal cord lesion; however this specialist intervention is beyond the scope of this text.

Special considerations for exercise in chronic neurological conditions

In addition to the normal precautions and contraindications to exercise training the factors below need to be considered when prescribing exercise in these patient groups.

Stroke

- Cardiac disease is prevalent in this patient group, and patients should be screened for undetected cardiac disease before commencing an exercise programme.
- Care should be taken with intense isometric work as it can cause a marked rise in blood pressure.
- Exercise in the acute period following stroke: there are no absolute guidelines, but literature suggests that exercise can commence 14 days post stroke, and blood pressure should be monitored to maintain systolic pressure <250 mmHg and diastolic pressure <115 mmHg. It is recommended that training HR should remain 10 bpm below the level that produces this maximum blood pressure.

Multiple sclerosis

- Some people with MS show an abnormal autonomic system response to cardiovascular exercise, which is seen as a blunted heart rate response and a drop in blood pressure. If such a reaction occurs the patient should be monitored, and a lower-intensity exercise programme may be needed.
- Thermal sensitivity is a significant problem in people with MS. The environment should be maintained at a cool temperature. A rise in core temperature can cause the onset of fatigue, balance problems and poor co-ordination.

Spinal cord injury

- Warm up is particularly important in this group due to blood pooling in inactive muscles and the decreased venous return to the heart.
- Autonomic dysreflexia. This is a potentially life-threatening increase in blood pressure occasionally seen in response to exercise in people with lesions above T6. The physiotherapist working with these people should be aware of the signs and symptoms, such as swelling, flushing and goosebumps above the lesion, pounding headache, blurred vision and nasal congestion. If a patient exhibits such symptoms they should be sat upright, their blood pressure monitored and they should be referred to the emergency department.
- Temperature regulation is often impaired; therefore close monitoring of temperature should take place during and after exercise and appropriate ventilation, towels and warm clothes should be available as needed.
- Patients with spinal cord injury often have a significant decrease in bone density due to disuse; therefore they are at risk of sustaining

a fracture in response to relatively minor trauma, so particular care should be taken to avoid this.

Recommendations for exercise prescription

There are no specific exercise prescriptions for people with chronic neurological conditions; therefore training should be adapted from the recommendations for cardiovascular and muscular fitness training for healthy people bearing in mind the points below.

Stroke

- Strength training should be carried out on both affected and unaffected sides of the body.
- The ability to participate in cardiovascular training may be limited due to poor trunk and lower limb control. If walking is the desired mode of training the body weight support harness may be used to support the patient while they are exercising.

Spinal cord injury

- In lesions above T6 maximum heart rate is limited to between 110 and 130 bpm.

Multiple sclerosis

- Studies investigating the effects of exercise in people with MS have focused on those with mild–moderate MS, and the benefits and risks of exercise in those with more severe disease are not clear.
- Resistance training should start at 15 RM and increase to 8 RM, 2 or 3 days a week, with priority being given to lower limb training.
- Cardiovascular training should start at 10 minutes and increase gradually, working at 50–70% maximun HR. It is recommended that the exercise is progressed over the first 6 months of training by increasing the duration of the training session and the number of sessions per week. A further increase in intensity can be considered with caution after that time.

EXERCISE FOR PEOPLE WITH OSTEOARTHRITIS

Exercise is a key intervention in the management of osteoarthritis (OA), and has been demonstrated to decrease pain and increase function in people with OA. This section outlines recommendations for exercise in OA; however it should be highlighted that the majority of the evidence for exercise in OA is based on OA of the knee, and the evidence base to support exercise for OA affecting other joints is sparse.

The impact of osteoarthritis on exercise ability

Cardiovascular exercise

People with OA tend to have a general decline in activity levels as the condition progresses. Patients with severe OA have been shown to have a significantly decreased maximal oxygen uptake. This decrease in cardiovascular fitness has been found to be reversible following joint replacement surgery, with continuing improvements demonstrated up to 2 years post surgery.

Muscle strength

Muscle strength has been shown to be reduced around joints affected by OA by as much as 45% in comparison with strength in aged-matched controls. This decrease in muscle strength is often attributed to the reduction in activity levels as a result of an increase in pain on movement or loading of the affected joint. However this is not the sole mechanism, as decreased muscle strength has been found around symptom-free joints with radiographic changes indicating OA. More recently arthrogenic muscle inhibition, a reflex inhibition of muscle contraction around a damaged joint to prevent further damage occurring, has been thought to be a cause of decreased muscle strength.

Flexibility

Joint movement in OA may be limited due to pain, altered biomechanics in the joint and decreased short tissue length. A study investigating the flexibility of the lower limbs in people with symptomatic OA of the knee found that they had decreased flexibility in both the affected and unaffected limb, suggesting that limitation of movement is not only due to specific joint changes.

Benefits of exercise in osteoarthritis

Cardiovascular training

Clinical guidelines for people with OA recommend the use of aerobic exercise training.

Cardiovascular training programmes have been found to have beneficial effects on pain, muscle strength and functional ability in people with OA. The small number of studies that have compared the effects of aerobic and strength training have found no significant difference in the benefits of the two modes of exercise.

In addition to the effects on pain and muscle strength, regular cardiovascular exercise can contribute to a weight-loss programme. A decrease in body weight reduces loading through the joints and is recommended in people with OA.

Resistance training

There is some evidence in the literature to suggest that strength training the muscles around a joint may decrease the development and progression of OA. However there is also evidence that strength training can result in redistribution of the load through a joint, and can contribute to the degeneration of a joint. It is recommended that the effects of strength training are monitored on an individual basis to prevent these possible detrimental effects.

Decrease in quadriceps strength has been correlated with pain in OA affecting the knee, and has also been associated with decreased activity levels. Strength training is effective in this patient group, has been shown to decrease pain and increase function, and is recommended in the clinical guidelines.

Isokinetic, isometric and dynamic resistance training have all been shown to be effective in people with OA, and there is some debate in the literature as to which mode of training should be used.

Isometric resistance muscle work, such as 'static quadriceps' exercises, are often used. Isometric exercise may be beneficial in OA, as they do not produce movement and avoid loading the joint; therefore they are often less painful for the patient to perform. However, it should be remembered that isometric exercises only train the muscle in the specific part of the range in which they are performed and this may not carry over into functional activity.

Conversely dynamic exercise trains the muscle through the full range of the exercise; however this movement may produce pain.

Isokinetic exercise has been demonstrated to increase muscle strength and walking speed, although accessing the exercise equipment may restrict the used of this mode of training.

In addition to increasing strength, it has been suggested that resistance training in OA also re-educates motor control and improves proprioception, although the evidence base for the benefits of these changes has not been established.

Flexibility

Flexibility exercises are not included in the recommendations for the management of OA; however there are several studies that demonstrate activities such as Tai Chi can increase flexibility in people with OA.

Special considerations for exercise in osteoarthritis

- Patients should be educated to recognize the signs and symptoms of acute inflammation in their joint, and be advised not to exercise if the joint is showing any signs of swelling, heat, redness and increased levels of pain.

- Patients should stop exercising and seek advice in the event of new, sharp pain, as this may be a sign of injury.
- High-impact activities that cause jarring or excessive loading to the joints should be avoided.
- The use of hydrotherapy in people with OA has been shown to be effective, and this mode of exercise should be particularly considered in this group.
- Co-morbidities should be considered when designing an exercise programme in this patient population, as OA generally affects people over the age of 45 years.

Recommendations for exercise prescription

Cardiovascular exercise

Cardiovascular exercise is recommended in line with guidelines for the healthy population (see Chapter 3). It should be remembered that this group is generally deconditioned, and the prescription should start at a low level and build up.

- Intensity: Low to moderate intensity (50–75% HR_{max}) is recommended, to avoid excessive loading through the joints.

Resistance training

There are no specific guidelines for strength training in OA; therefore it should be prescribed in accordance with guidelines for healthy individuals (see Chapter 4).

EXERCISE FOR PEOPLE WITH OSTEOPOROSIS

Osteoporosis is a common systemic disease of older people, characterized by low bone mass with micro-architectural deterioration, leading to increased risk of fractures. It is suggested that one-third of women and one in 12 men over the age of 50 years will sustain an osteoporotic fracture. People with osteoporosis have been shown to have decreased quality of life even in the absence of fractures, reporting chronic pain and decreased physical activity levels. Although a significant proportion of an individual's risk of developing osteoporosis is thought to be dependent on their genetic makeup, it is possible to influence the remaining 20% of their risk through diet and exercise. Exercise programmes have been shown to have benefits in both the prevention and management of this condition.

The impact of osteoporosis on exercise ability

Cardiovascular exercise

Self-reported physical activity levels have been found to be decreased in people with osteoporosis. This may be due to pain, but also to the fear of physical activity resulting in a fracture. High-impact activities should be avoided in this group, as there is a risk of sustaining a fracture; however people should be reassured that low- to moderate-impact exercise does not pose a specific risk, and may be beneficial. In addition to the exercise itself causing a fracture directly, the fear of falling during activity may also limit a person's activity, as falls lead to a significant proportion of fractures in this group.

Muscle strength

Osteoporosis has no direct effect on muscle strength, although muscle strength may be decreased as a consequence of the general decrease in physical activity and as a direct result of a fracture. Unlike cardiovascular exercise, high-intensity training for muscular fitness has been found to be safe in this patient group.

Flexibility

Flexibility may be reduced if movement is limited due to pain, and vertebral fractures can lead to the development of kyphosis. Some movements performed during the course of activities of daily living can result in vertebral fractures, and excessive spinal flexion and rotation should be avoided.

Benefits of exercise in osteoporosis

Cardiovascular training

Prevention

Much of the literature advocates aerobic exercise as important in the prevention of osteoporosis as it promotes the laying down of bone. For maximum benefit this must be done during childhood and adolescence, as more than half of the peak bone mass is accumulated during the adolescent years, although there is some evidence to show that higher activity levels in older people may help to prevent osteoporosis. Activities such as jogging, aerobic classes, dancing and walking are recommended. Although these activities are cardiovascular in nature, the benefit gained from them in terms of osteoporosis is due to their moderate- to high-impact weight-bearing characteristics.

Management

Low-impact weight-bearing activities can be used to try to decrease the rate of decline in bone density. It is recommended that activities particularly target the hip and spine as these are the main fracture sites seen in this group.

In addition maintaining activity levels may reduce the chance of falls, and thus decrease risk of fracture. However owing to the complex relationship between these factors it is difficult to demonstrate this link.

Resistance training

Prevention

It has been suggested that the action of the tendon pulling on the bone during activity produces an increase in bone mineral density, although it is difficult to separate the effects of resistance and weight-bearing impact activities in practice.

Management

High-intensity strength training over a period of at least 6 months has been demonstrated to produce a significant increase in bone mineral density in women with osteoporosis. Several studies have shown resistance training to maintain bone density in comparison with control groups.

In addition increased muscle strength may also decrease the risk of falls and subsequent fracture.

Special considerations for exercise in osteoporosis

- High-impact activities should be avoided in people with osteoporosis due to the risk of fractures as a result of the activity itself.
- When selecting exercises the risk of falls should be considered and minimized.
- Excessive spinal flexion and rotation should be avoided.
- The person should be advised to stop exercising and seek advice in the event of pain due to the possibility of a fracture.

Recommendations for exercise prescription

Cardiovascular training

For prevention moderate- to high-impact aerobic activities are recommended, to be carried out in line with the recommendations for cardiovascular training in healthy people (see Chapter 3). These should be reduced to low-impact activities, such as walking, for people with osteoporosis.

Resistance training

For both prevention and management of osteoporosis high-intensity strength training is recommended at a level of 80% 1 RM, with prescription in accordance with the guidelines for strength training in healthy people (see Chapter 4). This should be targeted towards the hip, spine and wrist.

Flexibility

Patients should be encouraged to maintain their available range of movement, although movement into pain should be avoided.

Further reading

Obesity and diabetes

American College of Sports Medicine (ACSM) (2001) American College Sports Medicine position stand on the appropriate intervention strategies for weight loss and prevention of weight regain for adults. Medicine and Science in Sports and Exercise 33(12): 2145–2156.

American College of Sports Medicine (ACSM) (2000) American College Sports Medicine position stand on exercise and type two diabetes. Medicine and Science in Sports and Exercise 32(17): 1345–1360.

Blair SN, Brodney S (1999) Effects of physical inactivity and obesity on morbidity and mortality: current evidence and research issues. Medicine and Science in Sports and Exercise 31(11 Suppl): S646–S662.

Curioni CC, Lourenco PM. Long-term weight loss after diet and exercise: a systematic review. International Journal of Obesity (London) 29(10): 1168–1174.

Havas S, Donner T (2006) Tight control of type 1 diabetes: Recommendations for patients. American Family Physician 74(6): 971–983.

Riddell M, Perkins B (2006) Type 1 diabetes and vigorous exercise. American Family Physician 74(6): 971–983.

Riddell M, Perkins B (2006) Type 1 diabetes and vigorous exercise: Applications of exercise physiology to patient management. Canadian Journal of Diabetes 30(1): 63–71.

Wing RR (1999) Physical activity in the treatment of the adulthood overweight and obesity: Current evidence and research issues. Medicine and Science in Sports and Exercise 31(11 Suppl): S547–S552.

Cardiovascular disease

AACVPR (2004) Guidelines for Cardiac Rehabilitation and Secondary Prevention Programs: 4th Edition. Human Kinetics.

BACR (1995) Guidelines for cardiac rehabilitation: Blackwell Science.

Department of Health Coronary Heart Disease. http://www.dh.gov.uk/en/Policyandguidance/Healthandsocialcaretopics/Coronaryheartdisease/index.htm (accessed 19/08/08).

Feigenbaum M, Pollock M (1999) Prescription of resistance training for health and disease. Medicine and Science in Sports and Exercise 31(1): 38–45.

Shamley D (ed.) (2005) Pathophysiology: An Essential Text for the Allied Health Professions. Edinburgh, UK: Elsevier.

Respiratory disease

British Thoracic Society (2001) BTS statement on pulmonary rehabilitation. British Thoracic Society standards of care sub-committee on pulmonary rehabilitation. Thorax 56(11): 827–834.

Reis A, Bauldoff G, Casaburi R, et al (2007) Pulmonary rehabilitation: Joint ACCP/AACVPR evidence-based clinical practice guidelines. Chest 131: 4–42.

Wasserman K, Hansen JE, Sue DY, et al (1999) Principles of Exercise Testing and Interpretation Including Pathophysiology and Clinical Applications: 3rd edition. Baltimore, MD: Lippincott Williams & Wilkins.

Neurological conditions

Dalgas U, Stenager E, Ingemann-Hansen T (2008) Review: Multiple sclerosis and physical exercise: recommendations for the application of resistance-, endurance- and combined training. Multiple Sclerosis 1: 35–53.

Gordon N, Gulanick M, Costa F, et al (2004) Physical activity recommendations for stroke survivors: An American Heart Association scientific statement from the Council on Clinical Cardiology, Subcommittee on Exercise, Cardiac Rehabilitation, and Prevention: the Council on Cardiovascular Nursing: the Council on Nutrition, Physical Activity and Metabolism: and the Stroke Council. Circulation 109: 2031–2041.

Hicks A, Martin K, Ditor D, et al (2003) Long-term exercise training in persons with spinal cord injury: Effects on strength, arm ergonometry performance and psychological well-being. Spinal Cord 41: 34–43. http://www.nature.com/sc/journal/v41/n1/full/3101389a.html (accessed 17/03/08).

Hoffman M (1986) Cardiorespiratory fitness and training in quadriplegics and paraplegics. Sports Medicine 3(5): 312–330.

National Centre for Physical Activity and Disability, NCPAD, Disability/Condition Multiple Sclerosis and Exercise. www.ncpad.org (accessed 3/01/08).

Newman MA, Dawes H, van den Berg M, et al (2007) Can aerobic treadmill training reduce the effort of walking and fatigue in people with multiple sclerosis: A pilot study. Multiple Sclerosis 13(1): 113–119.

Reitberg MB, Brooks D, Uitdehaag BMJ, Kwakkel G (2004) Exercise therapy for multiple sclerosis. Cochrane Database of Systematic Reviews(4). Art no CD003980.

Taylor NF, Dodd KJ, Prasad D, Denisenko S (2006) Progressive resistance exercises for people with multiple sclerosis. Disability and Rehabilitation 28(18): 119–126.

Zoellern RF, Riechman SE, Dabayebeh IM, et al (2005) Relation between muscular strength and cardiorespiratory fitness in people with thoracic-level paraplegia. Archives of Physical Medicine and Rehabilitation 86(7): 1441–1446.

Osteoarthritis

Hambly K. What is the evidence that muscle strength training matters in the management of osteoarthritis? www.library.nhs.uk (accessed 11/05/08).

Hurley M, Dziedzic K, Bearne L, et al (2002) The Clinical and Cost Effectiveness of Physiotherapy in the Management of Older People with Common rheumatological conditions. London, UK: Chartered Society of Physiotherapy.

Jamtvedt G, Thuve Dahm K, Christie C, et al (2008) Physical therapy interventions for patients with osteoarthritis of the knee: an overview of systematic reviews (CARE IV Series). Physical Therapy 88(1): 123–137.

Messier SP, Loeser RF, Hoover JL, et al (1992) Osteoarthritis of the knee: effects on gait, strength, and flexibility. Archives of Physical Medicine and Rehabilitation 73(1): 29–36.

NICE Guidelines (2008) Osteoarthritis: The Care and Management of Osteoarthritis in Adults. London, UK: NICE.

NICE Guideline CG59 Feb 2008. www.nice.org.uk (accessed 11/05/08).

Philbin EF, Groff GD, Ries MD, Miller TE (1995) Cardiovascular fitness and health in patients with end-stage osteoarthritis. Arthritis and Rheumatism 38(6): 799–805.

Ries MD, Philbin EF, Groff GD, et al (1996) Improvement in cardiovascular fitness after total knee arthroplasty. The Journal of Bone and Joint Surgery 78: 1696–1701.

Stitik TP, Kaplan RJ, Kamen LB, et al (2005) Rehabilitation of orthopedic and rheumatologic disorders. 2. Osteoarthritis assessment, treatment, and rehabilitation. Archives of Physical Medicine and Rehabilitation 86(Supplement 1): 48–55.

Thorstensson CA, Henriksson M, von Porat A, et al (2007) The effect of eight weeks of exercise on knee adduction moment in early knee osteoarthritis – a pilot study. Osteoarthritis and Cartilage 15: 1163–1170.

Topp R, Woolley S, Hornyak J III, et al (2002) The effect of dynamic versus isometric resistance training on pain and functioning among adults with osteoarthritis of the knee. Archives of Physical Medicine and Rehabilitation 83(9): 1187–1195.

Osteoporosis

Bianchi ML, Orsini MR, Saraifoger S, et al (2005) Quality of life in post-menopausal osteoporosis. Health and Quality of Life Outcomes 3: 78. http://www.hqlo.com/content/3/1/78 (accessed 5/05/08).

Bonaiuti D, Shea B, Lovine R, et al (2004) Exercise for preventing and treating osteoporosis in post menopausal women (Cochrane Review) in The Cochrane Library: Issue 4. Chichester, UK: Wiley.

Nelson M, Fiatarone M, Morganti C, et al (1994) Effects of high intensity strength training on multiple risk factors for osteoporotic fractures. Journal of the American Medical Association 272: 1909–1921.

Scottish Intercollegiate Guidelines Network (2003, updated 2004). A National Clinical Guideline. Management of Osteoporosis. www.sign.sc.uk (accessed 3/05/08).

CHAPTER THIRTEEN

Case Studies

These case studies have been developed to illustrate exercise prescription in practice. They demonstrate how appropriate exercise programmes can be developed to treat an individual patient's presenting problems, giving the rationale for the exercise and noting any precautions and special considerations needed for the patient's stage of rehabilitation. Each exercise programme has been designed to show how they may be progressed as the patient's condition changes.

The exercise programmes outlined in this chapter have been developed specifically for the patient cases described, and are not intended to be used as standard treatment for patients with these conditions. Each patient should be assessed and prescribed treatment on an individual basis.

CASE STUDY 13.1. An older person following total hip replacement

Mary is a 70-year-old lady who has a long history of OA in her left hip. She had a total hip replacement 2 days ago, with no complications. She is otherwise fit and well, and lives alone in a terraced house.

Since her surgery she has sat out in a chair, and is able to walk short distances with the aid of a walking frame.

Problem	Exercise/Activity	Rationale	Precautions/ Considerations
↓ ROM L hip abduction	Supine, hip abd with sliding board Use target markers on board to encourage movement to end of available range 10 reps × 1 day	↑ ROM hip abd ↑ Motor unit recruitment in abductors	Pain – Move within pain tolerance. Surgical incision – monitor condition. Risk of dislocation – avoid excessive hip add and flex according to local protocol
↓ ROM L hip flex	Supine, hip flex with sliding board Use target markers on board to encourage movement to end of available range 10 reps × 1 day	↑ ROM hip flex ↑ Motor unit recruitment in hip flexors	As above
Risk of ↓ lower limb strength and endurance	Daily walking over increasing distances with walking aid	Maintain muscular fitness and independence	Pain – Walk within limit of pain tolerance Surgical incision – monitor condition Risk of dislocation – ensure any chair used for resting is high enough to prevent excessive hip flex

Mary is now at home, 4 weeks after her surgery. She is walking independently with two sticks. Her recovery has been uncomplicated.

Problem	Exercise/ Activity	Rationale	Precautions/ Considerations
↓ mm strength hip abd	Standing with one hand support at side; hip abd. 8 reps, building to 15 reps. × 1 day, alternate days	Early strength training against gravity	Balance – ensure support used is stable Supporting leg – should be pain free and strong enough Risk of dislocation – avoid excessive swing into add
↓ mm strength hip ext	Standing with one hand support at side or front; hip ext 8 reps, building to 15 reps. × 1 day, alternate days	As above	As above Risk of dislocation – avoid excessive swing into flex
↓ lower limb muscle endurance and ↓ cardiovascular fitness	Walking increasing distances with sticks Walking outside Climbing stairs Build up to 20 min/day, can be 3 × 10 min, 5 days a week	It is likely that her cardiovascular fitness level was decreased before surgery, due to the hip limiting her activity levels Placing demand on aerobic pathways Using functional activity	Incorrect exercise intensity – exercise to point of slight fatigue to reach overload, but not to the point of exhaustion Pain – activities should not irritate pain Balance – assess environment for slip/trip hazards

At 12 weeks post surgery Mary has been discharged by the orthopaedic surgeon and is walking for 20 minutes a day without the use of walking aids.

Problem	Exercise/ Activity	Rationale	Precautions/ Considerations
↓ lower limb muscle strength and endurance	Step-ups on low step Sit → stand 8–15 reps for strength, building to 20 reps for endurance as able	When weak 8–15 reps provides overload to muscles to ↑ strength With increasing mm strength progress to endurance training with greater reps utilizing aerobic pathways	Balance – use handrail near the step. Ensure safe to step backwards down the step Assess environment for slip/trip hazards Risk of dislocation – ensure chair height for sit to stand does not produce excess hip flex
↓ lower limb muscle power	↑ walking speed for short periods during daily walk and introduce speed element to muscle fitness exercises	Speed element required to train muscle power. Muscle power is required for normal function	Balance – extra caution advised, as introduction of speed will further challenge balance Practicality of exercise programme – suggest alternate venues or options for walking in poor weather

It is important that Mary maintains her activity levels once discharged from the supervision of a physiotherapist, and she should be encouraged to continue her walking programme and some lower limb muscle-conditioning exercises in order to maintain her new fitness level.

CASE STUDY 13.2. A man with acute illness requiring ITU admission

Bernard is a 42-year-old businessman who was admitted to ITU 3 weeks ago with Legionnaire's disease following a recent business trip. He was previously fit and well.

He is now being weaned from ventilatory support and he is breathing via a tracheostomy with minimal support from the ventilator. During his ITU admission regular passive and active assisted movements have maintained his full ROM. He has been sitting out of bed for short periods of time.

Problem	Exercise/Activity	Rationale	Precautions/Considerations
Globally ↓ muscle strength, power and endurance	Sitting; knee ext. Sitting; shoulder flex 8–12 reps, add weight as required Sitting; elbow ext to lift bottom using chair arms. 8–12 reps Standing transfer bed → chair. Daily	Increase muscle strength focusing on those muscle groups required for functional activities such as transferring and standing Need to build up muscle strength before training for endurance	Adverse cardiovascular response to exercise – monitor cardiovascular systems closely before, during and for a period after exercise Damage to tissues – care of pressure areas and prevention of decreased circulation when adding weight to lower limb Disconnection of tubes and lines – temporarily disconnect from tubes and lines as able before transfer, monitor all tubes and lines during activity
↓ Cardiovascular fitness	Sitting; foot pedals Start as able, build up to 3 × 10 minutes, 5 days/week. Intensity Borg 13. 'Somewhat hard'	Overloading aerobic pathways to train for return to function	Adverse cardiovascular response to exercise – monitor cardiovascular systems closely before, during and for a period after exercise due to increased oxygen requirement during exercise

Once weaned from the ventilator, Bernard was transferred from ITU to a general ward and his tracheostomy was removed. After a week on the ward he is no longer requiring oxygen and is able to transfer independently and walk short distances.

Problem	Exercise/Activity	Rationale	Precautions/Considerations
Globally ↓ muscle strength	Using the Westminster pulley strengthen: Knee extensors Hip flexors Hip extensors 8–12 reps Toe standing 8–12 reps Do on alternate days	Strength training for walking, stair climbing and other functional activities	Nutrition and fluid – ensure that he is taking on adequate nutrition and fluid to meet the additional demands of the exercise programme Rest – ensure periods of rest in between activity Psychological issues – be aware of the impact of an acute illness resulting in an ITU admission
Globally ↓ muscle endurance and ↓ Cardiovascular endurance	Sit → stand Step-ups on low step Cycle ergonometer Exercise to fatigue, building to 10 min per exercise 3 × week Walking – encourage daily	Overload both cardiovascular system and local muscle endurance activity to place demand on aerobic pathways Functional activities	As above Adverse cardiovascular reaction to exercise – monitor heart rate, O_2 saturation and BP during initial exercise sessions

On discharge form hospital Bernard was invited to participate in an exercise rehabilitation programme for people who had been on ITU. The programme was based on a circuit training programme including a balance of cardiovascular and strength training exercises as is commonly used in cardiac rehabilitation. After attending the programme for 6 weeks Bernard was fit to return to work.

CASE STUDY 13.3. A child with a scald to the leg

Tom is a 6-year-old boy who sustained a scald to the lateral aspect of his left leg, including his knee and ankle joints. This scald did not require skin grafting and is healing. Tom is reluctant to move his knee and ankle and this is affecting his gait pattern.

Problem	Exercise/Activity	Rationale	Precautions/ Contraindications
Fear of moving left knee and ankle causing decreased ROM at both joints, in particular knee flex/ext ankle inversion and plantar flexion	Sitting; – moving ball under foot, forward & back, side to side – using foot to slide beanbag between markers – scrunching up a piece of paper with toes and placing on marker – picking up a bean bag and throwing it with foot	Increase ROM of – knee flex/ext and DF/PF, inv/ev – knee flex/ext and DF/PF – knee flex/ext and DF/PF – knee flex/ext and DF/PF Focus for Tom is on the fun of the activity rather than the specific movements of his leg and foot The physiotherapist monitors the ROM achieved during the activities and adapts to maximize ROM	Working into pain is not contraindicated; however Tom should not become distressed as this will reinforce avoidance of movement He may need pain relief before physiotherapy session
Abnormal gait pattern	Standing on left leg to kick football with right leg Games such as 'Simon says' Obstacle course encouraging normal movement	Focus of activity on unaffected leg Achieves full weight-bearing and stance phase of gait Concentrating on game whilst achieving movement	As above

Tom responded well to these exercises and became confident at moving his leg during normal activity within the session. He returned to the physiotherapy department 2 days later. His mother reported that he has been playing indoors with his older brother and did not seem to be so conscious of his leg, although he is still reluctant to join in with the other children when playing outside.

Problem	Exercise/Activity	Rationale	Precautions/Contraindications
↓ ROM and ↓ normal function	Games incorporating; – toe standing – DF/PF in long sitting – kneel sitting – wobble board – kneeling – side sitting – cross leg sitting – running – jumping – skipping – balancing – trampette	Full stretch to scar tissue knee extension with PF Full knee flex Inversion/eversion All producing stretch, full ROM in normal functional positions for 6 year old Functional physical activities for 6 year old Increase confidence	If the scald is continuing to heal activities to produce a stretch on the healing tissue should be incorporated to encourage the collagen to lay down in an organized manner Activities should be age-appropriate and related to the functional activities of a 6-year-old

After a further 2 weeks Tom regained full active range of movement and had resumed his normal activities. Tom was discharged from treatment and his parents were advised to monitor his range of movement and gait over the following 12 months, during the period of active scar tissue formation.

CASE STUDY 13.4. A person with chronic obstructive pulmonary disease

Frederick is a 67-year-old man who has shortness of breath on exertion due to his long-standing chronic obstructive airways disease. He has recently completed a 6-week outpatient pulmonary rehabilitation programme. Following the programme his exercise tolerance has increased from a baseline 6-minute walking distance of 210 m to a post rehabilitation distance of 320 m. He has asked for some advice to help him continue his exercise programme independently.

Problem	Exercise/Activity	Rationale	Precautions/Contraindications
Decreased cardiovascular exercise capacity, limited by SOB and leg muscle fatigue	Outdoor walking Start as able, build up to 20 min, 3 days/week At intensity level Borg 13 'Somewhat hard' Once easily achieving 20 min start to include hills Alternatives for variety: – Stair climbing or step ups – Repeated Sit → stand – Rapid throwing and catching of a ball – Static bike – Shadow boxing – Half jumping jacks Start as able, build up any combination for 20 min, 3 days/week at intensity level Borg 13 'Somewhat hard'	Overload both cardiovascular system and local muscle endurance activity to place demand on aerobic pathways Functional activities Includes upper limbs in activities, as people with COPD become particularly SOB during UL activity	Maximize respiratory function Exercise is best carried out after any required physiotherapy for chest clearance and inhaled medication to give maximum opportunity for gas exchange Decreased SaO_2 Frederick's oxygen saturation levels during exercise will have been monitored whilst attending PR, and he will have home oxygen to wear during exercise if needed Acute exacerbation He should be advised to stop exercising if he is unwell. He should return to activity at a lower level of intensity and build up again

Continued...

Problem	Exercise/Activity	Rationale	Precautions/Contraindications
Decreased mm strength	Sitting, apply resistance band at ankle and fasten behind, knee ext, fasten above and in front, knee flexion Standing holding firm support, apply resistance band at ankle and fasten in front, hip ext, fasten behind, hip flex Sitting, use hand-held weight for wrist flex, ext, elbow flex, ext, shoulder flex, shoulder abd Select resistance band and weights for 8–12 reps, 2–3 × week Use functional activities such as lifting and carrying for increasing grip strength	Increased muscle strength has been shown to increase exercise ability in people with COPD. Muscle atrophy is a distinctive feature of COPD	Usual precautions for use with resistance bands Avoid breath holding during effort as exacerbates SOB. Breathe out on concentric phase of muscle activity

Frederick can also be advised to attend a local gym to have access to a greater range of equipment, as variety is important in developing a sustainable exercise programme. He may increase his activities of daily living now that he has increased his exercise ability. If he participates in activities that produce an overload on his aerobic system, such as dancing or gardening, these activities can be used as a substitute for the 'formal' exercise programme.

CASE STUDY 13.5. An elite badminton player following shoulder stabilization surgery

Dave is a 28-year-old elite badminton player. He had right shoulder stabilization surgery 2 days ago. He is now at home wearing a sling and body belt to protect his arm. He has been prescribed these exercises by the physiotherapist before discharge from hospital. This early stage of rehabilitation will last from 0 to 6 weeks.

Problem	Exercise/Activity	Rationale	Precautions/Contraindications
Immobility and pain R shoulder and arm	Finger, hand and wrist movements – flex/ext, abd/add, circumduction Forearm pronation and supination Sh girdle elevation/depression, protraction/retraction Elbow flex/ext – remove sling for this exercise 10 repetitions of each 3 × a day	Maintains ROM of other joints in R arm	Exercise as pain allows so healing process is not disrupted
Decreased cardiovascular fitness due to reduced activity	Static bicycle 30 min 5 × a week at 13 on Borg Scale	Maintains some cardiovascular fitness for sport	Stable position for cardiovascular activity to avoid undue strain on healing shoulder Exercise intensity as pain allows

Three weeks after his operation Dave's body belt and stitches are removed. He continues his early exercise programme but is now able to begin gentle shoulder mobilization.

Problem	Exercise/Activity	Rationale	Precautions/Contraindications
Decreased ROM R shoulder	Remove arm from sling, small range pendular exercises – sh flex/ext and circumduction, 10 repetitions, 3 × a day	Start mobilizing R shoulder	Exercise in small range of specified movements only and as pain allows so that healing process is not disrupted

Six weeks after his operation, Dave's sling is removed and he begins attending the physiotherapy department for further rehabilitation. He is now in the intermediate stage of rehabilitation.

Problem	Exercise/Activity	Rationale	Precautions/Contraindications
Decreased ROM R shoulder	Continue pendular exercises as before working into more range Active assisted sh flex in crook lying Active assisted sh add and med rot in standing Progress to active movements through range and against gravity 10 repetitions each, 3 × a day Functional activities	Increase ROM R shoulder	Exercise within pain limits Do not exercise R shoulder into external rotation at this stage as this may disrupt healing process

Continued...

Inhibition of and decreased muscle strength of major muscles around R shoulder	Isometric exercises for major muscle groups around R shoulder – push R arm against wall in the direction of movement, all in inner range and hold 5 s and relax, repeat 10 × Progress to active movement through range, against gravity and then resisted activity 10 RM on alternate days Functional activities	Improves muscle function and recruitment to increase shoulder stability by working sh flexors, extensors, abductors and medial rotators	As above
Decreased proprioception R shoulder joint	3 point kneeling L arm, raise right arm and hold for 5 s, repeat 5 × Increase complexity by carrying out exercise with eyes closed	Increases proprioceptive input to R shoulder joint	Should be able to lift R arm against gravity before carrying out exercise Should be stable in 3 point kneeling to avoid falling onto shoulder
Decreased cardiovascular fitness	Continue with static bicycle 30 min 5 × a week at 13–16 on Borg scale. Increase intensity in intervals to 16 on Borg scale	Maintains cardiovascular fitness for sport	Stable position for cardiovascular activity to avoid undue strain on healing shoulder
Increase lower limb muscle strength	Major leg muscle groups – e.g. kn ext/flex, ankle PF and DF 8–10 RM on alternate days	To improve muscle strength for sport	Only exercise on a weight machine with a partner who can adjust resistance to avoid undue strain on healing wound

It is now 3 months since Dave had his operation. He has full, pain-free ROM in his R shoulder and the major muscle groups around his shoulder have been assessed as grade 4 on the MRC scale.

Problem	**Exercise/Activity**	**Rationale**	**Precautions/Contraindications**
Decreased muscle strength and power of major muscles around R shoulder	Resistance training of major muscle groups around R sh 4–8 RM on alternate days Fast force resistance training of muscle groups around R sh – add 1 set of 6 reps at 30–60% 1 RM at fast speed	Return R shoulder muscle strength and power to normal for sports participation	Make sure that there is a good base of strength in the shoulder muscles before adding in exercise at speed
Decreased proprioception R shoulder joint	3 point kneeling on sit – fit (L and R arm) Raise other arm and hold for 5 s with eyes closed Add small movements into more flex/ext/abd/add when arm is lifted and hold Standing on wobble board throwing and catching ball	Increases proprioceptive input to R shoulder joint	Should have adequate strength in R shoulder to bear weight through shoulder before attempting to lift L arm
Decreased cardiovascular fitness	Running, cycling, step machine for 30–50 min (carry out exercise for average length of badminton match) at varying intensities of 13–16 on Borg scale on most days of the week	Improves aerobic energy production in preparation for return to sport Preparation for return to playing badminton	Ensure warm-up period at start of cardiovascular exercise and cool down at the end

Continued...

Decreased sport specific fitness	Circuit training to include press-ups, tricep dips, sit-ups, throwing ball overarm and underarm to hit targets, jumping jacks, shuttle runs, etc Badminton drills and training Practice matches	Preparation for return to playing badminton Ensures confidence to play badminton again is built up gradually Ensures necessary skills are in place before return to sport	Do not return to sport until rehabilitation is complete–full ROM and muscle strength around shoulder, cardiovascular fitness, agility and power

Dave completed his rehabilitation and played in his first tournament 8 months after his operation.

CASE STUDY 13.6. An overweight woman referred for an exercise programme for health

Julia is a 45-year-old woman who works as a school receptionist. She recently saw her GP, who was concerned about her obesity and her blood pressure, which is consistently at the upper end of the normal range.

Julia has been referred for a supervised exercise programme to manage these risk factors, which predispose her to the development of diabetes and cardiovascular disease.

Problem	Exercise/Activity	Rationale	Precautions/Contraindications
Obesity, borderline blood pressure and generally low activity levels	Warm up 10 min Walking on treadmill Static bike Basket ball dribbling up and down the gym Stair climbing or step-ups Half jumping jacks Trampette Throwing and catching ball against a wall Circuit training including the above activities Circuit lasts 30 min, with rest at 10-min intervals Borg intensity 13 Cool down Attend supervised class × 2 week for 6 weeks, advise additional independent walk at Borg 13 × 1–2 week	Gradual increase in blood supply to cardiac muscle Activities overloading the aerobic system, to increase HR and RR To prevent blood pooling in periphery and potential fainting	Start the programme gradually by allowing rest periods during the circuit and increase exercise up to recommended amount Exercise restricted to moderate intensity due to deconditioned state and to avoid excessive overload on cardiovascular system Exercise generally low impact to avoid excessive stress through joints

At the end of her 6-week supervised programme Julia is encouraged by the fact that she has lost some weight and is keen to continue with exercise.

Problem	Exercise/Activity	Rationale	Precautions/ Contraindications
Obesity, difficulty establishing an independent exercise programme	Identify areas of Julia's daily life that could be easily changed to incorporate additional activity Walking briskly to work or going out for a walk during lunch time Use some of the school exercise facilities during or after school, become involved in supervising after school clubs, e.g. netball Take up new hobby with friends such as a form of dancing, swimming or dog walking Transfer exercises from programme to local gym, e.g. treadmill, cycle or join exercise class As further weight loss occurs the intensity of exercise can be increased and higher impact activities included such as skipping	To develop a more active lifestyle and reduce the need for specific exercise sessions Increasing the intensity of activity will facilitate weight loss in addition to gaining health benefits	It is important that the activities are carried out at sufficient intensity to gain benefits

INDEX

B

C

D

E

F

N

O